Conveyancing

Conveyancing

Second edition

I R Storey, MA
Solicitor, Principal Lecturer in Law
at Trent Polytechnic

London
Butterworths
1987

UNITED KINGDOM Butterworth & Co (Publishers) Ltd, 88 Kingsway, LONDON WC2B 6AB and 61A North Castle Street, EDINBURGH EH2 3LJ

AUSTRALIA Butterworths Pty Ltd, SYDNEY, MELBOURNE, BRISBANE, ADELAIDE, PERTH, CANBERRA and HOBART

CANADA Butterworths. A division of Reed Inc., TORONTO and VANCOUVER

NEW ZEALAND Butterworths of New Zealand Ltd, WELLINGTON and AUCKLAND

SINGAPORE Butterworth & Co (Asia) Pte Ltd, SINGAPORE

USA Butterworths Legal Publishers, ST PAUL, Minnesota, SEATTLE, Washington, BOSTON, Massachusetts, AUSTIN, Texas and D & S Publishers, CLEARWATER, Florida

Reprinted 1988

British Library Cataloguing in Publication Data

Storey, I.R.
Conveyancing.——2nd ed.
1. Conveyancing——England
I. Title
344.2064'38 KD979

ISBN 0 406 01064 1

Typeset, printed and bound in Great Britain by
Butler & Tanner Ltd, Frome and London

Preface

This second edition, like the first edition before it, has been written with the Law Society Final conveyancing examination in mind. It therefore includes a combination of theory and practice, and covers not only freehold and leasehold domestic conveyancing, but also the various provisions giving protection to residential and business tenants. However, I do hope that the book will also be found to be useful on other conveyancing courses, in particular the courses for licensed conveyancers.

I have dealt in the first section on domestic conveyancing with both freehold and leasehold conveyancing, but I have also included a separate chapter devoted to leases. I hope thereby to accommodate both those who wish to study freehold and leasehold conveyancing together, and those who wish to consider them separately.

I have tried to state the law as at 1 March 1987, although it has been possible to include a few more recent developments. To avoid constant repetition of 'he or she' and 'his or her', I have used the male pronoun to include the female.

I would like to thank Lin, who helped in some ways, and Daniel, who helped in others.

IAN STOREY
Nottingham
March 1987

Contents

Table of statutes

References in this Table to *Statutes* are to Halsbury's Statutes of England (Fourth Edition) showing the volume and page at which the annotated text of the Act may be found.

List of cases

Part one
Domestic Conveyancing

1 Introduction

The law of conveyancing is essentially the law relating to the creation and transfer of estates and interests in land. Typically, conveyancing involves buying – or selling – a house. The tendency is to employ a solicitor to do this. Why is this, when one does not normally use a solicitor on other sales or purchases; for example, when buying a book?

The first difference between the two transactions lies in the nature of what is being sold. A vendor cannot 'own' land in the same way that he can 'own' a book, that is to say that he cannot own land absolutely, but only have an estate in it. Since 1925 there have been only two legal estates in land.[1] Firstly there is the fee simple absolute in possession, which is the freehold estate and which represents the closest one can come to owning land absolutely. Secondly there is the term of years absolute which is the legal leasehold estate. That is not all. A freehold or leasehold estate may be subject to a whole range of other interests. These include legal interests such as easements, rentcharges and mortgages, and equitable interests such as covenants. Land could also be subject to planning restrictions or a Compulsory Purchase Order. In addition, the subject matter of the sale is normally not a vacant piece of land, but land with a house, garage and other buildings on it. These may be in a poor state of repair or they may have been built without planning permission. We can see then, that the subject matter of the sale is quite complicated and indeed much of the purchaser's solicitor's efforts will be directed towards finding out as much as possible about the property.

A second difference lies in the method of transfer of estates in land. A book is normally bought by taking possession and paying the purchase price. This is not a suitable method of transfer of land. The Law of Property Act 1925 provides, with a few exceptions, that the transfer or creation of a legal estate or interest must be by a deed.[2] A deed is a written document which will include the names of the parties to the transaction as well as a description of the property and a statement of the estate or interest being created or transferred. So, for example, a deed may transfer a legal freehold or leasehold estate from vendor to purchaser, or create a new legal easement such as a right of way, or

1 Law of Property Act 1925, s. 1(1).
2 Ibid, s. 52.

create a new leasehold estate. The deed is not only signed by the parties but also sealed.

A third difference between buying a book and buying land is in the proof of ownership provided. A purchaser buying a book normally neither demands nor receives any proof from the shop that they do own the book; he assumes that they do from their possession of it. Such an assumption would be extremely foolish in the case of land. One cannot really be in possession of land in quite the same way that one can be in possession of a book. One can be in occupation of it but that does not necessarily suggest that the occupant is the owner of a freehold or leasehold estate. He could be a mortgagee, a tenant under a weekly tenancy, a licensee, or even a mere squatter. Also, land is inevitably 'second-hand'. A purchaser of land will thus demand some proof from the vendor that he does own what he is selling. How can the vendor provide this? Let us take as an example a vendor selling his freehold house. As a deed is needed each time the property is transferred, a collection of deeds will have accumulated. There will be, in addition, other documents under which the property has passed. For example where the owner has died there will be a Grant of Probate or Administration as evidence that the property has passed to his personal representatives, and there may then be an assent transferring the legal estate in the property to a beneficiary under the will or intestacy. This bundle of deeds and other documents is called collectively the title deeds to the property, or more correctly to that particular estate in the property, and is passed on to successive owners. A vendor will demonstrate his ownership of the estate being sold by giving the purchaser details of the more recent of the deeds and other documents and events affecting the property. The purchaser will then be able to trace a chain of ownership from the chosen starting point through to the vendor.

This demonstration by the vendor that he does own what he is selling – or deducing title as it is called – does have disadvantages. It is repetitive, because title must be deduced each time the property is sold. More fundamentally, it provides no guarantee to a purchaser that the vendor does own what he is selling, for there may be some defect prior to the point at which the chain of title commences. If allowed to continue, the number of title deeds would eventually become unmanageable. It was as a result of such criticisms that a process was originated whereby the ownership of a particular estate in a piece of land could be registered, with the register then becoming the proof of ownership. The pre-registration title deeds lose their importance and a transfer of ownership can be recorded by changing the name of the owner in the register. This system of registered conveyancing is governed by the Land Registration Act 1925 as amended.

There are, then, two systems of conveyancing in operation at present, the traditional system based on title deeds and the more modern system where ownership of the estate has been registered. The main difference lies in the way that title is deduced to the purchaser.

2 Basic principles

A discussion of conveyancing must inevitably assume a certain knowledge of the theoretical land law principles upon which conveyancing is based. The purpose of this chapter is to reiterate these principles, including the law relating to registration of title.

1 Land law

We have already seen that there are only two legal estates in land, the freehold estate and the term of years absolute.[1] In addition there are a number of legal interests in land including easements, rentcharges and mortgages.[2] An easement is a right, such as a right of way or a right of light, which exists for the benefit of one piece of land over another piece of land. A legal easement will be for an interest equivalent to a legal freehold or leasehold estate. That is to say, a right of way for the benefit of freehold land will be a 'freehold' easement whilst if for the benefit of leasehold land it will be a 'leasehold' easement and come to an end at the same time as the lease. A rentcharge is a periodical payment charged on a particular piece of land. Put simply, it is rather like rent, but relates to freehold land. (The Rentcharges Act 1977 provides for the eventual extinction of most rentcharges but one that will continue is the estate rentcharge; this may arise if a house on a building estate, or flat in a block of flats, is subject to a rentcharge representing a contribution to the cost of maintaining shared facilities such as the grounds of a block of flats.) A mortgage over property is normally taken as security for a loan and it gives the lender certain rights over the property, including a power of sale.

There are also various equitable interests in land including covenants and equitable mortgages.[3] A covenant will be imposed on land for the benefit of other land. If restrictive, it will prevent some use or other activity in relation to the land affected. If positive, it will impose a positive obligation on the owner of the land, for example to contribute to the maintenance of a road.

1 Law of Property Act 1925, s. 1(1).
2 Ibid, s. 1(2).
3 Ibid, s. 1(3).

(Strictly speaking, positive covenants are not normally interests *in land*, but they are of as much concern to the conveyancer as restrictive covenants.) There are various rules which regulate the running of the benefit and burden of covenants with the land respectively benefitted and burdened. An equitable mortgage is a mortgage which is prevented from being a legal mortgage due to the lack of the formalities necessary to constitute a legal mortgage. For example, a legal mortgage must be by deed but an equitable mortgage could be created by a document merely signed and not sealed.

The main difference between legal and equitable interests lies in their effect on a purchaser of the legal estate affected by the interest. The general rule is that a purchaser of a legal estate will take subject to legal interests affecting the estate quite irrespective of whether he knows about them or not, but he will only be bound by equitable interests if he has notice of them. This could be actual, constructive or imputed notice.

However, if the interest is capable of registration as a land charge under the Land Charges Act 1972 the purchaser will take subject to it if it is registered but not if it is not registered, in both cases irrespective of notice.[4] An example of a registrable legal interest is a puisne legal mortgage. This is a mortgage not protected by deposit of title deeds and in practice will normally be a second mortgage. Examples of registrable equitable interests are restrictive covenants created after 1925 and estate contracts.

2 Registration of title

i Introduction

As we saw in the last chapter, the main disadvantages of the traditional system of conveyancing, based on use of the title deeds, are that the investigation of the vendor's title by the purchaser must be repeated on every transaction and that the investigation is purely historical and not conclusive. The system of registration of title seeks to overcome these difficulties by providing a once and for all registration of title to a particular estate in a particular piece of land, at the Land Registry. The register becomes the conclusive evidence of the estate owner's title and contains the information which would be found in the title deeds such as the estate owner's name, a description of the property and the estate held by the owner.

Before dealing with the system of registration of title in detail, it should be emphasised that the register is a register of title not of land, and that there may be two or more titles registered in respect of the same piece of land; for example a freehold estate, a headlease, and an underlease. Each estate would be registered with a separate title.

ii Registration with separate title

Only certain estates or interests are capable of being registered with separate title, or capable of 'substantive registration' as it is called; they are the 'estates capable of subsisting as legal estates'.[5] This expression includes not only the

4 Land Charges Act 1972, s. 4. See further in ch. 11, section 1i.
5 Land Registration Act 1925, s. 2(1).

legal freehold and leasehold estates but also the legal interests and charges under the Law of Property Act 1925, s. 1(2) and so would include legal easements, rentcharges and mortgages.[6] However the Land Registration Rules 1925 provide that the benefit of an easement cannot be registered separately but can only be registered as appurtenant to the dominant estate, title to which is registered.[7] Mortgages cannot be registered with separate title where there is an existing right to redeem the mortgage,[8] as there will be in the vast majority of cases, and although rentcharges are capable of registration with separate title they are only rarely encountered.

In practice, then, the only estates or interest capable of substantive registration are the freehold estate of fee simple absolute in possession and the leasehold estate of a term of years absolute. There are two leasehold estates which *cannot* be registered with separate title:[9]

(a) a mortgage term with a subsisting right of redemption;[10]
(b) a lease with twenty-one years or less left to run.[11]

To the extent that interests – such as easements, covenants and leases (whether registered with separate title or not) – adversely affect a freehold or leasehold estate which is registered then, apart from mortgages, they can be classified as either overriding interests or minor interests in relation to the title affected. They can, if necessary, be protected by some entry on the register of that title. Mortgages of registered titles can also be protected by an entry on the register of the title.

1 *First registration* We have said that registration of title to a particular estate is a once and for all process, and we have seen which estates are capable of substantive registration. We can now examine the rules which govern when title to a particular unregistered estate can, or must, be registered. This process of first registration can be either compulsory or voluntary.

2 *Compulsory registration* Whether substantive registration of title to a particular estate is compulsory depends on whether there is a Compulsory Registration Order in force for the area in which the land is situated. Such orders are made by Order in Council,[12] and their existence will be revealed by a search of the Public Index Map at the Land Registry and by enquiries of the Local Authority in the standard form.[13] There is also a pamphlet available from the Land Registry showing the areas currently covered by CROs.

6 Ibid, s. 3(xi).
7 Land Registration Rules 1925, r. 257. Easements which adversely affect land title to which is registered are dealt with at section vi, below.
8 Land Registration Act 1925, ss. 4(b), 8(1).
9 Prior to the Land Registration Act 1986, which amended s. 8(2) of the Land Registration Act 1925, leases which contained an absolute prohibition against assignments inter vivos were not registrable. Section 3 of the 1986 Act now provides for registration provided that the restriction on alienation is noted on the register.
10 See fn. 8, above. A mortgage term is in theory a term of years absolute, subject to cesser on redemption.
11 Land Registration Act 1925, s. 8(1).
12 Under ibid, s. 120.
13 See ch. 6.

Once a CRO has come into force, the following rules apply:[14]

(a) following the conveyance on sale[15] of a freehold, the purchaser must apply for first registration within two months of the conveyance;

(b) following the assignment of sale[15] of a lease, a purchaser must apply for first registration of his leasehold title within two months of the assignment if the lease has more than twenty-one years left to run at the date of the assignment;

(c) following the grant of a lease, the purchaser/lessee must apply for first registration of his leasehold title within two months of the grant if the lease is for a term of more than twenty-one years[16].

The sanction for not applying for registration within two months is that the transaction becomes void so far as the legal estate is concerned, until registration is effected.[17] The two month period can be extended and applications for registration outside the period will always be allowed provided some reasonable explanation is given. Application for first registration is made to the District Land Registry for the area in which the property is situated. Most urban areas are now covered by CROs but even in such a compulsory area the process whereby title to all land in the area becomes registered is slow, depending as it does on the land being sold.

On the sale of a council house to a tenant under the Housing Act 1985, first registration of title is compulsory whether or not the land is situated in a compulsory registration area.[18]

There is a further aspect of compulsory registration which must be considered. Once title to an estate is registered, then on any disposition of it, the legal estate only passes on registration of the disposition.[19] This is a fundamental principle of the system of registration. So if a registered title is sold, or given away, the legal estate only passes to the purchaser or donee once he is registered as proprietor in place of the vendor or donor. However the word 'disposition' which we have used above, and which is used in the Land Registration Act 1925, is defined to include not only the transfer of the whole or part of a registered freehold or leasehold estate, but also the grant of a lease out of such an estate.[20] If the superior title out of which the lease is being granted is registered, then the grant of the lease is a disposition of that title and the lease must be registered or no legal estate will pass to the lessee. The lease, if capable of separate registration, must be so registered.[1] Thus, whether or not the land is in an area of compulsory registration, if a lease for over twenty-one years[2] is granted out of a registered title then it must be registered

14 Land Registration Act 1925, s. 123(1).

15 By ibid, s. 123(3), this does not include an exchange where no money changes hands.

16 Prior to the Land Registration Act 1986, registration was only compulsory under headings (b) and (c) if the lease was granted for forty years or more or had forty years or more left to run.

17 Land Registration Act 1925, s. 123(1).

18 Housing Act 1985, s. 154.

19 Land Registration Act 1925, ss. 19(1), 19(2), 22(1), 22(2).

20 Ibid, ss. 18, 21.

1 Notice of the lease may also be entered on the register of the superior title; see section vi, below.

2 And therefore capable of substantive registration.

with separate title and until it is, no legal estate will pass; there is no two month time limit. An intending lessee can discover whether the superior title is registered from his search of the Public Index Map.

3 *Voluntary registration* This is possible in areas where a CRO is in force. For example, title to a freehold estate could be registered at any time and not just on sale, when it would be compulsory. Voluntary registration is not possible in areas where no CRO is in force,[3] with certain exceptions[4] which are principally:

(a) Where all or some of the title deeds have been destroyed or lost by enemy action, natural disaster, fire, theft or other criminal act; or have been destroyed or lost whilst in the custody of a solicitor, building society of clearing bank;

(b) where the property is to form a building estate consisting of twenty or more houses, flats or maisonettes.

iii Classes of title

On applying for first registration, there are a number of alternative classes with which the applicant's title may be registered. These are:

absolute (freehold or leasehold)
possessory (freehold or leasehold)
qualified (freehold or leasehold)
good leasehold

1 *Registration with Absolute Title* The effect of first registration with Absolute Title is to vest in the estate owner (or 'registered proprietor' as he becomes) the freehold or leasehold estate together with all rights appurtenant to the land[5] and subject *only* to:[6]

(a) matters which are entered on the register of the title;[7]

(b) overriding interests;[8]

(c) (if the proprietor is not entitled to the land for his own benefit, for example if he holds as a trustee) minor interests[9] of which he has notice; as between himself and the persons entitled to such interests, he will be bound by those interests;[10]

(d) (if the estate is leasehold) all express or implied covenants and obligations in the lease.[11]

These are the only interests that affect the registered proprietor and so first registration can have what is referred to as a 'curative' effect. For example, if

3 Land Registration Act 1966, s. 1.
4 These are specified by the Chief Land Registrar from time to time and can be found in a Land Registry Practice Note.
5 For example, easements existing for the benefit of the land.
6 Land Registration Act 1925, ss. 5, 9.
7 For example, covenants affecting the land; see section vi, below.
8 See section vi, below.
9 See section vi, below.
10 For example, a trustee or personal representative is bound by the interests of the beneficiaries, even though they are not mentioned on the register and are not overriding interests.
11 Perhaps rather oddly, the lease does not form part of the register.

the unregistered title was subject to a covenant which is not an overriding interest, and which is by error not mentioned on the register, then the proprietor will hold the land free from it, unless the person who has the benefit of the covenant can have the register rectified.[12] Rather more importantly, there is a discretion under section 13(c) of the Land Registration Act 1925 to allow registration, even with absolute title, of a title which though technically defective is nevertheless a title under which there is no prospect of the owner's possession and enjoyment of the land being affected; in other words where the owner has a 'good holding title'.

2 *Registration with other classes of title* The effect of registration with other classes of title is described in the Land Registration Act 1925 by reference to the effect of registration with absolute title. Registration with possessory title has the same effect as registration with absolute title save that the registration does not prejudice the enforcement of any right affecting the title which was in existence at the date of first registration.[13] In other words, the registered proprietor is additionally subject to all rights affecting the title in existence at the date of first registration and the guarantee provided by the register does not extend to any such rights. A possessory title might be granted if the applicant had lost all his title deeds. With a qualified title, it is some specified interest which is excepted from the effect of registration and to which the guarantee of the register does not extend; specified, that is, either by date (for example all interests arising before a specified date) or by reference to a specific document (for example all the interests arising under a particular deed).[14] A qualified title is rare in practice and arises most commonly where there has been a breach of trust in the past.

Much more common is a good leasehold title. Registration has the same effect as registration with absolute leasehold title save that the registration does not prejudice the enforcement of any right affecting the lessor's title to grant the lease.[15] In other words the guarantee of the register does not extend to the freehold and any superior leasehold titles and the registered proprietor is subject to any rights, such as covenants or easements, affecting these titles[16] and to any rights affecting the lessor's power to grant the lease.[17] Absolute leasehold title will only be given where all superior titles can be examined by the Land Registry, either because they are already registered or because the applicant for first registration with absolute leasehold title can also deduce the superior titles. In practice many Building Societies view good leasehold titles, and also any unregistered leasehold title where the superior titles are not also deduced, with an understandable degree of circumspection. A solicitor acting for a Building Society may be asked to investigate the superior titles and confirm that they are in order. As will be seen later, unless the purchaser has

12 Rectification is considered at section vii, below.
13 Land Registration Act 1925, ss. 6, 11.
14 Ibid, ss. 7, 12.
15 Ibid, s. 10.
16 A lessee is only subject to such rights as are in existence at the time of the grant of the lease.
17 For example, a provision in a mortgage entered into by the lessor, prohibiting him from granting any leases.

provided in his contract with the vendor that he can investigate the superior titles, he will be in no position to satisfy the Building Society's requirement.

3 *Upgrading title* The Land Registration Act 1925 as amended by the Land Registration Act 1986 provides for a title to be upgraded in certain circumstances:

(a) the Registrar, if satisfied as to the title, or if the land has been registered for at least twelve years and the Registrar is satisfied that the registered proprietor is in possession (meaning in actual occupation or in receipt of rents and profits),[18] may and must, on application[19] by the proprietor, convert possessory freehold title to absolute freehold;[20]
(b) the Registrar, if satisfied as above, may and must, on application[1] by the proprietor, convert possessory leasehold title to good leasehold;[2]
(c) the Registrar, if satisfied as to the freehold and any superior leasehold title may, and on application by the proprietor must, convert good leasehold title to absolute leasehold;[3]
(d) the Registrar, if satisfied as to the title, may and, on application by the proprietor, must convert a qualified title to absolute freehold or good leasehold as the case may be.[4]

iv Form of the register

The register for each title is split into three different parts; the property register, the proprietorship register and the charges register. Each title is given an individual title number.

1 *Property Register* This describes the land, normally with a brief verbal description and a reference to an official plan called the filed plan which is based on ordnance survey maps.[5] It will state the estate held – freehold or leasehold – and if the latter, it will give brief details of the lease, including its date, parties, term, rent and any provision prohibiting assignment or subletting without consent. It may also include a statement of any rights which exist for the benefit of the land[6] although registration does automatically vest such appurtenant rights in the proprietor.[7]

2 *Proprietorship Register* This states the class of title and the name and address of the registered proprietor. It will also contain any entries restricting the proprietor's rights of disposition, for example where the proprietor is the tenant for life of settled land.

When the property is transferred the name of the new proprietor will

18 Land Registration Act 1925, s. 3(xviii).
19 Conversion is commonly done on registration of a transfer on sale.
20 Land Registration Act 1986, s. 1(2).
1 See fn. 19, above.
2 Land Registration Act 1986, s. 1(2).
3 Ibid, s. 1(1).
4 Ibid, s. 1(3).
5 Land Registration Act 1925, s. 76(a).
6 Land Registration Rules 1925, r. 254.
7 See section iii, 1 above.

be added and the name of the previous proprietor struck out or removed altogether.

3 *Charges Register* This contains details of encumbrances adversely affecting the title, for example rights of way over the land, covenants, leases and mortgages.

Unless such third party rights are overriding interests, then in general terms they will not bind the proprietor (nor any purchaser from him) unless they are mentioned on the register,[8] and the charges register is the appropriate place for them to be recorded. So on first registration mention must be made in the charges register of all such adverse interests[9] and as they arise in the future they can be similarly noted. If an interest, for example a mortgage, is discharged, the entry is struck out or removed altogether.

4 *Land Certificates and Charge Certificates* The actual Land Register, that is the collection of registers of individual titles, is kept at the various District Land Registries around the country, which also deal with all registrations and other applications. On first registration the registered proprietor will be issued with a Land Certificate. This is a copy of the register of that title, including the plan, contained in an outer folder, which constitutes the actual Certificate and bears the Land Registry seal. The Certificate shows the date upon which it was last brought up to date with the entries in the register, which normally happens whenever the Certificate is produced to the Registry. If the property is subject to a mortgage or legal charge, protected by an entry in the charges register and thus called a 'registered charge', then the Land Certificate will be retained by the Registry[10] and the mortgagee will be issued with a Charge Certificate which is in similar form to the Land Certificate and has attached to it the mortgage deed. If there are further registered charges then further Charge Certificates will be issued to the further mortgagees.

v Dealings with registered titles

We have mentioned that all dispositions of land, the title to which is registered, must themselves be registered for the legal estate to pass.[11] On a straightforward sale of the registered title the purchaser's name will then be added to the proprietorship register and the vendor's name struck out or removed.

The effect of a registered disposition is, as might be expected, similar to the effect of first registration in that the purchaser, or donee, has vested in him the legal estate together with all appurtenant rights and subject only to entries on the register, overriding interests and, in the case of a leasehold title, all express or implied covenants and obligations in the lease.[12] If the title is possessory, qualified or good leasehold then the purchaser or donee is also subject to the additional matters thereby excepted from the effect of regis-

8 Ibid.

9 Land Registration Rules 1925, r. 40. By the Land Registration Act 1925, s. 70(2), this includes easements even if they are overriding interests.

10 Land Registration Act 1925, s. 65.

11 See section 2 ii 2, above.

12 Land Registration Act 1925, ss. 20, 23.

tration. If the disposition is made without valuable consideration, for example a gift, the donee is also bound by any minor interests subject to which the donor held the property.[13]

By section 64 of the Land Registration Act 1925, the Land Certificate must be produced on the application for registration of any disposition of the title. If there is a registered charge then the Land Certificate will already be at the Land Registry but the Charge Certificate will have to be produced if the registered charge is to be discharged.

vi Third party interests in registered land

Third party interests in land, title to which is registered, can be:

(a) registered with separate title, for example leases capable of such registration;
(b) overriding interests;
(c) minor interests;
(d) registered charges.

The first category has already been dealt with; the other categories have been mentioned in passing and must now be fully explained.

1 *Overriding interests* The crucially important characteristic of overriding interests is that they are binding on the registered proprietor and anyone who deals with him (for example a purchaser) irrespective of notice, and in particular, irrespective of whether they are mentioned on the register or not. As a result the majority of overriding interests will not be mentioned on the register.[14]

Overriding interests are a blot on the landscape of the system of registration title. If the ideal is a register which shows conclusively the land and all interests affecting it, then the existence of overriding interests is far from desirable. However they are necessary in practical terms, as it may not be possible to ascertain all the interests that do affect land at the time of first registration. The categories of overriding interests are in theory closed and they are listed in section 70(1) of the Land Registration Act 1925.[15] However, recent judicial decisions interpreting section 70(1) have broadened at least one of the categories.[16]

The categories of overriding interests are set out below.

Section 70(1)(a): A varied collection of rights comprising principally profits à prendre and legal easements. Certain easements such as rights of way, water and drainage are mentioned specifically. In addition, rule 258 of the Land Registration Rules 1925 provides that all rights appurtenant to land[17], which adversely affect land the title to which is registered, are also overriding interests.

13 See section 2 iii, above.
14 By the Land Registration Act 1925, s. 70(2) easements adversely affecting land should be entered on the register on first registration even though they are overriding interests.
15 The rights of the National Coal Board are also overriding interests; Coal Act 1938, s. 41, Coal Industry Nationalisation Act 1946, s. 5.
16 In particular *Williams & Glyn's Bank Ltd v Boland* [1981] AC 487, [1980] 2 All ER 408, HL.
17 Including, apparently, most equitable easements; *Celsteel Ltd v Alton House Holdings Ltd* [1985] 2 All ER 572, [1985] 1 WLR 204.

The effect of this is to ensure that the rights which impliedly pass on a conveyance by virtue of the Law of Property Act 1925, section 62 are overriding interests as regards the land adversely affected.

This category of overriding interests is obviously of great practical importance.

Section 70(1)(b): Certain tenurial liabilities, now virtually obsolete.

Section 70(1)(c): The liability to repair the chancel of a church.

Section 70(1)(d): Liabilities in respect of embankments and sea and river walls.

Section 70(1)(e):[18] Payments in lieu of tithe and tithe redemption annuities, now in effect extinguished by Finance Act 1977, s. 56.

Section 70(1)(f): Rights being acquired under the Limitation Acts. If this provision were not included one could only acquire title to registered land by prescription with great difficulty; the prescriptive right in the course of acquisition would have to be protected by some entry on the register, which would clearly be impracticable.

Section 70(1)(g): The rights of every person in actual occupation of the land or in receipt of the rents and profits thereof, save where enquiry is made of such person and the rights are not disclosed. This category has potentially very far-reaching effects. The rights must be rights in land, but they need not be in any way connected with the occupation of the land and could be rights which would otherwise rank as minor interests. Moreover the occupation does not have to be reasonably discoverable; there is no equivalent here to the unregistered conveyancing doctrine of notice. It is sufficient that the right is an interest in land and that the owner of the right is in occupation or in receipt of rents and profits. The following are all examples of rights which have been held to be overriding interests:

(a) a lessee's right to purchase the freehold reversion, contained in his lease;[19]
(b) a vendor's lien for unpaid purchase money;[20]
(c) the rights of a beneficiary under a trust for sale.[1]

However, certain rights are incapable of being overriding interests even though the owner of the right is in possession. Such rights include:

(a) the statutory right of occupation under the Matrimonial Homes Act 1983;[2]
(b) the rights under the Leasehold Reform Act 1967;[3]
(c) the rights of a beneficiary under a Settled Land Act 1925 settlement.[4]

Section 70(1)(h): In the case of a possessory, qualified or good leasehold title the interests excepted from the effect of registration. This accords with the definition of the effect of such registration.

Section 70(1)(i): Rights under local Land Charges unless and until protected on the register.

18 See also Tithe Act 1936, s. 13(11).
19 *Webb v Pollmount Ltd* [1966] Ch 584, [1966] 1 All ER 481.
20 *London and Cheshire Insurance Co Ltd v Laplagrene Property Co Ltd* [1971] Ch 499, [1971] 1 All ER 766.
1 *Williams & Glyn's Bank Ltd v Boland* [1981] AC 487, [1980] 2 All ER 408, HL.
2 S. 2(8).
3 S. 5(5).
4 Land Registration Act 1925, s. 86(2).

Section 70(1)(j): Various manorial rights.

Section 70(1)(k):[5] Leases for a term of twenty-one years or less. Such a lease will be thus an overriding interest as against any registered superior title. This is the corollary of the rule that leases for over twenty-one years are capable of registration with separate title.

Section 70(1)(l): Various mineral and mining rights.

A purchaser of a registered title takes subject to overriding interests which are in existence at the date of registration of his purchase, which under the Land Registration Rules 1925[6] is taken as the date of his application for registration. In assessing whether or not the purchaser is subject to overriding interests under section 70(1)(g), it is that date at which one must establish whether anyone who may have such an overriding interest was in occupation or in receipt of rents and profits.[7] As registration must obviously occur some time after completion of the purchase, problems can thereby be caused for both purchasers and their mortgagees which will be fully explored in later chapters.

2 *Minor interests* If an interest affecting a registered title is not an overriding interest, nor a mortgage protected as a registered charge, it must be a minor interest. A purchaser will take free of it, that is to say it will be overridden on a disposition for value of the registered title affected, unless it is protected in the appropriate way on the register. Minor interests include some leases, interests arising under trusts and settlements, interests arising under dispositions capable of substantive registration but not yet so registered[8] and the more familiar litany of third party interests such as estate contracts and restrictive covenants.

3 *Protection of minor interests by notice* The normal method of protecting a minor interest is by entry of a notice in the Charges Register of the title affected. This method can be used to protect leases,[9] restrictive covenants,[10] rights of occupation under the Matrimonial Homes Act 1983, estate contracts and other specified interests.[11] The effect is that the registered proprietor is subject to the interest[12] and any disposition by him is similarly subject but only of course so far as the interest is itself valid – if the Charges Register contains notice of a restrictive covenant, the burden must still be shown to pass under general land law principles for a purchaser to be bound by it.

The entry of a notice depends on the applicant producing the Land Certificate.[13] If this is not available because the registered proprietor will not co-operate, a caution may be the appropriate means of protection. If the property

5 As amended by Land Registration Act 1986.

6 R.83(2).

7 *Re Boyle's Claim* [1961] 1 All ER 620, [1961] 1 WLR 339.

8 For example the interest of a purchaser of a registered title who has not yet applied for registration of his purchase.

9 Land Registration Act 1925, s. 48.

10 Ibid, s. 50.

11 Land Registration Act 1925, s. 49.

12 Ibid, s. 52.

13 Ibid, s. 64(1)(c).

is subject to a registered charge, the Land Certificate is retained at the Registry; it is treated as being available and a notice can be entered. Exceptionally, the Land Certificate need not be produced on an application for entry of a notice to protect the Matrimonial Homes Act 1983 right of occupation.

The position of leases deserves special mention. We have seen that leases for over twenty-one years are capable of registration with separate title and that leases of twenty-one years or under are overriding interests. More fundamentally, the grant of a lease out of a registered title is a 'disposition' and must be registered for the lessee to obtain a legal estate. If the lease is capable of registration with separate title then the lessee must apply for this but in addition the lessee should apply for notice of the lease to be entered on the Charges Register of the reversionary title if that is registered. This then completes the process of registration. The Land Certificate *need not* be produced, provided that the lease was granted at a rent without a fine.[14] Unfortunately, many leases in practice are granted at a fine, for example the long lease of a newly built dwelling house on a housing estate. In such a situation the prospective lessee ought to ensure that his contract includes a provision compelling the lessor to make his Land Certificate available if his title is registered.

Finally, it should be noted that s. 70(1)(k) only covers a legal lease as opposed to an equitable lease or an agreement for a lease. The latter could be overriding interests under s. 70(1)(g) but should otherwise be protected by notice.

4 *Protection of minor interests by caution* The Land Registration Act 1925[15] provides that any person interested in a registered title may lodge a caution in the Proprietorship Register, the effect being that before any disposition of the land can be registered the cautioner is given an opportunity to establish his interest.[16] The Land Certificate does not have to be produced when lodging a caution and this is an alternative method to entry of a notice, where the Land Certificate is not available. It may well be the appropriate method of protecting an estate contract or a writ or order relating to the land. Before 1981 it was the commonly used method of protecting the (then) Matrimonial Homes Act 1967 right of occupation, but since 1981 this is to be done only by notice.[17] A registered proprietor can try and have cautions removed, if he thinks they are unjustified, by having them 'warned off', rather than waiting until there is a disposition of the property.[18]

It is also possible to register a caution against first registration where title to land is not yet registered.[19] This may be done if, for example, the title deeds have been lost and the owner wishes to be informed of any application for first registration so that he can establish his prior claim.

14 Ibid, s. 64(1)(c); *Strand Securities Ltd v Caswell* [1965] Ch 958, [1966] 1 All ER 820, CA.
15 S. 54.
16 Ibid, s. 55.
17 Matrimonial Homes and Property Act 1981, now Matrimonial Homes Act 1983.
18 Land Registration Rules 1925, r. 218.
19 Land Registration Act 1925, s. 53.

5 *Protection of minor interests by restriction* Unless there is anything on the register to the contrary, anyone dealing with a registered proprietor can assume that his powers of disposition are unlimited. In particular, the Land Registration Act 1925 provides that no one dealing with a registered title shall be affected by notice of a trust,[20] although this is subject to the possibility of the beneficiary's interest being an overriding interest.[1] In fact, the powers of the registered proprietor may be limited; for example if the registered proprietor is a trustee, or a tenant for life of settled land, or a charity. The appropriate method of recording this on the register, and protecting the minor interests involved, is by means of a restriction in the Proprietorship Register.[2] Thus where two persons who are beneficial tenants in common apply for registration, the survivor will have no power to deal with the property and the following restriction will be entered:[3]

> No disposition by one proprietor of the land (being a survivor of joint proprietors and not being a trust corporation) under which capital money arises is to be registered except under an Order of the Registrar or the Court.

A similar restriction will be imposed on registration of the tenant for life of settled land as proprietor, preventing registration of any disposition unless it is authorised by the Settled Land Act 1925 and capital money is paid to the trustees of the settlement.[4]

It is also possible to make an independent application for the entry of a restriction. This could arise where the matrimonial home is in the sole name of the husband, but the wife has an equitable interest. The wife may apply for the entry of the joint proprietorship restriction. The Land Certificate must normally be produced and in such a situation it may not be available. There are three other alternatives. Firstly her interest may be an overriding interest under section 70(1)(g) of the Land Registration Act 1925. Secondly, she could apply for entry of a notice on the register under section 49(1)(d) of the Act requiring payment of capital money to at least two trustees, although again this depends on production of the Land Certificate. Thirdly, she can apply to lodge a caution to protect her interest for which of course the Land Certificate need not be produced.[5]

6 *Protection of minor interests by inhibition* An inhibition in the Proprietorship Register completely prohibits the registration of any dealings with the land[6] and is normally only used consequent on the registered proprietor's bankruptcy. The bankruptcy order is registered in the Land Charges Registry in the register of writs and orders and an inhibition automatically entered in the Proprietorship Register of any registered land owned by the bankrupt.[7] The bankruptcy petition will have been similarly protected by a pending

20 Ibid, s. 74.
1 *Williams & Glyn's Bank Ltd v Boland* [1981] AC 487, [1980] 2 All ER 408, HL.
2 Land Registration Act 1925, s. 58.
3 Ibid, s. 58(3); Land Registration Rules 1925, r. 213.
4 Ibid, s. 86(3).
5 *Elias v Mitchell* [1972] Ch 652, [1972] 2 All ER 153.
6 Land Registration Act 1925, s. 57.
7 Ibid, s. 61(3).

action being registered in the Land Charges Registry and a creditor's notice automatically entered in the Charges Register.[8]

7 *Mortgages of registered titles* The normal method of creating a mortgage or legal charge over land, the title to which is registered, is by a registered charge, which is registered in the Charges Register of the title. The mortgagee is then issued with a Charge Certificate. A registered proprietor may in fact mortgage his land in any way appropriate to unregistered land although until it is protected as a registered charge the mortgage only takes effect in equity and is a minor interest, requiring protection by notice or caution.[9]

It is also possible to create a charge over land, the title to which is registered, by depositing the Land Certificate with the lender.[10] The lien so created can be protected by entry of notice of deposit (or notice of intended deposit if the Land Certificate is not yet available because for example it is still at the Registry for registration of a purchase). The Land Certificate need not be produced on application for entry of a notice of deposit which, confusingly, takes effect as a caution.[11]

8 *Comparison of third party interests in registered and unregistered conveyancing* In the earlier part of this chapter we dealt with the effect of third party interests on a purchaser of unregistered land. We can now see that the scheme of protection in relation to registered titles is quite different. A purchaser takes subject to overriding interests and to minor interests protected on the register but free from other interests. Although there is a superficial resemblance in the effect of legal interests in unregistered conveyancing and overriding interests in registered conveyancing, and in the effect of interests registrable under the Land Charges Act 1972 in unregistered conveyancing and minor interests in registered conveyancing, these categories do not coincide one with the other and should be considered quite separately.

A first legal mortgage of unregistered land will be protected by deposit of the title deeds with the mortgagee, subsequent legal and equitable mortgages being registrable as land charges under the Land Charges Act 1972. As we have just seen, the normal method of mortgaging registered land, whether it be a first or subsequent mortgage, is by registered charge. The deposit of the Land Certificate, protected by notice of deposit on the register, is roughly comparable with the deposit of title deeds in relation to unregistered land, creating an equitable mortgage

vii Rectification and indemnity

Although the main advantage of a system of registration of title is the guarantee that the register provides, there is the ever-present possibility that the register may be rectified if it contains an error.[12] However, if it is rectified then anyone suffering loss as a result may be able to claim compensation.

8 Ibid, s. 61(1).
9 Ibid, s. 106 as substituted by the Administration of Justice Act 1977, s. 26.
10 Ibid, s. 66.
11 Land Registration Rules 1925, r. 239.
12 See, for example, *Argyle Building Society v Hammond* (1984) 49 P&CR 148, CA.

The grounds on which the register can be rectified are set out in section 82(1) of the Land Registration Act 1925 and include not only specific situations but also a general discretion to rectify when it is deemed just. There is a restriction on rectification which will adversely affect the title of a registered proprietor who is in possession. Rectification in such circumstances can only be ordered[13] to give effect to an overriding interest (such as a prescriptive right); to give effect to an order of the court; if the proprietor has caused or substantially contributed to the error by fraud or lack of proper care; or if it would be unjust not to rectify.

An indemnity, ie compensation, is available if a person suffers loss by reason of rectification or by reason of an error on the register that is not rectified.[14] No indemnity is payable if the applicant (or someone through whom he claims otherwise than for value) caused or substantially contributed to the loss by fraud or lack of proper care. Neither would an indemnity be payable to a registered proprietor if the register were rectified to reflect an overriding interest; the proprietor would not be adversely affected by the rectification as he would have been bound by the overriding interest anyway. The amount of the indemnity is the value of the lost interest at the time of rectification if the register is rectified, but at the time of the making of the error on the register if the register is not rectified.[15]

13 Land Registration Act 1925, s. 82(3).

14 Ibid, s. 83. An indemnity is also payable if loss is suffered by reason of an error in an official search certificate, or by the Registry losing or destroying documents.

15 Ibid, s. 83(6).

3 Outline of a typical transaction

For the rest of the first part of this book we will be looking chronologically at the various stages of a conveyancing transaction. It is important to have an initial overall view of the typical transaction in order to put into context its constituent parts. The normal conveyancing transaction, loosely called buying and selling a house, will fall into one of three categories; the conveyance on sale of a freehold, the assignment on sale of an already existing lease, and the grant of a new lease out of a freehold or leasehold. A lease granted out of the freehold is normally called a headlease and a lease granted out of another lease is called an underlease. For example if a builder is selling an estate of new houses he may, if he owns the freehold, sell the freehold of the individual houses or grant long leases of them. If he holds the estate on a lease, he can either assign the lease in respect of each house or, as is perhaps more likely, he could grant underleases. If leases or underleases are granted, then when the original purchasers of the houses in their turn sell, they will in effect be assigning the lease or underlease.

The outline of the typical transaction that follows is applicable to all three types of transactions and when we deal with the transaction in detail in the following chapters we shall examine various possibilities. The assignment of a lease, in particular, is very similar to the conveyance of a freehold and both are examined fully in the following chapters. The grant of a lease stands to some extent on its own, involving, as it does, the creation of a new legal estate rather than the transfer of an existing one, although the conveyancing procedure is essentially similar. Thus, whilst the following chapters do make reference to the grant of a lease, this transaction and, in particular, the contents of the lease are examined further in chapter 17, which also reiterates the differences dealt with in the earlier chapters, between the assignment of a lease and a freehold conveyance.

The transaction is usually divided into two distinct stages – the stage leading up to the formation of a binding contract for the sale of the property, and the stage following that in which the vendor deduces title and which culminates in the legal estate vesting in the purchaser. The legal estate does not pass to the purchaser on the formation of the contract of sale; the parties merely become contractually bound to buy and sell on the terms contained in the contract. The second stage can be seen as the performance of these contractual obligations. The steps in the transaction can be summarised as follows.

(1) The vendor must first of all find a purchaser, either himself or by using an estate agent.

(2) A purchaser having been found, the vendor's solicitor will want to draft a contract. He must first of all be satisfied that the vendor can sell what he wants to and he will therefore examine the vendor's title, in much the same way as the purchaser's solicitor will eventually do. He will need the title deeds, or if title to the property is registered he will want the Land Certificate, or Charge Certificate if there is a registered charge. In fact if the title is registered he will probably also apply to the District Land Registry for a set of official photocopies of the entries on the register (called 'office copies'), which will be more up to date than the copy entries in the Certificate.

(3) The draft contract which the vendor's solicitor prepares will describe the property (both physically and by stating the estate being sold) normally by reference to the deeds, or to the register if title is registered. The contract will mention any matters subject to which the property is held and similarly any matters of which the property has the benefit. For example, the property may be subject to, or have the benefit of, easements or covenants. The draft contract will also include the terms upon which the property is sold, including of course the price.

(4) The draft contract is normally prepared in duplicate and both copies sent to the purchaser's solicitor for approval. At this time the parties are under no obligation whatsoever[1] and the draft contract is merely a basis for negotiating the terms which will be included in the actual contract.

(5) The purchaser's solicitor will examine the draft contract to ensure that it is acceptable and accords with the purchaser's requirements and, if the purchaser is taking out a mortgage to provide part of the purchase price, that it will accord with the mortgagee's requirements as well.

(6) The purchaser may have a survey done. Unless the vendor built the property, it is sold as it stands and it is up to the purchaser to satisfy himself as to its physical condition.

(7) The purchaser's solicitor makes a number of searches and enquiries, with the object of finding out all he can about the property. These include enquiries of the vendor through his solicitor, a local land charges search and additional enquiries of the Local Authority, an inspection of the property and perhaps other searches and enquiries in particular cases.

(8) If the purchaser is taking out a mortgage to provide part of the purchase price, he must be satisfied that a mortgage offer has been made and that the money will be available when he needs it.

(9) Assuming both parties still want to proceed, and are agreed on the terms, they can now enter into the formal contract. They are free to choose the method by which the contract is formed, but the normal way is by physical exchange of two identical signed contracts. Each party signs one copy. Normally the draft contract as amended is used although if there have been substantial amendments it may be re-typed. These two parts are then phys-

1 Except in the rare case where the parties have already entered into an informal binding contract.

ically exchanged either at the office of one of the solicitors or through the post, and only when the exchange is complete is the contract formed. The contract usually provides for a deposit to be paid on exchange, normally 10 per cent of the purchase price. As a result of the exchange each party has a contract signed by the other party.

(10) There is inevitably a delay between a purchaser seeing a property he wishes to buy and exchange of contracts. This is caused by the necessity to make searches and enquiries, agree on the contract and arrange finance. The purchaser may also have a property to sell and wish to synchronise the two transactions. As the parties are not under any binding obligation during this pre-contract period, there is the possibility of 'gazumping'.[2] This is where the vendor, having received a better offer, threatens to sell elsewhere unless the purchaser agrees to increase the purchase price. In a slow-moving market the purchaser could threaten to buy another property unless the purchase price were reduced. There may of course be genuine reasons why the purchaser does want the purchase price reduced; he may have discovered on his survey that the property is in a poor state of repair and needs money spent on it.

(11) Following exchange the parties are bound to buy and sell and the vendor is thus bound to convey the property described in the contract. He must first demonstrate to the purchaser that he can do so, and deduce title. If the title is unregistered the vendor's solicitor prepares and sends to the purchaser's solicitor details of the recent deeds and other events under which the property has passed. This can be in the form of an abbreviated precis called an 'Abstract of Title' or in the form of a list of the deeds and other documents together with photocopies, called an 'Epitome of Title'. If the title is registered then the vendor's solicitor sends copies of the entries on the register, normally using office copies.

(12) The purchaser's solicitor examines the title to ensure that the vendor can comply with the contract and convey what he has contracted to. If he cannot, then prima facie he is in breach of contract; for example if the property is subject to a restrictive covenant which was not revealed in the contract. If the purchaser's solicitor wants clarification of any point he will raise an enquiry called a Requisition on Title, pointing out the defect and requiring the vendor to remedy it.

(13) If the purchaser is taking out a mortgage, the title will also have to be investigated by the solicitors for the mortgagee. A mortgage is in effect just another sort of conveyancing transaction, like a conveyance on sale or a lease. The purchaser, having purchased the property, immediately mortgages it by a mortgage deed to the mortgagee, as security for a loan from the mortgagee which is used in order to help pay the purchase price of the property. The mortgagee will be just as concerned as the purchaser that the title to the property is good and will wish to examine the title before making the mortgage advance. Duplication in the examination of title is often avoided by the solicitor for the purchaser also acting for the Building Society or other mortgagee, so that he only investigates the title once, for both his clients.

2 The Law Commission has suggested a voluntary scheme for payment by both parties of a 0·5% deposit at a very early stage in the transaction, returnable only in certain circumstances to a party who withdraws before exchange of contracts. See 1987 Law Soc Gazette p. 791.

(14) The next stage in the process of investigation of title is for the purchaser's solicitor to make certain searches, with the object of discovering whether there are any third party interests of which he is not aware, which are going to be binding on the purchaser. These searches will differ according to whether the title is registered or not. If the title is registered, the main search will be at the District Land Registry; if not, it will be a search of the Land Charges Register under the Land Charges Act 1972. If a third party interest, such as a restrictive covenant, is revealed, then the vendor will again be prima facie in breach of contract unless the covenant was revealed in the contract. Similar searches may also be done on behalf of a mortgagee.

(15) The purchaser's solicitor will now prepare the purchase deed. In unregistered conveyancing the deed will be a conveyance (of freehold land), an assignment (of an existing lease) or a lease. In registered transactions it will be a 'transfer' of registered freehold or leasehold land, or a lease. The deed will describe the land, in a similar way to the contract, and name the parties to the transaction. The deed is submitted to the vendor's solicitor for approval and return and is then engrossed ie the final copy is typed. If the purchaser has to execute the deed he will normally do so at this stage and the deed is then sent to the vendor's solicitor for execution ie signing and sealing by the vendor.

The word 'conveyance' is often used to mean not just the unregistered freehold deed but in a wider sense to mean any purchase deed including an assignment and transfer and also a lease, mortgage or assent. In particular, this is the meaning of the word in the Law of Property Act 1925[3] and the word will normally be used in its wider sense in this book, unless the context shows otherwise.

(16) The mortgagee's solicitor, who may also be the purchaser's solicitor, will prepare the mortgage deed if the purchaser is taking out a mortgage. This must be executed by the purchaser and the mortgage advance obtained from the mortgagee in readiness for completion.

(17) The final stage in the transaction is called 'completion'. The purchaser's solicitor hands over the balance of the purchase price and the vendor's solicitor hands over the executed purchase deed, all the other deeds and the Land Certificate or Charge Certificate if the title is registered. If the purchaser is entering into a mortgage, the mortgagee receives all these documents of title and the executed mortgage deed, in return for the mortgage advance. The date for completion is normally agreed in the contract. If the property was mortgaged, as is likely, the vendor's solicitor will pay off the mortgage(s) out of the proceeds of sale, and the mortgage(s) will be discharged.

(18) After completion the deed must be produced to the Inland Revenue and possibly Stamp Duty paid. If the title is registered the purchaser's solicitor will have to apply for the disposition to be registered. The purchaser will not get the legal estate until this is done, whereas on an unregistered transaction the legal estate passes to the purchaser on completion. If title is unregistered, but the property is in an area now subject to a Compulsory Registration Order, the purchaser's solicitor will have to apply for first registration of title. If the

3 S. 205(1)(ii).

purchaser's solicitor is also acting for the mortgagee, then on registering the purchase application will also be made to register the mortgage.

(19) It often happens that a person is both selling one house and buying another, and normally exchange of contracts and completion must be co-ordinated to avoid leaving, or risking leaving, that person with two houses or no house at all. If the person to whom a purchaser is selling his own house is himself selling, one has the beginnings of a chain, which can make co-ordination of the transaction a major administrative problem for the solicitors involved.

4 Enforceability of the contract

1 Introduction

We have seen from the preceding chapter that the parties of a conveyancing transaction will normally enter into a contract which binds them to buy and sell; this contract is then performed, culminating in completion when the deed necessary to transfer the legal estate is handed over. There is nothing to prevent the parties proceeding straight to the completion stage, without entering into either a formal or informal contract. This might be thought to be a method of reducing the length of time taken by a conveyancing transaction but its main disadvantage is that a party can never be sure that the other party will complete until the very last minute. The possibility of gazumping increases with a consequently greater effect on a long chain of transactions if one of the transactions should 'go off'.

If we assume that the parties do follow the conventional procedure of first entering into a contract, there is a specific requirement which this contract must satisfy in order for it to be enforceable. It must either be in writing or evidenced in writing. The Law of Property Act 1925, section 40 states:

> (1) No action may be brought upon any contract for the sale or other disposition of land or any interest in land, unless the agreement upon which such action is brought, or some memorandum or note thereof, is in writing, and signed by the party to be charged or by some other person thereunto by him lawfully authorised.
> (2) This section ... does not affect the law relating to part performance ...

'Land' is defined in detail in section 205(1)(ix) of the Act. The section also applies to a contract part only of which relates to the sale of land.[1] In addition, in *Daulia Ltd v Four Millbank Nominees Ltd*,[2] an agreement to exchange contracts for the sale of land was itself held to be subject to section 40.

Under the conventional procedure, the contract itself is in writing. After exchange of contracts each party has the part of the contract signed by the other party and it is this which meets the requirement of the section that for

1 *Steadman v Steadman* [1976] AC 536, [1974] 2 All ER 977; *Ram Narayan s/o Shankar v Rishad Hussain Shah s/o Tasadua Hussain Shah* [1979] 1 WLR 1349, PC.

2 [1978] Ch 231, [1978] 2 All ER 557, CA.

a party to enforce such a contract by action there must be a document signed 'by the party to be charged', ie the party against whom the contract is being enforced. However even in the context of the conventional transaction it is necessary to study section 40 more closely.

The section states that if the contract is not in writing, there must be some written memorandum of it for it to be enforceable; the existence of the memorandum presupposes the existence of a valid contract. There is no need to consider whether a memorandum exists if there is no contract of which it can be evidence. However it may be that the parties have entered into an oral contract, perhaps before they have instructed solicitors. That contract will be enforceable if there is a written memorandum of it complying with the requirements of section 40. The memorandum need not have been intended to be evidence of the contract and it can arise by accident. In *Dewar v Mintoft*[3] the memorandum was a letter which actually repudiated the contract. The danger for solicitors is illustrated by a series of Court of Appeal cases which concern the practice of solicitors of heading their correspondence before exchange of contracts 'subject to contract'. This has the dual purpose of preventing an exchange of letters forming a contract and also of preventing the correspondence being used as a memorandum of a contract, which might conceivably already exist.[4]

In *Thirkell v Cambi*[5] it was suggested that the memorandum must contain some admission that there was a contract in existence. In *Law v Jones*,[6] *Thirkell v Cambi* was distinguished as being a case where the memorandum contained an actual denial of liability under the contract; there was nothing to prevent a letter headed 'subject to contract' from constituting a sufficient memorandum. *Law v Jones* was not followed in *Tiverton Estates Ltd v Wearwell Ltd*[7] which held that the memorandum must contain an acknowledgement of the existence of the contract and that a document containing the words 'subject to contract' could *not* constitute a memorandum. In *Daulia Ltd v Four Millbank Nominees Ltd*[8] the judges who had formed the majority in *Law v Jones* took the opportunity to reiterate their point of view. However, in *Cohen v Nessdale Ltd*,[9] *Tiverton Estates Ltd v Wearwell Ltd* was followed in preference to *Law v Jones*.

There seems to be some uncertainty on this point and also on whether an acknowledgment, if necessary, will be readily implied into a memorandum.[10] As it is fairly clear that a letter which denies the existence of a contract cannot form the basis of a memorandum it may be safer in practice for solicitors to use a 'contract denied' formula rather than the usual 'subject to contract'.[11]

3 [1912] 2 KB 373.
4 Such an informal contract between the parties would be rare in practice.
5 [1919] 2 KB 590, CA.
6 [1974] Ch 112, [1973] 2 All ER 437, CA.
7 [1975] Ch 146, [1974] 1 All ER 209, CA.
8 Above.
9 [1981] 3 All ER 118.
10 See for example *Tweddell v Henderson* [1975] 2 All ER 1096, [1975] 1 WLR 1496.
11 See Farrand *Contract and Conveyance* (4th edn) p. 36.

2 Contents of the memorandum

The memorandum must contain all the terms of the agreement, which can be summarised as the four P's – parties, property, price, plus any other agreed terms.

i Parties

The memorandum must state the names of the parties or at least describe them sufficiently to allow them to be identified. So in *F Goldsmith (Sicklesmere) Ltd v Baxter*,[12] the plaintiff was adequately described as Goldsmith Coaches (Sicklesmere) Ltd, a slightly incorrect version of the company's name. A description of the vendor simply as 'the owner' or 'the proprietor' might be sufficient if it is not ambiguous.

It must also be apparent from the memorandum which party is buying and which party is selling.[13]

ii Property

As with the parties, the property must be described so as to allow it to be identified. For a dwelling house, the postal address would normally be sufficient. Even 'my house' will be sufficient if the vendor has only one house; parol evidence is admissible to describe it precisely.[14] If on the other hand the vendor has more than one house, parol evidence will not be admissible to show which house is being sold and the memorandum will fail to satisfy section 40. Where land and chattels are sold together at a price not apportioned between them, a memorandum not mentioning the chattels may fail to satisfy section 40.[15]

iii Price

The memorandum must state either the price or the means by which it can be fixed.

iv Plus any other terms

The memorandum must also include any other terms of the agreement between the parties, for example the completion date if it has been fixed or a term that one party will pay another's costs. There have been suggestions that only important terms of the agreement have to be in the memorandum,[16] but the better view would seem to be that all relevant terms must be included for the contract to be enforceable. However, terms which will be implied into the contract do not have to be mentioned in the memorandum.[17]

A memorandum relating to the grant of a lease must also contain the

12 [1970] Ch 85, [1969] 3 All ER 733.

13 *Dewar v Mintoft*, above.

14 *Cowley v Watts* (1853) 17 Jur 172.

15 *Ram Narayan v Rishad Hussain Shah*, above.

16 In *Tweddell v Henderson*, above, at 1102, Plowman VC states that the memorandum must contain 'all the material terms of the alleged contract'; there is then a suggestion that material terms means 'terms of substance or importance'.

17 *Timmins v Moreland Street Property Co Ltd* [1958] Ch 110, [1957] 3 All ER 265, CA.

commencement date and term of the lease in addition to any other agreed terms.[18]

v Signature

The memorandum must be signed by the party to be charged, that is the party against whom the contract is being enforced. A rubber stamp may suffice[19] as may the name of a party in a document written or even dictated by that party,[20] but not if there is a space for signature at the end of the document which has been left blank.[1]

Section 40 also permits signature by an agent, who may be authorised orally. An auctioneer has implied authority from both parties to sign a memorandum although signature on behalf of the purchaser must be at the time of the sale; a week afterwards has been held to be too late.[2] His authority to sign for the vendor is not so limited and extends throughout the period he is instructed to sell the property. It appears that a solicitor may have implied authority to sign a memorandum of an already existing contract,[3] but not to sign the actual contract itself.[4] An estate agent has no such implied authority[5] although he could of course be given express authority.

vi Subsequent alterations

The danger here is that if the document is altered after signature it may not be 'signed' for the purpose of section 40 and the contract may then be unenforceable. The signature can be 'extended' to the alterations by initialling the alteration. In the conventional transaction the contract will be prepared and signed before exchange. It is not strictly essential for any alteration made before exchange to be initialled,[6] but if the alteration is made after exchange, because the parties have agreed to vary the terms of the contract, the original signature must be reauthenticated, normally by initialling the alteration.[7] In practice alterations should be initialled whenever made.

vii Joinder of documents

It may be that there is no one document which satisfies section 40. In certain circumstances two or more documents can be read together so as to constitute a memorandum. There must be some express or implied reference in a document signed by the party to be charged to some other document or transaction. If so, parol evidence is admissible to identify the other document referred to or to explain the other transaction and identify any document relating to it.[8]

18 *Harvey v Pratt* [1965] 2 All ER 786, [1965] 1 WLR 1025, CA.
19 *Bennett v Brumfitt* (1867) LR 3 CP 28.
20 *Knight v Crockford* (1794) 1 Esp 190; *Hucklesby v Hook* (1900) 82 LT 117.
1 *Hubert v Treherne* (1842) 3 Man & G 743.
2 *Bell v Balls* [1897] 1 Ch 663.
3 *North v Loomes* [1919] 1 Ch 378.
4 *Smith v Webster* (1876) 3 Ch D 49.
5 *Wragg v Lovett* [1948] 2 All ER 968.
6 *Koenigsblatt v Sweet* [1923] 2 Ch 314, CA.
7 *New Hart Builders Ltd v Bindley* [1975] Ch 342, [1975] 1 All ER 1007.
8 *Timmins v Moreland Street Property Co Ltd*, above, approved in *Elias v George Sahely & Co (Barbados) Ltd* [1983] 1 AC 646, [1982] 3 All ER 801, PC.

Documents brought to light in this way can be read with the original signed document so as to together constitute a memorandum. This rule seems to have replaced the similar 'side by side' rule under which documents could be read together if on laying them side by side they clearly referred to the same transaction,[9] although the latter rule probably still applies if both documents are signed by the party to be charged.[10]

In *Timmins v Moreland Street Property Co Ltd*[11] a cheque for the deposit signed by the purchaser was held not to refer expressly or impliedly to a receipt given by the vendor, which contained all the terms of the contract. The cheque referred merely to the payment of a sum of money and not the reason for that payment. The vendor could not enforce the contract against the purchaser, although because of the existence of the receipt signed by the vendor, presumably the purchaser could enforce against the vendor.

3 Non-compliance with section 40

Non-compliance with section 40 does not affect the validity of the contract but merely makes it unenforceable by action. It may be enforceable in other ways; the vendor can still forfeit the purchaser's deposit if the purchaser unjustifiably refuses to complete.[12] If an action is brought on a contract which is unenforceable by virtue of section 40, the defendant must expressly plead this[13] although it is unlikely that he would fail to do so. Further, despite the absence of a section 40 memorandum the contract may still be enforceable in equity, by a decree of specific performance, if there has been a sufficient act of part performance by the plaintiff.[14]

i Part performance

To amount to part performance, an act must be capable of explanation only by the existence of a contract, and must be consistent with the particular contract alleged to exist. In *Kingswood Estate Co Ltd v Anderson*[15] a widow agreed to give up a protected tenancy and move into alternative accommodation, of which she would have a life tenancy. Her landlord later served notice to quit the new accommodation alleging that she merely had a weekly tenancy. She was able to enforce her agreement for a life tenancy, as her act in occupying the new accommodation could only be explained by the existence of a tenancy agreement and was consistent with the tenancy agreement she alleged to exist.

The most common acts of part performance in the context of the sale of land will be the vendor giving up possession or the purchaser taking possession. Payment of money, for example the deposit, will not normally amount to part

9 *Sheers v Thimbleby & Son* (1897) 76 LT 709, CA.
10 *Timmins v Moreland Street Property Co Ltd*, above, at 130.
11 Above.
12 *Monnickendam v Leanse* (1923) 39 TLR 445.
13 RSC Ord 18, r. 8.
14 Law of Property Act 1925, s. 40(2).
15 [1963] 2 QB 169, [1962] 3 All ER 593, CA.

performance, although in *Steadman v Steadman*[16] the House of Lords held that the payment of arrears of maintenance did amount to part performance of an agreement between a husband and wife in respect of maintenance and the transfer of the matrimonial home. This rendered the latter part of the agreement enforceable. There is also a suggestion in this case that the purchaser instructing his solicitors to prepare and submit a draft conveyance would be a sufficient act of part performance. In *Sutton v Sutton*[17], a wife's consent to a divorce petition was held to be a sufficient act of part performance of an agreement providing, inter alia, for such consent and for the transfer of the matrimonial home to her.

The court will not enforce the contract unless the act of part performance is such that it amounts to a fraud on the defendant's part to take advantage of the unenforceability of the contract. There must be proper (although presumably at least partly oral) evidence of the contract, and specific performance could still be refused on equitable grounds.

ii Missing term

There is a further way in which the contract can be enforced, despite the lack of a sufficient memorandum. If the memorandum is only defective because some term or terms agreed between the parties have been omitted, then if the omitted term is solely for the benefit of the plaintiff he can waive it and enforce the contract as evidenced ie without that term.[18] Similarly, if the omitted term is solely to the detriment of the plaintiff he can undertake to perform it and enforce the contract.[19] One example of a term solely to the detriment or benefit of one party or the other is a term that one party should pay the other's conveyancing costs. Terms such as the date for completion will not be solely to the benefit or detriment of either party.

16 [1976] AC 536, [1974] 2 All ER 977, HL
17 [1984] Ch 184, [1984] 1 All ER 168.
18 *North v Loomes* [1919] 1 Ch 378.
19 *Scott v Bradley* [1971] Ch 850, [1971] 1 All ER 583.

5 Drafting the contract

1 Introduction

There is no special form that the contract must take; thus it could be formed by offer and acceptance either orally or in correspondence. Because of the requirements of section 40 of the Law of Property Act 1925 as to the enforceability of the contract, the conventional procedure is for a written contract to be prepared. Such a formal contract will consist very broadly of two parts; the particulars, which describe the subject matter of the sale, and the conditions, which state the terms on which it is being sold. This chapter deals with the preparation of such a formal contract.

A solicitor will in fact probably base the contract on a standard form, supplied by law stationers. This will include a comprehensive set of general conditions, for example the Law Society's general conditions of sale (LSC) or the national conditions of sale (NC).[1] These can then be amended or added to as the particular case demands.

When a contract contains no conditions to cover a particular situation, the contract is said to be 'open' on that point and the rights of the parties are normally prescribed by common law or statute. A completely open contract would contain no conditions whatsoever.

2 Preparation for drafting

It is the vendor's solicitor's job to draft the contract. In order to do this he must firstly establish in consultation with the vendor exactly what the vendor proposes to sell, and on what conditions, and secondly ensure that the vendor can do so by examining the vendor's title. He must therefore obtain the title deeds or, if the title is registered, details of the register entries. The vendor himself may have the deeds or the Land Certificate, or they may already be in the possession of the vendor's solicitor, if he acted on the purchase. They might be held by the vendor's previous solicitor, who will probably require a

1 The current Law Society Conditions are the 1984 edition; the current National Conditions are the 1981 edition. Both are reproduced in the appendix.

written authority from the vendor before releasing them. If the vendor's property is in mortgage, then the deeds or Charge Certificate will be with the first mortgagee. The solicitor will have to ask the mortgagee whether the deeds or Certificate can be released to him on his undertaking to return them on demand, or else to repay the amount owing under the mortgage. A Building Society mortgagee will normally release the deeds against such an undertaking, if the solicitor is on the panel of the solicitors whom the Society has authorised to act for it on repayment of the mortgage. If not, the vendor's solicitor will have to be content at this stage with an abstract or epitome prepared and supplied by the mortgagee's solicitor. If the title is registered, the vendor's solicitor can always apply for office copies of the register entries and will normally do so even if the Land or Charge Certificate is immediately available. They give the up-to-date state of the register and will be needed in due course to deduce title, if not to amplify the description of the property in the contract. A further possibility is that the deeds or Land certificate may be with a bank. If the bank is merely holding them for safe keeping, they will be released on the vendor's authority. If on the other hand they are security for a loan or overdraft, the solicitor may have to give some undertaking in respect of the proceeds of sale; perhaps to pay the net proceeds to the credit of the vendor's account at the bank. As with all undertakings, the solicitor should ensure that he gets his client's instructions before giving the undertaking and that he will be able to comply with its terms.

The vendor's solicitor will then examine the vendor's title to ensure that the vendor can convey what he proposes to. If there are any defects in the title,[2] the solicitor can then draft the appropriate condition in the contract to cover the situation. The examination of title will involve not only an inspection of the deeds (or abstract or epitome) or register entries, but also the appropriate searches; in fact the vendor's solicitor is following the same procedure as will be followed by the purchaser's solicitor in due course after exchange of contracts, and detailed consideration of this will be left until we deal with that stage of the transaction.

3 The particulars

The particulars will include both a 'physical' and a 'legal' description of the property to be sold. For unregistered land[3] there will normally be an existing physical description in the deeds, or more particularly in the most recent conveyance of freehold property or in the lease in respect of leasehold property. The vendor's solicitor must consider whether this is accurate and adequate and, if it refers to a plan, whether the plan is accurate and up to date. If so, the existing description can be utilised in the particulars in the contract, either by reproducing it, or by making reference to the deed containing it (in which case a copy will have to be provided with the draft contract – and if the deed containing the description will form part of the abstract or epitome, it may be

2 Defects in title are explained at section 4 ii, below.

3 The shortened terms 'registered land' and 'unregistered land' will be used to indicate that the relevant title to the land is registered or unregistered, respectively.

more convenient to send the whole of the abstract or epitome with the draft contract). If the existing description or plan are insufficient, then a fresh description must be inserted in the contract and/or a new plan prepared. If a new plan is prepared then the vendor's solicitor may wish to negotiate with the purchaser's solicitor as to the sharing of the cost of the plan. An appropriate condition – for example that the cost be shared equally – can then be inserted in the contract.

For land the title to which is registered, the vendor's solicitor will normally rely on the description in the Property Register (which includes a reference to the filed plan) and state in the particulars that the property is that which is comprised under the particular title number. He would then have to send with the draft contract at least a copy of the entries in the property register and the filed plan, and more probably a full set of office copies of all the entries in the register, as the conditions in the contract will no doubt refer to the entries in the Charges Register, and copies of the register entries will have to be provided in due course to deduce title.

If the sale is of only part of the property comprised in the deeds or the register then a fresh description will be essential and probably also a plan. If the title is registered the filed plan could be used, suitably adapted.

The 'legal' description will normally be a statement that the property is freehold, or leasehold held for the remainder of the term granted by the lease. If the latter, the contract should state whether it is a headlease or an underlease.[4] The lease will probably have been referred to in the particulars as containing the physical description and will be referred to again in the conditions, so a copy or abstract will accompany the draft contract. Again, this is no hardship as the lease will have to be sent as part of the abstract of title anyway.

On the grant of a lease, the full description and plan will be inserted in the draft lease, which will normally be sent with the draft contract, which will then simply refer to the draft lease for the description.

If there is no statement as to the estate being sold it is implied that it is freehold, unless the purchaser knows that it is not.[5] If the title to the land is registered, the description 'registered land' implies that the title is absolute freehold.[6] The class of title should therefore always be stated.[7]

4 The conditions

The conditions contain the terms upon which the property is sold. There will be general conditions, which will be applicable to most contracts – for example the Law Society and National Conditions – and there will be conditions which will vary from contract to contract, being peculiar to a particular contract, which are often called special conditions. Before looking at both of these we must examine the rule which lays down what matters, despite anything else,

4 *Re Russ and Brown's Contract* [1934] Ch 34, CA.
5 *Timmins v Moreland Street Property Co Ltd* [1958] Ch 110, [1957] 3 All ER 265, CA.
6 *Re Brine and Davies' Contract* [1935] Ch 388.
7 See for example Law Society Special Condition E.

must be included in the conditions; that is the rule prescribing the vendor's duty of disclosure.

i The vendor's duty of disclosure

The vendor is under no general duty of disclosure and this is the reason that the purchaser must make pre-contract searches and enquiries. However, the vendor must disclose latent defects in title, that is to say defects in title that are not apparent on inspection.[8] It is vital that the property is inspected by or on behalf of the purchaser, as he will be taken to know about patent defects, so discoverable.[9] The range of possible defects of title is discussed below, but one defect which might be patent is an easement. A right of way could be patent,[10] although not necessarily.[11] The safest course for the vendor is to disclose any such adverse interest in the contract and not to rely on the fact that it may be apparent on inspection.

The purchaser cannot complain about the non-disclosure of an interest which he knew about at the date of the contract,[12] although there is an exception in the case of a mortgage which is a removeable defect of title in the sense that the vendor can remove it by paying it off and having it discharged, and the purchaser is entitled to assume that this will be done. Again, the vendor's solicitor would not rely on the purchaser's knowledge of a defect of title, which may be difficult to prove, but would disclose the defect in the contract. The vendor's duty of disclosure is limited to defects of title and does not extend to physical defects and defects in the quality of the land unless they are also defects in title. The purchaser, '... if he does not protect himself by an express warranty [must] satisfy himself that the premises are fit for the purposes for which he wants to use them, whether that fitness depends on the state of their structure or the state of the law or any other relevant circumstances'.[13] A similar rule applies to planning matters, so that unless the vendor makes some positive statement that the present or intended use is authorised under the planning legislation the purchaser has no claim against the vendor should this not turn out to be the case.[14] The vendor's duty of disclosure is also limited to matters which will bind the purchaser. If in unregistered conveyancing there is a restrictive covenant created after 1925 which has become unenforceable due to non-registration as a Land Charge, or if a pre-1925 restrictive covenant has become unenforceable following a bona fide purchase without notice of it, then the vendor need not disclose the covenant.

The provisions in the Law Society and National Conditions make little change to the vendor's duty of disclosure, although the vendor's liability is

8 See for example *Re Puckett and Smith's Contract* [1902] 2 Ch 258.
9 See for example *Yandle & Sons v Sutton* [1922] 2 Ch 199.
10 Ibid.
11 *Ashburner v Sewell* [1891] 3 Ch 405.
12 *Timmins v Moreland Street Property Co Ltd* [1958] Ch 110, [1957] 3 All ER 265, CA.
13 Per Devlin J in *Edler v Auerbach* [1950] 1 KB 359 at 374, approved in *Hill v Harris* [1965] 2 QB 601, [1965] 2 All ER 358, CA. Of course on the sale of freehold land, the vendor's solicitor would have to disclose the existence of a restrictive covenant, as a defect in title.
14 This is discussed further in ch 7.

limited to defects of title of which the vendor knows or, in the case of the Law Society's Conditions, ought to know.[15] However one or both of the sets of Conditions do make additional provision in respect of the contents of the lease (and superior leases) of leasehold property;[16] existing tenancies of the property;[17] the authorised use of the property under the planning legislation;[18] and communications from the local authority.[19]

It is important that the vendor's solicitor does investigate the vendor's title before drafting the contract, so as to enable him to disclose in the contract any defects in title discovered; the danger is that he assumes the title is in order without making a full investigation. The purchaser's remedies should the vendor fail to discharge his duty of disclosure are dealt with in chapter 16.

We can now consider the conditions which may be included in the contract commencing with a statement of the defects in the title.

ii Defects in title

Consequent on the vendor's duty of disclosure, there will be a statement – normally in the conditions, although sometimes included in the particulars – of the interests subject to which the property is being sold. What then are these defects of title which the vendor must disclose? They fall broadly into two categories. Firstly, there are defects which relate to the property. These include covenants affecting the land, easements over the land, and agreements, for example for the maintenance of a party wall or a shared passageway.[20] They will be noted on a proper examination of title from the deeds or the register and from the appropriate searches. As with the physical description, they may be reproduced in the conditions or merely referred to in the conditions as being contained in a particular deed, an abstract or copy of which is then attached to the contract. For registered land, reference to the Charges Register may be appropriate, with office copies accompanying the draft contract, although the solicitor must not ignore the possibility of there being overriding interests. The Charges Register will also include details of any existing mortgage over the property and as the sale is presumably not subject to this, it should be excluded from the reference in the conditions to the Charges Register. If there are matters such as restrictive covenants affecting the property, but for some reason no details of them were available at the time of first registration, then the Charges Register will say so. A defect such as this should be drawn specifically to the attention of the purchaser in the contract.[1]

If the property is leasehold it is likely that the lease, which is being assigned, will contain a large number of covenants and other provisions. If so, reference to the lease in the conditions, with a copy sent with the contract, is the only

15 LSC 5(1), NC 14. LSC 5(1) also excludes from the duty of disclosure those defects of title which a 'prudent purchaser' would have discovered. The duty of disclosure under NC 14 apparently does not extend to the vendor's constructive knowledge; *Celsteel Ltd v Alton House Holdings Ltd (No 2)* [1986] 1 All ER 598, [1986] 1 WLR 666.

16 See the next section, ii.

17 See section xvi.

18 See ch 7, below.

19 Ibid.

20 And tenancies of the property – see section xvi, below.

1 *Faruqi v English Real Estates Ltd* [1979] 1 WLR 963.

practicable way of disclosing them. The vendor's duty under an open contract is to disclose any onerous or unusual covenants in the lease[2] but normally all will be disclosed in the manner mentioned. The Law Society's Conditions provide that copies of the lease, and any superior leases, the contents of which are known to the vendor, should be supplied to the purchaser who is then deemed to purchase with full notice of the contents thereof.[3]

Similarly on the grant of an underlease, the lessor must disclose covenants of an unusual nature. Law Society Condition 8(3) and National Condition 11(2) do not apply to the grant of an underlease.

The vendor's duty under an open contract is to convey free from encumbrances. This first category of defects of title constitute what can loosely be called encumbrances over the property and this is why the vendor must disclose them.[4] The second category of defects of title affect the vendor's right to convey the property rather than the property itself. An example would be where there has been in the past a sale by a mortgagee whose power of sale may not have arisen, or a sale of trust property to a trustee. Such situations will be more readily appreciated when we have dealt with the whole question of examining title in chapter 10. They are clearly of great importance because they mean that the vendor may not be able to convey the property at all, rather than just that the vendor can only convey subject to an undisclosed encumbrance. They will normally only occur in unregistered conveyancing for, as we have seen, a purchaser of registered land is entitled to assume that the registered proprietor does have the power to deal with the land in the absence of any entry to the contrary on the register.[5]

How should the vendor's solicitor deal with such a defect? He may provide in the contract that the purchaser will 'accept such title as the vendor has' or 'will make no objection to the vendor's title'. In order to rely on such a condition the vendor must have disclosed any defects of title of which he knew. Additionally, even though the vendor may be able to rely on such condition, he will be refused specific performance if he can only show a thoroughly bad title, although he would still be allowed to forfeit the purchaser's deposit if the purchaser refused to complete.[6]

Similarly the vendor cannot conceal a defect in title by stipulating that the title to be deduced to the purchaser shall commence after the defect. In *Becker v Partridge*[7] a contract for sale of property held under an underlease did not disclose that there were breaches of a covenant in a superior lease, giving rise to the possibility of forfeiture, and of which the vendor knew or ought to have

2 *Re White and Smith's Contract* [1896] 1 Ch 637.

3 LSC 8(3). The equivalent National Condition, 11(2), refers to provision merely of a copy of the lease being assigned, not superior leases.

4 It may be that these encumbrances are not in the nature of easements and covenants which will be acceptable to a purchaser, but are matters which makes it extremely unlikely that anyone will purchase the property, such as options or rights of pre-emption. The vendor would have to disclose them, and may thereby be unable to sell.

5 Subject to overriding interests.

6 *Re Scott and Alvarez's Contract* [1895] 2 Ch 603. The title in that case rested on a forged deed. There is now discretion to order repayment of the deposit under s. 49(2) of the Law of Property Act 1925.

7 [1966] 2 QB 155, [1966] 2 All ER 266, CA.

known. The superior lease was not to be included in the title to be abstracted to the purchaser but he found out about the breaches of covenant and was entitled to rescind the contract.

The correct procedure, then, is for the contract to include a full disclosure of the position in the conditions and *then* to provide that the purchaser buys with full notice of the defect and shall raise no objection on account of it. The purchaser can then evaluate the risk (and if necessary try and arrange insurance cover in respect of it) before deciding whether to proceed.

iii Capacity of the vendor

The conditions will often contain a statement of the vendor's capacity.[8] There are a number of alternatives which include:

(a) beneficial owner – where the vendor owns the whole legal estate and equitable interest in the property eg a sole owner or joint tenants;
(b) trustee – for example trustees for sale or a tenant for life of settled land;
(c) personal representative;
(d) mortgagee;
(e) settlor;
(f) under an order of the court.

The importance of these expressions is that the capacity in which the vendor conveys and is expressed to convey in the deed dictates the covenants for title which the vendor impliedly gives to the purchaser in the deed. This will be dealt with in more detail in chapter 16, but the expressions which when used in the deed give rise to implied covenants for title are those listed above. Joint tenants and tenants in common may be able to convey either as beneficial owners or as trustees. They hold the property on trust for sale and clearly they can sell as trustees, but if the trustees also between them own all the equitable interests then they could convey as beneficial owners; they would not then be overreaching the equitable interests but in effect making title with the concurrence of the beneficiaries (themselves!). However, this would not be the case if on the death of one of two tenants in common, the new trustee appointed was not the person who took the deceased's equitable interest under his will or intestacy.[9] A purchaser would prefer a conveyance by beneficial owners rather than trustees because the covenants for title given by beneficial owners are more wide-ranging. It appears that a purchaser might not be able to object if the vendor cannot convey in the capacity stated in the contract.[10]

The word 'capacity' can of course be used in another perhaps rather more literal sense, to describe the vendor and so demonstrate his power to deal with the property. For example, the vendor may be a limited company, or charity, or the tenant for life of settled land, or a mortgagee. This aspect of the vendor's right to convey will be considered in chapter 10 as part of the process of examining the vendor's title.

8 Law Society Special Condition D, statement on front page of National Contract form.

9 Nor if there were more than four joint tenants, as the first four named would hold the legal estate on trust for sale for all of them and so the trustees would not own all the equitable interests.

10 *Re Spencer and Hauser's Contract* [1928] Ch 598; but see *Green v Whitehead* [1930] 1 Ch 38, CA.

iv Rights appurtenant to the property sold

We have dealt with the need for disclosure of existing covenants, easements and other interests affecting the property. There may of course be easements existing for the benefit of the property, for example a right of way over adjoining property or up a shared passageway. There may be covenants of which the property enjoys the benefit, for example that the adjoining property must only be used as a private dwelling house. These should also be mentioned in the contract, either in the conditions or the particulars. If the title is unregistered then, as before, the simplest way will be by reference to the deed or deeds containing the details. If the title is registered, and if they are mentioned in the Property Register, they may be incorporated in the particulars by a reference to the Property Register. On the grant of a lease, they would normally be included in the draft lease which would be referred to in the contract.

v Sale of part

In addition to disclosing *existing* easements affecting property, when the vendor is selling only part of the property he owns and is retaining property adjoining or nearby, he may wish to impose new easements over the property he is selling for the benefit of the property he is keeping. He must also consider what, if any, easements the sold property is to have over the retained property.

To take the latter point first, the vendor's solicitor in drafting the contract must be aware of the effects of the rule in *Wheeldon v Burrows*.[11] This states that on a 'grant' (which includes a contract for sale) by an owner of part of his property, he will impliedly grant to the purchaser all quasi-easements which are:

(a) continuous and apparent;
(b) necessary to the reasonable enjoyment of the property sold; and
(c) used prior to and at the time of the sale by the owner for the benefit of the part sold.

One must talk in terms of quasi-easements as one cannot have an easement over one's own land. However if there are rights which satisfy the above three conditions, then the contract impliedly includes them and the purchaser is entitled to have them in the deed. To take an example, if the owner of a house and large garden is selling the house but keeping part of the garden on which to build himself a bungalow, and if the owner was in the habit of crossing the part of the garden he is keeping to gain access to the house, he may find that he has impliedly contracted to grant this right of way to the purchaser of the house. The vendor's solicitor may wish to negate the effect of *Wheeldon v Burrows*[12] and this he can do by an appropriate condition in the contract. The National Conditions contain a condition providing that the purchaser shall not be entitled to any right of light or air over any adjoining or neighbouring property retained by the vendor,[13] but the Law Society Conditions do not contain even this restriction on the operation of the rule in *Wheeldon v Burrows*

11 (1879) 12 Ch D 31, CA.
12 Above.
13 NC 20.

and the vendor's solicitor should insert an appropriate special condition if the need arises.

The rule in *Wheeldon v Burrows* is only a rule of implied grant and does not operate to imply reservations, that is easements reserved by the vendor over the property he is selling. In the above example, if the vendor were keeping the house and selling part of the garden there would be no implied reservation of the right of way over the part sold off. If the vendor does wish to reserve easements over the property he is selling there must be some specific provision in the contract. Both the Law Society and National Conditions contain a condition to cover this situation and both deal with the problem in the same way, which is to state that the vendor reserves such easements over the land sold off as would have been implied had the retained land also been sold simultaneously to another purchaser.[14] In that case, the rule in *Wheeldon v Burrows* would apply to both sales and what would be grants of easements in favour of one part would be reservations of easements over the other part.[15] The effect is that *Wheeldon v Burrows* is made to operate 'in reverse' to impliedly reserve easements over the land sold, as well as impliedly grant them for the benefit of the land sold over the land retained. The National Condition refers to the vendor's 'adjacent or neighbouring' property, but the Law Society Condition provides that if the retained land is only near to the property sold and not adjoining it then the retained land must be specified in the special conditions for the general condition to apply.[16]

Some doubt will remain as to whether existing quasi-easements do meet the conditions set out in *Wheeldon v Burrows* or not, so perhaps the best course for the vendor's solicitor is to exclude in the special conditions both the effects of *Wheeldon v Burrows* and the appropriate general condition and then state specifically in the special conditions what easements are to be granted and reserved.

vi Imposition of new covenants

We have dealt with existing easements and new easements, both over the property and for its benefit, and we have also similarly dealt with existing covenants. When the vendor is selling part of his land he may wish to impose *new* covenants over the part being sold for the benefit of the land he is keeping, or vice versa. He can thereby retain some control over the use to which the land he is selling is put. In particular if the vendor is a builder developing a new housing estate, he may wish to impose covenants on the sale of the individual plots in order to preserve the character of the development.

Assuming that the covenant is to be given by the purchaser, a special condition must be inserted in the contract stating that the purchaser will in the deed enter into the covenant, the full wording of which is then given. The wording of the covenant will be important as the vendor's solicitor will wish to ensure both that the burden of the covenant will run with the land if possible and also that the benefit of the covenant will run with the vendor's land. To take first of all the position on the sale of part of freehold (or of an existing

14 LSC 5(3), NC 20.

15 *Hansford v Jago* [1921] 1 Ch 322.

16 Special Condition B.

leasehold), the benefit of the covenant will run with the vendor's land in most circumstances if the covenant touches and concerns that land and either the benefit is assigned to the vendor's successor in title or the benefit has become annexed to the vendor's land. Annexation may be deduced from surrounding circumstances or may be achieved by the language used in the original covenant; for the latter the covenant should actually state that it is for the benefit of the whole *or any part or parts* of the vendor's retained land.[17] The burden of a covenant does not run with the land at law, but the burden of a restrictive covenant will run in equity if either it was made for the benefit of the vendor's retained land[18] or there is a Building Scheme as defined in *Elliston v Reacher*.[19] This is where purchasers of individual plots on a building estate have all given restrictive covenants on the basis that they are to be enforceable by all the other purchasers, the intention being that the covenants will be for the benefit of all the plots sold. If there is a Building Scheme then the covenants are mutually enforceable between the various purchasers and their successors in title. If the builder is selling the freehold of the individual plots his solicitor should ensure that the estate does qualify as a Building Scheme.[20] The alternative would be for the builder to grant leases of the individual plots which will then avoid the problems of the covenants running with the land, because the benefit and burden of both restrictive and positive covenants *in leases* will normally pass to the assignees.[1] If there is a Letting Scheme – requirements similar to a Building Scheme – the covenants in the lease will also be mutually enforceable between the various purchaser lessees and their assignees.

The position regarding positive covenants in relation to freehold land is more acute; the burden does not run with the land at law or in equity. On the development of a freehold housing estate; positive covenants can be made to run with each individual plot by imposing a rentcharge,[2] either for a purely nominal amount to serve as a 'peg' on which to hang positive covenants[3] or, if the covenant is for payment of a sum of money – perhaps a contribution to the maintenance of some common area – the rent charge can be for that variable sum.[4] Apart from this a positive covenant may be enforced on the basis that if the property has the benefit of a right of way with a positive covenant to contribute to its maintenance, the owner will not be allowed to take the benefit – the right of way – without also submitting to the burden – paying the contribution.[5] Otherwise enforcement of a positive covenant may

17 *Marquess of Zetland v Driver* [1939] Ch 1, [1938] 2 All ER 158, CA, cf *Re Ballard's Conveyance* [1937] Ch 473, [1937] 2 All ER 691. See also *Federated Homes Ltd v Mill Lodge Properties Ltd* [1980] 1 All ER 371, [1980] 1 WLR 594, CA, and *Roake v Chadha* [1983] 3 All ER 503, [1984] 1 WLR 40. The law is somewhat uncertain, and to be on the safe side the formula suggested in the text should be included to ensure annexation.

18 *Tulk v Moxhay* (1848) 2 Ph 774; this requirement will normally be satisfied on a sale of part.

19 [1908] 2 Ch 665, CA.

20 Other conditions are laid down in *Elliston v Reacher* (above), apart from that mentioned.

1 The running of covenants in leases is dealt with in more detail ch 17, below.

2 A rentcharge is a legal interest, which is thus binding on purchasers irrespective of notice. Covenants imposed in support of the rentcharge can thus effectively run with the land.

3 Rentcharges Act 1977, s 2(4)(a).

4 Ibid, s. 2(4)(b).

5 *Halsall v Brizell* [1957] Ch 169, [1957] 1 All ER 371.

depend on the existence of a chain of indemnity covenants, which are considered below. Again, if a housing estate is developed by granting leases of the individual plots, these problems can be avoided.

We have discussed the imposition of new covenants for the benefit of the vendor's land but it is quite possible, particularly on the development of a block of flats, that the vendor will enter into covenants with the purchaser for the benefit of the purchaser's property. Thus, the vendor might covenant to maintain the common parts and the purchasers of the individual flats would covenant to each pay a proportionate amount of the cost.

vii Indemnity covenants

If a covenant is so expressed that the original covenantor will remain liable even after he has parted with the property – for example a covenant to erect 'and ever thereafter maintain' a fence – then he ought to take an indemnity, in the form of an indemnity covenant, from the person to whom he disposes of the property. He will remain liable for any breach of the covenant and ought to be indemnified against the consequences of any future breach. The person to whom the covenantor disposes of the property, having given an indemnity covenant, will then take a similar covenant when he in turn disposes of the property, and so on. A chain of indemnity covenants is thus built up and if the original covenant is a positive covenant, on a sale of freehold it may still be possible for the covenantee to enforce the covenant against the present owner of the property 'down the chain'. This method of enforcement is not ideal as the intervening owners may have disappeared or failed to take an indemnity covenant and thus broken the chain. It is, though, better than nothing and if the covenantee desires to take advantage of it then the original covenant should be appropriately worded so as to ensure the covenantor's continuing liability.

On an assignment for value of leasehold land title to which is not registered, there will be implied in the deed of assignment a covenant for indemnity by the purchaser in respect of the covenants in the lease.[6] The vendor need not stipulate for such a covenant in the contract. In the case of leasehold land the title to which is registered, the indemnity covenant is implied whether the assignment is for value or not.[7] If the property is freehold there is some authority for saying that under an open contract the vendor can require the purchaser in the purchase deed to indemnify him against any continuing liability.[8] The safest course is to insert a condition in the contract to provide that the purchaser will in the deed give an indemnity covenant and both the Law Society and National General Conditions stipulate that the purchaser shall indemnify the vendor in respect of any continuing liability on any covenant or other matter, subject to which the property is sold.[9]

On the grant of a lease, as on the sale of freehold, no indemnity covenant will actually be implied and so if an indemnity covenant is appropriate – eg on the grant of a lease out of a freehold subject to a covenant – the appropriate

6 Law of Property Act 1925, s. 77(1)(c).
7 Land Registration Act 1925, s. 24(1)(b).
8 See for example *Moxhay v Inderwick* (1847) 1 De G & Sm 708.
9 LSC 17(4), NC 19(6).

condition should be inserted in the contract and an indemnity covenant included in the lease.

viii Licence to assign

If the property being sold is leasehold, or in other words there is to be an assignment of the lease, then it may be that the lease contains a provision that there be no assignment without the consent or licence of the lessor.[10] If so then under an open contract, the vendor is under a duty to use his best endeavours to obtain the licence.[11] If it is not forthcoming by the time for completion then the purchaser can – and presumably will – rescind the contract, recovering his deposit and interest and also the costs of investigating the title.[12] The rule in *Bain v Fothergill*[13] prevents him from obtaining full damages unless the vendor has not used his best endeavours to obtain the licence, for example if he has induced the lessor to withhold the licence.[14]

The contract may well include a condition to cover the point. The Law Society Conditions provide that the vendor shall use his best endeavours to obtain the consent, the purchaser shall co-operate in providing any necessary references, and that if the consent is not granted five working days before the contractual completion date, either party can rescind the contract.[15] The purchaser would then get his deposit back but interest would only start to run four working days after rescission.[16] The National Conditions contain a broadly similar provision, making the sale 'subject' to the consent being obtained and providing that if it is not obtained, the vendor can rescind.[17] No time limit is given and the time limit may apparently extend beyond the contractual completion date.[18] The purchaser would then get his deposit back. The purchaser is not given a specific right to rescind although presumably retains his open contract right to do so.[19] In *Bickel v Courtenay Investments (Nominees) Ltd*,[20] it was held that the vendor can rescind under National Condition 11 (5) if the lessor refuses consent, even though the refusal is apparently unreasonable. (There is a statutory restriction on the lessor unreasonably refusing consent, considered in Chapter 17, but it is immaterial to the question of rescission that the consent is unreasonably refused.)

10 See further ch 17.
11 *Day v Singleton* [1899] 2 Ch 320, CA.
12 *Re Marshall and Salt's Contract* [1900] 2 Ch 202.
13 (1874) LR 7 HL 158.
14 *Day v Singleton*, above.
15 LSC 8(4).
16 LSC 16(2)(a).
17 NC 11(5). By NC 10(2), the purchaser would not receive interest on the deposit, nor the costs of investigating title.
18 See *29 Equities Ltd v Bank Leumi (UK) Ltd* [1987] 1 All ER 108, [1986] 1 WLR 1490, CA. If the consent is refused, the vendor could presumably rescind at that stage.
19 In any event the purchaser could force the vendor to act by serving a notice to complete; see ch 16, below.
20 [1984] 1 All ER 657, [1984] 1 WLR 795.

ix Deposit

Under an open contract no deposit is payable. Normally the vendor will require a deposit to be paid on exchange of contracts, both as part-payment of the purchase price and as some sort of guarantee that the purchaser will complete; for if the purchaser unjustifiably refuses to complete, the vendor can forfeit the deposit even though he has suffered no loss.[1] If the deposit is paid to the vendor's solicitor then he will hold it, in the absence of any provision to the contrary in the contract, as agent for the vendor.[2] This means that the purchaser loses control of the deposit and it can be paid over to the vendor. An alternative capacity in which the vendor's solicitor – or any other deposit holder – may take the deposit is as stake-holder.[3] A stake-holder is effectively an agent for both the parties; he cannot pay the money to either party unless and until that party has become lawfully entitled to it, as for example the vendor would be, following completion. Obviously the purchaser would prefer the deposit to be held by a stake-holder, for if he becomes entitled to rescind and have the deposit returned, it is ready and waiting for him; if held by a solicitor it would be paid into a special stake-holder account. If on the other hand the deposit has been held by the vendor's solicitor as the vendor's agent, it may have been paid to the vendor and the purchaser will merely have a right of action against the vendor for that sum. (The purchaser would also have a lien over the property he had contracted to buy, to the extent of the deposit.[4]) The vendor may have a very good reason for wanting the deposit to be paid to his solicitor as agent; he may wish to use it before completion, usually to put towards the deposit on a property he is buying. The capacity in which the vendor's solicitor holds the deposit is therefore a matter for negotiation between the parties.

The Law Society Conditions provide for a deposit of 10 per cent of the purchase price (excluding any amount payable for chattels, fixtures and fittings) to be paid on exchange to the vendor's solicitor as stake-holder.[5] The relevant National Condition is of similar effect[6] although both are often amended in the Special Conditions to provide for the solicitor to hold as the vendor's agent, for the reason just mentioned. If the purchaser will not agree to such an amendment, the vendor can either find another purchaser who will agree, or finance the deposit on his own purchase from some other source such as a bank loan which will involve him paying interest.

If the purchaser becomes entitled to the return of the deposit on rescission, he may find that the person holding the deposit has gone bankrupt or is otherwise unable to pay. After the formation of a binding contract, the position is clear; whether the deposit is held by a stake-holder or by an agent, the loss

1 See further ch 16, below.

2 *Ellis v Goulton* [1893] 1 QB 350, CA.

3 The Law Society has recommended that the contract should deal with the question of who is entitled to the interest on a stake-holder deposit, and that in the absence of such provision the interest should normally be payable, less any appropriate charges, to the stakeholder solicitor's client, ie normally the vendor.

4 See ch 16, below.

5 LSC 9.

6 NC 2(1).

must be borne by the vendor and he would have to reimburse the purchaser.[7] The position where there is not yet a binding contract – for example as a result of the common practice of paying a small deposit to an estate agent when the parties agree to proceed 'subject to contract' – the position is less clear. It would seem following *Sorrell v Finch*[8] that because a purchaser is entitled to demand repayment and was under no obligation to pay any deposit, the risk should be borne by the purchaser. The Estate Agents Act 1979 provides that deposits are to be held on trust for the person entitled to them,[9] which on the above principles would presumably mean the purchaser before exchange of contracts.

If a contract provides for payment of a deposit which is then not paid, it could either be said that payment was a condition precedent to the formation of the contract or that payment was a term of the contract, the breach of which entitles the vendor to rescind.[10] The practical effect will be the same whichever interpretation is preferred; the vendor will be able to re-sell. However if the latter interpretation is adopted, the vendor does have the option of affirming the contract and in due course suing for the deposit if necessary. Subsequent cases have favoured this latter interpretation. In *Millichamp v Jones*,[11] it was held that the vendor could rescind the contract for non-payment (*and* sue for the unpaid deposit). This was also the approach in *Damon Cia Naviera SA v Hapag–Lloyd International SA, The Blankenstein*,[12] a shipping case.

Non-payment of the deposit will most often arise when a deposit is paid by cheque which is subsequently dishonoured. Solicitors should be wary of the form in which the deposit is paid and in particular should be most hesitant about accepting the purchaser's personal cheque – or if they do they should delay exchange until the cheque has been presented and cleared. The Law Society Conditions provide that except in the case of a sale by auction, the deposit must be paid either by a banker's draft or by a solicitor's cheque. They further provide that if any deposit cheque should be dishonoured, the vendor has the right within seven working days to serve a notice on the purchaser and treat the contract as repudiated by the breach,[13] the implication being that if he does not do so he has affirmed the contract. The National Conditions on the other hand simply provide that if a cheque for the deposit is dishonoured the vendor can elect either to treat the contract as discharged by the breach or to enforce payment of the deposit.[14] If a deposit is paid by a number of

7 *Rowe v May* (1854) 18 Beav 613; *Ellis v Goulton*, above. If the deposit-holder was the vendor's solicitor, the purchaser may be able to make a claim on the Law Society Compensation Fund.

8 [1977] AC 728, [1976] 2 All ER 371, HL.

9 S. 13. By s. 14 the estate agent must pay the deposit into a client account and by s. 16 must arrange insurance in respect of it.

10 *Myton Ltd v Schwab-Morris* [1974] 1 All ER 326, [1974] 1 WLR 331. The case does not decide which.

11 [1983] 1 All ER 267, [1982] 1 WLR 1422.

12 [1985] 1 All ER 475, [1985] 1 WLR 435, CA.

13 LSC 9.

14 NC 2(2).

cheques, the case of *Trustbridge Ltd v Bhattessa*[15] – on the National Condition – confirms that the vendor can still rescind if only one of the cheques is dishonoured. The position would be the same under the Law Society Condition.

It may be that the vendor will agree to accept a deposit of less than 10 per cent – if for example the purchaser is buying with the aid of a 95 per cent mortgage and will not have a full 10 per cent of the purchase price available on exchange (unless he borrows the money on a bridging loan until completion). If so, the vendor will want to be sure of recovering the full 10 per cent if he is ever in a position to forfeit the deposit. This is achieved by Law Society Condition 9(2), whereby if the vendor serves a completion notice,[16] he immediately becomes entitled to the difference between the deposit actually paid and the full 10 per cent. There is no similar provision in the National Conditions, and so a special condition would be needed to cover the point in an appropriate case.

It would be negligent not to advise the vendor of the benefits of taking a deposit,[17] although there is some discussion currently about whether the taking of 10 per cent deposits – or any deposit at all – is justifiable and should be retained. As an alternative to actually paying a deposit, particularly for a purchaser who is not readily able to pay on exchange the deposit required by the vendor and who would therefore otherwise have to borrow the money on a bridging loan, there are deposit guarantee schemes available. On payment of a premium by the purchaser, the insurer agrees to pay the specified deposit to the vendor should the purchaser fail to complete; the vendor will naturally wish to ensure that in that situation the insurer will pay the deposit quickly. If the insurer does have to pay the deposit, he can recover it from the purchaser.

x Exchange of contracts

If the contract is to be brought into existence by the conventional method of exchange, it is important to establish the precise moment at which such exchange takes place. If it occurs in one of the solicitors' offices there is no problem but there may be difficulties if as is common the exchange takes place through the post. Normally the purchaser's part, plus deposit, is posted to the vendor's solicitor who will in return post the vendor's part back to the purchaser's solicitor. In *Eccles v Bryant and Pollock*[18] it was held that exchange takes place not before the second part is posted. This is fairly obvious, but it was specifically not decided whether the exchange would be complete at the time of posting the second part or only on its receipt. The former would be the case if the normal contractual postal rule applied,[19] but this is unclear[20] and there are grounds for arguing that the contract should not come into existence until the second part is received by the purchaser. If the contract came into existence at the time of posting of the second part and the purchaser never in fact received it, he might find proof of compliance with section 40 of the Law of

15 [1985] LS Gaz R 2580.
16 Completion notices are discussed in ch 14, below.
17 *Morris v Duke-Cohan & Co* (1975) 119 Sol Jo 826.
18 [1948] Ch 93, [1947] 2 All ER 865, CA.
19 See for example *Household Fire and Carriage Accident Insurance Co Ltd v Grant* (1879) 4 Ex D 216.
20 See for example *Holwell Securities Ltd v Hughes* [1974] 1 All ER 161, [1974] 1 WLR 155, CA.

Property Act 1925 awkward if he tried to enforce the contract against the vendor. He would also be without an important document of title should he wish to sub-sell. Both the Law Society and National Conditions provide that the contract shall be made when the last part is posted if exchange is by post,[1] although there is a difficulty in a term of a contract stating how that contract is to come into existence as until the contract does exist, the term is of no effect.

As an alternative to the conventional method of exchange, the parties may agree over the telephone or in telex messages that the contract shall become immediately effective and that if the solicitors still hold the part of the contract signed by their own client, then this shall be held irrevocably to the order of the other party.[2] Both the Law Society and National Conditions contain provision for such a procedure[3] but it will be dealt with in more detail when we look at the process of exchange of contracts in chapter 8.

xi Vacant possession

In the absence of any provision to the contrary – ie under an open contract – the vendor is bound to give vacant possession on completion.[4] This presumption is probably rebuttable by for example the property not being vacant when inspected by the purchaser, but the vendor's solicitor ought to state quite clearly in the contract that vacant possession is not to be given if that is indeed the case. Both the Law Society and National forms of contract provide for vacant possession to be given,[5] thus placing quite firmly on the vendor the onus of disclosing in the contract any leases or tenancies to which the sale is subject. Moreover, it is not only tenancies which will amount to breaches of a term for vacant possession. In *Wroth v Tyler*[6] the breach was a class F land charge registered against the vendor in respect of the statutory right of occupation of the vendor's spouse.[7] In *Cumberland Consolidated Holdings Ltd v Ireland*[8] it was a large quantity of solidified cement in the basement of a warehouse, which formed a substantial interference with the enjoyment of a substantial part of the property. In *Topfell Ltd v Galley Properties Ltd*[9] there was held to be a breach when the vendor of a two-storey property, the top floor of which was tenanted but the lower sold with vacant possession, did not disclose an order made by the Local Authority to the effect that the building could only be used to house one household. There already was one household on the top floor, meaning that the vendor could not give vacant possession of the lower floor.

1 LSC 10(1), NC 1(7)(ii).
2 *Domb v Isoz* [1980] Ch 548, [1980] 1 All ER 942, CA. The Law Society has published guidelines for solicitors intending to exchange in this way.
3 LSC 10(2), NC 1(6).
4 *Cook v Taylor* [1942] Ch 349, [1942] 1 All ER 85.
5 Law Society Special Condition F, National Special Condition C. Both are drafted in the alternative to allow for vacant possession or the existence of tenancies; see section xvi, below.
6 [1974] Ch 30, [1973] 1 All ER 897.
7 Matrimonial Homes Act 1983.
8 [1946] KB 264, [1946] 1 All ER 284, CA. Compare *Hynes v Vaughan* (1985) 50 P & CR 444, where there were piles of rubbish on the property, but not enough to mean that the vendor could not give vacant possession.
9 [1979] 2 All ER 388, [1979] 1 WLR 446.

xii State and condition of the property

We have already seen that the vendor is under no duty to disclose physical defects in the property. The common law rule applicable to an open contract is 'caveat emptor'.[10] This is confirmed by conditions in both the Law Society and National Conditions, which provide that the purchaser shall buy with full notice of the actual state and condition of the property save where it is to be constructed or converted by the vendor.[11] In that case there may be liability under the Defective Premises Act 1972 and/or the National House Building Council Agreement,[12] or indeed in negligence,[13] the latter possibly even where the vendor has himself made relatively minor improvements and alterations and provided that the purchaser shall buy with full notice of the actual state and condition of the property.[14] A Local Authority which negligently approves defective work may also be liable.[15]

The purchaser would be well advised to have a professional survey made as part of his pre-contract enquiries.

If however the vendor has deliberately concealed a physical defect, this may amount to a fraudulent misrepresentation that the property is not defective in that respect, and the vendor may thus be liable. In *Gordon v Selico Co Ltd*,[16] the vendor had covered up dry rot in the property, and was held liable to the purchaser (in fact, an intending lessee).

xiii Auction sales

At an auction the contract is made by the acceptance of the final bid. Nevertheless, bearing in mind the requirements of section 40 of the Law of Property Act 1925, a written contract is normally prepared by the vendor's solicitor in consultation with the auctioneer, and this is made available for inspection by a prospective purchaser for some time before the actual auction – normally at least a week. It is then this contract that the prospective buyers are offering to enter into by means of their bids. The contract is normally exchanged immediately after the auction. An auctioneer will hold a deposit as stakeholder in the absence of any agreement to the contrary.

The Sale of Land by Auction Act 1867 provides that the contract must:

(a) state whether the property is sold without reserve or subject to any reserve price.[17] A reserve price is a price below which the property will not be sold (ie if the bidding does not reach the reserve price the vendor can withdraw the property). The reserve price itself does not have to be disclosed;

(b) state whether any right to bid is reserved.[18] If so, then assuming the sale is subject to a reserve price the vendor or any one other person may bid.[19]

10 See for example *Terrene Ltd v Nelson* [1937] 3 All ER 739.
11 LSC 5(2)(a), NC 13(3).
12 See section xxi, below.
13 *Anns v Merton London Borough Council* [1978] AC 728, [1977] 2 All ER 492, HL.
14 *Hone v Benson* (1978) 248 Estates Gazette 1013.
15 *Dutton v Bognor Regis UDC* [1972] 1 QB 373, [1972] 1 All ER 462, CA.
16 [1986] 1 EGLR 71.
17 Sale of Land by Auction Act 1867, s. 5.
18 Ibid, s. 5.
19 Ibid, ss. 5, 6.

Both the Law Society and National Conditions provide that:[20]
(a) the property is subject to a reserve price;
(b) the vendor reserves the right to bid up to the reserve price;
(c) the auctioneer can refuse to accept a bid;
(d) the auctioneer can resolve any dispute, or put the property up again at the last undisputed bid;[1]
(e) the highest accepted bidder shall be the purchaser;[2]
(f) the purchaser shall forthwith sign the contract and pay the deposit.

A solicitor may have to advise the vendor whether to sell by auction or in the more normal manner which is called a sale 'by private treaty'. At an auction the vendor can be sure of obtaining the best price from those present, but if the vendor is also buying a property there may be serious problems of synchronisation if he sells at auction and he may also be limiting the number of potential buyers, as not everyone will be in a position to attend an auction and enter a contract immediately. As a prospective purchaser's solicitor will warn his client, there may be similar problems of synchronisation for the purchaser if he is also selling a property. As the purchaser at an auction is committing himself to pay the deposit immediately and the balance of the purchase price on the completion date, his financial arrangements including any mortgage must be finalised before the auction, and this may not be possible for some prospective purchasers.

Auctions are commonly used by persons other than the ordinary domestic houseowner, who may be under some sort of duty to obtain the best price available, for example a mortgagee exercising a power of sale or personal representatives selling property which forms part of the deceased's estate.

xiv Fixtures, fittings and chattels

If an item is a fixture, then it will pass with the land without any express mention of it in the contract – for example, plants in the garden of a house. If the vendor wishes to keep for himself any fixtures, some specific condition should be inserted in the contract excluding them from the sale. It is sometimes difficult to decide whether a particular item is a fixture or not – for example fitted cupboards or a gas fire – and in such cases it is safer to put a special condition in the contract. The difficulties are illustrated by the case of *Hamp v Bygrave*,[3] in which some garden ornaments were held to be chattels, but that because the vendor regarded them as included in the sale they were to be treated as fixtures. (They were not mentioned in the contract.)

Similarly if the vendor is also selling chattels, such as curtains or carpets, which will not pass with the land automatically, the purchaser will want these to be specifically mentioned in the conditions, and may also want the price to be apportioned between the property and the chattels to achieve a possible saving of stamp duty. In *Dean v Andrews*,[4] a prefabricated greenhouse, bolted

20 LSC 25, NC 1; there are minor differences.
1 The efficacy of such a term was confirmed in *Richards v Phillips* [1969] 1 Ch 39, [1968] 2 All ER 859, CA.
2 Not specifically stated in LSC, though obviously a necessary inference.
3 (1983) 266 Estates Gazette 720.
4 (1985) Times, 25 May.

to a concrete plinth which then rested on its own weight, was held to be a chattel and the purchaser who had refused to surrender it had to compensate the vendor.

The National Conditions state that the vendor warrants that any chattels included in the sale are his to sell.[5] The Law Society Conditions contain no such specific warranty, but this will be implied anyway under the Sale of Goods Act 1979 or the Supply of Goods and Services Act 1982; there is provision that the purchaser will only become owner of the chattels on actual completion, thus ensuring that he does not acquire the chattels before he acquires the property.[6] As a result it seems that the chattels are at the vendor's risk until completion which as we shall see is not the case for the property itself.[7] The National Conditions do not deal with title to the chattels and the purchaser should thus insure the chattels from exchange, as title (and risk) will pass then.

xv Identity and boundaries

Conditions can be put in the contract covering the identity of the property and its boundaries. The Law Society Conditions state that the vendor shall not be required to define the exact boundaries, and both the Law Society and National Conditions provide that the vendor is not bound to show the ownership of boundary fences, hedges or walls nor to identify parts of the property held under different titles.[8]

Whilst it might be difficult to establish the exact boundaries and their ownership, the vendor should be encouraged to make every effort to do so.[9] Many disputes between neighbours arise as a result of imprecise boundaries and uncertainty as to their ownership.

xvi Evidence of tenancies

In pursuance of the vendor's duty of disclosure and the implication that vacant possession will be given, the contract may not only disclose the existence of any tenancies of the property but also stipulate the evidence of them which the purchaser will receive. Both the Law Society and National Conditions provide that the vendor shall supply copies of all such agreements and the purchaser will then be deemed to buy with full knowledge of them and of the rights of the tenants.[10]

xvii Title

The question of the title which will be deduced to the purchaser following exchange of contracts is of fundamental importance. We must deal in turn with freehold and leasehold property, both unregistered and registered.

5 NC 4.
6 LSC 24.
7 As regards the property, risk passes on exchange of contracts.
8 LSC 13(1), NC 13(2).
9 See *Scarfe v Adams* [1981] 1 All ER 843, CA.
10 LSC 6, NC 18.

1 *Sale of freehold, the title to which is not registered* We have seen in chapters 1 and 3 that title is deduced by providing the purchaser with an abstract or epitome of recent dealings under which the property has changed hands: a history of the property, including not only sales but also, for example, the death of a joint tenant or the grant of probate to the estate of a deceased owner. How far back should this history go, or in other words what is to be the length of the title? With what sort of deed or other document must it start? Statute provides a partial answer, and the open contract rule. The Law of Property Act 1925, section 44(1) as amended by the Law of Property Act 1969 provides that the purchaser can require the title to be deduced for at least the last fifteen years; thus the instrument with which the abstract starts, or the root of title as it is called, must be *at least fifteen years old at the date of the contract.* Under an open contract the root must also be a 'good root'; there is no statutory definition of this but the common law definition[11] is an instrument which:

(a) deals with or shows title to the whole legal and equitable interest contracted to be sold (although the equitable interests need not be dealt with if they are over-reached, eg on a sale by trustees for sale);
(b) contains an adequate description of the property (in theory, the description should probably not refer to a description or plan in an earlier deed, but in practice such roots are often accepted and the earlier deed also abstracted);
(c) contains nothing to cast any doubt on the title.

Adopting this definition, the best root will be a conveyance on sale and this is certainly the most common root in practice. However a voluntary conveyance (ie deed of gift) can also be a good root as can an assent by personal representatives, and it seems to be accepted in practice that a post-1925 mortgage can be a good root even though in theory it should not be, not dealing with the whole of the legal estate. A post-1925 will, on the other hand, cannot be a good root.

After the root, all dealings and other events affecting the property must be deduced and an unbroken chain of ownership shown, culminating in the vendor.[12]

The root is normally specified in the conditions;[13] if not, the open contract rules apply and a good root at least fifteen years old must be shown. Neither the Law Society nor the National Conditions contain any alteration of the open contract position. There is nothing to prevent the parties agreeing in the conditions on a root less than the statutory fifteen years old, although in *Re Marsh and Earl Granville*[14] it was held that the nature of the root must then be clearly stated. In that case, it was not made sufficiently clear in the contract that the root was a voluntary conveyance and the court refused to award the vendor a decree of specific performance. There are serious disadvantages for the purchaser in accepting a title of less than the statutory fifteen years, for the purchaser will be taken to have constructive notice of all equitable interests

11 Taken from *Williams on Vendor and Purchaser* (4th edn) p. 124.
12 Or someone whom the vendor can compel to convey – see ch 9, section 1, below.
13 For example, Law Society Special Condition E, National Special Condition B.
14 (1883) 24 Ch D 11.

of which he would have had notice had he insisted on a full statutory title.[15] This can best be illustrated by reference to an example:

1920 – Conveyance on sale A to B imposing restrictive covenants
1950 – Conveyance on sale B to C stated to be subject to the restrictive covenants
1966 – Conveyance on sale C to D but with no mention of the restrictive covenants (the conveyance would of course have mentioned the covenants if it had been properly drafted)
1987 – Contract on sale D or E specifying the 1966 conveyance as the root of title and again not mentioning the restrictive covenants

The root satisfies the statutory fifteen year rule; it is over fifteen years old at the date of contract. The enforceability of covenants created before 1926 depends on the equitable doctrine of notice. E will not, it would appear, have notice of the covenants because they have not been disclosed in the contract and nor will they be discovered on an examination of the title starting with the root in 1966. The covenants will not be enforceable against E.[16]

If in the above example the conveyance from C to D had been in 1976 rather than 1966, but still specified in the contract as the root, then it would not satisfy the statutory requirement being only eleven years old at the date of the contract. Again E will not have actual notice of the covenants, but had he insisted on a statutory title, the root would have been the 1950 conveyance – the most recent conveyance over fifteen years old at the date of the contract – and he would have had notice of the covenants as they are mentioned in the 1950 conveyance. In accepting the short title, he is taken to have constructive notice of the covenants and they will be enforceable against him.

A similar rule applies to interests which depend for their enforceability on registration as land charges, for example post-1925 restrictive covenants. If in the example above the conveyance creating the restrictive covenants had been in 1930 rather than 1920, we would have:

1930 – Conveyance A to B imposing restrictive covenants, which are then protected by registration against B's name
1950 – Conveyance B to C stated to be subject to the covenants
1966 – Conveyance C to D with no mention of the covenants
1987 – Contract D to E specifying the 1966 conveyance as the root and again not mentioning the covenants[17]

Again, the root satisfies the statutory fifteen year requirement. E will have no actual knowledge of the covenants and will not discover their existence when he does a land charges search before completion. He will not search against B's name, against which the covenants are registered, because the title deduced to him does not include B's name. He will none the less be bound by the covenants because they are registered. He will be entitled to receive compensation under the Law of Property Act 1969, section 25.[18] If in the example

15 *Re Nisbet and Pott's Contract* [1906] 1 Ch 386, CA.

16 Or his successors in title, *Wilkes v Spooner* [1911] 2 KB 473, CA.

17 The covenants should have been disclosed by the vendor as they will be binding on the purchaser in any event.

18 See ch 16, below; he may also have a claim against the vendor for breach of the duty of disclosure. Land Charges Searches are considered in detail in ch 11, below.

we again assume that the conveyance from C to D was in 1976 rather than 1966, and specified as the root, then as before if E had insisted on his statutory entitlement, the root would have been the 1950 conveyance. In that case E would have discovered the existence of the covenants, both because the 1950 conveyance mentions them and because B's name is now included in the title, and a land charges search could be made against him. E will therefore not be entitled to compensation under section 25.

2 *Grant of a lease out of an unregistered title*[19] The open contract position can be summarised as follows:

(a) On the grant of a headlease (ie a lease granted out of the freehold) the lessee is not entitled to have the freehold title deduced at all.

(b) On the grant of an underlease (ie granted not out of the freehold but out of another (superior) leasehold), the under lessee is entitled to have deduced the lease out of which his underlease is being granted (ie the under lessor's lease) and also an abstract or epitome of title to that lease going back at least fifteen years (but obviously not going back before the date it was granted).[20] In other words, the abstract will start with the lease out of which the underlease is being granted and will then show a chain of ownership of that leasehold estate culminating in the present under lessor, but with the proviso that because of the operation of the fifteen year rule, if the under lessor's lease was granted more than fifteen years before the date of the contract, there may be a gap in the abstract between that lease and the most recent disposition that is at least fifteen years old at the date of the contract. The fifteen year rule is really the same rule that applies on the sale of a freehold.

The under lessee does not get any other superior title deduced; for example the freehold title is not deduced.

It is in the interests of a lessee to be able to investigate all the superior titles and in particular the freehold title. This may have been subject to some adverse interest such as an easement or covenant to which the lessee will also be subject, although he will not be able to discover its existence.[1] If the adverse interest is registered as a land charge, then neither will the lessee be able to claim compensation under the Law of Property Act 1969, section 25, because the section does not apply to this situation.

Similarly if he cannot examine the superior title, the lessee cannot discover whether superior leases and in particular the head lease were validly granted or not (for example, the requisite consent of a mortgagee to the grant of a lease may not have been obtained). Further, on first registration, only good leasehold title would be registered rather than absolute leasehold.

Whether the lessee will attempt to have a condition inserted in the contract to the effect that the freehold and other superior titles should be deduced probably depends on the nature and length of the lease. If a purchaser/lessee is buying a new house on a building estate, or a flat in a newly built or converted block, the developer may as we have already seen grant a long lease

19 See ch 17, below.

20 Law of Property Act 1925, ss. 44(1), (2), (4).

1 See for example *White v Bijou Mansions Ltd* [1937] Ch 610, [1937] 3 All ER 269.

of the individual flat or house rather than sell the freehold. The transaction will proceed on normal conveyancing lines with a contract followed by the grant of the lease, and the purchase price (which is in effect a premium on the grant of the lease) will be more or less the same as would be paid were the freehold being sold. The purchaser/lessee would be unwise to part with his money without being satisfied that the developer had a good title. If the purchaser were financing his transaction by means of a mortgage, then a Building Society or a bank would be unlikely to lend unless the freehold title and any superior leasehold title were deduced, so that they could ensure that the property was good security for the loan.

Perhaps rather surprisingly, neither the Law Society nor the National Conditions make any amendment to the open contract position. Any amendment to the open contract position must be negotiated and included as a special condition.

3 *Assignment on sale of a lease, the title to which is not registered* The open contract rule is really the same as that applicable on the grant of an underlease – rule (b) above. The purchaser (assignee) is entitled to have deduced the lease that he is buying together with an abstract of epitome of title to it going back at least fifteen years (but again obviously not going back before the date of grant of the lease).[2] This rule applies whether the lease is a headlease or an underlease, but the purchaser cannot investigate the superior title, leasehold or freehold, and therefore is faced with the same problem as has been outlined in the previous section.

The Law Society Conditions do recognise that the statutory position is not very generous. An assignment of a lease will be a fairly common transaction in the domestic conveyancing field – once there has been a long lease of a house or flat of the kind mentioned in the previous section, every sale of it will of course be an assignment of the lease. The Law Society Conditions provide that the purchaser is entitled to have title deduced for at least fifteen years prior to the date of the contract, so long as the lease is for a term exceeding twenty one years.[3] If the lease was granted over fifteen years before the date of the contract then the purchaser under the Law Society Conditions obtains no more than he would under the open contract rule. On the other hand if the lease was granted less than fifteen years before the date of the contract then the purchaser is in addition entitled to some superior title; freehold, leasehold or both, depending on exactly how long ago the lease and any superior leases were granted

We can now look at some examples of the operation of these rules starting with the statutory open contract rules contained in this and the previous section.

1936 – 99 year headlease granted out of the freehold by F to L
1946 – Assignment on sale of the headlease by L to A
1956 – Underlease granted by A to B
1966 – Assignment on sale of the underlease by B to C
1976 – Sub-underlease granted by C to D

2 Law of Property Act 1925, s. 44(1), (3).
3 LSC 8(2).

1987 – Assignment on sale of the sub-underlease by D to E

To represent this diagrammatically:

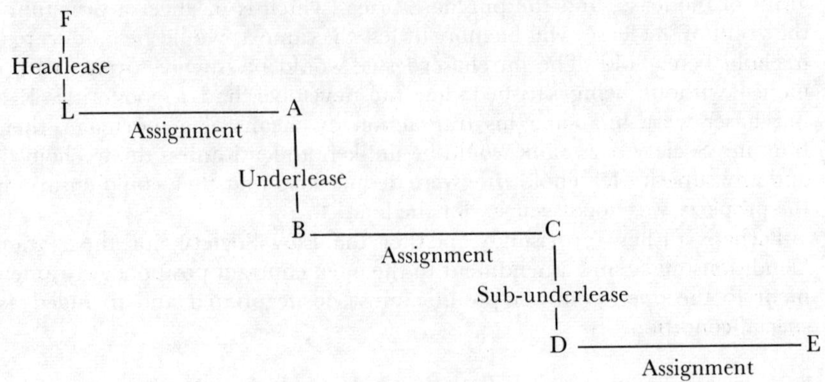

Under an open contract the various purchasers would have been entitled as follows:

L in 1936 – Nothing
A in 1946 – Headlease F to L
B in 1956 – Headlease F to L, assignment L to A
C in 1966 – Underlease A to B
D in 1976 – Underlease A to B, assignment B to C
E in 1987 – Sub-underlease C to D

To give a further example of the rule applying to an assignment, or to the grant of an underlease:

1936 – 99 year headlease granted out of the freehold by F to L
1940 – Assignment on sale L to A
1950 – Assignment on sale A to B
1960 – Assignment on sale B to C
1970 – Assignment on sale C to D
1980 – Assignment on sale D to E
1987 – Underlease E to G

Diagrammatically:

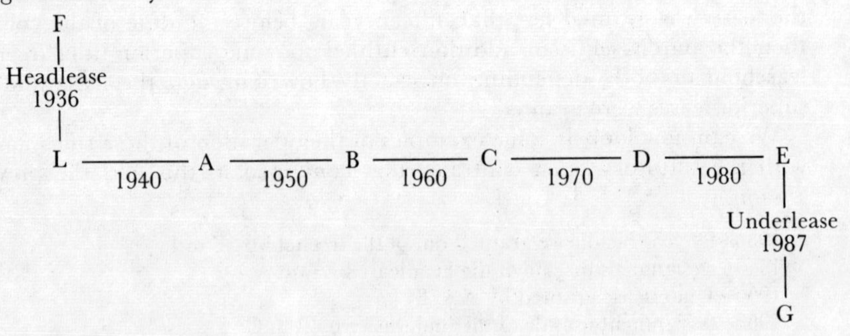

Title deduced under an open contract to:

L in 1936 Nothing
A in 1940 – Headlease F to L
B in 1950 – Headlease F to L, assignment L to A

C in 1960 – Headlease F to L, assignments L to A, A to B
D in 1970 – Headlease F to L, assignments A to B, B to C
E in 1980 – Headlease F to L, assignments B to C, C to D
G in 1987 – Headlease F to L, assignments C to D, D to E

Now an example of the operation of the Law Society Condition:

1940 – Conveyance on sale by A to B
1960 – Conveyance on sale by B to C
1975 – Conveyance on sale by C to D
1976 – Headlease granted by D to E for 99 years
1977 – Assignment on sale of headlease by E to G
1980 – Underlease granted by G to H for remainder of term of headlease (less the last day)
1982 – Assignment on sale of underlease by H to J

Diagrammatically:

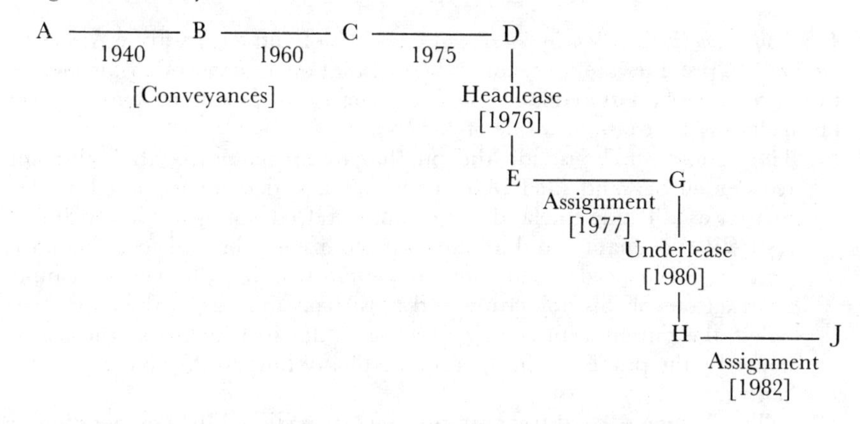

If in 1987 J contracts to assign the underlease to K, then under the Law Society Condition K will be entitled to have deduced all the deeds mentioned with the exception of the 1940 conveyance. Fifteen years prior to 1987 is 1972 and this takes us back through the superior leasehold title and into the freehold title. K is entitled to an abstract or epitome starting with the first deed prior to 1972 – ie the 1960 conveyance – and continuing with both the freehold and the superior leasehold title. However the freehold title is only deduced up to the date of grant of the headlease and the head leasehold title only up to the date of the grant of the underlease. Under the open contract rule K would only have been entitled to see the 1980 underlease, which he is buying, and the 1982 assignment of it. This would probably not have been satisfactory to K's Building Society or bank, if he were buying with the aid of a mortgage. The purchaser's solicitor should, before exchanging contracts, ascertain that the title offered in the contract is satisfactory not only to his client the purchaser, but also to any prospective mortgagee, for whom he may also be acting.[4]

If the vendor is unwilling or unable to comply with the Law Society Condition then his solicitor should ensure that the condition is deleted from the contract by a special condition, if the contract is expressed to be subject

4 See further in ch 13, below.

to the Law Society General Conditions. For example, the vendor may be the original lessee of the lease which he is now assigning to the purchaser; if it is a headlease granted only five years ago, the Law Society Condition stipulates that the vendor must deduce some freehold title. However if when the vendor took the lease he did not insist on and was not provided with any abstract of the freehold title, he is clearly in no position to deduce the freehold title to the purchaser now. From the purchaser's point of view, he will want a special condition giving him a full 15 year abstract of the freehold title either if Law Society Condition 8(2) does not apply because the lease is over 15 years old or if Condition 8(2) would not give him a full 15 year freehold abstract.

The National Conditions contain no amendment to the open contract position stated at the beginning of this section although of course a purchaser buying subject to the National Conditions may negotiate for the inclusion of a special condition varying the open contract position.

4 *Sale of freehold, the title to which is registered* The Land Registration Act 1925, section 110 provides the open contract rule, that on a sale or other disposition to a purchaser of registered land (not including a lease or a mortgage or charge but including for example a sale of part):

(a) The vendor shall provide the purchaser with copies of the subsisting register entries and filed plan, copies of any documents noted on the register as affecting the land (for example a deed containing a schedule of restrictive covenants) and an authority to inspect the register (which the purchaser will need for his pre-completion search). The vendor cannot contract out of this obligation and must bear the cost of the copies etc. unless the purchase price is £1,000 or under in which case the cost is borne by the purchaser in the absence of anything to the contrary in the contract.

The National conditions simply rely on section 110, not mentioning how the title is to be deduced, but the Law Society Conditions are a little more generous to the purchaser, providing that all copies shall be office copies and that the vendor shall also provide authorities to inspect for prospective mortgagees, lessees or sub-purchasers.[5] Law Society Special Condition E also incorporates an authority to inspect.

(b) The vendor shall at his own expense supply the purchaser with the necessary evidence of rights and interests as to which the register is not conclusive[6] and of any other matters excepted from the effect of registration,[7] to the extent that the purchaser would have been entitled were title to the property not registered. This obligation is subject to any provision in the contract to the contrary; there is nothing in either set of General Conditions on the point and the matter should be dealt with in the special conditions according to the particular circumstances of the individual case.

5 LSC 12(1)(b).

6 Including rights existing for the benefit of the land as well as adverse rights such as overriding interests.

7 For example under a qualified or possessory title.

5 *The grant of a lease out of a registered title* If the lease to be granted is a headlease ie is to be granted out of a registered freehold, the Land Registration Act 1925 does not affect the general principle that the lessee is not entitled to examine the lessor's title under an open contract. The position is the same as under heading 2 above; the lessee gets nothing and section 110 of the Land Registration Act 1925 expressly does not apply. If the lessee does want to examine the lessor's title and to be provided with office copies of the register entries then he must negotiate for the inclusion of a special condition to this effect in the contract.

If the lease to be granted is an underlease, ie to be granted out of a lease the title to which is registered, then the position is not so straightforward. We have seen that in relation to unregistered land, the under lessee is entitled to examine the under lessor's title, commencing with the under lessor's own lease. So it might be expected that in respect of registered land, the under lessee would be entitled under section 110 to details of the under lessor's title and if so, the position would be similar to that prevailing on the assignment of a registered lease discussed in the next section. However section 110 itself states that it does not apply to a 'lessee' and in the Act 'lease' is defined to include 'underlease',[8] so section 110 may not apply. On the other hand section 110 does apply to a 'disposition', an expression which would otherwise include an underlease.[9] On the basis that section 110 probably does not apply, the solicitor for the vendor/under lessor would be well advised to include a special condition in the contract stating exactly what title is to be deduced.

Even if a lessee or under lessee cannot investigate the superior title or titles, if the latter are registered he may still be granted an absolute leasehold title as the superior titles may be examined internally by the Registry.

6 *Assignment on sale of a lease the title to which is registered* This is a disposition to which the Land Registration Act 1925, section 110 does apply and therefore the position is the same as for a registered freehold title discussed under heading 4 above, with the difference that the vendor must also supply, as in unregistered conveyancing, a copy or abstract of the lease being sold; the lease does not form part of the register. The Act makes no difference to the position regarding the superior title; in other words under an open contract the purchaser is not entitled to examine it. For the reasons already mentioned above, the purchaser's solicitor may wish to insert a condition in the contract providing for the superior title to be deduced, although if the leasehold interest being sold is registered with absolute leasehold title there is no need for this. However if the purchaser is buying a good leasehold title then he is subject to the same uncertainties concerning the validity of the grant of the lease and the existence of adverse interests affecting the superior title as have already been mentioned in relation to unregistered leases.

The amendments to the open contract rule made by the Law Society Conditions mentioned in section 3 above are equally applicable where the title is registered, save that the purchaser is not entitled to call for any superior title if the lease he is buying is registered with absolute leasehold title.

8 Land Registration Act 1925, s. 3(x).
9 Ibid, s. 21(5).

7 *Production of Land Certificate* Difficulties can arise on the grant of a lease out of a registered title because unless the lease is granted at a rent without a fine, the Land Certificate must accompany the application for registration of the lease.[10] The lessor is apparently under no obligation to make the Land Certificate available and in such a situation the solicitor for the purchaser/lessee should negotiate for the inclusion in the contract of a condition providing that the vendor/lessor will make the Certificate available for production.

xviii Lost deeds

Where title deeds to unregistered land have been lost, the open contract rule is that the vendor must produce secondary evidence – by means of statutory declarations, copies, drafts etc. – of the contents and execution of the lost deeds and the circumstances surrounding their loss.[11] In such a situation the vendor's solicitor will normally insert a special condition in the contract stating exactly what proof of title will be provided. If all the deeds have been lost, the vendor's solicitor may state in the contract that a statutory declaration of undisturbed possession for a particular period of time will be supplied, showing what is in effect a possessory title.[12]

xix Completion

Under an open contract, completion must take place within a reasonable time.[13] It is unclear whether it must take place at the vendor's solicitor's office, or anywhere the vendor specifies. The National Conditions state that the completion date is the twenty-sixth working day after the date of the contract or of the delivery of the abstract, whichever is the later, and that completion shall take place at such place as the vendor's solicitor 'shall reasonably require' or by post.[14] The Law Society Conditions provide that the completion date shall be the twenty-fifth working day after the date of the contract, and that it shall take place at the vendor's solicitor's office or the office of the vendor's mortgagees or their solicitors if notice to this effect is given to the purchaser.[15] Again provision is made for completion by post.[16] The time of day before which completion must take place is stated in both sets of Conditions. This is to ensure that completion takes place before the banks shut so the vendor's solicitor can bank the money. LSC 21 states 2.30 pm; NC 5(5) states 2.15 pm, but only if completion is on the last working day of a week. Non-compliance means that completion is deemed to take place the following working day, so under NC5(5) the vendor may get interest, and under LSC 21 the vendor may get compensation; the vendor must give notice within five working days if he wishes to claim such compensation. If the vendor is buying as well as selling, the condition may need to be amended to bring the time forward so he has the money from the sale to complete the purchase on the same day. As regards

10 Ibid, s. 64; *Strand Securities Ltd v Caswell* [1965] Ch 958, [1965] 1 All ER 820, CA.
11 *Re Halifax Commercial Banking Co Ltd and Wood* (1898) 79 LT 536.
12 See for example *George Wimpey & Co Ltd v Sohn* [1967] Ch 487, [1966] 1 All ER 232, CA.
13 *Johnson v Humphrey* [1946] 1 All ER 460.
14 NC 5(1), (4).
15 LSC 21(1).
16 LSC 21(3).

payment on completion, both sets of Conditions provide for payment by any method which is agreed to by the vendor's solicitor. The Law Society Conditions specifically mention payment by legal tender (which will be rare) or by a banker's draft,[17] whereas the National Conditions additionally mention payment by a cheque drawn on and guaranteed by a designated bank or payment by telegraphic transfer.[18] The open contract rule is probably that payment must be made by legal tender, although the conventional procedure is for payment to be made by a banker's draft. Under the National Condition, the banker's draft must also be drawn on a designated bank, which means a bank designated under the Building Societies Act 1962, section 59;[19] most high street banks are so designated. Under the Law Society Condition, the banker's draft must be drawn on 'a settlement bank for the purposes of the Clearing House Automated Payments System' (CHAPS).[20] Again, most, if not all, high street banks qualify.

The completion date will often be specified in a special condition,[1] thus overriding any general condition, and may only be fixed immediately before exchange. If the completion date is written in after exchange, then the alteration ought to be initialled by the parties, which would be inconvenient. There is some authority for saying that insertion of a completion date is merely an administrative matter and will not affect the validity or enforceability of the contract.[2]

If a client is both selling and purchasing, then unless he is not dependent on the sale proceeds to provide part of the purchase money, or can lodge elsewhere and store his furniture, the two transactions will have to be completed on the same day.

The date for completion will not normally be taken as being of the essence of the contract, unless the property is of a particular character such as the sale of a public house as a going concern.[3] In the normal domestic conveyancing transaction it would be intolerable for time to be of the essence of completion as there are a number of reasons why completion may be delayed for a day or two or even longer, particularly where completion of a purchase is dependent on the sale of another property. The contract will however provide for the rights of the parties when there is delay in completion.[4]

17 LSC 21(2).

18 NC 5(3); the vendor must agree to a telegraphic transfer.

19 NC 1(7). Section 59 is repealed by the Building Societies Act 1986.

20 LSC 21(2b).

1 For example Law Society Special Condition B, statement on front page of National form of contract.

2 *Smith v Mansi* [1962] 3 All ER 857 at 865, CA per Russell LJ; approved by Lord Denning MR in *Storer v Manchester City Council* [1974] 1 WLR 1403 at 1408. Neither will a special condition for completion, included in the contract form and neither deleted nor completed on exchange, but left blank, override the general condition so as to leave either an open or even an unconcluded contract (ibid). In *Walters v Roberts* (1980) 258 Estates Gazette 965 the parties left the completion date to be agreed in the future; it was held that in the absence of such agreement, there was an implied term that completion would take place as under an open contract, within a reasonable time.

3 *Lock v Bell* [1931] 1 Ch 35.

4 See ch 16, below.

On the purchase of a new property which is in the course of being built, it is unlikely that the vendor/builder will agree to a specific completion date being inserted in the contract, as there are a number of factors which could delay the building of the property which would be outside the immediate control of the builder. In such a contract there will normally be a condition that the builder will finish the property with reasonable expedition and that the purchaser will then complete within a particular period, say one or two weeks, of being notified that the property is finished. This period will allow both the purchaser and his prospective mortgagee to inspect the property and make arrangements for completion.

xx Other common general conditions

There are a number of other matters commonly dealt with by conditions, and on which both the Law Society and National Conditions do make provision. These include insurance; the time for delivery of the abstract and requisitions; additional rights of rescission and restrictions on other remedies such as those for misdescription and misrepresentation; the position where the purchaser is given possession before completion; the apportionment of out-goings on completion; and the rights of the parties if completion is delayed including the payment of interest. These matters will be dealt with at the appropriate stage of the examination of the conveyancing transaction in subsequent chapters.

The vendor's solicitor should not lose sight of the need to amend or delete general conditions, as the occasion demands. This has already been mentioned in relation to areas such as the grant and reservation of easements on a sale of part and the title to be deduced on the assignment of a lease, but there are other conditions which are commonly amended. The Law Society Conditions specifically provide, in Special Condition B, for amendment of conditions covering the contractual interest rate; the completion date; a banker's draft emanating from a non-CHAPS bank; the time of day by which completion must take place; and the definition of 'working days' by which time limits are calculated. Any other amendments can be effected by an appropriately worded special condition. For example, if the completion date is much earlier than the five weeks envisaged by the general conditions, some of the other time limits, covering submission of requisitions and the draft purchase deed, will need to be altered.

Finally, it is worth noting the comment on general conditions in the recent case of *Lyme Valley Squash Club Ltd v Newcastle under Lyme Borough Council*[5] that where a general condition was included (dealing with the grant of easements on the sale of part; an old Law Society Condition similar to the first part of National Condition 20) and 'no one gave it a thought', then it was right to go behind the condition; indeed the outcome of the case was that the plaintiffs did have a right to light which would have been expressly excluded had the condition been allowed to operate. This attitude does seem to undermine some of the purpose of having an all-embracing set of general conditions, but the implication, that the solicitor should be aware of the effect of the general conditions in a particular case, is clear.

5 [1985] 2 All ER 405 at 411, 412.

xxi Other special conditions

No discussion of special conditions can be exhaustive as by definition they are peculiar to a particular transaction. For example, in a mining area there may be a condition that the vendor will assign to the purchaser the benefit of any right to claim compensation for damage caused by subsidence. It is part of the vendor's solicitor's job to advise the vendor on appropriate conditions, both in the sense of matters to be included in the deed such as the imposition of new easements and covenants, and conditions regulating the conduct of the sale. By way of an example we will look briefly at one quite common transaction, the sale by a builder of a new house on an estate, or flat in a new block of flats.

If the vendor owns the freehold, the initial decision must be whether he will be selling the freehold of the individual units or granting long leases. If the vendor himself owns a leasehold interest he could assign the lease in respect of each unit but it would be far simpler to grant underleases. In addition to advantages in respect of the enforceability of covenants, a leasehold scheme does bring in some income to the vendor in the form of rent.[6]

The contract for sale will have to contain a fresh description of the property, probably by reference to an estate plan. The latter can also be deposited with the Local Authority and the District Land Registry if title is registered, to simplify the purchaser's solicitor's task when making searches. There will be provision for the grant and reservation of easements including rights of drainage, passage of cables and common rights of way such as shared pathways. There may be a quite lengthy list of covenants with the object of preserving the character of the development, and in the case of flats there will be some provision for the maintenance of any common parts such as stairs and gardens, and for payment of a service charge to meet the cost of such maintenance. Rather than include all these provisions separately in the contract it may be easier to draft a model form of conveyance (or transfer or lease) and provide in the contract that the deed shall be in that form. If the title is registered, the model can be submitted to the Registry in advance for approval. Instead of a filed plan, which may be large, the vendor may instead supply a form 102 which certifies that the purchaser's plot is comprised in the vendor's title.

If the house or flat has not yet been built, there will be a condition in the contract – or a separate contract – regulating this. The builder may agree to erect the property 'in a workmanlike manner'[7] according to a specification, or he may simply provide that the parties shall contemporaneously enter into a National House Building Council (NHBC) Agreement. This Agreement will almost invariably be entered into by the parties in any event, as in practice it is highly unlikely that a Building Society or bank will lend money on the security of a new property which does not have the benefit of the NHBC scheme. Briefly, in the NHBC Agreement, the builder – who must be registered with the NHBC – agrees to build the property in a workmanlike manner in accordance with the NHBC standards, and also warrants that a notice of insurance cover will be issued in respect of the property, the insurance policy

6 See further in ch 17. A mortgagee such as a Building Society may be reluctant to lend on the security of a freehold, as opposed to leasehold, flat.

7 This will be implied; *Hancock v B W Brazier (Anerley) Ltd* [1966] 2 All ER 901, [1966] 1 WLR 1317, CA.

being in a standard form. The builder agrees to remedy defects appearing within two years, and the policy protects the purchaser against the builder's bankruptcy or other breach by the builder of his obligations to remedy defects, and also provides a ten year guarantee in respect of major structural defects. There are some exclusions and limitations but in practice the scheme costs the purchaser nothing.[8] The contract must make quite clear what is included in respect of decoration, fitted units, paths, boundary walls and similar matters. The time for completion will be fixed by reference to the finishing of the work rather than any specific date.

The vendor's solicitor must also consider whether he should ask the purchaser to make 'stage' payments at various times before the property is actually finished. This will benefit the vendor's cash flow position although the purchaser may find it financially awkward, even with a cooperative Building Society.

xxii Void conditions

In dealing with the contents of a contract, it should be mentioned that there are some conditions considered so unfair to a purchaser that even if the vendor includes them in the draft contract and they are not removed at the purchaser's request, they will be void. The most important are:

(a) a condition precluding the purchaser from objecting to the lack of or insufficient stamping on a document forming part of the title, or providing that the purchaser is to pay for the proper stamping of such a document;[9]

(b) a condition precluding the purchaser from examining a power of attorney under which a document of title has been executed;[10]

(c) a condition restricting the purchaser in his choice of solicitor or providing that the conveyance will be prepared by the vendor's solicitor at the purchaser's expense;[11]

(d) a condition that the purchaser shall accept title made by the concurrence of the persons entitled to equitable interests, if title can be made discharged from those interests by them being over-reached, for example on a trust for sale or Settled Land Act 1925 settlement.[12]

5 Communication with the vendor

It will be obvious that the vendor's solicitor will need a good deal of information from his client in the early stages of the transaction. Matters such as the whereabouts of the deeds and, if the property is mortgaged to a Building Society, the Society's reference number so that the deeds can be requested; the easements to be granted and reserved on a sale of part; the name of the vendor's estate agent; details of the purchaser and the price agreed; any fixtures to be

8 The NHBC produces literature on the scheme both for solicitors and purchasers.
9 Stamp Act 1891, s. 117.
10 Law of Property Act 1925, s. 125(2).
11 Ibid, s. 48.
12 Ibid, s. 42(1).

retained or chattels to be sold; the anticipated completion date; these are just some of the matters dealt with in this chapter.

In addition the solicitor should confirm with the vendor the financial basis of the transaction. If the property is in mortgage, he will need to know the amount owing on the mortgage and indeed on any second mortgages; this information can be obtained from the mortgagees if necessary. The existence of second mortgages will be revealed on a proper investigation of title, even if the vendor omits to mention them. In unregistered conveyancing they will be protected as land charges and in registered conveyancing there will be some mention of them on the register. The solicitor will need to know whether the vendor plans to purchase another property and if so whether the two transactions must be co-ordinated. He will also have to advise the vendor on any liability to capital gains tax or any other relevant tax. In practice capital gains tax is rarely payable because of the exemption which applies to the sale of a dwelling house which is the vendor's main or only residence. If the vendor owns more than one house, he can elect which is his main residence. The exemption covers the grounds of the dwelling house up to one acre and also a separate disposal of part of the grounds provided it takes place prior to the sale of the dwelling house.[13] The exemption still applies for up to two years after the vendor has ceased to reside in the property. If part of the property has been used exclusively for business, the exemption will not apply to part of the gain.

Although most of these matters can be covered in the initial interview between the solicitor and his client, the solicitor should never lose sight of his fundamental obligation to keep his client fully informed at all times.

6 Procedure

The contract will be drafted in duplicate and both copies sent to the purchaser's solicitor for approval. The draft forms a basis for negotiation between the parties. The particulars or conditions may make reference to earlier deeds or in the case of a registered title to the register entries. For that reason it is quite common for the whole of the abstract or epitome, or office copy entries, to be sent to the purchaser's solicitor with the draft contract. As the purchaser cannot object to defects of title of which he is aware, there is a danger that the purchaser's solicitor may be taken to have examined the abstract and be aware of any defects in title apparent from it. The purchaser's solicitor should make quite clear that he has only looked at the documents provided for the purpose of enlarging on the references made in the contract. There is a specific provision to this effect in the Law Society Conditions.[14]

In view of the inevitable delay before contracts are exchanged and the ever-present possibility that a prospective purchaser may withdraw, a vendor may wish to send out draft contracts to more than one prospective purchaser, so that he can exchange contracts with the first purchaser who is in a position to do so. The Law Society has issued rules for a vendor's solicitor involved in

13 Capital Gains Tax Act 1979, ss. 101, 102.
14 LSC 12(3).

such a 'contract race'. The vendor's solicitor must disclose in writing to each prospective purchaser's solicitor that they are involved in the contract race or if the vendor refuses to authorise such disclosure, the solicitor must cease to act for him.[15] The vendor's solicitor should, however, avoid creating a binding contract obliging him to exchange contracts with the first purchaser in a position to do so.[16]

15 See *Law Society's Gazette*, 28 November 1979, p. 1177.

16 See *Daulia Ltd v Four Millbank Nominees Ltd* [1978] Ch 231, [1978] 2 All ER 557, CA.

6 The purchaser's pre-contract searches and enquiries

It will be apparent from the vendor's limited duty of disclosure that the purchaser's solicitor will have to instigate a number of searches and enquiries, with the object of collecting information about the property which the vendor is not under a duty to disclose but which may influence the purchaser in his decision whether or not to proceed with his purchase and exchange of contracts. Some searches and enquiries are done in all cases and others only where circumstances demand.

1 Local Land Charges search

This search should be made on the purchase of both unregistered and registered land (local land charges are over-riding interests in relation to registered land[1]). The matters that are protected as local land charges are as the name implies essentially local in nature and are set out in the Local Land Charges Act 1975. They include planning matters such as enforcement notices and conditional planning permissions; tree preservation orders; certain compulsory purchase orders; the listing of buildings as being of special historical or architectural interest; various financial charges for expenses incurred by the Local Authority; and others. A register of local land charges is kept by District Councils and London Borough Councils. The register is in twelve parts all of which should be searched. A matter protected as a local land charge may not be within the scope of the vendor's duty of disclosure.[2]

i The search

The search can be done personally or by applying for an official certificate of search on a standard form. In both cases a fee is payable. A personal search is quicker, but there are advantages in the official search certificate, including for the solicitor the protection given by the Local Land Charges Act 1975,

1 Land Registration Act 1925, s. 70(1)(i).

2 The Law Society Conditions are quite specific in placing on the purchaser the onus of doing a local land charges search and the additional enquiries of the local authority; LSC 3(1), (2). See also ch 7, section vii, below.

section 13, which provides that a solicitor is not answerable for any loss caused by reliance on an erroneous official certificate. Another disadvantage of a personal search, whether by the purchaser's solicitor or by an agency specialising in such searches, is that it might not be very easy for the purchaser to establish liability against the person making the search who has apparently made an error.

As registration is by reference to the land affected, a description of the land, preferably with a plan, must be submitted with the application for an official search. The official certificate of search is not conclusive. An interest registrable as a local land charge is binding whether or not it is revealed on a search and indeed whether or not it is even registered. There is provision for compensation for persons acquiring an interest for valuable consideration in the land searched against; this would cover a lessee and a mortgagee as well as a purchaser. Compensation is payable if an interest registrable as a local land charge is not revealed on a personal search because it was not registered, or is not revealed on an official certificate of search either because it was not registered or because of an error in the preparation of the certificate.[3] To obtain compensation, the search must have been made before 'the relevant time' which is the date of the contract for sale, unless either the contract is in some way conditional on the outcome of the search or there is no contract, in which case the relevant time is the date of the conveyance. For the purpose of obtaining compensation, a purchaser can take the benefit of a search requisitioned by someone else, for example the vendor or an earlier abortive purchaser, provided he knew of the contents of the search before the relevant time.[4] The amount of the compensation will be the loss suffered by reason of the interest not being registered or revealed. If the property is mortgaged, the compensation can be claimed by the mortgagee, who would apply it in reduction of the amount owing under the mortgage.[5]

The search is essentially an information-gathering exercise and gives no protection against the future creation of local land charges. It would be negligent for a solicitor not to effect such a search for a purchaser and there are clearly dangers in relying on an out-of-date search.

2 Additional enquiries of the Local Authority

Many matters affecting the property which are of a local nature are not registrable as local land charges. The purchaser's solicitor invariably sends with the local land charges search a list of additional enquiries of the District Council or London Borough Council. Again, a fee is payable. There is a standard form of enquiries agreed between the Law Society and the Local Authority associations. There is one form for enquiries of District Councils and a slightly different form for enquiries of London Borough Councils. Some of the questions are quite detailed and it may be fair to say that even some practising solicitors are unaware of their precise nature; it is only when a

3 Local Land Charges Act 1975, s. 10.
4 Ibid, s. 10(3).
5 Ibid, s. 11.

question to which one would have expected a negative answer receives a positive answer, or vice versa, that the alarm bells ring.[6] There follows a brief description of the eighteen questions on the District Council's form:

(1) This question asks whether the roads and paths, being the postal address or additionally specified on the form, are maintainable at the public expense. This will normally be the case as they will have been adopted by the local authority. If not, the purchaser will wish to enquire of the vendor both to confirm the rights of way that do exist over the roads and paths and to establish who is responsible for their maintenance. If the roads and paths are not maintained at public expense, the problem for the purchaser lies not only in probably being liable for a contribution to their maintenance, but also the risk that the local authority may by resolution decide to make up the roads in which case the purchaser would be liable for a proportion of the cost thereof, calculated by reference to the length of the frontage of the property onto the road. The question on the form also asks whether any such resolution has been made.

When a new housing estate is built the roads will often not be made up by the builder until after some or all of the houses have been sold. The purchaser of a new house on a building estate should thus ensure that in the conveyance from the builder, the latter covenants to make up the roads and paths on the estate. However, this is not really sufficient for the purchaser as if the builder should go into liquidation or for some other reason fail to make up the roads, they may be made up by the local authority and the purchaser charged a proportion of the cost. To guard against this possibility, the purchaser should ensure that the builder has entered into an agreement with the local authority under section 38 of the Highways Act 1980, agreeing to make up the estate roads and paths. This agreement should be supported by a financial bond of a sufficient amount to cover the cost of the work should the builder default. The question on the form does ask whether there is any such agreement and bond in existence. Although the purchaser's prime concern will be that the agreement and bond relates to the road in front of the house being bought, the purchaser should also ensure that the agreement and bond covers the other estate roads; it would be most inconvenient for the purchaser if he had to drive across muddy unmade roads to reach his house and it would certainly decrease the value of his property until the roads were made up.

(2) This asks whether the Council has been notified by the Secretary of State of any proposed new trunk road or motorway or of construction of a subway flyover or footbridge, in either case within 200 metres of the property. There are further questions about the existence of any proposals for highway construction.

(3) This question asks whether there are any outstanding statutory or informal notices issued by the Council under the Public Health Acts, Housing Acts, or Highways Acts.

6 In *JGF Properties Ltd v Lambeth London Borough* (1985) 277 Estates Gazette 646, it was suggested that the questions and answers are unintelligible to the layman. The case also illustrates the dangers of relying on a telephoned inquiry of the Local Authority, not least being the difficulty of proof.

(4) This question asks whether there are any proceedings in respect of infringement of Building Regulations.

(5) This question concerns drainage from the property. It asks whether the property drains into a public sewer for both foul drainage and surface water. When a new sewer is built, then by a scheme similar to that applicable when a new road is made up, the developer and the Water Authority will enter into an agreement (with supporting bond). The question also asks whether the Council is aware of such a scheme. If the property does not drain into a public sewer, the question asks whether there is a public sewer within 100 feet of the property. If the property drains into a private sewer, the purchaser's solicitor should check both the existence of an easement, and maintenance costs.

(6) This is a question concerning planning; it asks whether there are any enforcement or stop notices other than those shown in the official search certificate and it also asks where the register of enforcement and stop notices can be inspected.

(7) This also deals with planning and asks whether there are any structure, local or development plans and if so what the plan indicates as the use of the area in which the property is situated.

(8) This asks whether the Council has resolved to make a direction under article 4 of the Town and Country Planning General Development Order 1977 restricting permitted development, except where this is shown in the official Certificate of Search.

(9) This asks whether the Council has made any orders revoking or modifying planning permission, requiring the discontinuance of use and alteration or removal of buildings, or any tree preservation orders.

(10) This asks whether the Council has paid any compensation where the Secretary of State has refused to grant permission for development within the existing use of the property. This will affect the compensation paid on any subsequent compulsory acquisition of the property.

(11) The Council keeps a register of planning applications and the result of each application. This question asks whether there are any entries relating to the property in that register and where it can be inspected.

(12) This question asks whether the property is within a conservation area.

(13) This question asks whether the Council has served a Building Preservation Notice in respect of the property which would temporarily make the property a listed building; it would then be an offence to alter the building without listed building consent.

(14) The question asks whether the Council has made any Compulsory Purchase Orders except those shown in the official certificate of search.

(15) This question asks whether the property is included in a programme of slum clearance or in a general improvement area. In the latter case the property will be eligible for certain grants.

(16) This question asks whether the property is in an area subject to a smoke control order except where this is shown in the official certificate of search.

(17) This question asks whether there has been a resolution that rates be charged on unoccupied property after a period of three months.

(18) This question asks whether the property is in an area subject to a Compulsory Registration Order under the Land Registration Act 1925.

There are a further thirteen optional enquiries on both forms, which will only be answered if a specific request to do so is made and at an additional fee over and above the fee for the standard enquiries. These are questions which will only be relevant to particular types of property. For example, questions ask whether the property is an enterprise zone. The purchaser's solicitor should consider whether in a particular case any of these additional enquiries, and indeed any other enquiries not covered by the standard form, should be made of the Local Authority. In particular if the purchaser is buying tenanted residential property he may wish to know whether there are any rents registered under the Rent Act 1977, because these would represent the maximum rent recoverable. The register of such rents is kept not by the Local Authority but by the local Rent Officer; a personal search may be made or a written or possibly telephoned enquiry may be made.

It is not always necessary to submit the complete form; it is possible to submit a much briefer form which incorporates the questions on the full form by reference only.

i Replies to the enquiries

When the replies to the enquiries are received they should be scrutinised carefully to see whether any of the information disclosed is prejudicial to the purchaser and whether any further enquiries need to be made. The majority of enquiries are so drafted that the purchaser's solicitor will be hoping for a negative answer. Should anything untoward be revealed than the purchaser's solicitor should inform the purchaser as soon as possible and obtain instructions.

The form contains a statement that the Local Authority and its officers will only be liable for an error in answering the enquiries if there has been negligence. It would seem that there could be not only tortious liability in negligence but also liability in contract, as a fee has been paid for the answers to the enquiries.[7] This 'exclusion clause' might then possibly have to be read subject to the reasonableness test in the Unfair Contract Terms Act 1977. As with the local land charges search, it is not necessary that the purchaser made the enquiries, for the purchaser can take the benefit of replies to enquiries requisitioned by some other person provided he was aware of their contents before the relevant time.

These enquiries should be made in respect of every purchase of land, registered or unregistered. Of course, the replies to the enquiries give no guarantee that the situation covered by the question will not change at some time in the future, so again there is a danger in relying on out-of-date replies. The Law Society Conditions make it quite clear that the property is sold subject to matters which would be revealed by a local land charges search and enquiries of the Local Authority and go even further in providing that the purchaser must rely on the Local Authority's replies rather than on any information provided by the vendor;[8] however this limitation of the vendor's

7 *Coats Patons (Retail) Ltd v Birmingham Corpn* (1971) 69 LGR 356.
8 LSC 3(2), (3).

liability may be subject to the reasonableness test in the Misrepresentation Act 1967, section 3 as amended.[9]

3 Enquiries of the vendor

The need for enquiries directed at the vendor through his solicitor is a very obvious consequence of the vendor's limited duty of disclosure. The purchaser's solicitor will probably again use a standard form as the basis for his enquiries, such as those produced by the various law stationers.[10] This will commonly include enquiries on matters such as the ownership of boundary walls and fences; the existence of any disputes relating to the property, for example about the exact position of a boundary; whether the property has the benefit of the NHBC scheme; the existence of any guarantees in relation to the property, eg for wood that has been treated for rot or insect attack; the route of services to the property such as gas, electricity and drainage; the arrangements for shared drives and any other easements; whether all covenants affecting the property have been observed; planning matters, including whether there has been any recent development which would have required planning permission; the fixtures and fittings that are to pass with the property, including oil remaining in the storage tank where the property has oil-fired heating; the exact scope of the vendor's liability for paths, drives and laying out the garden on the purchase of a newly constructed property; and details of any service charge payable.

The enquiries on the standard form are not intended to be exhaustive and the purchaser's solicitor's duty is to raise all appropriate enquiries; if the standard form is used then such further enquiries must be added as may be appropriate in each particular case. Similarly, inappropriate enquiries should be deleted. So if the property is subject to a tenancy, be it residential, business or agricultural, the purchaser may require further information. If the property is centrally-heated, the purchaser may wish to enquire about the state of repair and maintenance of the system. If vacant land is being sold for building or other purposes, the purchaser may wish to know if the land is subject to flooding. The enquiries can also be used to clarify a provision in the draft contract, although negotiation as to the terms of the contract may be dealt with more conveniently in correspondence.

The usefulness of the enquiries depends on the attitude of the vendor and his solicitor. The vendor is under no obligation to answer any enquiries, although he will normally do so. The replies given may be so equivocal as to be virtually useless to the purchaser. For example, if the purchaser raises enquiries about the physical state of repair of the property, and the central heating, he may be told simply to rely on his own inspection and survey. Other replies may only be answered 'so far as the vendor is aware'. The reason for such vague replies is that a reply may amount to a representation and if false

9 However under the Law Society Conditions, the vendor must disclose communications received from the Local Authority; see ch 7, section vii, below.

10 For example, the forms produced by Oyez, Unilaw, Fourmat, Stat-plus and Shaw and Sons.

involve the vendor in liability for misrepresentation. The *Oyez* standard form of enquiries contains a disclaimer stating that the accuracy of replies is not guaranteed and that other appropriate searches and enquiries and inspections should be made, but this is of little effect and will not prevent answers being representations of fact.[11] The Law Society and National Conditions also purport to restrict the vendor's liability for misrepresentation.[12] In addition to the vendor's potential liability, the vendor's solicitor could be liable in negligence to the purchaser for incorrect replies to enquiries;[13] the disclaimer on the *Oyez* standard form also purports to exclude this liability. In practice, the vendor's solicitor should at the very least take instructions from the vendor and try to be as informative as possible in the replies to enquiries. The purchaser's solicitor can then examine the replies given and, if dissatisfied with any reply, can take the point up again with the vendor's solicitor. The danger is that the process of raising and answering preliminary enquiries becomes a mere charade; the only effective solution to this would then be to in some way extend the vendor's duty of disclosure.

4 Search of the Public Index Map

This search is made at the District Land Registry. It will reveal whether the land is an area of compulsory registration of title, whether title to the freehold or leasehold estate in all or any part of the land is already registered, and whether there are any cautions against first registration. The search ought to be made in all cases where title to the land sold is unregistered.[14] There is a prescribed form of search which should be accompanied by a plan unless the land is in a compulsory registration area.[15]

5 Commons registration search

A search in the Register kept under the Commons Registration Act 1965 will reveal whether all or any part of the land is registered as a common, or town or village green. This would mean that certain local rights existed over the land which would almost certainly adversely influence the purchaser's decision to buy. All land which is so affected must be registered under the Act. A search should be made if the land being bought has never been built on or if it has ever belonged to the Local Lord of the Manor, unless the purchaser's solicitor is acquainted with the land and knows that it is not affected.[16] There is a standard form of search which is sent to the appropriate County Council or to the district or borough council in an area previously covered by the Greater

11 *Walker v Boyle* [1982] 1 All ER 634, [1982] 1 WLR 495. See also *Cremdean Properties Ltd v Nash* (1977) 244 Estates Gazette 547, CA. Other standard forms contain similar disclaimers.
12 See ch 16, below.
13 *Wilson v Bloomfield* (1979) 123 Sol Jo 860, CA.
14 On the grant of a lease, the search should be made against the reversionary title.
15 Form 96.
16 *G & K Ladenbau (UK) Ltd v Crawley and de Reya (a firm)* [1978] 1 All ER 682, [1978] 1 WLR 266.

London Council or Metropolitan County Council with a plan and a small fee. The search should be made whether the land is unregistered or registered as rights of common are overriding interests in respect of registered land.[17]

6 Enquiries of British Coal

If the land is in an area of past, present or potential future mining, the purchaser's solicitor should write to the area office of British Coal to discover the position as regards mining underneath the property and whether there have already been any claims in respect of damage caused by subsidence. Although British Coal will compensate in respect of such damage, the purchaser may wish to have this information available and also to check whether the property is adequately constructed to minimise subsidence damage, before he makes his final decision to proceed. The purchaser will also want to discover, either from British Coal or the vendor, whether any compensation has been paid in respect of subsidence damage. If so, it will not be paid again and the purchaser should ensure that the damage has been repaired.

7 Search in the Central Land Charges Registry

The Law of Property Act 1925, section 198 provides that registration of a land charge in the Central Land Charges Registry is notice to all persons for all purposes. The Law of Property Act 1969, section 24 makes it clear that this provision does not apply to a purchaser before exchange of contracts. If section 198 had been applicable, the vendor would have been able to argue that since the purchaser had notice of the land charge by virtue of its registration, the vendor would be under no duty to disclose it, as his duty of disclosure does not extend to defects of title of which the purchaser is aware. Section 24 makes it clear that the vendor remains under a duty to disclose a land charge and therefore in theory at least there is no need for the purchaser's solicitor to make a search of the Land Charges Registry at this stage.

If there is a land charge registered which the vendor has failed to disclose then the purchaser would normally have an action for damages for breach of contract or possibly rescission. This will inevitably involve the purchaser in some inconvenience and delay. It may be in the purchaser's interest to actually find out whether there are any charges in existence *before* exchange of contracts. If there are, he can then refuse to proceed and exchange contracts unless and until the matter is satisfactorily resolved. This could be particularly appropriate if there was a Class F land charge registered, which protects a non-owning spouse's statutory right of occupation of the matrimonial home.[18] This could arise if the vendor was a spouse who was the sole owner of the legal estate in the matrimonial home being sold; the other spouse may have registered a Class F. Although the vendor would be under a duty to procure the cancellation of

17 Land Registration Act 1925, s. 70(1)(a).
18 Matrimonial Homes Act 1983.

the registration[19] or else be in breach of contract and have to pay damages,[20] the purchaser may prefer to find out by a search of the Land Charges Registry before exchange of contracts whether there is any such charge registered and then simply not proceed and look for another property to buy if there is a registration of which the vendor is unable to arrange for cancellation. The purchaser may have wasted some money in abortive conveyancing costs but this may be preferable to a lengthy action for damages for breach of contract. The ways by which the purchaser can be satisfied that the Class F will be cancelled are dealt with in chapter 8. However, even if a clear search is obtained before exchange of contracts there is always the possibility of a registration being made before completion.

The search, if done, need normally only be made in respect of unregistered land. In respect of a registered title, the Matrimonial Homes Act 1983 charge is protected by notice, the existence of which would be apparent from the register. Assuming the purchaser is sent a full set of up to date office copy entries of the register, there will be no need to make any search.

8 Inspection of the property

There are a number of reasons why it is important for the property to be inspected before exchange of contracts.

i Physical defects

The vendor is under no duty to disclose any defects in, and makes no warranty about, the state and condition of the property being sold.[1] The purchaser must satisfy himself about this and would be well advised to employ a professional surveyor to prepare a report.[2] The scope of such a survey would be agreed in advance but would usually cover the structure of the property, the incidence of dry and wet rot and insect attack, the electrical wiring, the plumbing system and other similar matters.[3] The surveyor could be liable in negligence for any errors in his report, subject to any exclusion clause and to the effects of the Unfair Contract Terms Act 1977.

If the purchaser is taking out a mortgage to provide part of the purchase price, he may be unwilling to go to the expense of a surveyor's report when he knows that the Building Society or the bank will themselves have had a surveyor's report on the property, and indeed the purchaser will have paid for this. There are a number of reasons why the purchaser may be better advised not to rely on this survey but to have one done for himself. The scope of the mortgagee's survey may be quite limited, in that the mortgagee is only inter-

19 Ibid, s. 4.

20 *Wroth v Tyler* [1974] Ch 30, [1973] 1 All ER 897.

1 See, however, *Gordon v Selico Co Ltd*, ch 5, section 4xii, above.

2 In *Low v RJ Haddock Ltd* [1985] CILL 162, it was even held, surprisingly, that a purchaser suing in respect of damage caused by spreading tree roots might be contributorily negligent if he had not arranged a survey at the time of purchase.

3 The RICS provide a standardised survey and valuation report which falls short of a structural survey but which is sufficient for most properties.

ested in ensuring that the property is adequate security for the amount of the loan, which may be substantially less than the purchase price. Past practice has been for Building Societies not to allow purchaser to even see their survey report. Many Building Societies have now changed this practice and are willing to allow the purchaser to see the report, although its scope may still be quite limited. Moreover it does appear that a surveyor who negligently prepares a report for a mortgagee may be liable not only to the mortgagee but also to the purchaser.[4] As a result, Building Societies (and other mortgagees) have introduced a clause in the mortgage application form, excluding liability for (negligent) surveys. Such clauses would seem to be effective.[5] The purchaser should therefore be made aware of the benefits of having his own survey done. Some saving in cost could be achieved by using the same surveyor who is preparing the mortgagee's report; some work will be duplicated and the purchaser should be able to negotiate a reduced price for his own survey. On the purchase of a new property with the benefit of the NHBC scheme it will not normally be necessary for the purchaser to have his own survey done, but the mortgagee will still normally arrange for a surveyor to inspect the property once it is finished.

Under section 30 of the Building Societies Act 1962, the making of an advance by a Building Society implied a warranty that the purchase price was reasonable; however, section 30 was in practice invariably excluded by a statement on the mortgage offer that no such warranty was to be implied. Section 30 is to be repealed by the Building Societies Act 1986, but it is anticipated that it will be replaced by a Building Societies Association Code of Practice of similar effect.

There is another compelling reason why the property should be inspected before exchange of contracts. This is to check that the property as described in the contract accords with the property as enclosed by the physical boundaries on site. If a boundary wall has been erected in the wrong place, this may mean that a neighbour has acquired title by adverse possession to land to which the vendor has the paper title and which is being transferred to the purchaser.

ii Patent defects in title

The vendor is not under a duty to disclose defects in title if they are patent, that is to say if they are apparent on reasonable inspection. The property should be inspected to ascertain whether there are any such defects, for example rights of way. If this inspection is carried out by the purchaser rather than his solicitor, then the solicitor must ensure that the purchaser knows what he is looking for.

iii Other defects in title

There may be other defects in title which are not patent (and which the vendor must therefore disclose), but which may in fact be discoverable by the purchaser by investigation of the occupier of the property. For unregistered land, there is a rule that as between the purchaser and an occupier who has some interest in the property, the purchaser has constructive notice of interests reasonably

4 *Yianni v Edwin Evans & Sons* [1982] QB 438, [1981] 3 All ER 592.

5 *Stevenson v Nationwide Building Society* (1984) 272 EG 663: but see *Smith v Eric S Bush (a firm)* (1987) Times, 18 March, CA.

discoverable from enquiry of the occupier.[6] This will mean that the interests will be binding on the purchaser. For example if the occupier is a tenant, the purchaser may have constructive notice of the existence and terms of the tenancy agreement. However as between the vendor and the purchaser such a defect in title may not be patent and the vendor would have to disclose it or else be in breach of contract.[7] In the case of registered land, under the Land Registration Act 1925, section 70(1)(g), the rights of persons in possession (including both occupation and receipt of rents and profits) are overriding interests and will be binding on a purchaser unless enquiry is made of such person and the rights are not disclosed. Again as between vendor and purchaser some such rights may well not constitute patent defects in title. The vendor may also be in breach of contract if the contract specifically provides for vacant possession.

As we have already seen in connection with the central land charges search, a purchaser may prefer to try and obtain actual knowledge of an interest by which he will be bound, so that he can decide on that basis whether to proceed to exchange, rather than relying on being able to sue the vendor if he fails to comply with his duty to disclose the interest. On this basis it may be advisable to make enquiries of occupiers at this stage.

There are differences in the rules applying to registered and unregistered land. The Land Registration Act 1925, section 70(1)(g) covers the rights of persons not only in occupation of the property but also in receipt of rents and profits and would therefore include the rights of a lessor of the property. The rule in *Hunt v Luck*[8] for unregistered land does not extend so far. Also, the enquiries necessary in respect of unregistered land are limited by section 199[9] of the Law of Property Act 1925, which provides that a purchaser shall not be fixed with constructive notice of any matter unless it would have come to his knowledge if such enquiries and inspections had been made as ought reasonably to have been made. There is no such limitation on the operation of section 70(1)(g); the occupation need not be discoverable from reasonable enquiry and inspection. Further, for registered land, the time at which one looks to see who is in occupation for the purpose of s. 70(1)(g) is quite specific. For registered land, it is those persons who are in occupation at the date of registration of the purchase who may have overriding interests;[10] the date of registration of the purchase is inevitably after the completion of the purchase. All the purchaser and his solicitor can do at this stage is find out who is in occupation now and take precautions in case those people are still in occupation on completion and after.

The first task for the purchaser and his solicitor is to find out who is in occupation. The registered land position is illustrated by the case of *Williams & Glyn's Bank Ltd v Boland*[11] which decided that a wife's equitable interest in

6 *Hunt v Luck* [1902] 1 Ch 428, CA; Law of Property Act 1925, s. 199(1)(ii)(a).
7 *Caballero v Henty* (1874) 9 Ch App 447, CA.
8 [1902] 1 Ch 428, CA.
9 S. 199(1)(ii)(a).
10 *Re Boyles Claim* [1961] 1 All ER 620, [1961] 1 WLR 339, though this is open to some doubt – see dicta in *Paddington Building Society v Mendelsohn* (1985) 50 P & CR 244, CA.
11 [1981] AC 487, [1980] 2 All ER 408, HL.

a matrimonial home which was in her husband's sole name could be an overriding interest under section 70(1)(g) if she was in possession. Furthermore she would still be in occupation for the purposes of section 70(1)(g) even though her husband was also in occupation.[12] In these circumstances her equitable interest, acquired for example by some financial contribution and giving a right to possession of the property, would be an overriding interest and be binding on a purchaser or, in the actual case, a mortgagee. This principle is not confined to spouses but will extend to anyone with an equitable interest, for example an aged relative who has contributed to the cost of building a 'granny flat'. The task of discovering whether anyone of this nature is in occupation is difficult if not impossible. Consider the position if the spouse or cohabitee or granny or whoever has an equitable interest is out shopping or at work when the purchaser calls to look at the property. Or if he or she is away on holiday or has been driven from the property by the violence of someone else in the property. The person with the equitable interest may still be in occupation for the purposes of section 70(1)(g) and the equitable interest will still be an overriding interest, but it will be extraordinarily difficult for the purchaser or his solicitor to find out about the occupier. The position as it relates to unregistered land is slightly better from the purchaser's point of view in that as we have seen, for the purchaser to have constructive notice of the equitable interest and therefore be bound by it, the interest must be discoverable from reasonable enquiries. However, there will still be problems. The effect of section 199 was considered in *Kingsnorth Trust Ltd v Tizard*,[13] where it was held that an inspection at a time pre-arranged with the vendor was not sufficient. The case also confirms that the necessary presence for occupation is not negatived by regular and repeated absence. The case actually concerned the position of a mortgagee (and is considered further in chapter 13) but is presumably equally applicable to a purchaser; the task of the purchaser and his solicitor, in relation to both registered and unregistered title, is difficult and, as the law stands, unrealistic.

There may be a question on the standard form of enquiries of the vendor which asks for details of anyone in occupation and any rights they may have in the property. This is not that much use for the purchaser, save for probably making the vendor liable for misrepresentation should he answer incorrectly. In particular under section 70(1)(g) the enquiry must be addressed to the occupier for the purchaser to be able to take free of the interest if it is not revealed. The purchaser cannot rely on the vendor's word. This, then, is the second task for the purchaser and his solicitor; having discovered who is in occupation, to ascertain what if any rights the occupier may have. Although we have said that under section 70(1)(g) if the rights are not revealed on enquiry of the occupier they are not overriding interests and will not be binding on the purchaser, in practice it may well be that the spouse or cohabitee is quite unaware of the equitable interest which he or she has. Indeed the occupier may refer the enquiry to the vendor's solicitor, who is then placed in an awkward position. Looking at matters *purely* from the point of view of the vendor, he would rather the rights were not disclosed to the purchaser because

12 Apparently overruling *Caunce v Caunce* [1969] 1 All ER 722, [1969] 1 WLR 286.
13 [1986] 2 All ER 54, [1986] 1 WLR 783.

there would then be no danger of the purchaser being bound by them. There would be a conflict of interest between the vendor and the occupier and it might not be appropriate for the vendor's solicitor to advise the occupier as well.

What if the inspection does reveal an occupier with an interest in the property? The purchaser's solicitor will need to take steps to ensure that the purchaser is not bound by the interest. The ways in which this could be done in respect of an occupier's equitable interest are discussed in chapter 8, section 1 iv below. For registered land, if the occupier leaves when the vendor leaves and is not in possession on completion (or afterwards) then the whole problem disappears, because the occupier's rights will not be binding on the purchaser. Unfortunately the purchaser cannot see into the future and must still be protected against the occupier's interest.

The equitable interest of a spouse, which has been discussed above, must be distinguished from a spouse's statutory right of occupation of the matrimonial home,[14] which must be protected as a Class F land charge, or a notice if the title is registered. Although the search for and enquiry of occupiers should be pursued in every case, perhaps the most common situation in which there may be problems along these lines is where the vendor is a sole spouse, the other spouse having an equitable interest. This will then also raise the problem of a registration of the other spouse's statutory right of occupation.

9 Other enquiries

The list of enquiries cannot be exhaustive. The purchaser's solicitor should make all the searches and enquiries appropriate to the particular case. To take two examples, if power lines run over or under the property, an enquiry may be made of the electricity board as to the terms on which this is done and the route, if underground; if the property is adjacent to a railway line then a similar enquiry could be made of British Rail which will reveal whether fences bounding the track are maintainable by British Rail.

10 Communication with the purchaser

It is of the utmost importance that the purchaser's solicitor informs the purchaser immediately of any matter revealed by the various searches and enquiries which could affect the purchaser's decision to proceed.

14 Under Matrimonial Homes Act 1983.

7 Planning law in conveyancing

1 Introduction

In broad terms there are three controls over the erection and alteration of buildings and the use to which land and buildings can be put. These are:

(a) any provisions such as easements and more particularly covenants subject to which the property is held;

(b) the Town and Country Planning Legislation and the need for planning permission:

(c) Building Regulation consent.

The purchaser will be concerned on two counts. Firstly he will want to establish that what he is buying is in no way in breach of the foregoing, or in other words that the vendor has complied with any restrictions and obtained all necessary consents. The purchaser's enquiries before contract are aimed at establishing this. The vendor will be asked in preliminary enquiries to state the present use of the property and also to state whether there has been any work done at the property which might have required planning permission. The vendor should also be asked to supply copies of planning permissions and building regulation consents. If the property is subject to restrictive covenants, the vendor should be asked to confirm that they have been complied with and to produce any necessary consents or approvals. The local land charges search and additional enquiries of the Local Authority are also directed in part at establishing whether there has been any breach of planning control.[1]

The purchaser's second consideration will be to establish whether his proposals for the property will fall foul of the controls mentioned. If he wants to extend a dwelling house, will this be in breach of any restrictive covenant? Will he require planning permission or building regulation consent? This is really part of a more general question of whether the property is suitable for the purchaser's purposes, which both the purchaser and his solicitor will have to consider before exchange of contracts.

If on the sale of freehold land there is a restrictive covenant affecting the

1 Question 6 on the current (1982) District Council form. Question 4 enquires about breaches of building regulations.

property then as we have seen the vendor is under a duty to disclose this.[2] It may be a covenant restricting the type of building which can be erected on the land, or its size, or the number of buildings. It may provide that no building can take place without the prior approval of plans by the covenantee. It may restrict the use to which the land or any buildings are put. The existence of an easement may also restrict development of the property; it is inadvisable to build over a right of way unless it can be re-routed to the satisfaction of parties concerned. Again, we have seen that the vendor is under a duty to disclose such easements unless they are apparent on inspection. However apart from the above, the vendor gives no general implied warranty that the use of the property is authorised, either as regards his own use or the purchaser's intended use.[3]

Building regulations are made under the Public Health Acts. They are not local but cover the whole country and deal with the way in which new buildings and alterations are constructed. They regulate such matters as the preparation of the site, the materials to be used, ventilation and the structural stability of the building. Put simply, whereas planning permission covers what is to be built, building regulations cover how it is to be built. Building regulation consent is sometimes called byelaw approval, because building control is administered by the local authority, but under the Building Act 1984, a private 'approved inspector' can be engaged to supervise building control, rather than the local authority. One such approved inspector is a subsiduary of NHBC. The approved inspector will be appointed by a notice which suspends the local authority powers. The inspector ultimately issues a 'final certificate' of compliance with building regulations.

Planning permission cannot be dealt with quite so briefly.

2 Planning control

i Background

The policy of the planning authorities will be reflected in a development plan. This consists of two elements, the structure plan and the local plan. The structure plan is prepared by the County Council and contains the Council's detailed policy for the area. Local plans cover a much smaller area and are prepared by District Councils. They will go into more detail than the structure plan and will deal with the policy for individual pieces of land. In Greater London and the six metropolitan counties, structure and local plans are to be replaced by unitary development plans, prepared by the London Borough Councils and the Metropolitan District Councils (following the abolition of

2 Also, where the property sold is leasehold, any onerous or unusual covenants in the lease should be disclosed, see ch 5, above; the purchaser's solicitor will of course examine the whole of the contents of the lease.

3 In *Hill v Harris* [1965] 2 QB 601, [1965] 2 All ER 358, CA, an underlessee was permitted by his lease to use the premises for certain purposes. This use was in fact prohibited by the head lease but the under lessee had no claim against the under lessor. (An under lessee's solicitor should examine the contents of the headlease; he has the contractual right to do so under an open contract, though this could be excluded by special condition.)

the Greater London Council and the six metropolitan County Councils). The standard form of additional enquiries of the Local Authority does include a question about the existence and contents of the various plans.[4]

ii When is planning permission needed?

The general principle is that planning permission is needed for 'development'. This is defined as:

(a) the carrying out of building, engineering, mining or other operations in, on, over or under land,
or

(b) the making of any material change in the use of any buildings or other land.[5]

It is specifically provided that the change of the use of a dwelling house to use as two or more dwelling houses is a material change of use and thus development. However certain matters are specified as not constituting development and therefore not needing permission. These include works of alteration, improvement or maintenance which do not materially affect the external appearance of a building;[6] the use (not construction) of any buildings or other land within the curtilage[7] of a dwelling house for any purpose incidental to the enjoyment of the dwelling house as such;[8] the use of land for agriculture and forestry;[9] and in the case of buildings or other land used for a purpose contained in a class specified in an order made by the Secretary of State, the use thereof for any other purpose contained in the same class.[10] That order is presently the Town and Country Planning (Use Classes) Order 1972. This contains 18 detailed classes, and the change of use from a use within one class to another use within the same class will not constitute development and not require permission. Class I comprises use as a shop, with certain exceptions including shops for the sale of hot food, pet animals or birds or motor vehicles. Thus a grocer's shop can become a butcher's shop without the need for planning permission. Class II comprises use as an office for any purpose including a bank or an estate agency or a building society, but excluding a post office or betting office. Class III comprises use as a light industrial building and Class IV use as a general industrial building for any purpose. The other classes are very specific in their content.

As well as the matters which the legislation provides do not constitute development, there are certain other matters which may constitute development but in respect of which permission is not required.[11] An example would be the resumption of the use of land for a previously authorised use following service of an enforcement notice.[12]

4 Question 7 on the current (1982) form.
5 Town and Country Planning Act 1971, s. 22(1).
6 Ibid, s. 22(2)(a).
7 This means the area surrounding the house which is regarded as part of the house. For a normal dwelling house, it includes the garden.
8 Town and Country Planning Act 1971, s. 22(2)(d).
9 Ibid, s. 22(2)(e).
10 Ibid, s. 22(2)(f).
11 Ibid, s. 23.
12 Ibid.

iii General Development Order

Permission is needed for development, with the exceptions just mentioned. There may be no need to actually apply for planning permission, because permission may be granted for certain sorts of development by a General Development Order. The current Order is the General Development Order 1977 as amended. The Order contains a number of classes of 'permitted' development in respect of which the General Development Order itself grants planning permission and there is no need for a separate application for permission. (The development may of course require building regulation consent.) Class I of the Order relates to development within the curtilage of a dwelling house. This includes the enlargement, improvement or alteration of a dwelling house, provided that a number of conditions are met. The size must not be increased by more than 70 cubic metres or 15 per cent whichever is the greater,[13] subject to a maximum of 115 cubic metres. The enlargement or extension must be no higher than the original dwelling house and it must not extend beyond the forwardmost part of any wall of the house fronting onto a highway. No part of the enlargement or alteration within two metres of the boundary of the curtilage must be over four metres high. The result of the enlargement or alteration must be that no more than 50 per cent of the original curtilage (excluding the area of the original house) is occupied by buildings. Garages are treated as coming within this part of the class if they are within 5 metres of the house. The class also includes porches and central heating oil storage tanks, both subject to size limits; hard standing for vehicles which is incidental to the enjoyment of the dwelling house as such; and the erection of and improvements and alterations to buildings within the curtilage, used for a purpose incidental to the enjoyment of the dwelling house. The latter are also subject to certain conditions concerning height, projection beyond the forwardmost wall fronting a highway, and area of the curtilage covered by buildings. This part of the class would include garages not within 5 metres of the house.

Class II covers the erection of fences and walls with certain height limits, and the painting of the exterior of a building. There are 28 other classes in the Order covering fairly specialised areas and not normally encountered in the ordinary domestic conveyancing transaction.

Under article 4 of the Order the Secretary of State or the Local Planning Authority (subject normally to confirmation by the Secretary of State) may make a direction that particular types of development are to be excluded from the classes of development permitted by the Order. The existence of such a direction will be revealed by the additional enquiries of the Local Authority.[14]

iv Application for planning permission

Unless permission is not needed or is granted by the General Development Order, it will be necessary to apply for planning permission. If there is some doubt as to whether express permission is needed or not, an application can be made to the Local Planning Authority for a determination.[15]

13 50 cubic metres and 10% for a terraced house.
14 Question 8 on the current (1982) form.
15 Town and Country Planning Act 1971, s. 53.

Application for permission is made to the Local Planning Authority, that is the District Council or London Borough Council. The application is made on a form supplied by the Local Planning Authority and it is accompanied by a plan identifying the land concerned and describing the development, and the appropriate fee. It must also be accompanied by a certificate stating that the applicant is either the sole owner of the land or that he has duly notified other owners of the application.[16] 'Owner' in this context includes the freehold owner and any person holding a leasehold interest with at least seven years still to run. Anyone who genuinely hopes to acquire an interest in land may apply for planning permission in respect of it. It is possible to apply merely for 'outline' planning permission. This is an application for approval in principle of the erection of a building subject to the subsequent approval by the Local Planning Authority of detailed matters such as the design of the building, external appearance, access, drainage and other similar provisions. The outline permission if granted will be subject to these 'reserved matters' which will be specified in the permission. Providing that application for approval of the reserved matters is made within three years of the outline permission,[17] the Local Planning Authority cannot go back on its original decision of principle.

The Local Planning Authority must decide whether to grant or refuse the application and give the applicant notice of the decision within eight weeks of the application. This period can be extended by agreement. If no such notification is made then the applicant is entitled to deem the application refused and pursue an appeal. The grant of permission may be made subject to conditions[18] but these must fairly and reasonably relate to the development.[19] The Local Planning Authority keeps a register of applications and the decisions made on them.[20] Details of entries in this register are revealed by the additional enquiries of the Local Authority.[1] Conditions imposed on permissions granted after 1 August 1977 are registrable as local land charges.[2]

There is appeal to the Secretary of State against a refusal of permission (including a deemed refusal) and against conditions subject to which approval is given.[3] Notice of appeal must be given within six months of the decision. The Secretary of State may allow or dismiss the appeal and can deal with the application as if it had been made to him in the first instance; so conditions could be added which were not imposed by the Local Planning Authority.

v Effect of permission

The permission attaches not to the applicant personally, but to the land.[4] Permissions are subject to an implied condition that development must com-

16 Ibid, s. 27.
17 Ibid, s. 42.
18 Ibid, s. 29.
19 *Pyx Granite Co Ltd v Ministry of Housing and Local Government* [1960] AC 260, [1959] 3 All ER 1, HL.
20 Town and Country Planning Act 1971, s. 34.
1 Question 11 on the current (1982) form.
2 Local Land Charges Act 1975, s. 2(1).
3 Town and Country Planning Act 1971, s. 36.
4 Ibid, s. 33.

mence within five years from the date of the grant of permission.[5] In the case of an outline permission, development must commence within five years of the grant of the outline permission or two years of approval of the reserved matters, whichever is the later.[6]

Additionally, if development has not been completed within the above periods, then the Local Planning Authority can serve a completion notice, stating that the planning permission will cease to have effect on a specified date, being not earlier than 12 months from the date of the notice.[7] The notice must be confirmed by the Secretary of State.

vi Enforcement

A breach of planning control occurs if development is carried out in respect of which the necessary permission has not been obtained or if conditions subject to which permission has been granted are not complied with. To enforce planning control, the Local Planning Authority may serve an enforcement notice. This must be served on the owner and occupier of the land affected.[8] If the breach of planning control consists of:

(a) the carrying out of building or other operations (ie the first limb of development as defined in section ii, above) either without permission or in breach of the conditions attached to a permission, or

(b) changing the use of any building to use as a single dwelling house,

then an enforcement notice can only be served within four years of the breach.[9] Otherwise – that is to say for all other changes of use – the only time limit is that the breach in respect of which the notice is served must have occurred after the end of 1963. The notice must state the alleged breach of planning control, the steps required to remedy the breach, the date on which the notice becomes effective (being not less than 28 days from the date of service) and the date by which the required steps must be taken, that is the compliance period.

Before the notice takes effect an appeal can be made to the Secretary of State and the notice will not then take effect until after the termination of the appeal. The grounds of appeal are specified in the Town and Country Planning Act 1971, section 88 and include that planning permission ought to be granted for the development which constitutes breach of planning control; that the compliance period is too short; and that the notice was served out of time. Non-compliance with an effective enforcement notice is a criminal offence.[10]

The Local Planning Authority may wish to stop the breach of planning control before the enforcement notice takes effect, particularly if there is an appeal pending to the Secretary of State. The Local Planning Authority can, at any time after service of an enforcement notice but before it has become effective, serve a stop notice.[11] This will state the activity which is to be stopped,

5 Ibid, s. 41.
6 Ibid, s. 42.
7 Ibid, s. 44.
8 Ibid, s. 87.
9 Ibid, s. 87(3).
10 Ibid, s. 89.
11 Ibid, s. 90 as amended by the Town and Country Planning (Amendment) Act 1977.

being some or all of the activities alleged by the enforcement notice to be a breach of planning control. The notice cannot prohibit certain activities, including the use of a house as a dwelling house. Non-compliance with a stop notice is also a criminal offence. If the enforcement notice is eventually quashed on appeal, any person who suffers loss as a result of a stop notice can claim compensation from the Local Planning Authority.[12] The existence of an enforcement notice or a stop notice is revealed by the local land charges search and the additional enquiries of the Local Authority.[13]

As no enforcement notice can be served in respect of a pre-1964 change of use, it is possible for any person with an interest in land to apply for a certificate of established use in respect of that land.[14] This will be granted if the use began before 1964 (without planning permission) and has been continuous since 1964. No certificate will be given in respect of use of land as a single dwelling house. A purchaser requiring reassurance that the use of land is authorised might ask the vendor to obtain such a certificate.

vii Contractual conditions

The vendor gives no implied warranty that the present use nor the purchaser's intended use are lawful and authorised under the planning legislation.[15] The purchaser's enquiries are directed towards establishing that the property can be used for his purposes. The National Conditions of Sale provide that the purchaser can deliver with his requisitions (ie after exchange of contracts) questions concerning the authorised use of the property, to which the vendor shall reply so far as he is able.[16] If the property is sold on the footing that the authorised use is a particular use specified in the special conditions then if it appears before completion that this use is not an authorised use, the purchaser can rescind. Otherwise the purchaser shall be deemed to buy with knowledge of the authorised use of the property, which is to say that the open contract position applies and the vendor is making no warranty concerning the use. The National Conditions also provide that the vendor must disclose any notice or other matter arising under the Planning Acts of which he knows,[17] and if any notice is served after the date of the contract the vendor must inform the purchaser.[18] In *Sakkas v Donford Ltd*[19] the vendor failed to disclose that the house was to his knowledge in an area zoned as open space; he fell foul of National Condition 15(4) and the purchaser could rescind. Under the Law Society Conditions, the vendor warrants that he has informed the purchaser of the contents of any written communication from the local authority received by or known to him *before* the date of the contract[20] and that if any such communication is received after the date of the contract, the vendor must

12 Ibid, s. 177 as amended by the Town and Country Planning (Amendment) Act 1977.
13 Question 6 on the current (1982) form.
14 Town and Country Planning Act 1971, s. 94
15 *Mitchell v Beacon Estates (Finsbury Park) Ltd* (1949) 1 P & CR 32.
16 NC 15. The purchaser's solicitor will normally raise this in preliminary enquiries of the vendor before exchange of contracts.
17 NC 15(4).
18 NC 16.
19 (1982) 46 P & CR 290.
20 LSC 3(3)(a).

inform the purchaser.[1,2] So under both sets of conditions the vendor would have to disclose to the purchaser the existence of any enforcement notice.

1 LSC 3(3)(c); this, and NC 16, would cover other local authority matters apart from just planning, for example a notice concerning the making up and adoption of a road.
2 The vendor's duty of disclosure is therefore considerably widened, particularly under the Law Society Conditions.

8 Exchange of contracts

1 Are the parties ready?

i Approval of the draft contract

Having found out as much as possible about the property, the purchaser's solicitor must consider the proposed contract and decide whether it is acceptable or whether he should try to negotiate some change. This is a two-fold process – making sure that both the property and the terms on which it is to be sold are satisfactory both from the purchaser's point of view and from the purchaser's solicitor's professional point of view. If there is negotiation about the terms then the vendor's solicitor will be bearing similar matters in mind in acting for his client, as indeed will have been the case when the contract was drafted in the first place. The purchaser's solicitor will examine terms such as the length of title offered, the amount of deposit required and the rights of the parties should completion be delayed in order to ensure that these are acceptable to the purchaser or at least the best terms available. As regards the property, the solicitor must consider whether in the light of his enquiries and the description of the property and interests affecting it in the contract, the property is suited to the requirements of the purchaser. By way of illustration, if the purchaser is a developer buying land on which to build a housing estate, the land would be of no use if there were no comprehensive right of access to a public road, or no right of drainage, or if there were a restrictive covenant preventing building. Similarly when a purchaser buys a new house on such an estate he will require a right of way over the estate roads until they become public roads, rights of passage of drains, pipes and cables and a scheme of restrictive covenants to preserve the character of the development. He may want a right to enter onto neighbouring property to repair drains. If he has a shared drive he will want a right of way over his neighbour's half and provision made for maintenance. On the same lines, if the purchaser is buying a house which has been built right up to the boundary of one side of a plot, without leaving a strip of land between the house wall and the boundary, the purchaser's solicitor should ensure that the property has the benefit of a right of entry onto the neighbouring property for the purpose of effecting repairs to the house.

If there should be a restrictive covenant affecting the property which will be enforceable against the purchaser and which will render it unsuitable for the purchaser's purposes, then instead of withdrawing, the purchaser could attempt to have the covenant discharged or take out insurance against it ever being enforced. The Lands Tribunal has power to discharge or modify any restrictive covenant affecting freehold land if:

(a) the restriction is obsolete due to changes in the character of the property or neighbourhood or other circumstances, or

(b) the restriction impedes some reasonable use of the land *and* either the persons entitled to the benefit of the covenant get no practical benefit from it or the restriction is contrary to public interest *and* in either case money will be an adequate compensation to the persons entitled to the benefit if the covenant is discharged or modified, or

(c) all persons of full age and capacity entitled to the benefit of the covenant have expressly or impliedly consented to the discharge, or

(d) the discharge will not adversely affect the persons entitled to the benefit of the covenant.[1]

The Tribunal can also award compensation for loss resulting from the modification or discharge. In practice, because of the cost and time factor, an application to the Tribunal may not be a realistic possibility for a potential purchaser.

It may be possible to arrange insurance against the covenant ever being enforced. Full disclosure would have to be made to the insurers who would for a single premium issue a policy for indemnity up to a specified amount. If a policy is already in existence the solicitor for the purchaser should ensure that the benefit will be assigned to the purchaser and that the amount of the indemnity is satisfactory; if it is too low, perhaps representing the value of the property when the policy was taken out, it may be possible to increase it by paying an additional premium.

Once the purchaser has given instructions to proceed then one part of the contract, which will have been sent to the purchaser's solicitor in duplicate, will be returned to the vendor's solicitor approved (as amended if necessary) in readiness for exchange. If the contract has been amended substantially then it may be retyped. If it has been amended then it is crucially important that both parts are similarly amended.[2]

ii Financial arrangements

The vendor's solicitor will need to ensure that the proceeds of sale will be sufficient to pay off all mortgages over the property and in addition meet any other expenses such as estate agent's fees and the vendor's solicitor's own costs. If capital gains tax is payable then provision should be made for this also. The solicitor will probably have discovered at an early stage what mortgages there are over the property and what amounts are owing on them. He will have had to approach the first mortgagee, often a Building Society or a bank, to obtain the deeds or charge certificate and he could if necessary request at that stage a statement of the amount owing. The investigation of title he does before drafting the contract will probably include, for unregistered land, a land

1 Law of Property Act 1925, s. 84. This also applies to covenants in certain leases.

2 See for example *Harrison v Battye* [1974] 3 All ER 830, [1975] 1 WLR 58, CA.

charges search against the vendor. This will reveal any mortgages not protected by deposit of the title deeds, which the vendor may have forgotten to mention to the solicitor. Again there is no harm in approaching the second mortgagees at this stage to check the amount owing under their respective mortgages.

The purchaser's solicitor should ensure that on the completion date the purchaser will be in a position to hand over the required money. If some of this is being generated by the contemporaneous sale of the purchaser's existing house, this will lead to problems of synchronisation, dealt with below. In calculating the amount needed by the purchaser, his solicitor should bear in mind his own costs and disbursements in acting on the purchase as well as the costs of the mortgagee's solicitors, if the purchaser is buying with the aid of a mortgage. These costs are payable by the purchaser. (The purchaser's solicitors may also be acting for the mortgagee but there will still be additional costs for so doing.)

As many clients will be both buying and selling property with the same solicitor acting on both transactions, the solicitor will have to consider both the proceeds of sale and also the amount required to complete the purchase, the balance of the former probably making up part of the latter.

A typical purchaser will require financial assistance with the purchase from some outside source and the purchaser's solicitor may be asked to advise on various sources of finance.

1 *Ordinary repayment mortgage* The essence of a mortgage is that a sum called the principal is advanced by the mortgagee on terms for repayment of the principal and payment of interest. These terms will be contained in the mortgage deed which will also mortgage (or charge) the property to the mortgagee. This gives the mortgagee certain rights, the most fundamental of which is a power of sale in certain circumstances. Under a repayment mortgage the term over which it is anticipated that the principal will be paid is fixed, although the mortgagor can of course pay off his mortgage at any time. With a fixed term, of say 15, 20 or 25 years, it is possible to calculate a monthly instalment which if paid for the whole of the term, and assuming a constant rate of interest, will pay off both principal and all interest accruing, by the end of the term. The mortgage deed will doubtless provide for variation of the interest rate and thus the monthly instalment necessary to pay off the mortgage over the agreed term will fluctuate. Individual instalments can be apportioned as between payment of interest and repayment of principal. It may be that the instalments paid over the first few years of the term are virtually all interest and the amount attributable to repayment of principal increases throughout the term but, because of the MIRAS system explained below, it is more likely that the payment of interest and repayment of principal is spread equally over the term and that each instalment represents a similar amount of interest and principal. The significance of this for the purchaser is that income tax relief is available for mortgage payments, but only on the *interest* on a loan for the purchase or improvement of property, not on repayments of principal. (The property must be the only or main residence of the mortgagor or his or her dependent relative or separated spouse. There is no relief for interest on the excess of any loan over £30,000.) Before April 1983, the mortgage interest payable was reflected in the mortgagor's PAYE code. However, since April

1983, under the MIRAS scheme (Mortgage Interest Relief at Source), the mortgagor pays his instalment to the mortgagee net of basic rate tax on the interest element of the instalment. (If the mortgagor pays higher rate rax, the extra tax relief is obtainable through the PAYE code or notice of assessment.) If each instalment is not similarly split between principal and interest, and the proportion due to interest falls as the term progresses, the actual amount paid will increase as the tax relief diminishes.

Repayment mortgages are obtainable from a variety of sources including Building Societies, Local Authorities, and, increasingly, from banks. It may be necessary to advise the purchaser on the relative merits of loans from banks and Building Societies or from two different Building Societies. In particular the solicitor can compare the possible fluctuations of bank and Building Society interest rates. In addition some Building Societies and banks will charge a higher rate of interest for loans in excess of a certain figure, eg £15,000.

Although a Local Authority might be more lenient, all mortgagees will limit the amount of the loan by reference to the income of the mortgagor or mortgagors and the value of the property to be mortgaged; applicants for a mortgage will have to pay for a survey and valuation for that purpose. If the loan is to be in excess of a certain proportion of the value of the property – often 80 per cent – then most mortgagees and certainly Building Societies will take out a single premium guarantee policy. This is to insure against the value of the property falling below the amount of the 80 per cent figure, thereby leaving the excess of the loan over that amount effectively unsecured. The premium for this policy is payable, needless to say, by the mortgagor.

The older the applicant the shorter the term of mortgage which is likely to be on offer. In certain circumstances, for example if the applicant's income might fluctuate, the mortgagee might require a guarantor (perhaps one of the applicant's parents if the applicant is particularly young) to join in the mortgage deed to guarantee that repayments will be made.

Building Societies have tended in the past not to be too enthusiastic about older property. A Local Authority on the other hand tends to have less stringent requirements but the amount of Local Authority funds available for mortgages may be extremely limited.

2 *Endowment mortgage* The difference between an endowment mortgage and an ordinary repayment mortgage is that as well as the mortgagor mortgaging the property, he – or they – will also assign to the mortgagee a life insurance policy on his – or their – life or lives. The policy is for a sum equivalent to the principal advanced under the mortgage and the term of the policy will be the same as the term of the mortgage. The mortgage instalment repayments are made up wholly of payments of interest, the principal being repaid at the end of the term (assuming the mortgage is not paid off earlier) with the sum produced by the life insurance policy. The mortgagor must also pay the premiums on this policy; policies taken out before March 1984 qualified for tax relief at 15% but policies taken out after that date do not qualify for tax relief. An advantage of this scheme is that the death of a mortgagor whose life is insured will automatically generate the funds to pay off the mortgage. Such a benefit is also available under an ordinary repayment mortgage by means

of a special insurance policy called a mortgage protection policy which guarantees, on death, repayment of the sum then outstanding on the mortgage.

A solicitor should give careful thought before he recommends either a type of repayment or a particular endowment mortgage to a particular client, and may need to call in independent specialist financial advice. He should consider the ultimate sums to be realised by the life policy, and whether these are guaranteed or merely estimated. He should consider the position if the property has to be sold after only a short while – the surrender value of the policy in the first few years. It also tends to be the case that as interest rates rise, endowment mortgages become less favourable than repayment mortgages.

If any commission is payable to the solicitor in respect of a policy the solicitor should account to the client for it, if it is over £10, unless the client agrees it can be retained.

Sometimes a slightly higher interest rate will be charged for an endowment mortgage as compared with an ordinary repayment mortgage. The MIRAS system applies to endowment mortgages, where of course the whole of each instalment represents interest.

3 *Mortgage offer* It is vital that the purchaser receives before exchange of contracts a mortgage offer, intimating that the advance will be available by completion. He otherwise runs the risk that the advance is not available on completion and that unless he can find the money from elsewhere, he may eventually lose his deposit and even have to pay damages to the vendor. Some Building Societies will not issue an offer until shortly before the advance is available but there has been a recent tendency to make an offer as soon as the property and the borrower are approved, possibly stating the future date at which the advance will be available, or even approving a loan of up to a particular amount to a borrower before he has yet found a property (subject of course to the property being satisfactory). This then avoids some delay and uncertainty on the purchaser's part.

The purchaser's solicitor must ensure that any conditions attached to the mortgage offer can be met. In certain circumstances there may be a provision that the mortgagee will retain some of the advance pending some specified condition. If on a newly built housing estate the roads are not yet adopted nor is there a Highways Act Agreement and Bond, the mortgagee may make a retention in case the builder defaults in making up the roads, in which case the cost of so doing is borne proportionately by the properties abutting the road making such properties worth that much less. This is also a valid reason for the purchaser in these circumstances making a retention from the balance of the purchase price payable on completion and indeed the purchaser's solicitor should try and agree before exchange of contracts that in such circumstances a retention, commonly of the amount retained by the mortgagee, can be made on completion.

The money can be released when the roads are adopted or a Highways Act Agreement and Bond comes into existence, whichever is the earlier. The mortgagee may also make a retention in respect of repairs which have to be done to the property. As it is unlikely that these will be done before completion, the purchaser's solicitor should check that the purchaser does not need the retained money in order to pay over the balance of the purchase price on completion.

Another condition of the mortgage offer may refer to payment of the single premium of the guarantee policy if the advance is in excess of a certain percentage of the mortgagee's valuation of the property. In fact Building Societies will commonly add the premium on to the advance. On a mortgage of leasehold property, the mortgagee may require the freehold and any superior titles to be deduced, unless the lease is registered with absolute title. The purchaser's solicitor should ensure that the contract with the vendor contains an equivalent provision.

4 *Deposit* As well as ensuring that sufficient money will be available to complete the purchase, the purchaser's solicitor must ensure that there will be sufficient money available on exchange of contracts to pay the deposit, normally fixed by the contract at 10 per cent of the purchase price. If the purchaser is selling a property at the same time, he may wish to use the deposit he receives on his sale to put towards the deposit he must pay on his purchase. This can be done if his solicitor holds that deposit as his agent but not if it is held as stake-holder. Even if this money can be used, there will probably be a balance to make up, if the price which the purchaser is paying on his purchase is greater than that for which he is selling his present property. If the purchaser is a first time buyer then he will have to find all of the deposit. The excess of the purchase deposit over a sale deposit, or the whole of the deposit in the case of the first time buyer, will normally come from the purchaser's savings. If the purchaser is obtaining a mortgage in excess of 90 per cent of the purchase price – say 95 per cent – he will not wish to pay a 10 per cent deposit. The mortgage is providing 95 per cent of the purchase price and the purchaser is therefore only finding, from other sources, 5 per cent. The mortgage is of course only available on completion and the purchaser will therefore wish to pay a deposit of only 5 per cent. His solicitor should negotiate for the inclusion of such a term in the contract. The alternative is a bridging loan. Similarly, if the purchaser cannot use the deposit on his sale because it is held as stake-holder, he may conceivably have to take out a bridging loan in order to help him pay the deposit on his purchase. This can then be repaid on completion (of the sale) when the money does become available but it does involve the purchaser in paying interest on the loan. Assuming the loan is from the purchaser's bank, the purchaser's solicitor would have to give an undertaking to the bank that the net proceeds of sale (after payment of outstanding mortgages, the amount needed to finance completion of the purchase, solicitor's costs etc.) would be paid to the credit of the purchaser's account at the bank; the bank would then need to be satisfied about the likely amount of these net proceeds. The bank may have a standard form of undertaking which the purchaser's solicitor would be asked to sign, but he must first check that the terms of such an undertaking are satisfactory. In particular the undertaking should be limited to money which is actually received by the purchaser's solicitor and which will be available for repayment of the bridging loan. An alternative to such a bridging loan would be a deposit guarantee scheme, discussed in chapter 5, section ix.

The purchaser's solicitor will need to ascertain whether any preliminary deposit has been paid, for example to the vendor's estate agent, as this will count towards the contractual deposit. On exchange, the deposit will normally be paid by means of the purchaser's solicitor's cheque. If some of the money is coming from the purchaser in the form of a cheque, the purchaser's solicitor should make sure he receives this well in advance of exchange so that it can be cleared before being drawn against.

iii Sale of part of mortgaged property

If the vendor is selling part of property the whole of which is subject to a mortgage, he can either pay off the whole mortgage in the usual way using the proceeds of sale, or, particularly if the proceeds will be quite small, he may approach the mortgagee to see if he will agree to release from the mortgage the part being sold. The mortgagee may do this, particularly if all or part of the proceeds of sale are paid in reduction of the amount owing under the mortgage. The vendor's solicitor should ensure that the mortgagee's approval is obtained before exchange because if the approval is not forthcoming, the vendor will have to pay off the whole of the mortgage in order to be able to convey the property to the purchaser free of it.[3]

iv Sale by a sole spouse

1 *Matrimonial Homes Act 1983* If the matrimonial home is in the sole name of one spouse then the other non-owning spouse can register a statutory right of occupation as a Class F land charge in respect of unregistered land or a notice in respect of registered land. Unless the vendor can procure the cancellation of the charge, he will be in breach of contract with the purchaser and liable to pay damages.[4] If the charge or notice is already registered before exchange of contracts then the vendor's solicitor should advise the vendor not to proceed until he is sure that the charge can be cancelled on or before completion. This will normally mean reaching some sort of agreement with the vendor's spouse or more probably the spouse's solicitors, perhaps involving some share of the proceeds of sale, although it must be said that the charge protects a right of occupation, not an interest in the proceeds of sale.[5] If the purchaser's solicitor has discovered that there is a charge registered then he will advise the purchaser not to exchange contracts until he is satisfied that the charge will be cancelled. He may require the other spouse to join in the contract with the vendor or sign some separate declaration not to enforce the charge against the purchaser. He will require an undertaking from the vendor's solicitors to hand over on completion an application for cancellation of registration of the charge signed by the vendor's spouse; ideally the signed application could be handed over on or before exchange of contracts. All this will only be possible if the vendor has managed to reach some agreement with the spouse. The case of *Holmes v H Kennard & Son*[6] illustrates the pitfalls. A purchaser's solicitor was held negligent for accepting an application to cancel a caution signed by the vendor's wife's solicitors rather than an application to cancel a notice signed

3 See eg *Re Daniel* [1917] 2 Ch 405.
4 See eg *Wroth v Tyler*, mentioned in ch 5, section xi above.
5 *Barnett v Hassett* [1982] 1 All ER 80, [1981] 1 WLR 1385.
6 (1985) 49 P & CR 202, CA.

by the wife personally; the notice was thereby not cancelled after completion and in the meantime the wife changed her mind.

Even if there is no charge registered before exchange of contracts, the vendor is still taking some risk in proceeding because if a charge should be registered after exchange of contracts but before the purchaser's solicitor has obtained his pre-completion search then the vendor will still be in the position of having to procure the cancellation of the charge or else of being in breach of contract. Where the vendor and spouse are living together quite happily there will be no problem but if the parties should be separated or separating, it might in some cases be advisable for the vendor's solicitor to suggest that the other spouse be approached before exchange of contracts rather than risk the possibility of a charge being registered after exchange.

2 *Spouse's equitable interest* Even though the matrimonial home may be in the sole name of one spouse, the other spouse may have an equitable interest, for example by having made a contribution to the purchase price. We have already seen that, in broad terms, if a spouse with an equitable interest is in occupation of the property being sold then that interest may be binding on the purchaser.[7] If the purchaser or his solicitor has discovered that the other spouse is in occupation before exchange of contracts, and has or may have an equitable interest, then again the purchaser should be advised not to proceed unless satisfied that he will take the property free from the equitable interest. The vendor might be willing to convey the property into the joint names of both spouses, who would then sell to the purchaser and the problem would be overcome. Otherwise, the purchaser may require the other spouse to join in the contract and to join in the conveyance if requested so as to transfer any interest to the purchaser. Alternatively the purchaser (or his solicitor) should obtain a form of consent to the sale, signed by the other spouse. This is discussed further in ch 11, section 1 iii, as is the question of appointing a second trustee and thereby overreaching the interest on the sale to the purchaser.

The foregoing applies not only to a sale by a spouse where the other spouse has an equitable interest and is in occupation but to any other sale where there is an occupier with an equitable interest, for example some other relative or a cohabitee.

v Co-ordination of two transactions

If a client is dependent on the sale of one property for the purchase of another, the two must proceed side by side. Exchange of contracts must be contemporaneous and the completion date in both contracts must be the same. To avoid losing a property he wishes to buy, the client may wish to exchange contracts on a purchase before exchanging contracts on his sale; and vice-versa. The dangers are obvious; if on the other transaction contracts never are exchanged – which is perfectly possible – the client is left with either two properties or no property at all. He would then need respectively, a bridging loan to fund his purchase; or somewhere to live and store his furniture!

7 See ch 6, section 8 iii, above.

vi Completion date

Before, and normally just before, exchange, the parties must agree on a completion date and insert it in both parts of the contract. If the transaction is one of a chain all of which must be completed on the same date, it could take some time and negotiation before arrangements are made which are satisfactory to all concerned. If a standard form of contract is used there is provision for the insertion of the completion date in the special conditions. If this is not done the appropriate general condition will apply.

vii Sale by auction

If the purchaser is intending to buy a property at an auction, all the steps which are normally taken before exchange of contracts must be taken before the auction. This includes all the pre-contract searches and enquiries and making financial arrangements for payment of the deposit and the balance of the purchase price on completion. It may be difficult if not impossible to coordinate two transactions one of which is proceeding by way of an auction.

2 Exchange of contracts

i Conditional contracts

The parties may wish to make the contract dependent on the satisfaction of some external condition. An obvious example would be on the purchase of land for building, where the purchaser would only want to buy if planning permission was available and the contract could thus be made conditional on planning permission being granted. If the parties propose entering a conditional contract, the condition must be sufficiently precisely stated otherwise the contract may be void for uncertainty. A contract which is 'subject to the purchaser obtaining a satisfactory mortgage' will be void for uncertainty,[8] although if surrounded by more precise stipulations it could be valid.[9] A contract 'subject to preliminary enquiries and searches' might be void for uncertainty or might be a valid contract conditional on the purchaser's solicitor being satisfied as to these matters.[10]

For the contract to actually take effect, the condition must be satisfied:

(a) by the date so specified, or if no date is specified
(b) by the date specified in the contract for completion, or if there is no such date
(c) within a reasonable time.[11]

For the first two time limits, (a) and (b), time is of the essence. Unless the condition is satisfied within the appropriate time limit, the contract fails and either party can treat it as discharged. This will be the case where within the time limit the condition positively failed (eg planning permission being refused) or there is no resolution of the condition one way or the other (eg no decision having yet been given on an application for planning permission). Unless the

8 *Lee-Parker v Izzet (No 2)* [1972] 2 All ER 800, [1972] 1 WLR 775.
9 *Junmohamed v Hassam* (1976) 241 Estates Gazette 609.
10 *Smith and Olley v Townsend* (1949) 1 P & CR 28.
11 *Aberfoyle Plantations Ltd v Cheng* [1960] AC 115, [1959] 3 All ER 910, PC.

condition has positively failed, the parties are bound and cannot withdraw from the contract until the time limit has passed, but must wait and see whether the contract is to become effective or not. As might be expected, neither the Law Society nor the National Conditions is in the form of a conditional contract. However both sets of Conditions do contain provision, which would be excluded on the ordinary run of the mill transaction, allowing the purchaser to rescind if within a specified period after exchange of contracts the purchaser discovers some matter which will materially affect the value of the property but which had not been disclosed by the vendor and of which the purchaser was unaware at the time of exchange of contracts.[12] Upon such rescission the purchaser merely gets his deposit back. These conditions would normally be only applicable where the purchaser was exchanging contracts before being able to complete the appropriate searches and enquiries, and the effect would be rather similar to making the contract conditional upon nothing untoward being discovered by those searches and enquiries.

If the condition of a conditional contract is entirely for the benefit of one party (eg a planning permission condition for the purchaser's benefit) apparently that party can waive the condition and enforce the contract.[13]

A conditional contract must be distinguished from a contract containing a term which imposes an obligation on one or other of the parties, such as obtaining the landlord's consent to the assignment of a lease.[14] It must also be distinguished from an agreement which is 'subject to contract'[15] or 'subject to the preparation and approval of a formal contract'[16] the effect of which is that there is no concluded binding contract between the parties at that stage. The 'subject to contract' qualification is often inserted by solicitors in their pre-exchange of contract letters so as to avoid inadvertently creating a contract by offer and acceptance contained in the correspondence. The 'subject to contract' qualification can be removed if the parties subsequently expressly or impliedly so agree.[17] There may, however, be exceptional circumstances in which an agreement expressed to be subject to contract is nevertheless held to constitute a binding contract. *Alpenstow Ltd v Regalian Properties plc*[18] was such a case, where a 'subject to contract' agreement provided a detailed timetable for submission and approval of a draft contract, and exchange of contracts;

12 LSC 4, NC3.

13 *Heron Garage Properties Ltd v Moss* [1974] 1 All ER 421, [1974] 1 WLR 148.

14 See eg *Property and Bloodstock Ltd v Emerton* [1968] Ch 94, [1967] 3 All ER 321, CA.

15 *Spottiswoode, Ballantyne & Co Ltd v Doreen Appliances Ltd* [1942] 2 KB 32, [1942] 2 All ER 65, CA.

16 *Winn v Bull* (1877) 7 Ch D 29.

17 In *Griffiths v Young* [1970] Ch 675, [1970] 3 All ER 601, CA, a 'subject to contract' qualification was held to have been waived by a subsequent telephone conversation. In *Sherbrooke v Dipple* (1980) 41 P & CR 173, CA, it was held that once negotiations are made 'subject to contract' then any agreement reached as a result of those negotiations will be subject to contract unless either expressly made otherwise or the circumstances are so exceptional as to lead to the implication that the subject to contract qualification has been abandoned. In that case, the agreement was reached after an interruption in negotiations of over 12 months but it was still governed by the subject to contract qualification originally imposed. See also *Cohen v Nessdale Ltd* [1981] 3 All ER 118.

18 [1985] 2 All ER 545, [1985] 1 WLR 721.

the normal meaning of 'subject to contract' was held to be incompatible with the nature and terms of the agreement. (There has also been a novel suggestion in *Salvation Army Trustee Co Ltd v West Yorkshire Metropolitan County Council*[19] that a defendant could be estopped from pleading that an agreement was 'subject to contract' if in the circumstances it would be inequitable to do so.) The effect of a contract made 'subject to survey' or 'subject to a surveyor's report' was thought to be the same as a subject to contract stipulation, indicating that there was no concluded contract between the parties.[20] However the recent case of *Ee v Kakar*[1] suggests that there could be a valid conditional contract made subject to survey.

In dealing with contracts created informally, for example by correspondence, there is one further possibility, which is that despite some qualifying words there is a provisional yet binding contract which it is intended will be replaced eventually by a formal contract. Thus in *Branca v Cobarro*[2] there was a 'provisional agreement until a fully legalised agreement' was drawn up and signed.

ii Exchange of contracts

Before the two parts of the contract are exchanged they must be signed by the vendor and purchaser respectively. The solicitor will normally take this opportunity of explaining to his client the contents of the contract. Signature will normally be by the client personally; the solicitor has no implied authority to sign the contract on his client's behalf but this can of course be given expressly. An auctioneer does have implied authority to sign for both parties One other matter to be checked on or before exchange is that the two parts of the contract are identical. In *Harrison v Battye*[3] one part was amended to show an agreed reduced deposit but the other part was not so amended. Exchange of these two would not effect a contract, subject to the equitable remedy of rectification.

Exchange of two identical parts of the contract is the normal method adopted by the parties of bringing the contract into existence and the method contemplated by both the National and Law Society Conditions. However there is more than one way in which the exchange can be effected.

1 *Exchange by personal attendance* The two parts of the contract can be exchanged in the office of one or other of the solicitors or in any other convenient place. This often happens if the two solicitors' offices are close to each other. The purchaser's solicitor hands over the purchaser's part and the deposit and in return the vendor's solicitor hands over the vendor's part.

2 *Exchange by post* This is probably the most common method of exchange. We have already mentioned the difficulty of knowing at what precise moment the contract does come into existence, a difficulty remedied by provision in

19 (1980) 41 P & CR 179. An unusual case, based on proprietary estoppel, where there was no contract.
20 *Marks v Board* (1930) 46 TLR 424.
1 (1979) 40 P & CR 223.
2 [1947] KB 854, [1947] 2 All ER 101, CA.
3 [1974] 3 All ER 830, [1975] 1 WLR 58, CA.

both the Law Society and National Conditions stating that it is on the posting of the second part.[4] Normally the purchaser's solicitor will post the purchaser's part and the deposit; when the vendor's solicitor receives this he will post the vendor's part. Of course even at this late stage there is no obligation on the vendor to send his part. He could if he wished instruct his solicitor to return the purchaser's deposit and call the whole deal off.

Mistakes happen even in the best run offices and it may be that the vendor's solicitor by mistake sends to the purchaser's solicitor not the vendor's part of the contract but the purchaser's part which has just been sent to him. There is a suggestion in *Harrison v Battye*[5] that this error would be overlooked and that the part retained by the vendor's solicitor would be appropriated to the purchaser by virtue of the covering letter sent to the purchaser's solicitor purporting to enclose it. This suggestion perhaps gains some support from the reasoning in *Domb v Isoz*,[6] below.

The Law Society Conditions specifically refer to exchange via a document exchange, and provide that the contract is made when the second part of the contract is delivered to the document exchange.[7]

3 *Exchange by telephone or telex* The practice of exchanging contracts by telephone has been given the blessing of the Court of Appeal. Each solicitor may still hold the part of the contract signed by his own client and the process of exchange may not yet have begun. It may be important that the parties enter into the contract at short notice, but exchange of contracts by personal attendance may be out of the question. It is possible for the two solicitors to agree over the telephone that the contracts be treated as exchanged, each part then being appropriated to the other party. This is seen as effecting an exchange of the two parts rather than as a separate oral contract for sale.[8] The Law Society have issued guide lines as to the procedure to be adopted.[9] These recommend that solicitors should carefully consider who in the firm is to have authority to exchange contracts in this way. Under Formula B, which covers the situation described at the beginning of this paragraph, the completion date is agreed, and each solicitor confirms that it is inserted in the part contract held by him and that the part contract is in the agreed form, with any amendments being identical, and signed. Each solicitor then undertakes to hold the part contract to the order of the other solicitor, thereby effecting exchange. Each solicitor also undertakes to send on that day the part contract (and deposit in the case of the purchaser) via first class post or a document exchange.

If one solicitor holds both signed parts of the contract, ie normally the vendor's solicitor where the process of exchange has begun, Formula A applies. The procedure is similar except that the solicitor who holds the contracts can

4 LSC 10(1), NC 1(7).
5 Above.
6 [1980] Ch 548, [1980] 1 All ER 942, CA.
7 LSC 10(1).
8 *Domb v Isoz* [1980] Ch 548, [1980] 1 All ER 942, CA. The same procedure can be used for an exchange by telex.
9 See *Law Society's Gazette* 9 July 1986 at p. 2139.

of course confirm that both parts are identical and signed. He then undertakes to hold the part signed by his client to the order of the other solicitor and to send it off the same day.

Each solicitor should make a note of the telephone conversation, including the date and time of exchange, the completion date and the identity of those involved in the conversation. It seems that this method of exchange is within a solicitor's implied authority from his client and so no express authority would be required. This method of exchange is contemplated by both the Law Society and National Conditions.[10] Efficacious though it is, there do seem to be some risks attached to the procedure. The two parts of the contract might by oversight not be identical, a particular risk under Formula B. The purchaser's solicitor might send no deposit.[11] It may be that by oversight one of the parts of the contract, at the time of the telephone exchange, is not signed. The procedure is very useful, but perhaps it should be reserved for occasions when there is no viable alternative method of exchanging contracts at short notice.

iii Payment of the deposit

The deposit will normally be paid by the purchaser's solicitor's cheque and the Law Society Conditions make specific provision for this as an alternative to a banker's draft.[12] If the deposit should be paid by the purchaser's personal cheque then the vendor's solicitor would be well advised to delay exchange until the cheque has been cleared. The consequences of non-payment of the deposit, ie a deposit cheque being dishonoured, have been dealt with in chapter 5.

iv Synchronisation

If his client is selling one property and buying another, a solicitor may have to synchronise exchange on both contracts. If exchange in both cases is to be effected personally, the solicitor could collect the purchaser's part of the contract and deposit on his client's sale, then exchange contracts on his client's purchase and finally return to hand over his client's part of the contract on his sale and so effect that exchange. The only area of risk is that after exchanging on his client's purchase and before concluding the exchange on his client's sale, the latter could 'go off' and his client's purchaser's solicitor could demand return of his part of the contract and the deposit. It is more likely that the exchanges will be effected by post. If the solicitor receives the contract from the purchaser on his client's sale, then exchanges contracts on his client's purchase and finally concludes the exchange on his client's sale by sending off his client's part of the contract, then the period during which there is some risk will be between the posting of the vendor's part on his client's purchase and its receipt; on receipt the solicitor can immediately post his client's part of the contract on his sale thus concluding that exchange. This period of risk can be minimised if he asks the vendor's solicitor on his client's purchase to telephone him as soon as the vendor's part of the contract has been posted so that he can then immediately post his client's part on his client's sale. This of

10 LSC 10(2), NC 1(6).

11 Although this would presumably amount to professional misconduct.

12 LSC 9.

course assumes that the effective date of exchange is the date of posting of the second part of the contract.

There is an alternative method which avoids the solicitor having to 'sit on' the purchaser's part of the contract which has been sent to him on his client's sale whilst he exchanges on his client's purchase. It also avoids the risks inherent in a telephone exchange. In advance of exchange, the solicitor sends off his client's part of the purchase contract to the vendor's solicitors, to be held by them to his order. When he receives the purchaser's part of the contract on his client's sale, he can by a telephone call release his client's part of the purchase contract and again ask to be informed by telephone when the vendor's part is posted, whereupon he can then conclude the exchange on his client's sale. However, he might not be able to send off the deposit in advance of exchange.

It is relatively straightforward to synchronise a telephone exchange and a postal exchange if the telephone exchange is on the client's purchase; the solicitor receives the purchaser's part contract on his client's sale, exchanges by telephone on the client's purchase, then immediately posts the client's part contract on the sale. It is not so easy to synchronise if the telephone exchange is on the sale, and in the case of two telephone exchanges, one must precede the other unless the solicitor can speak into two telephones simultaneously.

v Other methods of creating the contract

Exchange of a formal contract in two identical parts is only one way of bringing the contract into existence, although it is by far the most common way. It might be that there is to be only one contractual document, to be signed by both parties.[13] A contract could be formed by offer and acceptance either orally or in correspondence;[14] solicitors will take care to ensure that such a contract is not created inadvertently by their own correspondence. The main advantage of the conventional method of exchange is that it is the two parts of a formal contract which also satisfy the requirements of the Law of Property Act 1925, section 40 and that as a result of the exchange each party has in his control the document necessary to satisfy section 40 should he wish to enforce the contract.

3 The position after exchange

i Dating the contract

Once the solicitor receives the other party's part of the contract it should be dated with the date of exchange, ie the date of posting of the second (vendor's) part under both sets of general conditions. This is important because some time limits under the general conditions are calculated by reference to the date of the contract. The agreed completion date should have been entered in the contract before exchange; if not the general condition will operate. If an agreed completion date is entered after exchange then although this may not affect the validity of the contract there is a risk that if uninitialled by the party or

13 See eg *Smith v Mansi* [1962] 3 All ER 857, [1963] 1 WLR 26, CA.

14 See eg *Storer v Manchester City Council* [1974] 3 All ER 824, [1974] 1 WLR 1403, CA.

his agent there may be difficulties in showing that the document complies with the requirement of signature under the Law of Property Act 1925, section 40.[15]

ii Protecting the contract

The contract is an 'estate contract' and can be protected by entry of a Civ land charge (unregistered land) or a notice or caution (registered land). If the property is subsequently sold to another purchaser, then even if he has notice of the first contract he will not be bound by it unless it is so protected before completion of his purchase, or more accurately before his solicitor obtains his pre-completion search. If the contract is not protected and the vendor does sell the property to another purchaser, then although the first purchaser will be able to recover damages from the vendor he will not be able to enforce the contract and have the property conveyed to him. If his contract had been registered then it could be enforced against the second purchaser who in practice would then never have bought the property. The practice is not to register the contract in every case but only when there are particular circumstances which make it advisable, such as a long period of time between exchange of contracts and completion, or a suspicion of the vendor's intentions. However, the *safest* course is clearly to register in every case. For a registered title, a notice can only be entered if the land certificate is available, otherwise a caution is the appropriate method of protection. For unregistered land, the registration – like any other land charges registration – to be effective must be made against the name of the estate owner at the time of registration.[16] This will normally be the vendor. There is a presumption that the correct name of the estate owner is the name appearing in the deeds, but the purchaser's solicitor may not see the abstract or epitome until some time after exchange and therefore after the time at which he may want to apply for the registration. If a registration is made against a name which is in fact not the estate owner's correct name then this will give no protection against another purchaser who searches against the correct name. The problem is more acute if the purchaser is a sub-purchaser, that is if the vendor has himself entered into a contract (with the 'head vendor') to purchase the property, and that contract has not yet been completed (the usual course is that the conveyance is made directly by the head vendor to the sub-purchaser). At the time of registration of the sub-purchase contract the owner of the legal estate is still the head vendor and it is against his name that the sub-purchase contract must be registered, even though he is not directly affected by it.[17] The problem is that the sub-purchaser may not know his name or even be aware that his purchase is a sub-purchase, until he receives the abstract or epitome.

iii Insurance

On the sale of land, the risk passes at the time of the contract rather than completion and the purchaser should make arrangements for insurance of the property to take effect from exchange of contracts. The vendor will normally not cancel his insurance but maintain his policy until completion in case the

15 But see ch 5, section xix, above.
16 Land Charges Act 1972, s. 3(1).
17 *Barrett v Hilton Developments Ltd* [1975] Ch 237, [1974] 3 All ER 944, CA.

purchaser does not complete and the vendor is left with the property. If the purchaser is buying with the aid of a mortgage it is common for the mortgagee to arrange the insurance of the property, charging the premiums to the purchaser. This insurance cover might only commence on completion, as it is only at that stage that the mortgagee is subject to any risk, but if requested the mortgagee will arrange for the insurance cover to commence on exchange of contracts. If the property is leasehold and particularly if it is a flat, there may be some provision in the lease requiring the insurers to be approved by the lessor, or even specifying a particular insurance company. The mortgagee's approval would then have to be obtained to this arrangement. In this case it may be simpler for the purchaser to take over the vendor's existing policy rather than for him to take out a completely fresh policy.

If the purchaser does not take out insurance then in certain circumstances he can take the benefit of the vendor's policy if that is still in existence. The Law of Property Act 1925, section 47 states that money payable under the policy to the vendor after the date of the contract in respect of damage to the property shall be paid over to the purchaser on completion or when received if later, provided that there is no stipulation to the contrary in the contract, that the insurers give their consent and that the purchaser pays a proportionate part of the premium. Insurance companies commonly give their consent but both the Law Society and the National Conditions do contain provisions about insurance. The Law Society Conditions exclude section 47 and further provide that if any money payable to the purchaser under his policy of insurance is reduced because of the existence of the vendor's policy, the purchase price shall be correspondingly reduced,[18] if both parties have insured the property, both will not receive the full amount of the loss but this will be averaged between them. The National Conditions provide that the purchaser can have a note of his interest endorsed on the vendor's policy if he pays a proportionate part of the premium.[19] Both conditions specifically provide that the vendor is under no duty to the purchaser to maintain any insurance.

There is also an old statutory provision in the Fires Prevention (Metropolis) Act 1774 under which certain persons can compel an insurance company to spend the money due on reinstating the property, but the application of this Act to a purchaser is somewhat doubtful.

It is imperative for the purchaser to arrange for insurance cover from exchange of contracts. If he does not do so then, unless he can claim under either of the statutory provisions referred to above, or unless the damage is due to the vendor's default, he must complete and pay the full purchase price, and will have no claim on any insurance money paid to the vendor.[20] Of course if the vendor does receive the full purchase price he will have suffered no loss and will have to repay any insurance money he has received.[1]

18 LSC 11.
19 NC 21.
20 *Rayner v Preston* (1881) 18 Ch D 1, CA.
1 *Castellain v Preston* (1883) 11 QBD 380, CA.

4 The effect of a binding contract

i Position of the vendor

The vendor remains the owner of the legal estate until this passes to the purchaser as a result of the coneyance. Nevertheless the purchaser does have an equitable interest by virtue of the contract, and the vendor is in a position similar to that of a trustee. He has a duty of care towards the property, to exercise reasonable care to keep the property in the condition in which it was at the date of the contract.[2] This duty lasts until completion, whether the vendor remains in actual occupation or not (unless the purchaser takes up occupation). The vendor must not damage the property himself[3] nor allow others to damage it.[4] He must do ordinary repairs necessary to maintain the property, at his own expense. He should not let the property – for example if a subsisting tenancy is terminated – without consulting the purchaser, although there is a difficulty here. The vendor does retain a personal interest in the property as he will be left with it if the purchaser does not complete, so the purchaser's wishes cannot be paramount. However if the purchaser also offers an indemnity against loss then probably the vendor would have to follow his wishes. The Law Society Conditions contain a specific condition along these lines.[5]

The vendor's position also differs from that of a trustee in that he can retain the property until completion. He can also keep the income (eg rents) of the property until at least the date fixed for completion in the contract although he must also pay the outgoings (eg rates and any ground rent if the property sold is leasehold).[6]

ii Position of the purchaser

As risk passes on exchange of contracts, the purchaser must bear any losses occuring after that date and is also entitled to any gains which are of a capital nature. As we have seen, the vendor is entitled to retain the income and must bear the outgoings. The purchaser's liability for losses is amply illustrated by his liability for any damage to the property not caused by a breach of the vendor's duty of care. Similarly if the property is made subject to a compulsory purchase order after exchange, the purchaser must still complete.[7] The purchaser's entitlement to gains in the property of a capital nature is illustrated by his taking the benefit of any increase in the value of the property, the price having been fixed by the contract. This is shown by *Lake v Bayliss*[8] where the vendor, having contracted to sell the property to a purchaser, re-sold it to a second purchaser at a higher price. The first purchaser had not protected his contract and thus could not enforce it against the second purchaser. He could,

2 *Clarke v Ramuz* [1891] 2 QB 456, CA.

3 *Phillips v Lamdin* [1949] 2 KB 33, [1949] 1 All ER 770.

4 *Clarke v Ramuz*, above.

5 LSC 6(5); see also *Earl of Egmont v Smith* (1877) 6 Ch D 469; *Abdulla v Shah* [1959] AC 124, [1959] 2 WLR 12, PC.

6 See further at ch 14, section 2, below.

7 *Hillingdon Estates Co v Stonefield Estates Ltd* [1952] Ch 627, [1952] 1 All ER 853.

8 [1974] 2 All ER 114, [1974] 1 WLR 1073.

provided he acted promptly, take the proceeds of the second sale in lieu of the property. A purchaser also gets the benefit of any improvements the vendor may be unwise enough to make to the property before completion.

We have seen that prima facie the purchaser is not entitled to any insurance money paid out to the vendor in respect of damage to the property. Similarly where the vendor contracts to sell a tenanted property free of the tenancy, and the tenant on leaving the property before completion pays a sum to the vendor in respect of damage to the property, the vendor does not have to hand this over to the purchaser.[9] This seems sensible as the agreed price for the sale would presumably reflect vacant possession and the current state of the property. The property is being sold with vacant possession, and not subject to but with the benefit of the tenancy. On the same lines where property subject to a requisitioning order is sold free of the order, the compensation payable on derequisitioning can be kept by the vendor;[10] he is selling the property with vacant possession, not subject to but with the benefit of the requisitioning order.

Both the Law Society and National Conditions provide that the purchaser shall indemnify the vendor in respect of any requirement in respect of the property made by a Local Authority;[11] the Law Society Conditions extend this provision to requirements made before the date of the contract although this is subject to the vendor's duty of disclosure in respect of Local Authority matters mentioned in chapter 7 above.

iii The purchaser in possession before completion

If the vendor allows the purchaser access to an empty property so that he can start cleaning and decorating, there may be some slight risk to the vendor but this is perhaps off-set by the beneficial effect on the property. However if the purchaser takes actual possession, the danger for the vendor is that the purchaser may become a tenant and therefore difficult to remove, and will in any event lose the spur to complete on time, leaving the vendor in the meantime with neither the property nor his money. The danger for the purchaser is that he is taken to have accepted the vendor's title however defective it may be.

The open contract position is that the purchaser must pay interest on the outstanding balance of the purchase money from the time he goes into possession and the vendor's liability to maintain the property ceases. In addition the Law Society Conditions provide that the purchaser shall be a licensee not a tenant, must insure the property, shall leave when given notice to do so and shall not be deemed to have accepted the vendor's title.[12] The National Conditions contain broadly similar provisions.[13]

iv Death of one of the parties after exchange of contracts

The death of one of the parties between exchange of contracts and completion does not affect the contractual obligations. If the vendor is a sole beneficial

9 *Re Lyne-Stephens and Scott-Miller's Contract* [1920] 1 Ch 472, CA.

10 *Re Hamilton-Snowball's Conveyance* [1959] Ch 308, [1958] 2 All ER 319.

11 LSC 3(4), NC 16(1).

12 LSC 18.

13 NC 8.

owner then his personal representatives are bound by the contract. If the deceased is one of a number of joint owners of the legal estate, for example as trustees or personal representatives, then the survivors are still bound by the contract. If the vendor's death leaves a sole surviving trustee then another trustee may have to be appointed. If a purchaser dies, his personal representatives are bound to proceed with the purchase although if he was buying with the aid of a mortgage, there could be difficulties in finding the money. It is the person entitled to the property under the deceased's will or intestacy who is ultimately responsible for providing the purchase money.[14]

The position on the bankruptcy of either party is dealt with in chapter 10.

14 See Administration of Estates Act 1925, s. 35.

9 Deducing title

1 Vendor's obligations

The vendor, having contracted to sell the property to the purchaser, must now demonstrate that he does own and thus can sell exactly what he has contracted to sell. In other words he deduces title to the purchaser. He must either show that *he* owns and can convey the property or that someone else, whom he can compel to convey, owns it. The former is most common, but an example of the latter would be where the director of a company personally contracted to sell property which was in fact owned by the company. If he had a controlling interest in the company and could thus compel it to convey, the purchaser could not object to the title offered.[1] In *Re Bryant and Barningham's Contract*[2] trustees of settled land with no power of sale contracted to sell trust property. The tenant for life, who did have a power of sale, offered to convey to the purchaser but the court upheld the purchaser's refusal to accept this, as the trustees could not compel the tenant for life to convey. The trustees were thus in breach of their contract with the purchaser. In the rather similar case of *Re Baker and Selmon's Contract*,[3] beneficiaries requested a trustee to sell. The trustee had no power of sale but because title could be made with the concurrence of the beneficiaries, and the trustee could compel them to cooperate as they had requested the sale, the purchaser had to accept the title offered. The same principle applies if the contract is a sub-sale, that is where a vendor contracts to sell to a purchaser and before completion, the purchaser contracts to sell to a sub-purchaser. (The deed would normally be direct from vendor to sub-purchaser.) Having had title deduced to him, the purchaser can in turn deduce title to the sub-purchaser. He can show that the legal estate is in the vendor and that by his contract with the vendor he can compel the vendor to convey to the sub-purchaser. The contract thus forms part of the title he is deducing.

1 *(Harold) Elliott and H Elliott (Builders) Ltd v Pierson* [1948] Ch 452, [1948] 1 All ER 939.
2 (1890) 44 Ch D 218, CA.
3 [1907] 1 Ch 238. However the Law of Property Act 1925, s. 42(1) now provides that a stipulation in the contract that the purchaser shall accept a title made with the concurrence of beneficiaries is void if the equitable interests of the beneficiaries could be overreached under the Law of Property Act 1925 or the Settled Land Act 1925 (or any other statute).

He must ensure that his contract with the vendor contains nothing prohibiting this arrangement; for example the Law Society Conditions do contain a provision that the vendor shall on reasonable grounds be entitled to refuse to convey to anyone other than the purchaser.[4] The purchaser would also want to ensure that the completion dates in the two contracts coincided.

The title to be deduced to the purchaser, and the manner of deducing it, will be covered by the conditions in the contract or failing that by the appropriate open contract rule. The contract can affect the deducing of title in two ways. Firstly, it can reveal defects in the title to which the purchaser will not be able to object on examination of the title deduced to him. If the vendor fails to disclose a defect this does not mean that the purchaser can automatically reject the title and rescind the contract, for the defect may not be such as to involve the purchaser in any appreciable risk of his title being affected. In *MEPC Ltd v Christian-Edwards*[5] there was evidence of a contract to purchase the property in 1912, which was referred to as still in existence in 1930. The House of Lords held that at the time of the contract with the purchaser in 1973, it was beyond reasonable doubt that the purchaser was not at risk from the defect and that the vendor had shown a good title. Secondly, the contract can control the manner in which title is deduced, for example the length of title offered in the case of unregistered land; the root of title as we have seen is normally stated in the contract. In fact the vendor is not strictly bound to deduce title in the manner stated in the contract for if he can correct some post-root defect by showing adverse possession, the purchaser may be forced to accept this. A period of 12 years adverse possession is sufficient to defeat most claims. In *Re Atkinson and Horsell's Contract*[6] the contract provided for title to commence in 1842. In 1874 there was a serious defect – the wrong person took under a will – and therefore the title from that point on was wholly bad. However the vendor could show adverse possession by himself and his predecessors in title from 1874 to the time of the contract and the purchaser was forced to accept this title. This should be distinguished from the situation in *George Wimpey & Co Ltd v Sohn*[7] where the contract stipulated that title to a particular piece of land was to be a statutory declaration of 20 years adverse possession. The vendor was only able to give a declaration of 12 years adverse possession and the purchaser was not forced to accept this.

How then is title deduced to the purchaser? We must deal separately with unregistered and registered land.

2 Unregistered land

Title in unregistered land is evidenced by the title deeds, and title is deduced by letting the purchaser have details of the more recent of the title deeds, starting with the root of title and tracing a chain of ownership through to the

4 LSC 17(6).
5 [1981] AC 205, [1979] 3 All ER 752, HL.
6 [1912] 2 Ch 1, CA: in practice, if the vendor relies on a possessory title then this will normally be made clear in the contract.
7 [1967] Ch 487, [1966] 1 All ER 232, CA.

vendor (or someone he can compel to convey). We have already seen in chapter 5 how far back the title must go, and therefore how old the root of title must be, under open contract rules and Law Society and National Conditions for sales of both freehold and leasehold land. On a sale of freehold land for example, the open contract rule preserved by the Law Society and National Conditions is that title must commence with a good root of title which is at least 15 years old at the date of the contract.

i Abstract or epitome

The vendor's solicitor would be unwilling to hand the title deeds over to the purchaser's solicitor at this stage for examination; if not for fear that they might not be returned, at least because they might be lost. The traditional method of deducing title is to prepare a painstaking summary or precis of the various deeds and other documents, at the same time transposing them into the past tense. The document so prepared is called an abstract of title. The abstract effectively tells the purchaser what was included in all the deeds and other documents which have been abstracted. Abbreviations are used whenever possible and sometimes whole clauses in a deed, if in a standard form, can be abbreviated. The result is pretty incomprehensible to the layman and to the non-conveyancing lawyer too. Preparation of an abstract is very time-consuming; as it is almost impossible to dictate, it must be written out and then typed up. It is far quicker and indeed more accurate simply to photocopy the deeds and other documents and to attach to the bundle of photocopies an index or epitome which details each document. This method of deducing title, the epitome plus photocopies, is the modern method and one cannot imagine that many abstracts are prepared nowadays, certainly in run-of-the-mill domestic conveyancing. The copy documents should be numbered to correspond with each entry on the epitome and the copies must be legible and complete. Particular attention should be paid to ensuring that matters such as stamps or memoranda endorsed on the back of a deed are included in the photocopy. Any plans which are copied must be coloured to correspond with any colouring on the original. The copies must be durable. If the vendor is retaining deeds and not handing them over on completion, for example because he is only selling part of the land comprised in them, the abstract or epitome will be the only evidence of title that the purchaser will have in his possession, although he can call for production of the original deeds. When the purchaser in his turn sells, the abstract or epitome will normally be relied on and the original deeds not produced. It is thus important that the photocopies last at least 15 years, the statutory length of title.

The vendor's solicitor will probably not have to start from scratch in preparing the abstract or epitome because he will normally have the abstract or epitome which was supplied to the vendor when he bought. He can simply pass this on to the purchaser – having checked its accuracy – together with a supplemental epitome (or abstract) bringing the title up to date. In a typical case the supplemental epitome would contain details of the conveyance to the vendor and the vendor's mortgage(s). Although abstracts may not be prepared very often nowadays, a solicitor must still be adept at handling them as old abstracts will still be used to deduce title for years to come.

The abstract or epitome is prepared at the vendor's expense. Both the Law

Society and National Conditions reiterate the vendor's duty to provide an abstract or epitome.[8]

ii Contents of the abstract or epitome

The word abstract is commonly used to denote either an abstract or an epitome and, to avoid repetition, this practice will be followed hereafter. The abstract starts with the root of title and then traces in chronological order a chain of ownership through to the vendor or someone whom he can compel to convey. In theory title should be shown to both the legal estate and equitable interests and the chain of both should be traced, but as machinery exists for the over-reaching of equitable interests, for example, by trustees for sale, it will in practice only be necessary to deduce title to the equitable interests in the rare case when they are not over-reached (for example, where the survivor of two co-owners who hold on a beneficial tenancy in common sells as beneficial owner by deducing title to the deceased's equitable interest, which has been left by will to the survivor and vested in him by an assent).[9] All deeds, documents and other events affecting title to the property must be included in the abstract.[10] This will include the following.

(a) Conveyances, or for leasehold property, assignments – the legal estate passes under a conveyance and conveyances will predominate in most abstracts. Of course both conveyances on sale and voluntary conveyances must be abstracted.

(b) Discharged mortgages – the purchaser's solicitor will want to satisfy himself that the mortgage has been properly discharged. The mortgage and the receipt (which operates as a discharge) would both be abstracted. In general terms this rule also applies to second (puisne) legal mortgages, that is legal mortgages not protected by deposit of title deeds, which will be with the first mortgagee; and also to equitable mortgages. However, it is conceivable that exceptions could be found. A puisne legal mortgage is registrable as a Ci land charge. If that registration has been cancelled on the discharge, as it ought to have been, the mortgage could no longer bind the purchaser[11] and it is arguable that it need not be included in the abstract. It seems that the same argument could be applicable to discharged equitable mortgages which are registrable as Civ (or possibly Ciii) land charges.

(c) Subsisting mortgages – although these are presumably to be discharged on completion out of the proceeds of sale, they must be included in the abstract. The purchaser will not be unduly concerned for mortgages are an example of removable defects in title, which the purchaser is entitled to assume will be removed by the vendor; in the case of a mortgage, by

8 LSC 12(1)(a), NC 9(1).

9 See also *Barnsley's Conveyancing Law and Practice*, 2nd edn, p. 299.

10 If the vendor has lost some or all of the deeds, this would normally be disclosed in the contract. Even if this were not done, the purchaser would have to accept the situation if the vendor could produce satisfactory secondary evidence of contents and execution of the missing documents, such as copies, drafts and statutory declarations; *Re Halifax Commercial Banking Co Ltd and Wood* (1898) 79 LT 536.

11 Land Charges Act 1972, s. 4(5).

discharge. Again, both second legal mortgages and equitable mortgages should also be abstracted. Practice is sometimes not to abstract equitable mortgages, but if they are protected by registration they will show up when the purchaser's solicitor does his pre-completion search. If the abstract does not provide details of the mortgage, the purchaser's solicitor will raise a requisition.

On a sale by a mortgagee exercising his power of sale, the purchaser takes free of mortgages over which the vendor mortgagee has priority.[12] So on a sale by first legal mortgagee, the purchaser will take free of any second legal or equitable mortgages whether they are registered or not, and they need not be included in the abstract.

(d) Leases – subsisting leases or tenancies of the property must be included in the abstract. Both the Law Society and National Conditions provide for details of leases and tenancies to be provided to the purchaser before exchange.[13] Leases which have expired by effluxion of time need not be abstracted, but leases which have terminated by surrender should still be included in the abstract.

(e) Grants of probate or administration – but the will of a deceased estate owner need not be abstracted. The legal estate in the property of the deceased passes to his personal representatives and the evidence of this is the grant of probate or administration. The grant forms a link in the chain and should thus be abstracted where the estate owner has died.

(f) Assents by personal representatives – a deceased estate owner's personal representatives will either sell the property or else vest the legal estate in a beneficiary under the terms of the will or intestacy. The document used to transfer the legal estate to a person entitled under the will or intestacy, as opposed to a purchaser, is normally an assent; as such it should be included in the abstract.

(g) Death – when the estate owner has died, then although the death may be mentioned in the abstract, the point is effectively covered by the grant of probate or administration. However if one of two or more joint tenants holding the legal estate dies – meaning that the survivors acquire the legal estate by survivorship – it is the mere fact of the death that is important. The death would be mentioned in the abstract as it is an event under which the legal estate passes. The vendor would have a death certificate available and, if preparing an epitome, would include a copy. If the vendor coincidentally had access to the deceased's grant of probate or administration then this could of course be used instead. Theoretically the vendor can just supply the purchaser with the date of the death and leave it to the purchaser to obtain the death certificate, but the vendor usually has the certificate available.

(h) Contract – if the vendor is sub-selling, his own contract to purchase would be included as the final link in the chain of title.

We have already mentioned that it is not normally necessary to deduce the title to equitable interests. For example, on the sale of settled land by a tenant for life there is normally no need for the purchaser to see the trust instrument,

12 Law of Property Act 1925, s. 104(1).
13 LSC 6(2), NC 18(1).

and indeed he is not entitled to see it, but merely the vesting deeds or assents which trace the passage of the legal estate from one tenant for life to the next. The equitable interests will be overreached.

Land charges search certificates, obtained on past purchases of the property, are sometimes included in the abstract. There is no obligation on the vendor to do this but it can save the purchaser money if he can rely on the old searches instead of repeating them, and they can also be useful in discovering whether a land charge such as a Dii restrictive covenant has become void for non-registration.

Although the root of title under an open contract need only be 15 years old, if any of the documents in the abstract do refer back to pre-root deeds then the vendor must provide the necessary information.[14] For example if a deed in the abstract describes the property by reference to a plan contained in a pre-root deed then a copy must be provided. If an abstracted deed refers to covenants in an earlier pre-root deed then that deed must be abstracted. This means that the purchaser's solicitor may well be confronted by fairly elderly abstracts of these earlier deeds, prepared some time ago and possibly even handwritten.

3 Registered land

Deducing title to land the title to which is registered is, as we have seen in chapter 5, covered by the Land Registration Act 1925 section 110, as amended where permissible by conditions in the contract. Briefly, the purchaser normally gets office copy entries of the register and filed plan and an authority to inspect the register which he will need in order to make his pre-completion search. If appropriate, he will also get an abstract or epitome, as for unregistered land, of any matters on which the register is not conclusive or any matters excepted from the effect of registration.

Provision of office copy entries is a far simpler process than provision of an abstract or epitome. In addition it appears that there is no need to supply details of the vendor's existing mortgage which will be discharged on completion, even though this will appear on the charges register of the title. On a sub-sale, it is not possible to comply fully with the statutory requirements as the register will not show the (sub-)vendor as registered proprietor. The sub-purchaser will receive office copies of the proprietor's title and a copy of the contract between the proprietor and the sub-vendor.

4 Delivery of the abstract

For ease of reference, in this section the word abstract will be used to connote either an abstract, an epitome or the details supplied under the Land Registration Act 1925, section 110.

The open contract rule is that the abstract must be delivered within a reasonable time. Conditions in the contract should amplify this to provide a

14 Law of Property Act 1925, s. 45(1).

definite time limit. The Law Society conditions state that the abstract must be delivered forthwith upon exchange of contracts[15] and the National Conditions give the vendor eleven working days after the date of contract in which to deliver it.[16] Time is not of the essence of these requirements and any delay by the vendor would be reflected merely in the general provisions for delay in completion considered in chapter 16. It may be that the abstract, or part of it, is delivered before exchange of contracts, often with the draft contract. The draft contract may refer to a deed in the abstract or epitome or to the contents of the register in the case of registered land, for both a description of the property and for details of easements and covenants. This would be much less cumbersome than repeating a long description or list of covenants verbatim in the contract, but it does mean that the purchaser will want to see a copy of the deed or the register so that he can fully appreciate the provisions of the contract. Even if the abstract is not needed by the purchaser for this purpose, it may be sent with the draft contract simply for administrative convenience. The danger from the purchaser's point of view is that he may acquire constructive if not actual notice of defects of title discoverable by an examination of the abstract and, as the vendor is under no duty to disclose defects of title of which the purchaser is aware, the purchaser could not then object to such defects in title. The vendor could in this way neatly sidestep his duty of disclosure. To avoid this, the Law Society Conditions contain a provision[17] that the purchaser shall not be deemed to have notice of anything discoverable from the abstract before exchange except for

(a) matters specifically referred to in the particulars or special conditions;[18]
(b) the contents of any tenancy agreement relating to the property;[19]
(c) if the property is leasehold, the contents of the lease and any superior leases.[20]

If the contract does not contain such a condition, the purchaser's solicitor should make clear to the vendor's solicitor that he has not examined the abstract but has just referred to it to amplify the reference in the contract.

15 LSC 12(1).
16 NC 9(1).
17 LSC 12(3).
18 This exception, whilst a matter of necessary inference, was specifically mentioned in the 1980 edition of the General Conditions, but does not appear in the 1984 Conditions as printed in the contract for sale form.
19 LSC 6(2).
20 LSC 8(3).

10 Investigating title

1 Introduction

The purpose of the purchaser, by his solicitor, investigating title is simply to check that the vendor has deduced title properly, that is to ensure that the vendor can convey what he has contracted to convey. The purchaser's solicitor will be on the lookout for the types of defect in title which were mentioned in chapter 5. These are defects such as restrictive covenants or easements which relate to the property; if they have not been disclosed by the vendor, this means that although the vendor can convey property, he cannot convey the property that he has contracted to convey. The second sort of defect of title affects the vendor's ownership of the property and means that the vendor cannot really convey anything at all, at least not a good title. An example would be where the vendor is purporting to exercise his power of sale as a mortgagee, but that power of sale has not arisen. Because of the nature of registration of title, the second type of defect is mainly confined to unregistered conveyancing. If the vendor's solicitor has done his job properly in preparing the draft contract, then the investigation of title should not reveal any defects in title which have not already been disclosed by the contract.

Investigation of title is a process made up of a number of stages. In investigating an unregistered title, the purchaser's solicitor must examine the abstract, on the assumption that it has been correctly prepared. He will then check that assumption by verifying the abstract against the original deeds, and also make certain searches, principally a search in the central land charges register and an inspection of the property. For a registered title, the purchaser's solicitor will examine the register entries, but if the contract describes the property and matters affecting it by reference to the register entries, there will be no surprises. He must then bring up to date the copy entries from which he has been working, by means of a search at the district land registry, and also check for any over-riding interests and other matters on which the register is not conclusive. This will also entail an inspection of the property.[1]

We can now look at a number of problems which can occur, principally where the powers of an estate owner are limited in some way, whether the

1 Because of Land Registration Act 1925, s. 70(1)(g).

estate owner is the present vendor or, in the case of an unregistered title, he was one of the vendor's predecessors in title. We shall be concerned principally with unregistered titles but in each case we shall see how the problem is resolved in the context of a registered title. Before drafting the contract, the vendor should examine the title in order to discover any defects and then disclose them in the contract. We shall therefore examine not only provisions that exist for the protection of a purchaser in particular cases, but also pay regard to the approach of the vendor's solicitor to see how he deals with a particular problem.

2 Dispositions of settled land

i Basic framework

Since 1925 there can only be two legal estates, the fee simple absolute in possession and the leasehold term of years absolute in possession. So where for example there are successive interests, for example, to A for life remainder to B, the framework must be equitable. The definition of settled land in the Settled Land Act 1925 includes, inter alia, land limited to persons in succession.[2] The legal estate in settled land will be vested in a tenant for life. There will be a trust instrument which will contain the terms of the settlement, including the names of the beneficiaries and the trustees and any extension of the tenant for life's statutory powers. An example of a trust instrument would be a will creating a settlement. There will also be a vesting instrument, vesting the legal estate in the tenant for life. When the tenant for life dies, the trustees will become his special personal representatives by virtue of a special grant of probate or administration limited to the settled land. They will then execute another vesting instrument vesting the land in the person next entitled as tenant for life, and so on. The vesting instrument can be an assent if by personal representatives but otherwise must be a deed. A vesting instrument must contain the 'statutory particulars',[3] that is:

(a) a description of the land;
(b) a statement that it is vested in the tenant for life on the trusts;
(c) a statement of any extension of the tenant for life's powers;
(d) the names of the trustees;
(e) the name of anyone empowered to appoint new trustees.

If there is no tenant for life – for example where the tenant for life would be a minor – the legal estate is vested in the 'statutory owners' who are normally the trustees.[4] They have the powers of the tenant for life.[5]

The land may cease to be settled land on the death of the tenant for life, for example if the end of the 'chain' of beneficiaries is reached. If land is settled on A for life remainder to B then on A's death B becomes absolutely entitled. The land will then devolve on the deceased tenant for life's ordinary personal representatives who will vest the property in the person entitled to it – B in

2 Settled Land Act 1925, s. 1(1)(i).
3 Ibid, s. 5(1).
4 Ibid, s. 117(1)(xxvi).
5 Ibid, s. 23.

the above example – by an ordinary assent or deed. When the settlement is at an end the trustees can be called upon to execute a deed of discharge,[6] but there would be no need for this in the above situation as it would be clear that the land was no longer subject to the settlement and indeed a purchaser must assume that this is the case.[7]

ii Powers of tenant for life

By section 13 of the Settled Land Act 1925, where a tenant for life has become entitled to have a vesting instrument executed in his favour then until such instrument has been executed, no purported disposition by any person[8] can pass a legal estate. There is protection for a bona fide purchaser without notice of the tenant for life's entitlement, but the solicitor acting on a sale of settled land will ensure that the vendor *is* tenant for life and has a vesting instrument in his favour.

1 *Authorised dispositions* By section 18 of the Settled Land Act 1925 any disposition by the tenant for life (or statutory owners) must be authorised either by the Act or by an extension of the tenant for life's powers (which would be mentioned in the vesting instrument). Otherwise the disposition will be void. Where the tenant for life is disposing of the land, his solicitor must therefore ensure that the disposition is authorised. Provision for the protection of purchasers is dealt with in section iii 3, below.

2 *Power of sale or exchange* By section 38 of the Settled Land Act 1925 the tenant for life has a power to sell or exchange the land. By sections 39 and 40 the sale or exchange must be for the best consideration that can reasonably be obtained. This is of particular importance to the solicitor for a tenant for life who is selling.[9]

3 *Power of leasing* The tenant for life does have a power to grant leases of the settled land. These must be at the best rent reasonably obtainable. There are fairly detailed rules in the Act concerning the length and type of such leases.[10]

4 *Other powers* The Act lists other miscellaneous powers of the tenant for life including a power to mortgage the land for certain purposes.[11]

iii Provisions affecting purchasers[12] from the tenant for life

1 *Purchaser cannot see the trust instrument* The purchaser is not entitled to see the trust instrument and if the last vesting instrument contains the statutory

6 Ibid, s. 17.
7 Ibid, s. 110(5).
8 Other than a personal representative.
9 See section iii 3 below for protection of purchasers.
10 Settled Land Act 1925, ss. 41–48.
11 Ibid, ss. 49–71.
12 A purchaser in this context means a purchaser in good faith for value including a lessee and mortgagee; ibid, s. 117(1)(xxi).

particulars, he must assume that the vesting instrument was made to the correct person, that the persons named as trustees are the properly constituted trustees of the settlement, that the statutory particulars are correct and that the statements contained in any deed of discharge are correct.[13] This rule prevents the purchaser going 'behind the curtain' and concerning himself with the actual trust. (There are exceptions to the rule in certain relatively rare circumstances.) The purchaser can of course see from the vesting instrument that the land is settled, who the trustees are, and whether the tenant for life's statutory powers have been extended. The last point in particular may need to be checked if the tenant for life is granting a lease to the purchaser. If new trustees have been appointed, a purchaser will need to see a deed of declaration, declaring who the trustees are; the purchaser does not see the actual deed of appointment. The deed of declaration is in effect a supplement to the last vesting instrument, which will have contained the names of the then trustees as part of the statutory particulars.

2 *Over-reaching the interests under the settlement* A conveyance or other disposition by the tenant for life will over-reach all the provisions of the settlement and all interests arising under it including annuities, limited owners charges and general equitable charges even if registered as land charges.[14] However by section 18 of the Settled Land Act 1925 the purchaser must pay any capital money, for example the purchase price, or the premium on a grant of a lease, to the trustees of the settlement being at least two in number (or being a trust corporation). The vesting instrument will reveal who the trustees are.

3 *Compliance with the requirements of the Act* We have seen that a sale or exchange must be for the best consideration reasonably attainable. Section 110(1) of the Settled Land Act 1925 provides that on a disposition by the tenant for life or statutory owners, a purchaser in good faith shall be conclusively taken to have given the best consideration reasonably attainable, as against all other persons entitled under the settlement. However it may be that this provision does not protect the purchaser who does not realise he is dealing with a tenant for life, the latter having suppressed the settlement.[15]

iv Registered titles

The registered conveyancing approach to settled land is relatively simple. The registered proprietor will be the tenant for life (or statutory owners). Because of the limitation on powers of disposition, a restriction is entered in the proprietorship register.[16] Typically this will say:[17]

> No disposition by the proprietor of the land under which capital money arises is to be registered unless the money is paid to A and B (the trustees of a settlement of whom there must be not less than two nor more than four unless a trust corporation

13 Settled Land Act 1925, s. 110(2).
14 Ibid, s. 72.
15 *Weston v Henshaw* [1950] Ch 510, but this is inconsistent with *Re Morgan's Lease* [1972] Ch 1, [1971] 2 All ER 235.
16 Land Registration Rules 1925, r. 58.
17 Ibid, form 9; there is a similar form where the statutory owners are the registered proprietors.

is a trustee) or into Court. Except under an order of the Registrar no disposition by the proprietor of the land is to be registered unless authorised by the Settled Land Act 1925.

On the death of the tenant for life, his special personal representatives will execute a vesting assent in favour of the next tenant for life who will then apply for registration as proprietor.

3 Dispositions by trustees for sale

i Basic framework

A trust for sale may be created expressly or may be implied by statute in the following circumstances.

(a) Personal representatives hold the land of an intestate on trust for sale.[18]

(b) Where land is held jointly, it is held on a trust for sale.[19] The legal estate must be held on a joint tenancy since a tenancy in common cannot exist at law; the equitable interests may be held on a joint tenancy or a tenancy in common. For example, if land is conveyed to A and B as beneficial joint tenants then A and B hold the legal estate as joint tenants on trust for sale for themselves as joint tenants. If land is conveyed to A and B as tenants in common, they hold the legal estate as joint tenants on trust for sale for themselves as tenants in common. If land is conveyed to A and B jointly for life with remainder to C, there is no trust for sale; the land is settled land and A and B are the joint life tenants.

(c) Where trustees have lent money and have taken a mortgage over land as security, then if the mortgagor's right of redemption should be extinguished, the trustees hold the property on trust for sale.[20] This is rare in practice.

(d) Where a settlement of personal property or land held on trust for sale contains a power to invest in land, such land will be held on a trust for sale.[1] Again this is unlikely to be encountered in ordinary domestic conveyancing.

There can be no more than four trustees for sale, so if land is conveyed to A, B, C, D and E jointly, the effect is that A, B, C and D – the first four named in the deed – hold the legal estate on trust for sale for all five. The most common trust for sale encountered in practice is that which arises when property is held jointly by a husband and wife.

The essence of a trust for sale is that the trustees hold the legal estate on trust to sell and hold the proceeds for the beneficiaries – who may of course be, and often are, the same people as the trustees. The power to postpone the sale is implied.[2] This is common sense, as the usual reason why, say, married couples buy a house is to live in it not to sell it! However the decision by the trustees to postpone the sale must be unanimous. There will obviously be

18 Administration of Estates Act 1925, s. 33.
19 Law of Property Act 1925, ss. 34–36.
20 Ibid, s. 31.
1 Ibid, s. 32.
2 Ibid, s. 25.

difficulty if one trustee does not wish to sell, as he will be needed to execute the conveyance. There is provision therefore for an application to be made to the court under the Law of Property Act 1925, section 30 for an order of sale. Such an application might not be appropriate in the case of a husband and wife, being better made in matrimonial property proceedings in the Family Division.[3]

ii Powers of trustees for sale

The solicitor acting for vendors who are trustees for sale may in appropriate circumstances first have to check that the trust is still subsisting and that the correct persons have been appointed trustees although this would not be necessary in the case of a straightforward husband and wife joint tenancy. Trustees for sale have by the Law of Property Act 1925, section 28 all the powers of a tenant for life and trustees of a settlement.[4] This includes power to sell and lease. The document creating the trust for sale can extend the powers of the trustees. A conveyance to a husband and wife will quite often extend their powers as trustees to include all the powers of an absolute owner.[5] It may also be that the consent of some person or persons is necessary before the trustees can exercise their powers, although again this would not be relevant to the ordinary husband and wife situation. The provision for consent may be made expressly in an express trust for sale. Under a statutory trust for sale, the trustees must so far as is practicable consult all persons of full age who are beneficially interested, and give effect to the majority view.[6] In the typical husband and wife case, where the beneficiaries are the same persons as the trustees, this is clearly unnecessary.

iii Provisions affecting purchasers[7] from trustees for sale

1 *Subsistence of trust* In favour of a purchaser, the trust will be deemed to be still subsisting until the land has been conveyed to or under the direction of the beneficiaries.[8] Thus a purchaser is not concerned with this aspect.

2 *Postponement of sale* A purchaser is not concerned with establishing whether any directions about postponement of the sale have been complied with.[9]

3 *Appointment of trustees* A purchaser is not concerned to establish that the proper persons have been appointed trustees.[10]

3 *Williams v Williams* [1976] Ch 278, [1977] 1 All ER 28, CA, cf *Re Holliday* [1981] Ch 405, [1980] 3 All ER 385, CA and *Re Evers' Trust* [1980] 3 All ER 399, [1980] 1 WLR 1327, CA.
4 Under the Settled Land Act 1925.
5 The need for such a clause is discussed in ch 12, section 2 xiii.
6 Law of Property Act 1925, s. 26(3).
7 A purchaser in this context means a purchaser in good faith for valuable consideration, including a lessee and a mortgagee; ibid, s. 205(1)(xxi).
8 Ibid, s. 23.
9 Ibid, s. 25(2).
10 Ibid, s. 24(1).

4 *Consents to the disposition* If the consent of more than two persons is required then the consent of any two will in favour of a purchaser be deemed sufficient.[11] In addition the purchaser is not concerned with the consent of someone who is not sui iuris or who is subject to some disability.[12] However these provisions are only for the benefit of the purchaser and the vendor/trustees would still have to meet their obligations vis-à-vis the beneficiaries by getting all necessary consents including the consent of the parent or guardian of a minor, or the receiver of a person suffering from mental disorder. The purchaser is not concerned to see that the general requirement to consult the beneficiaries under a statutory trust for sale is carried out.[13]

5 *Over-reaching the equitable interests* A purchaser is not concerned with the trusts affecting the proceeds of sale.[14] The equitable interests under the trust for sale will be over-reached by a conveyance to a purchaser provided that he pays his purchase money to the trustees who must be at least two in number or a trust corporation.[15] Although a sole trustee for sale could pass a good title in a transaction where no capital money arises, such as a lease without a premium, on a sale it is vital that there be at least two trustees to whom the purchaser can pay the purchase money. If the purchaser completes with a sole trustee, the equitable interests under the trust for sale are not over-reached and the purchaser takes subject to them. If one of two tenants in common dies, the legal estate which must be held on a joint tenancy vests in the survivor but the deceased's equitable interest passes under his will or intestacy. The trust for sale thus continues with the survivor as sole trustee holding on trust for himself and whoever is entitled to the deceased's share. To deal with the property another trustee must be appointed. The power of appointment, if not specified when the trust was created, can be exercised by the remaining trustee.[16] The appointment should be made by deed.[17] If coincidentally the person entitled to the deceased's share is the survivor, then he has an alternative to appointing a new trustee and selling as trustees. He is now the sole beneficial owner. He has the legal estate by survivorship and once the deceased's equitable share has been vested in him by an assent from the deceased's personal representatives, he has the whole of the equitable interest too. Deducing title this way is rather clumsy though, involving as it does deducing title to the equitable interest. Any stipulation in the contract that title will be made by the beneficiaries of a trust for sale joining in the deed is void if title could be made by the trustees over-reaching the equitable interests of the beneficiaries.[18]

If one of two beneficial joint tenants dies, the survivor takes the whole legal and equitable interest and becomes a sole beneficial owner.

11 Ibid, s. 26(1).
12 Ibid, s. 26(2).
13 Ibid, s. 26(3).
14 Ibid, s. 27(1).
15 Ibid, ss. 2(1)(ii), 2(2), 27(2).
16 Trustee Act 1925, s. 36(1).
17 This will have the effect of vesting the legal estate in the (surviving and) new trustee(s), without the need for any separate conveyance of the legal estate.
18 Ibid, s. 42(1).

The requirement of payment of capital money to at least two trustees does not affect the right of a sole personal representative to give a valid receipt.[19]

iv Registered titles

In principle this is similar to the settled land position. The trustees, being the owners of the legal estate, will be the registered proprietors and there will be a restriction in the proprietorship register, typically:

> No disposition by one proprietor of the land (being the survivor of joint proprietors and not being a trust corporation) under which capital money arises is to be registered except under an order of the Registrar or of the Court.

However if the trustees are beneficial joint tenants, there is no need for this restriction, as the survivor will be a sole beneficial owner and can deal with the property as he wishes.

4 Sale by sole surviving beneficial joint tenant

i The problem

As mentioned in the previous section, the last surviving beneficial joint tenant becomes absolutely entitled as sole beneficial owner. The legal estate and the equitable interests are held as joint tenants and so the survivor takes the whole legal and equitable interest. The Law of Property Amendment Act 1926 confirmed that the survivor could deal with the land as if it were not held on trust for sale. The difficulty for a purchaser from the survivor, and subsequent purchasers, was in knowing whether the survivor was what he claimed to be; whether he was a survivor of beneficial joint tenant or of beneficial tenants in common. If the latter, then although he would have the legal estate, the trust for sale would continue and unless he could show that he had become entitled to the whole equitable interest as well, he would be a sole trustee and the equitable interest would not be over-reached on a sale to the purchaser. A problem arises because a beneficial joint tenancy can be severed quite simply and thereby converted to a beneficial tenancy in common. This is done by one joint tenant serving a written notice of severance on the other joint tenants[20] and it also occurs automatically on the bankruptcy of a joint tenant. A mortgage by a joint tenant of his interest will also sever the joint tenancy. How can a purchaser from someone who claims to be the survivor of joint tenants, or indeed a subsequent purchaser, be sure that the tenancy had not been severed? The answer is that the purchaser is given a measure of statutory protection.

ii Protection of purchaser

The protection is contained in the Law of Property (Joint Tenants) Act 1964, which is deemed to take effect at the same time as the 1925 property legislation (ie 1 January 1926). Where there has been a sale by a sole surviving joint tenant since 1925 then a purchaser can rely on the protection of the Act. The

19 Law of Property Act 1925, s. 27(2).
20 Ibid, s. 36(2).

Act states that in favour of a purchaser, the survivor of two or more joint tenants shall be deemed to be such and to be solely beneficially entitled to the property, provided that:

(a) he conveys as beneficial owner or the conveyance by him states that he is solely and beneficially interested – such a statement would commonly be made in the recitals in the conveyance; and
(b) no memorandum of severance of the joint tenancy has been endorsed on or annexed to the conveyance to the joint tenants – such a memorandum must be signed by at least one of the joint tenants and must record severance of the equitable interest on a specified date;[1] and
(c) no bankruptcy petition or receiving order has been registered as a land charge against any of the joint tenants at the time of the conveyance by the survivor.

The Act only applies where the original conveyance was to joint tenants not tenants in common. To ensure that the protection of the Act is available the solicitor for a purchaser from a survivor of beneficial joint tenants, or a subsequent purchaser, should check the following.

(a) That the original conveyance was to joint tenants; this should be apparent from the abstract.
(b) That the conveyance by the survivor contains or will contain the necessary statement, or the survivor conveyed or will convey as beneficial owner. If the conveyance is by the personal representative of a survivor of joint tenants who has then died, the Act still applies and the personal representative would make a statement in the conveyance that the survivor at his death was solely and beneficially entitled.[2] If a purchaser is faced in the abstract with a conveyance made by a survivor of beneficial joint tenants before 1964 which therefore does not contain the necessary statement, then a statement made subsequently by the survivor or his personal representative is to be treated as if it had been included in the conveyance.[3]
(c) That there is no memorandum of severance endorsed on or annexed to the conveyance to the joint tenants. This should be apparent from the abstract and it can be confirmed when the abstract is verified against the original deeds.
(d) That there are no bankruptcy proceedings registered under the Land Charges Act 1972 against any joint tenants. A land charges search can be made, and indeed would be made in any event against the joint tenants, and any bankruptcy proceedings would be revealed by this search. A subsequent purchaser could normally rely on the search made at the time of the purchase from the survivor.

If all these conditions are satisfied the survivor is deemed to be a sole beneficial owner even if in reality he is not, because for example there has been a severance of which there is no memorandum on the conveyance to the joint tenants. The protection applies to a purchaser, who is defined in the Law of Property Act 1925 as a purchaser in good faith, including a lessee and a

1 Law of Property (Joint Tenants) Act 1964, s. 1(1)(a).
2 Ibid, s. 1(2).
3 Ibid, s. 2.

mortgagee.[4] Presumably if a purchaser was *aware* that there had been severance then even though there was no memorandum of it endorsed on the conveyance, the purchaser would not be in good faith and could not claim the protection of the Act. If there should be any doubt, the simplest course is for the survivor to appoint another trustee when selling, to over-reach the equitable interests. The Act does not protect a vendor and if there has been severance then he should appoint another trustee. Even if he does not, he would still hold the proceeds of sale on trust for those entitled to them.

iii Registered titles

The 1964 Act does not apply to registered land.[5] The position is adequately dealt with by the restriction in the proprietorship register. If the proprietors are beneficial tenants in common then there will be such a restriction. If they are beneficial joint tenants there will not, and any purchaser can rightly assume that the survivor can deal with the land; on proof of the death of one of two or more joint proprietors, his name will be removed from the register. The application forms for registration do ask whether, if there are joint proprietors, the survivor can deal with the land. This will establish whether the restriction is necessary.

If a joint tenancy is severed then the proprietors can have a restriction entered.

5 Dispositions by personal representatives

i Basic framework

The deceased is replaced as estate owner by his personal representatives. If he left a will, the legal estate in his property passes to his executors on his death and they will apply for a grant of probate. If he died intestate, the legal estate passes to his administrators on the grant of administration. An executor could validly contract to sell property comprised in the deceased's estate before obtaining a grant of probate but a purchaser could not be compelled to complete until probate had been granted and it would be prudent for the executor to make the contract conditional on obtaining the grant. The term 'personal representatives' covers both executors and administrators. Their authority is joint as regards freehold or leasehold land and all personal representatives if there are more than one must execute a conveyance.[6] However one personal representative, if there is only one, can give a valid receipt and over-reach the beneficial interests under the will or intestacy.[7] One of two personal representatives can without the concurrence of the other bind them to sell land by entering into a contract for sale, but not if he purportedly contracts on behalf of the other personal representative when in truth he has no such authority.[8]

4 Law of Property Act 1925, s. 205(1)(xxi).
5 Law of Property (Joint Tenants) Act 1964, s. 3.
6 Administration of Estates Act 1925, s. 2(2).
7 Law of Property Act 1925, s. 27(2).
8 *Fountain Forestry Ltd v Edwards* [1975] Ch 1, [1974] 2 All ER 280.

ii Powers of personal representatives

Personal representatives have the same powers of disposition as trustees for sale.[9] This includes a power of sale. In simple terms there are two alternative courses of action for personal representatives to take in relation to land comprised in the deceased's estate. It can either be sold and the proceeds distributed in accordance with the will or intestacy or it can be vested in a beneficiary under the terms of the will or intestacy. There are two documents which a personal representative can use to transfer the property – an ordinary conveyance or assignment, or a document called an assent. To pass a legal estate an assent must be in writing, although before 1926 it could be inferred from conduct. It must be signed by all the personal representatives but it need not be sealed (although it could be) and is thus an exception to the general rule that a legal estate can only be transferred by means of a deed. It must also name the person(s) in whose favour it is made.[10] An assent is capable of being a good root of title provided it satisfies the standard requirements of a good root. Personal representatives can use an assent to vest property in a beneficiary but will use an ordinary conveyance or assignment if selling property. If a personal representative is himself entitled to the property in some other capacity, for example because it has been left to him in the deceased's will, there must still be an assent to vest the property in him in that capacity.[11] This even applies where there is a sole personal representative. If he has been left property in the will he must still sign an assent in his own favour, from himself as personal representative.

Personal representatives can only use an assent where the property has devolved on them.[12] In *Re Stirrup's Contract*[13] a beneficiary under a will died before an assent was made in his favour; an assent was made in favour of his personal representatives who then themselves made an assent in dealing with the property. Technically the second assent should have been a conveyance because the property did not devolve on the personal representatives but was vested in them by the original testator's personal representatives. However the court held that this did not amount to a defect in title although it should be noted that the assent in that case was sealed and not just signed.

When a sole or sole surviving executor dies then his executors become the executors of the original testator and providing this chain is unbroken, the last executor in the chain is the executor of every preceding testator. The chain is broken by an intestacy or a will not appointing an executor[14]. When the chain is broken there must be a grant de bonis non in respect of the part of the previous estate not dealt with.

iii Protection of purchasers

There are two major problems for purchasers who are either buying from personal representatives or who are buying property which is shown by the

9 Administration of Estates Act 1925, s. 39(1).
10 Ibid, s. 36(4).
11 *Re King's Will Trusts* [1964] Ch 542, [1964] 1 All ER 833.
12 Administration of Estates Act 1925, s. 36(1).
13 [1961] 1 All ER 805, [1961] 1 WLR 449.
14 Administration of Estates Act 1925, s. 7.

abstract to have been disposed of by personal representatives in the past. The first problem is that the personal representatives might by mistake or worse have already disposed of the property to someone else before selling it to the purchaser. The second problem is that personal representatives may in the past have made an assent in favour of the wrong person. In both these cases the purchaser is given some statutory protection.

1 *Administration of Estates Act 1925, section 36(6)* This provides as follows:

> A statement in writing made by a personal representative that he has not given or made an assent or conveyance in respect of a legal estate shall in favour of a purchaser, but without prejudice to any previous disposition made in favour of another purchaser deriving title mediately or immediately under the personal representative, be sufficient evidence that an assent or conveyance has not been given or made in respect of the legal estate to which the statement relates, unless notice of a previous assent or conveyance affecting that estate has been placed on or annexed to the probate or administration.
>
> A conveyance by a personal representative of a legal estate to a purchaser accepted on the faith of such a statement shall (without prejudice as aforesaid and unless notice of a previous assent or conveyance affecting that estate has been placed on or annexed to the probate or administration) operate to transfer or create the legal estate expressed to be conveyed in like manner as if no previous assent or conveyance had been made by the personal representative.

What does this mean? To take advantage of the protection, the purchaser from the personal representatives must obtain a statement in writing from them, that they have not made any previous assent or conveyance in respect of the legal estate in the property being sold. This statement is normally made in the recitals of the conveyance to the purchaser. If the original personal representatives have died, the statement can be made by their successors (either their executors or administrators de bonis non) and the statement will also protect the purchaser in respect of dispositions by the original personal representatives. From the personal representatives' point of view, the statement will of course only be made if it is true. However so far as the purchaser is concerned the statement is sufficient evidence of its own truth[15] and the purchaser will still get the legal estate even if the statement is false and the personal representatives have previously disposed of the property to someone else, unless:

(a) there is a memorandum of the previous assent or conveyance endorsed on the grant of probate or administration – the purchaser's solicitor should check that there is no such memorandum, or

(b) there has been a previous disposition (for valuable consideration) to another purchaser.[16] This could be an 'immediate' disposition if the personal representatives have previously conveyed the property to another purchaser, or a 'mediate' disposition if the personal representatives have vested the property in a beneficiary by an assent and the beneficiary has then sold the property to a purchaser before the present purported sale by the personal representatives. In both these cases the first purchaser

15 As to the meaning of this, see section 2, below.

16 A purchaser here includes a lessee and a mortgagee.

does not lose the legal estate and the statutory provisions do not assist the present purchaser from the personal representatives.

It follows that someone to whom an assent is made must protect the assent by having a memorandum of it endorsed on the grant of probate or administration, or else run the risk that if the personal representatives later (mistakenly) sell the property then the purchaser will acquire the legal estate and the assentee will lose it. The Administration of Estates Act 1925, section 36(5) provides that any person in whose favour an assent or conveyance of a legal estate is made by personal representatives can require that a memorandum of it be endorsed on the grant at the cost of the estate. It is not essential that a memorandum of a conveyance to a *purchaser* be so endorsed since, as we have seen, a purchaser is in no danger of losing the legal estate should the personal representatives subsequently sell the same property to another purchaser. However it would cause inconvenience, and solicitors for personal representatives should automatically endorse a memorandum of any disposition, be it assent or conveyance, on the grant.

Where the abstract reveals a conveyance by personal representatives in the past, the solicitor for the present purchaser will want to check that the necessary statement had been made by the personal representatives and that there was no memorandum on the grant, relating to the property sold, at the time of the conveyance by the personal representatives. This can be checked from the abstract and if necessary by raising a requisition. It is unlikely that the vendor will possess the original grant; the personal representatives would normally keep this although the vendor would have a right to production. The vendor will have an abstract or epitome of the grant which will have been checked against the original at the time of the purchase from the personal representatives. This is probably sufficient for the subsequent purchaser's purposes as he is only interested in the state of the grant at that time.[17]

The effect of section 36(6) can be summarised by four examples.

Example A

(1) Personal representatives make assent in favour of A. Memorandum of assent is endorsed on grant.

(2) Personal representatives sell same property to purchaser, giving section 36(6) statement.

Result

Purchaser does not get legal estate, A retains it.

Example B

(1) Personal representatives make assent in favour of A. Memorandum of assent is not endorsed on grant.

(2) Personal representatives sell same property to purchaser, giving section 36(6) statement.

Result

Purchaser gets legal estate, A loses it.

Example C

(1) Personal representatives sell property to purchaser P.

17 Although consider the advisability of relying on examined abstracts generally, discussed in section 20, below.

(2) Personal representatives sell the same property to purchaser Q, giving section 36(6) statement.

Result
Q does not get legal estate, P retains it irrespective of whether a memorandum of conveyance to P is endorsed on the grant.

Example D
(1) Personal representatives makes assent in favour of A. Memorandum of assent is not endorsed on grant.
(2) A sells to purchaser P.
(3) Personal representatives sell the same property to purchaser Q, giving section 36(6) statement.

Result
Q does not get legal estate, P retains it.

2 *Administration of Estates Act 1925, section 36(7)* Where a purchaser's solicitor sees from the abstract that there has in the past been an *assent* by personal representatives, his initial reaction would be to check that the beneficiary was under the terms of the will or intestacy the correct person to have the property. He might do this, for example, by looking at the will. However as we saw in the last chapter, the will is normally kept off the title and would not be deduced. Instead the purchaser is given statutory protection. Section 36(7) provides that an assent or conveyance by personal representatives in respect of a legal estate shall in favour of a purchaser be sufficient evidence that the person in whose favour the assent or conveyance is made is the person entitled to have the legal estate, unless there is a memorandum of a previous assent or conveyance relating to that property endorsed on the grant of probate or administration. In the last section we were dealing with a sale by personal representatives, to which section 36(6) applies; we are now dealing with the effect on a subsequent purchaser of an assent by personal representatives. The purchaser's solicitor should check that there is no memorandum of any *previous* assent or conveyance on the grant. If there is not, the purchaser can rely on the fact that the assent was made as sufficient evidence that it was made to the right person. This check will be made on each occasion that the title is examined in the future.

What is 'sufficient' evidence? Well, it is not conclusive evidence. If there is anything in the abstract which suggests that the assent *was* made to the wrong person then the purchaser is not protected. This is illustrated by the cautionary tale of *Re Duce and Boots Cash Chemists (Southern) Ltd's Contract.*[18] The testator appointed his son as his sole personal representative and left property to his son subject to his daughter's right to live there during her lifetime. The son signed an assent in his own favour, reciting in the assent the terms of the will. The son subsequently sold the property to X who later contracted to sell to Y. On examination of title by Y, it was pointed out that the assent should have been in the daughter's favour. The will created settled land and the daughter was the tenant for life. X replied that this may be so, but that Y must rely on section 36(7). The court held that Y could not do this as there was other evidence in the abstract – in the recitals to the assent, which recited the terms

18 [1937] Ch 642, [1937] 3 All ER 788.

of the will – from which it was quite clear that the assent had been made to the wrong person. Perhaps the moral is to avoid inserting unnecessary recitals!

3 *Other provisions protecting purchaser* One of the most basic protections for a purchaser from personal representatives is that a conveyance by the personal representatives over-reaches the interests of the beneficiaries under the will or intestacy.[19] This accords with the principle that the purchaser is not concerned with the beneficial interests and the will is kept off the title. There are two further provisions protecting purchasers from personal representatives; firstly, a conveyance to a purchaser shall not be invalidated by reason only that the purchaser has notice that all debts, legacies and other expenses of the estate have been discharged[20] and secondly, a conveyance to a purchaser is also unaffected by a subsequent revocation of the personal representatives' grant.[1]

iv Registered titles

1 *Death of sole or sole surviving registered proprietor* The proprietor's personal representatives have two alternatives. They can apply for themselves to be registered as proprietors in the place of the deceased, in which case the application would be accompanied by the grant of probate or administration.[2] Otherwise they can transfer the property, either to a purchaser by a deed of transfer or to a beneficiary by an assent, without themselves being registered in which case the purchaser or beneficiary must produce a certified copy of the grant on his application for registration.[3] Whether the personal representatives have been registered as proprietors or not, an assent by them of registered land must be in the form specified in the Land Registration Rules 1925.[4]

2 *Protection of purchaser* Neither the Administration of Estates Act 1925, section 36(6) nor section 36(7) are relevant to registered titles, because of the conclusive nature of the register. In addition the Registrar is not concerned as to the contents of the will and will assume that the personal representatives are acting correctly.[5]

6 Sales by mortgagees

i Power of sale

A mortgagee has an implied statutory power of sale of the whole or part of the mortgaged property if the mortgage is made by a deed which does not exclude the power.[6] This power arises when the mortgage money becomes due. Mort-

19 Administration of Estates Act 1925, s. 39(1).
20 Ibid, s. 36(8).
1 Ibid, s. 37(1).
2 Land Registration Act 1925, s. 41(1).
3 Ibid, s. 41(3); Land Registration Rules 1925, r. 170(1).
4 Land Registration Act 1925, s. 41(4).
5 Land Registration Rules 1925, r. 170(5).
6 Law of Property Act 1925, s. 101(1)(i).

gages will normally contain a provision that the mortgage must be repaid in a particular, often very short, period of time; perhaps one, three or six months. This is called the legal date for redemption of the mortgage – 'legal' because it is the date contained in the deed. In practice, of course, mortgages are not repaid on the legal date for redemption and indeed the whole idea of the mortgage is to spread repayments over a quite long period of time. The significance of the legal date for redemption is that once it has passed then the mortgagee's power of sale and other powers arise. Of course even though the legal date for redemption has passed the mortgagor can still redeem (ie pay off) the mortgage in reliance on his equitable right of redemption. (If the amount borrowed is repayable by instalments then the mortgage money can be said to have become due, for the purposes of the power of sale arising, if one instalment has become due.[7]) So the first matter to be checked both by the solicitor for a vendor mortgagee and for a purchaser (either directly from the mortgagee or where the abstract shows there has been a sale by a mortgagee in the past) is that the legal date for redemption has (or had) passed and the power of sale arisen. This ought to be apparent from the abstract of the mortgage.

A second mortgagee can only sell the property subject to prior mortgages. It is most unlikely that a purchaser will be willing to buy subject to a mortgage and in practice the second mortgagee may have to sell free from the prior mortgage and redeem it on completion of the sale. This is much the same as the ordinary vendor in the typical conveyancing transaction redeeming his existing mortgage on completion.

An equitable mortgagee may have a power of sale but he will not on the face of it be able to convey a legal estate to a purchaser.[8] He must be empowered to pass a legal estate in some other way. He may be given a power of attorney by the mortgagor under which he could pass a legal estate. He could be given a power of attorney to execute a legal mortgage in his own favour. Alternatively the mortgage could declare that the mortgagor held the property on trust for him and give him the power to remove the mortgagor and appoint new trustees. If there are joint mortgagors, the latter alternative may be preferable, in view of the effect of section 25 of the Trustee Act 1925, mentioned below in section 11, which limits the duration of a trustee's power of attorney.

ii Position of the vendor mortgagee

The solicitor for a vendor mortgagee must ensure that the power of sale has not only arisen but has also become exercisable. The Law of Property Act 1925, section 103 states that the statutory power becomes exercisable:

(a) when a notice requiring repayment of the mortgage money owing has been served on the mortgagor and has not been complied with in three months, or
(b) when some interest is in arrear and unpaid for at least two months, or
(c) when there has been a breach of some other express or implied provision in the mortgage. Building Society and other mortgages may contain a number of provisions such as a prohibition on the mortgagor granting

7 *Payne v Cardiff RDC* [1932] 1 KB 241.
8 *Re Hodson and Howes' Contract* (1887) 35 Ch D 668, CA.

leases or tenancies and a provision that the power of sale shall become exercisable on the mortgagor's bankruptcy.

There are further matters to be taken into account. The mortgagee is not a trustee of his power of sale but he must take reasonable care to obtain the true market value of the property at the time he chooses to sell.[9] If the mortgagee is a Building Society then it has a duty under the Building Societies Act 1986, Schedule 4 to obtain the best price reasonably obtainable for the property. This may mean that the Building Society is more likely to sell by auction than by private treaty. A mortgagee cannot sell to himself; there is no hard and fast rule that he cannot sell to a company in which he is interested, although the sale must be in good faith and the mortgagee must have taken reasonable precautions to get the best price reasonably obtainable.[10]

The mortgagee will presumably wish to sell with vacant possession; assuming the mortgagor is in possession then he must be evicted. The mortgagee is prima facie entitled to possession but if he cannot get possession peaceably he must obtain a court order for possession to avoid committing an offence under the Criminal Law Act 1977. If the property is or includes a dwelling house, the court has a discretion under the Administration of Justice Act 1970, section 36 to adjourn the action for possession or suspend a possession order. The court can exercise this discretion if it appears that the mortgagor is likely to be able to pay the sums (ie instalments) due or otherwise remedy a breach of his obligations under the mortgage within a reasonable time.[11] The court can make the adjournment or suspension subject to conditions and will commonly make a possession order suspended on condition that the mortgagor pay off his arrears at a specified rate calculated to clear the arrears within one to two years. It should be noted that the mortgagee is applying for possession (with a view to selling with vacant possession) rather than for an order for sale. The discretion is applicable to endowment as well as repayment mortgages,[12] and could apply to a charge to secure an overdraft if the overdraft is payable off in a reasonable time.[13]

iii Protection of purchaser

The Law of Property Act 1925, section 104(2) provides that a purchaser is not affected by the power of sale having been 'improperly or irregularly exercised'. The solicitor for the purchaser from the mortgagee, and any other subsequent purchasers examining the title, must check that the power has arisen but is not concerned to see that it is exercisable. If in fact the power is not exercisable the purchaser will still get a good title, although the mortgagee would be liable in damages to the aggrieved mortgagor. If the purchaser from the mortgagee actually knows that the power is being improperly exercised, his title may be bad and the mortgagor may be able to recover the property. However the purchaser is certainly under no duty to enquire about the exercise of the power

9 *Cuckmere Brick Co Ltd v Mutual Finance Ltd* [1971] Ch 949, [1971] 2 All ER 633, CA.

10 *Tse Kwong Lam v Wong Chit Sen* [1983] 3 All ER 54, [1983] 1 WLR 1349, PC.

11 The mortgagor must also be likely to be able to repay instalments which will fall due in the future; Administration of Justice Act 1973, s. 8.

12 *Bank of Scotland (Governor & Co) v Grimes* [1985] QB 1179, [1985] 2 All ER 254, CA.

13 *Habib Bank Ltd v Tailor* [1982] 3 All ER 561, [1982] 1 WLR 1218, CA.

and would be ill-advised to do so, unless the circumstances were such as to amount to constructive notice of the irregularity.[14]

The effect of the conveyance by the mortgagee is to pass the legal estate to the purchaser subject to prior mortgages if any but free from other subsequent mortgages even if they are registered as land charges (unregistered titles) or as registered charges (registered titles). Thus in the typical situation where a first legal mortgagee such as a Building Society is selling, the purchaser takes free from any second legal or equitable mortgages. The subsequent mortgagees have an interest in the proceeds of sale and provided these are sufficient, they will recoup the amounts they are owed.

iv Registered titles

The principles discussed above, including the incidence and exercise of the power of sale, apply equally to mortgages of registered land, with the necessary differences due to the particular methods of creation and protection of mortgages over registered land. By the Land Registration Act 1925, section 34(1), the proprietor of a registered charge has, subject to any entry on the register to the contrary, all the powers of a legal mortgagee.

7 Dispositions by charities

i Restrictions on dispositions

There are now no significant restrictions on the sale of land to a charity, but there is a statutory restriction on dispositions by a charity. The Charities Act 1960, section 29(1) provides that no property forming part of the 'permanent endowment' of a charity shall be sold, leased, mortgaged or otherwise disposed of without the consent of the court or the Charity commissioners. Section 29(2) provides that consent is also needed for the disposal of land which is or has at any time been occupied for the purposes of the charity. Certain charities are exempt from the provisions of section 29 and a charity can also be excepted from the provisions. Section 29 specifically permits, without the need for consent, the grant of a lease for not more than 22 years without a fine.

If consent is necessary, it should be obtained by the solicitor for the vendor charity before the contract is made, as otherwise the contract will be unlawful and the purchaser could withdraw and recover his deposit.[15] If the parties wish to enter into the contract before the consent is available, they could make the contract conditional on the consent being obtained. It appears that such a conditional contract is probably not invalidated by section 29.[16] If there is

14 The protection of s. 104(2) only applies to a sale under the statutory power of sale conferred by the Act, but by s. 104(3) a sale is deemed to be made under the statutory power of sale unless a contrary intention appears.

15 *Milner v Staffordshire Congregational Union Inc* [1956] Ch 275, [1956] 1 All ER 494.

16 *Michael Richards Properties Ltd v Corpn of Wardens of St Saviour's Parish, Southwark* [1975] 3 All ER 416, not following dicta in *Manchester Diocesan Council for Education v Commercial and General Investments Ltd* [1969] 3 All ER 1593, [1970] 1 WLR 241.

such a conditional contract, it is not open to the purchaser to apply for consent.[17]

ii Position of purchaser

From the vendor's point of view, if consent is necessary then it must be obtained. For a purchaser, there is no protection from the effect of section 29(1) so if consent is needed because the land is part of the charity's permanent endowment, the purchaser's solicitor must ensure that the consent is obtained. Enquiries may have to be made to discover whether the property is part of the charity's permanent endowment.[18] The solicitor for a subsequent purchaser would also be concerned to establish that consent if necessary had been given. There is some protection for a purchaser if consent is only needed by virtue of section 29(2), that is if the property does not form part of the permanent endowment but is or has been occupied for the purposes of the charity. A disposition in favour of a purchaser (including a mortgagee) in good faith for money or money's worth will still be valid even if consent is not obtained. However if the purchaser (or his solicitor) *knew* that consent was necessary on this ground then the purchase would not be valid. It seems that the purchaser is probably under no duty to actually enquire as to whether consent is necessary on this ground. This protection also applies to a subsequent purchaser; if he buys in good faith then he is protected by the section and gets a good title even if the original purchaser from the charity did not.

iii Registered titles

The trustees of the charity (or the charitable corporation) will be registered as proprietors in the normal way. Effect will be given to section 29 if it is applicable, and the powers of disposition limited, by the entry of a restriction in the proprietorship register. A typical restriction under section 29(1) might read:

> No disposition or other dealing is to be registered without the consent of the Charity Commissioners or an order of the Registrar.

Or under section 29(2):

> Except under an order of the Registrar no disposition or other dealing by the proprietor of the land is to be registered without the consent of the Charity Commissioners unless a certificate signed by the solicitor or secretary of the charity ... has been furnished that the land is not and has not at any time been occupied for the purposes of the charity.

17 *Haslemere Estates Ltd v Baker* [1982] 3 All ER 525, [1982] 1 WLR 1109.

18 A charity is deemed to have a permanent endowment (unless all property held for the charity's purposes can be expended for those purposes without distinction between capital and income), and the permanent endowment means property held subject to a restriction on it being so expended; Charities Act 1960, s. 45(3).

8 Dispositions to or by companies

i Power of the company

Dispositions to or by companies incorporated under the Companies Act 1985 are governed by the ultra vires rule. If the act of the company is not within its objects as set out in the memorandum of association, nor incidental to those objects, then it is void. The solicitor for a vendor company and indeed also a purchaser company must ensure that the company does have power to buy or sell the land.[19]

ii Protection of purchaser

So far as a person dealing with the company is concerned, the ultra vires doctrine has been modified by the Companies Act 1985, section 35. This states that:

> In favour of a person dealing with a company in good faith, any transaction decided on by the directors shall be deemed to be one which it is within the capacity of the company to enter into, and the power of the directors to bind the company shall be deemed to be free of any limitation under the memorandum or articles. A party to a transaction so decided on is not bound to enquire as to the capacity of the company to enter into it or as to any such limitation on the powers of the directors and is presumed to have acted in good faith unless the contrary is proved.

This protection does depend on the person dealing with the company being in good faith and so would not apply if he knew that the company was acting ultra vires. The section does however state that there is no duty to enquire into the memorandum or articles to establish the company's capacity. The protection also depends on the transaction being 'decided on by the directors', whatever that means.[20] There is also a difficulty in the protection in relation to subsequent purchasers; they can rely on the presumption of good faith on the part of the person dealing with the company, but how are they to satisfy themselves that the transaction was decided on by the directors? If there is any doubt it will be safer for the purchaser and subsequent purchasers to actually satisfy themselves that the company did have the power to acquire, and does have the power to dispose of the land. This could be done by a search at the Companies Registry to examine the memorandum of association.[1] Another piece of information which may be revealed by such a search is the date of incorporation of the company. It is not totally unknown for property to be conveyed to a company before its incorporation; this would be a defect in title which a purchaser would require to be remedied.

iii Registered titles

When a company applies for registration as proprietor of land, the application form requires details to be given of the company's powers to ensure that it does have the power to hold the land. The need for a restriction in the proprietorship register will also be considered if the company's powers of

19 The memorandum will almost inevitably include powers to buy, sell, lease and mortgage land.

20 Obviously a decision by the board of directors would be covered.

1 See further at ch 11, section 1 ii, below.

disposal are limited. In the absence of any such restriction a purchaser can assume that the powers of disposal are not limited.

9 Dispositions involving minors

i Capacity of minor

Before 1970 a person under 21 was a minor. From 1 January 1970 the age of majority was reduced to 18 and now a person under 18 is a minor.[2] A minor cannot hold a legal estate, although he can hold an equitable interest, in land.

ii Dispositions to a minor

As a minor cannot hold a legal estate, a conveyance to a minor does not transfer the legal estate but instead operates as an agreement for value to create a settlement in the proper form – by a trust instrument and vesting deed – and in the meantime to hold the land on trust for the minor.[3] If a conveyance is made jointly to a minor and an adult then the latter takes the legal estate and holds it on a statutory trust for sale for himself and the minor.[4] A minor should not be registered as the proprietor of registered land; a purported disposition of registered land to a minor does not entitle the minor to be registered until he attains majority, but in the meantime operates as a declaration that the land is to be held on trust for the minor.[5] This would be protected by a restriction on the register. If a minor is by mistake registered as proprietor, the register is subject to rectification. The correct method of giving a minor an interest in land is by means of a Settled Land Act 1925 settlement or a trust for sale with the legal estate vested in trustees.

A contract for sale to a minor is binding unless repudiated during minority or within a reasonable time of attaining majority. On repudiation the minor can recover money paid under the contract only if there has been a total failure of consideration. Thus where the minor repudiates the contract before completion he can recover his deposit[6] but if he has completed and taken possession he probably cannot recover the purchase money on repudiation.

iii Dispositions by a minor

As a minor cannot hold the legal estate he clearly cannot convey it. He can dispose of his equitable interest although this is subject to his right to repudiate the transaction during minority or within reasonable time of attaining majority. A mortgage by a minor is void (not voidable) under the Infants Relief Act 1874, section 1. The mortgagee could not sue for the loan but would have a lien over land purchased with the aid of it.[7]

2 Family Law Reform Act 1969, s. 1.
3 Law of Property Act 1925, s. 19(1), Settled Land Act 1925, s. 27(1).
4 Law of Property Act 1925, s. 19(2).
5 Land Registration Act 1925, s. 111(1).
6 *Corpe v Overton* (1833) 10 Bing 252.
7 *Nottingham Permanent Benefit Building Society v Thurstan* [1903] AC 6, HL.

iv Presumption of full age

By the Law of Property Act 1925, section 15, the parties to a conveyance (including a lease and a mortgage) are presumed to be of full age at the date thereof unless the contrary is proved. A purchaser will rely on this presumption but where there is some suspicion that, for example, the present vendor may be a minor then perhaps the purchaser's solicitor should ask to see the vendor's birth certificate to confirm. In view of the rule mentioned above, mortgagees will be particularly concerned to ensure that the purchaser/borrower is not a minor.

10 Mentally disordered persons

i Before the appointment of a receiver

A contract for sale by a person suffering from mental disorder will be valid unless it can be shown that the purchaser knew of the incapacity in which case it will be voidable at the instance of the patient (or his receiver or personal representatives).[8] A similar rule applies to a conveyance for valuable consideration by the patient, and to a purchase. However a gift, ie a voluntary conveyance by the patient, is void.[9]

ii After the appointment of a receiver

A receiver may be appointed under the Mental Health Act 1983, section 99. Thereafter any disposition by the patient is void, as the effect of an order under section 99 is that the patient's property passes out of his control and into the control of the receiver. The receiver, before selling, would have to obtain the approval of the court to the transaction.

iii Registered titles

If the patient is a registered proprietor then on appointment of a receiver no restriction is normally entered as the receiver will have control of the land certificate. On a dealing, the Land Registry would require evidence of the receiver's power to act for the patient ie a copy of the order. If the receiver *is* registered as proprietor there will be a restriction on the proprietorship register, that no disposition by the proprietor be registered unless made pursuant to an order of the court.

11 Dispositions by an attorney

i Basic framework

For the purpose of conveyancing, a power of attorney must be signed and sealed by the donor of the power,[10] and will authorise the donee of the power – the attorney – to act on the donor's behalf in dealing with his property. The power of attorney might state quite specifically what powers the attorney is to

8 *Broughton v Snook* [1938] Ch 505, [1938] 1 All ER 411.

9 *Elliot v Ince* (1857) 7 De G M & G 475.

10 Powers of Attorney Act 1971, s. 1(1).

have, for example to do all things necessary to sell a particular named property, or merely to execute a particular conveyance. There is provision in section 10(1)[11] of the Powers of Attorney Act 1971 for a general form of power of attorney which operates to confer on the attorney authority to do on behalf of the donor anything which can lawfully be done by an attorney. (This does not extend to functions which the donor has as trustee or personal representative, or as tenant for life or statutory owner of settled land.[12] The general power should therefore not be used if it is intended that the attorney should have power to act for the donor in the disposition of land held by the donor as one of two or more joint tenants, as trustees for sale.[13] If the donor does wish the attorney to perform his functions as a trustee then he can delegate them by a specific power of attorney for a period not exceeding 12 months, provided that the power of attorney is attested by at least one witness.[14] The attorney must not be the donor's only other co-trustee. The donor must give written notice to the other trustees, although failure to do this will not prejudice anyone dealing with the attorney.)

The wording of the general power is as follows:

> I appoint X to be my attorney in accordance with section 10 of the Powers of Attorney Act 1971.

A power of attorney might be used when the owner of land wishes to sell it but will not be available to sign and execute the necessary documents, perhaps because he will be abroad or physically ill in hospital. The attorney might be his solicitor, or a relative. To cover the situation where the donor is physically incapable, the 1971 Act provides that the power may be signed and sealed by the direction of and in the presence of the donor in which case two witnesses must be present and attest the execution.[15]

ii Revocation

A power of attorney once given can be revoked. There can be express revocation by the donor and revocation will occur automatically on the donor's death, incapacity or bankruptcy. The Powers of Attorney Act 1971 has introduced a special rule in relation to what are called powers given by way of security. Security is used here in the sense of security for a loan. An example would be a power of attorney given in connection with an equitable mortgage to enable the mortgagee to pass a legal estate on exercising his power of sale as mortgagee. The Powers of Attorney Act 1971, section 4 provides that if such a power is expressed to be irrevocable (which it normally would be, there being little point if the mortgagor can revoke it at will) then so long as the interest of the attorney – the equitable mortgage in the above example – exists, the power is not revoked by the donor/mortgagor's death, incapacity or

11 And Sch. 1.
12 Ibid, s. 10(2).
13 The position was confirmed in *Walia v Michael Naughton Ltd* [1985] 3 All ER 673, [1985] 1 WLR 1115.
14 Ibid, s. 9, amending Trustee Act 1925, s. 25.
15 Ibid, s. 1.

bankruptcy but can only be revoked by the donor *with the consent of* the attorney/mortgagee.

iii Purchase from the attorney

As a first step a proprietor or other person dealing with the attorney should ensure that the power does cover the transaction which the attorney is to undertake. This applies equally to a subsequent purchaser where the abstract reveals a disposition by an attorney. The purchaser's solicitor will wish to examine the wording of the power of attorney and to this end a purchaser is always entitled to see free of charge any power of attorney which affects his title, or a copy thereof.[16] This provision applies notwithstanding any stipulation to the contrary in the contract. The copy should be a photocopy certified by the donor or a solicitor[17] to be a true copy of the original. The purchaser's solicitor would also check the execution of the power (in common with all other deeds abstracted). The purchaser is still entitled to see a power of attorney or a copy even if the power dates from a period before the root of title, notwithstanding the normal rule that no requisition can be raised on pre-root matters.[18]

The main problem for the purchaser buying from an attorney is that the power may have been revoked before completion. This will be difficult for a purchaser to ascertain and so he is now protected by the Powers of Attorney Act 1971, section 5(2), which states that when a power of attorney has been revoked and a person without knowledge of the revocation deals with the attorney, the transaction between them shall in favour of such a person be as valid as if the power had then been in existence. Section 5(5) provides that knowledge of an event giving rise to revocation amounts to knowledge of the revocation itself. In the case of an ordinary power, the relevant knowledge is of express revocation or of the donor's death, incapacity or bankruptcy. If the purchaser does not have this knowledge then he will get good title even if the power has been revoked. In the case of a power given by way of security the only relevant knowledge is of revocation by the donor with the consent of the attorney since, as we saw in the previous section, this is only in this way that the power can be revoked.[19] The Powers of Attorney Act 1971, section 5 also gives protection to the attorney in similar circumstances. If he has no knowledge that the power has been revoked then he will not be under any liability if he acts in pursuance of the power.[20]

iv Subsequent purchasers

We can now consider the position of a purchaser from the person who acquired the property from the attorney, and subsequent purchasers. The title depends on whether the person who dealt with the attorney had knowledge of revocation at that time. On the face of it subsequent purchasers would have to try and find this out, but again this would be most difficult in practice and the Powers

16 Law of Property Act 1925, s. 125(2); see also ibid, s. 45(1).
17 Or a stockbroker; Powers of Attorney Act 1971, s. 3(1).
18 Law of Property Act 1925, s. 45(1).
19 S. 5(3).
20 S. 5(1).

of Attorney Act 1971 gives protection. This protection only applies to a purchaser in good faith for valuable consideration (including a mortgagee and lessee).[1] The relevant provision is contained in section 5(4) of the Act. When the interest of a purchaser depends on whether the transaction between the attorney and the person dealing with him is valid, it is in two situations conclusively presumed in favour of the purchaser that the person who dealt with the attorney did *not* know of revocation at the relevant time. The first of the circumstances giving rise to the conclusive presumption is when the transaction between the attorney and the person who dealt with him was completed within 12 months of the date the power came into operation. If this is inapplicable, because the power was not exercised within 12 months, the purchaser must turn to the other circumstance giving rise to the conclusive presumption. This is where the person who dealt with the attorney makes a statutory declaration that he did not know of revocation at the material time. The declaration must be made before or within three months after completion of *the subsequent purchase* ie the sale by the person making the declaration, the person who dealt with the attorney. However it would be good practice for the person who dealt with the attorney to make the declaration immediately rather than waiting until he subsequently sells the property.

The solicitor for the purchaser from the person who dealt with the attorney must be satisfied that the proprietor can rely on one of these presumptions and if necessary obtain the statutory declaration. The solicitors for subsequent purchasers will also check that a presumption is applicable either by virtue of the date of the transaction with the attorney or the existence of the statutory declaration.

v Dispositions before 1971

The Powers of Attorney Act only came into force on 1 October 1971. Briefly, the position before that date was as follows. A statutory declaration *by the attorney* as to *his* lack of knowledge of revocation had to be obtained.[2] This would be made within three months after the disposition *by the attorney*, and would be conclusive proof of non-revocation in favour of a purchaser in good faith.

vi Registered titles

The position is governed by the Land Registration (Powers of Attorney) Rules 1986. When an application for registration is made as a result of an instrument executed under a power of attorney, the applicant must also send the original or a certified copy of the power. If the transaction was not completed within 12 months of the coming into operation of the power, the applicant must also send the statutory declaration necessary to give rise to the appropriate conclusive presumption. This would in all likelihood be a declaration by the applicant for registration.

1 Powers of Attorney Act 1971, s. 5(6).
2 Law of Property Act 1925, s. 124(2).

vii Enduring powers of attorney

As has already been mentioned, an ordinary power of attorney is automatically revoked by the donor's mental incapacity. To overcome the problems caused by this rule, the Enduring Powers of Attorney Act 1985 provides for a so-called enduring power of attorney; this is not revoked by the donor's subsequent incapacity,[3] and indeed the point of giving such a power might be specifically to allow the donor's property to be dealt with subsequent to his incapacity. The enduring power must be in a specified form executed by donor and attorney[4] and containing prescribed information explaining the effect of the power.[5] Like an ordinary power, the enduring power can be general or specific in its scope,[6] but unlike the ordinary power, an enduring power may also extend to the donor's functions as a trustee.[7] The Act contains specific provisions about the scope of the authority of the attorney under a power, including for example the power to make gifts in certain circumstances.[8]

Prior to the donor's incapacity the power will take effect in a similar fashion to an ordinary power. On incapacity occurring, the attorney ceases to have authority under the power[9] and there must be an application for registration of the power with the Court of Protection.[10] Pending such registration, the attorney has authority, but limited to maintaining the donor and preventing loss to the donor's estate.[11] Before applying for registration, the attorney must give notice to the donor and to at least three of the donor's relatives.[12] The Act contains a list of categories of relatives in order of priority, starting with the donor's spouse and including the donor's children, parents, brothers and sisters, grandchildren etc.[13] Commencing at the head of the list, at least three relatives must be informed (or all the members of a particular class if there are more than three). Following notification, the donor or relatives have four weeks in which to object to registration. The grounds of objection, set out in the Act, include the invalidity of the power, the fact that the application is premature (ie the donor is not mentally incapable), and the unsuitability of the attorney.[14] Assuming that any objection is not upheld by the Court of Protection, the power will be registered and the attorney resumes his full authority under the power. Once registered, the power cannot be revoked without the consent of the Court.[15]

The position of persons dealing with the attorney and subsequent purchasers is similar to the position under the Powers of Attorney Act 1971 mentioned above. Prior to the donor's incapacity, and after incapacity but before an

3 Enduring Powers of Attorney Act 1985, s. 1(1)(a).
4 Ibid, s. 2(1).
5 Ibid, s. 2(2).
6 Ibid, s. 3(1). The scope of a general power is defined in s. 3(2).
7 Ibid, s. 3(3). This may mean that enduring powers will be popular with co-owners.
8 Ibid, ss. 3(4), 3(5).
9 Ibid, s. 1(1)(b).
10 Ibid, s. 4(2).
11 Ibid, s. 1(2).
12 Ibid, s. 4(3).
13 Ibid, Sch 1.
14 Ibid, s. 6(5).
15 Ibid, s. 7(1)(a).

application for registration, section 5 of the 1971 Act applies and the position is as for an ordinary power,[16] ie dependent on the lack of knowledge, by the person dealing with the attorney, of revocation or incapacity. Section 5, it will be remembered, also protects subsequent purchasers. Between application and registration, an act outside the limited scope of authority of the attorney will be valid so far as a person dealing with the attorney is concerned if that person did not know that the attorney was acting outside his authority;[17] however, there does not appear to be any protection here, along the lines of section 5 of the 1971 Act, for a subsequent purchaser.

If a power is registered, which later turns out not to have been a valid power (eg where the donor was already mentally incapable when giving the power), any transaction by the attorney will still be valid provided that the person dealing with the attorney did not know that there was no valid enduring power, and did not know of any event which would have revoked the power had it been a valid enduring power.[18] Similarly where there is a valid power of attorney, which is for some reason not a valid *enduring* power, any transaction by the attorney will be valid unless the person dealing with the attorney knows that there is no valid enduring power or that the donor has become mentally incapable.[19] In respect of these two situations, the 1985 Act contains provisions protecting subsequent purchasers exactly similar to the provisions in section 5 of the 1971 Act.[20]

Section 5 of the 1971 Act will continue to apply to revocation by the donor's death or bankruptcy, or express revocation, but in respect of the latter, it is knowledge of the court's confirmation of revocation of a registered power, rather than the express revocation, that is relevant.[1]

The provisions of the Land Registration (Powers of Attorney) Rules 1986 also cover enduring powers.

12 Voluntary dispositions

A voluntary disposition, that is to say a deed of gift (be it a conveyance of freehold land or an assignment of leasehold land) can of course form a perfectly adequate link in the chain of unregistered title. However there are certain circumstances in which a voluntary disposition can be set aside and the solicitor for the purchaser – and vendor – must check that the title is not so affected.

16 Ibid, s. 1(1)(c).
17 Ibid, s. 1(3).
18 Ibid, ss. 9(2), 9(3).
19 Ibid, s. 9(6) and Sch 2.
20 Ibid, s. 9(4).
1 Ibid, s. 9(5). There is one area of doubt under the 1985 Act, which is the extent to which knowledge of an application for registration, of registration itself, and of revocation of registration is to be implied; it is possible to make a search at the Court of Protection on payment of a small fee, and a person dealing with an attorney should presumably make such a search, although it does not confer any priority period within which completion could take place in reliance on the search.

i Subsequent bankruptcy

The Insolvency Act 1986, section 339[2] provides that any deed of gift is voidable by the trustee in bankruptcy of the donor if the donor should become bankrupt within two years of the gift.[3] The section also applies to a transaction at an undervalue and a preference to a creditor. This period is extended to five years in relation to gifts or transactions at an undervalue unless at the time of the gift the donor was solvent. On the face of it, if there is a voluntary conveyance within the last five years then the purchaser should refuse to complete. There is a protection for the purchaser in good faith without notice of the relevant circumstances; the deed conveyance cannot be avoided by the trustee in bankruptcy.[4] The relevant circumstances are those by virtue of which a s. 339 order could be made if the donor became bankrupt. (If this includes knowledge of the deed of gift, there is no protection for purchasers of unregistered land, who have such knowledge from the abstract.) Even after the time period has expired a purchaser will not be protected if he has notice of the donor's prior bankruptcy; thus in respect of unregistered title a land charges search should be made against the donor to reveal any bankruptcy registration, which will amount to notice.

ii Dispositions to defraud creditors

The Insolvency Act 1986, section 423[5] states that deeds of gift or transactions at an undervalue made with intent to put assets beyond the reach of creditors shall be voidable at the instance of the person prejudiced.[6] Section 425 excepts from the operation of this rule a conveyance made (not by the debtor) for value to a purchaser in good faith with no notice of the relevant circumstances. This protection covers to subsequent purchasers without notice. So far as a purchaser is concerned, if he is buying in good faith without notice of relevant circumstances, he need not be concerned further.

iii Dispositions to avoid spouse's claims

The Matrimonial Causes Act 1973, section 37(4) provides that any disposition made by a spouse with the intention of defeating the other spouse's claim for financial relief under the Act may be set aside, unless made for a valuable consideration to a purchaser in good faith without notice of such intention. If a spouse has made a claim for a property adjustment order in matrimonial proceedings, the pending action and eventual order should be protected by registration under the Land Charges Act 1972 for unregistered land or by entry of a caution for registered land.

2 Formerly Insolvency Act 1985, ss. 174 and 175.

3 The Act provides that the trustee can apply to the Court, which will make such order as it thinks fit to restore the original position. Other time limits apply to preferences.

4 S. 342.

5 Formerly Insolvency Act 1985, s. 212.

6 The Act provides that a person prejudiced can apply to the Court, which will make such order as it thinks fit to restore the original position.

13 Discharged mortgages

i Manner of effecting discharge

It is not sufficient merely to pay all the sums due under a mortgage. The mortgage must also be discharged. The basic method of discharge as provided by the Law of Property Act 1925, section 115, is by receipt. This must be endorsed on, written at the foot of, or annexed to the mortgage. It must also state the name of the person paying off the mortgage and must be executed by the mortgagee. It operates to discharge the mortgage and no further reconveyance, surrender or release is necessary. The form of the receipt is set out in the third schedule of the Act and is as follows:

> I .... hereby acknowledge that I have this (date) received the sum of .... representing the balance remaining owing in respect of the principal money secured by the within written mortgage together with all interest and costs, the payment having been made by ....
> As witness ....

It is not strictly necessary that the receipt be under seal and so an individual mortgagee could simply sign the receipt although it is probably preferable that it be sealed. The majority of mortgages in practice are to Building Societies. A Building Society receipt under section 115 should be sealed by the Society and counter-signed by any person acting under the authority of the Board of Directors. There is also a special form of receipt which can be used by a Building Society and which the Building Society is more likely to use than a section 115 receipt. This is a receipt under the Building Societies Act 1986, section 13(7) and Schedule 4. It must be endorsed on or annexed to the mortgage and it too must be sealed by the Society and counter-signed by any person acting under the authority of the Board of Directors. The chief difference from the section 115 receipt is that the Schedule 4 receipt does not name the person making payment. The form in Schedule 4 is as follows:

> The .... (Note 1) Building Society hereby acknowledge to have received all monies intended to be secured by the .... (Note 2) deed.
> .... (Note 3).
> .... (Note 4).
>
> Note 1: Insert remainder of name.
> Note 2: Insert 'above written', 'within written' or 'annexed'.
> Note 3: Insert words of attestation.
> Note 4: Seal is to be affixed and countersigned.

The receipt should follow the wording of the scheduled form exactly.

A discharge need not necessarily be in the form of a receipt and could be in the form of a deed of release. This might be appropriate if a small part of the mortgaged property was being sold off, with the mortgagee agreeing to release the part sold from the mortgage, perhaps on terms as to the purchase price being paid towards the mortgage debt. A receipt would not be appropriate and the mortgagee would either execute a separate deed of release or would join in the conveyance to the purchaser to release the part sold from the mortgage.

ii Position of purchaser

Apart from the vendor's mortgage or mortgages, which will be discharged on completion, the purchaser's solicitor will check that all mortgages revealed by the abstract have been properly discharged. He will examine the receipts to ensure that they comply with the appropriate statutory requirements. There is one particular difficulty which may arise if the receipt is made under the Law of Property Act 1925, section 115. Section 115(2) provides that if it appears from the receipt that the money was paid by someone who was not the person immediately entitled to redeem the mortgage, then in the absence of any provision to the contrary the receipt does not operate to discharge the mortgage but as a transfer of the mortgage to the person making the payment. The effect of this transfer is that the person making payment 'steps into the shoes' of the mortgagee and the mortgage continues to subsist. For example, the person immediately entitled to redeem a mortgage will be the mortgagor only if there are no subsequent mortgages; if there are, it will be the person with best claim to priority amongst the subsequent mortgagees.[7] If the purchaser's solicitor sees from examining the abstract that a mortgage has only been transferred and not discharged because of the effect of section 115(2), he should in theory require that the mortgage be properly discharged. However the case of *Cumberland Court (Brighton) Ltd v Taylor*[8] shows that a purchaser may not in fact be adversely affected by this apparent defect in title. A sold property to B, B mortgaged it to M and B later sold it to V, the vendor. The discharge of the mortgage from B to M was dated two days after the conveyance from B to V. The effect of the conveyance was to convey the property to V subject to the mortgage. After the conveyance the person immediately entitled to redeem the mortgage was V. But of course the mortgage was paid off by B. Under section 115(2) the receipt did not operate as a discharge but as a transfer of the mortgage to B. However in the conveyance to V, B had included standard recital that he owned the property free from incumbrances. He was thereby estopped from setting up the mortgage against V and his successors in title and the purchaser, whose solicitor pointed out the defect, would still get a good title.

There are also three statutory exceptions to the effect of section 115(2). A receipt will not impliedly operate as a transfer even though the person named as making payment is not the person immediately entitled to redeem the mortgage if:

(a) it is expressly provided that the receipt shall not operate as a transfer,[9] or
(b) the payment is by a trustee or personal representative out of money applicable for the redemption of the mortgage,[10] or
(c) the payment is made by the mortgagor even though there are subsequent mortgages.[11]

7 However see (c) below. The priority of subsequent mortgages will be the order in which they were registered, either under the Land Charges Act 1972 for unregistered land or the Land Registration Act 1925 for registered land.
8 [1964] Ch 29, [1963] 2 All ER 536.
9 Law of Property Act 1925, s. 115(2)(a).
10 Ibid, s. 115(2)(b).
11 Ibid, s. 115(3).

The contract for sale may contain some restriction on the purchaser's right to enquire into the discharge of mortgages. The Law Society conditions provide that the purchaser must assume that the receipt on a Building Society mortgage which appears to have been duly executed was indeed duly executed by all proper persons and is valid.[12]

iii Registered titles

A registered charge when discharged will be deleted from the charges register. The Law of Property Act 1925, section 115 is inapplicable[13] and the charge can only be discharged by presenting an application for its removal from the register. There is a prescribed form of application for this, which is form 53 in the Schedule to the Land Registration Rules 1925.[14] The same form is also used for a discharge of part of the charge, ie where part of the property is released from the charge. The form must be signed by the mortgagee (or sealed by a corporation) and then sent to the District Land Registry along with the Charge Certificate and the appropriate application form. The wording of form 53 is as follows:

> County and District ....
> Title Number ....
> Property ....
> Date ....
> .... hereby admits that the charge dated .... and registered .... of which he is the proprietor has been discharged.

If the mortgagee is a Building Society it may still discharge the registered charge by a receipt under the Building Societies Act 1986, Schedule 4, which will then be sent to the Registry instead of the form 53, with the Charge Certificate. If it does use a form 53 this can be executed either in the same way as the Schedule 4 receipt or as provided for in the Land Registration Rules 1925, that is sealed by the Society and counter-signed by its secretary.[15]

14 Bankrupts

i Basic framework

Bankruptcy proceedings are commenced by a bankruptcy petition. This is essentially based on the inability of the potential bankrupt to pay his debts. The petition could be presented by a creditor or by the debtor himself. If the petition is successful a bankruptcy order is made and the Official Receiver takes control of the bankrupt's property. A trustee in bankruptcy is then appointed and the bankrupt's property vests in him. A bankruptcy petition is registrable under the Land Charges Act 1972 in the register of pending actions and a bankruptcy order is registrable in the register of writs and orders. The petition and bankruptcy order are automatically so registered. As soon as practicable after the registration of the petition or bankruptcy order a creditor's

12 LSC 14.
13 S. 115(10).
14 Land Registration Rules 1925, r. 151.
15 Ibid, r. 152.

notice (in respect of a petition) or a bankruptcy inhibition (in respect of a bankruptcy order) will be entered automatically in the register of title of any registered land that appears to be affected, ie that the (potential) bankrupt appears to own.[16]

ii Position of purchaser

The Insolvency Act 1986, section 284, provides that any disposition of property made after the presentation of a petition (in the case of a petition which does lead to a bankruptcy order) is void unless made with the consent of the court. However, there is protection for a purchaser; any person dealing with the (potential) bankrupt during the period between presentation of the petition and the making of the bankruptcy order will still acquire good title if he acts in good faith for value and without notice of the presentation of the petition. Any person who subsequently acquires property from such a person is also protected. The petition may, of course, be registered. To take unregistered title first, registration of the petition in the register of pending actions will amount to notice of the petition. However, a petition which is not registered will not bind a purchaser of a legal estate in good faith for money or money's worth.[17] (The registration of a petition or bankruptcy order lasts for five years and must then be renewed.[18]) Additionally, the title of the trustee in bankruptcy is void against a purchaser of a legal estate in good faith for money or money's worth unless the bankruptcy order is registered,[19] and if a petition is registered the title of the trustee in bankruptcy is void against a purchaser in good faith of a legal estate for money or money's worth claiming under a conveyance made after the date of registration unless at the time of the conveyance either the registration of the petition was still in force or the bankruptcy order is registered.[20]

What this means for a purchaser[1] of a legal estate for money or money's worth in good faith is that if neither a petition nor a bankruptcy order are registered he can proceed. He will need to check for such registrations by doing a land charges search before completion. (If he discovers before exchange of contracts that the vendor is being made bankrupt he will not exchange contracts with the vendor but either discontinue his interest in the property or await the outcome of the petition and if need be deal with the trustee in bankruptcy, or get the consent of the court.) If the purchaser discovers the impending bankruptcy after the exchange of contracts but before completion, eg from his search, he will again await and deal with the trustee in bankruptcy, assuming the petition is successful.

The position in relation to registered titles is similar. We have seen that the creditor's notice and bankruptcy inhibition take the place of registration under the Land Charges Act 1972. Registration under the Land Charges Act 1972 does not constitute notice in connection with registered titles and so no land

16 Land Registration Act 1925, s. 61.
17 Land Charges Act 1972, s. 5(8).
18 Ibid, s. 8.
19 Ibid, s. 6(5).
20 Ibid, s. 6(6).
1 Including a mortgagee or lessee; ibid, s. 17.

charges search need be done. The Land Registration Act 1925, section 61 contains protection for a purchaser which is the rough equivalent of the protection given under the Land Charges Act 1972 in relation to an unregistered title. It provides that where a purchaser is registered as proprietor following a disposition in good faith for money or money's worth, the title of the trustee in bankruptcy will be void against such a purchaser unless a creditor's notice or bankruptcy inhibition was registered at the date of the disposition.[2] Prior to completion, the purchaser's solicitor will check that there is no creditor's notice or bankruptcy inhibition on the register as indeed he will check that no other adverse entry has been made on the register since the date of the office copy entries with which he has been provided.

iii Dealing with the trustee in bankruptcy

The vendor's trustee in bankruptcy can compel the purchaser to complete the contract. In theory, the purchaser cannot compel the vendor's trustee to complete because the trustee has a power to disclaim unprofitable contracts.[3] However, as the purchaser already has an equitable interest in the property as a result of the contract disclaimer by the vendor's trustee is extremely unlikely. If a purchaser is dealing with the vendor's trustee he will wish to see as part of the abstract of title proof of the trustee's power to act, that is to say the adjudication and the certificate of appointment of the trustee. In the case of registered titles the trustee can be registered as proprietor on production of such documents. Otherwise the purchaser must produce them on his application for registration.

iv Bankruptcy of purchaser

Section 284 of the Insolvency Act 1986 applies to the vendor on the bankruptcy of the purchaser because it is applicable to payment of money as well as to dispositions of property. Thus, if the vendor has notice of presentation of a petition against the purchaser he should not complete – nor indeed exchange – with the purchaser as he may be liable to refund the purchase money to the purchaser's trustee in bankruptcy. If he does exchange contracts and then discovers that a petition has been presented he must wait and if need be complete with the purchaser's trustee in bankruptcy. If the vendor does have to deal with the purchaser's trustee he may fall foul of the latter's right to disclaim. The vendor can serve a notice requiring the trustee to decide whether he will disclaim within 28 days. If he does disclaim then the vendor can forfeit the deposit and prove in the bankruptcy for any further loss.

15 Transactions involving persons in a fiduciary relationship

There are a number of situations in which a transaction may be voidable because it involves someone in a fiduciary position, and there is a risk that he may have unfairly exploited that position. A prime example is the sale by

2 Land Registration Act 1925, s. 61(6); however, a purchaser who has notice of the petition or adjudication will not be in good faith.

3 Insolvency Act 1986, s. 315.

trustees or personal representatives of the trust (or estate) property to one or more of their own number. Prima facie, the transaction is voidable at the instance of the beneficiaries. There are circumstances in which the transaction will be perfectly valid, for example if the sale was expressly authorised by the trust instrument (eg will); if the consent of the court was obtained; if all the beneficiaries consented; or in the case of a personal representative if he was acquiring the property under a contract made with the deceased before he died.

A similar rule applies to parties who are in a fiduciary relationship. For example, a solicitor and his client are in a fiduciary relationship. A presumption of undue influence arises and unless the solicitor can prove that the client was fully informed, understood the nature of the transaction and that the transaction was fair, the client may be able to have the disposition between them set aside.

These are matters to which a vendor's solicitor must be alive, for example if he is asked to act for trustees selling trust property to one of their number. What, though, of subsequent purchasers following a disposition which may be voidable? A subsequent purchaser for value without notice of the position will take free of the equitable right to have the disposition set aside and will get a good title.[4] However if the purchaser is aware of the circumstances surrounding the disposition – for example if these are apparent from the abstract – he should object to the title. The defect can often be remedied by a conveyance confirming the voidable conveyance, in which all interested parties could join, having had the benefit of independent advice.

16 Marriages and deaths

i Marriages

It may be that the marriage of a person forms part of the chain of title and so is abstracted. This would happen if for example a couple bought a house before they were married, and later sold it. The woman's name in the purchase deed would not correspond with that on the sale deed, assuming she had taken her husband's name on marriage. In the case of a registered title, the register may still show the vendor wife's maiden name, if the vendors bought before they married. The marriage is proved by the certificate obtained from the appropriate registrar.

ii Deaths

If the estate owner dies then as we have already seen, the grant of probate or administration will be abstracted followed by the assent or conveyance by the personal representatives. If the abstract has to show just the death, as would be the case if one of a number of joint tenants had died, this is proved by a certificate from the appropriate registrar.

4 If the title is registered, the register will be rectified if the disposition is set aside, subject to the limits on rectification against a registered proprietor in possession.

A death or marriage could also be proved by a recital in a deed over 20 years old.[5]

17 Stamp duty

Many of the deeds and other documents in the abstract will bear stamp duty. When stamp duty is paid, stamps showing the amount of duty are impressed on the deed. The abstract should indicate this. Stamping is dealt with in detail in chapter 15. Suffice to say here that the purchaser's solicitor must check that all documents in the abstract which attract stamp duty are properly stamped. This will require a knowledge of the various rates of stamp duty in the past, which can be obtained from sets of stamp duty tables. The consequence of a document which attracts stamp duty not being stamped or being insufficiently stamped is that it is inadmissible in evidence and thus inadmissible to prove the title. The purchaser should require the vendor to correct any deficiency by applying for late stamping. Any condition in the contract which purports to preclude the purchaser from objecting to the absence or insufficiency of stamps, or to throw the cost of late stamping on the purchaser, is void.[6]

Even if a deed does not attract stamp duty, particulars of it may have to be delivered to the Inland Revenue.[7] A stamp called a 'P.D.' (particulars delivered) stamp is impressed on the deed when this is done. The penalties for non-compliance are the same as for not stamping with stamp duty and so this too must be checked by the purchaser's solicitor. Again this is dealt with in detail in chapter 15.

The vendor's solicitor ought to note any deficiencies in stamping when he examines the title prior to drafting the contract and deal with them immediately.

18 Execution

The purchaser's solicitor – and of course the vendor's solicitor too – will want to check that all the deeds and other documents have been properly executed, particularly where it is not a simple matter of signing and sealing by an individual but sealing by a company or Building Society. The requirements on execution are dealt with in detail in chapter 14.

19 Statutory presumptions in respect of leasehold land

Finally in this category of potentially problematical areas in the abstract of title, we should mention some matters about which the purchaser may be precluded from enquiring. We have seen that in the case of leasehold land the purchaser's right to examine the superior title is very limited, particularly

5 See ch 12, section 2iii, below.
6 Stamp Act 1891, s. 117.
7 Finance Act 1931, s. 28.

under an open contract. Hand in hand with this restriction are certain statutory presumptions. The Law of Property Act 1925, section 45(2) and (3) provide that on the assignment on sale of leasehold land, the purchaser must assume unless the contrary appears that the lease and any superior leases were duly granted. On production of the receipt for the last payment of rent due before completion, the purchaser must assume, again unless the contrary appears, that all the covenants and other provisions in the lease and any superior leases have been performed and observed. Of course if the purchaser has been able to include a condition in the contract allowing him to examine the superior title, this will be done. Even if he has not, if he discovers from some other source that the superior title is defective then he may still be able to object to the title unless the defect was disclosed by a proper condition in the contract.[8]

Both the Law Society and National Conditions provide that the purchaser shall assume that the last receipt for rent was given by the person then entitled to receive rent.[9]

The purchaser is also given some protection by the Law of Property Act 1925, section 44(5), which states that where the purchaser is precluded by the Act from examining the superior title, he is not deemed to have notice of matters of which he would have had notice had he contracted to examine the title. However this is subject to section 198 of the Act, so if something affecting the superior title is registered as a land charge, the purchaser is bound by it (and cannot claim compensation under the Law of Property Act 1969, section 25).

20 Investigating title – unregistered land

i Examination of the abstract[10]

The first stage in the purchaser's solicitor's investigation of an unregistered title is the examination of the abstract (or epitome). In so doing the purchaser's solicitor will be ensuring that there is an unbroken chain of ownership of the estate being sold, from the root of title right up to the present day. There must be no breaks in the chain whereby it is impossible to trace the passage of the legal estate from one owner to another; a break would occur for example if a conveyance on sale, or the death of one of two joint tenants, was not abstracted. Even a change in the spelling of the name of an estate owner from the deed whereby he bought to the deed whereby he sold may be sufficient to raise a doubt in the mind of the purchaser's solicitor as to whether the person who sold was indeed the same person who had previously bought the property. There should be no defects in the abstract of the kind already mentioned in this chapter.

If the title is in order then the vendor has, on the face of it, shown that he does own what he is selling. However in examining the abstract, the purchaser's solicitor will also be on the lookout for mention of adverse interests such as

8 *Becker v Partridge* [1966] 2 QB 155, [1966] 2 All ER 266, CA; see section 22i, below.
9 LSC 8(7), NC 11(3).
10 If the title is leasehold, then the purchaser's solicitor may also be examining the superior title(s), which may be registered or unregistered.

covenants and easements, which the vendor has not disclosed in the contract; the first sort of defect in title mentioned at the beginning of this chapter. If such a defect is revealed by the abstract then unless the purchaser was aware of it on exchange of contracts – or it was apparent on inspection[11] – the vendor will be in breach of contract in that he will not be able to convey what he has contracted to convey. The purchaser's solicitor will also be checking the abstract for the easements and covenants that are disclosed in the contract, to ensure for example that the wording of a covenant disclosed in the contract is correct. He will also check the description of the property.

If any point does arise on examination of the title then it is taken up with the vendor's solicitor by means of a requisition. The manner in which this is done will be dealt with later in this chapter. However, there is a general rule that not only is the purchaser not entitled to see the title prior to the root, but neither can requisitions be raised on matters prior to the root.[12] There are three exceptions to this general rule.

(a) The purchaser is entitled to have abstracted the power of attorney under which an abstracted document has been executed, even if the power was given prior to the date of the root of title.

(b) The purchaser is entitled to have abstracted 'any document creating or disposing of an interest power or obligation which is not shown to have ceased or expired and subject to which any part of the property is disposed of by an abstracted document'. Under this provision the purchaser could require pre-root leases to be abstracted if the property is sold subject to them. Similarly if an abstracted document refers to restrictive covenants still affecting the property, which are contained in an earlier deed; the purchaser would still be entitled to have the covenants abstracted even if the deed containing them was dated prior to the root of title. Likewise, if an abstracted document describes the property by reference to a plan on an earlier deed; the purchaser would still be entitled to a copy even if the deed were dated prior to the root.[13]

(c) The purchaser is entitled to have abstracted any document creating any limitation or trust, by reference to which any part of the property is disposed of by an abstracted document. This does not extend to any trust that will be over-reached.

Even though the purchaser cannot normally raise requisitions on matters prior to the root of title, the vendor cannot conceal a defective title by specifying a later deed as the root of title, and the purchaser can still rescind if he does discover that the title is defective even though the defect is prior to the root.

If the vendor refuses to answer a properly raised requisition then on the face of it this will entitle the purchaser to rescind.

11 See ch 5, section 4 i.

12 Law of Property Act 1925, s. 45(1).

13 NC 12(1) provides that in respect of a plan or covenants contained in a pre-root document, a copy will be supplied by the vendor *if the document is in his or his trustee's or mortgagee's possession.*

ii Searches

Before completion the purchaser's solicitor will do a number of searches, principally searches in the Central Land Charges Registry and an inspection of the property. These are dealt with in detail in the next chapter.

iii Verification of the abstract

The purchaser's solicitor has examined the abstract or epitome on the basis that it is a full and accurate representation of the original deeds and other abstracted documents. He must as some stage verify this assumption by checking the abstract against the original deeds. He will be particularly alert to such matters as execution and stamping which may be difficult to ascertain from an abstract and also as to the existence of any memoranda, such as a memorandum on a grant of probate or administration or a memorandum of severance on a conveyance to joint tenants. He may also pay particular attention to the description of the property and the wording of the covenants which may have been abbreviated in the abstract. Of course if he was provided with an epitome rather than a true abstract then the process of verification is rather easier, but it must still be done. It is easy for the back page of a conveyance containing a memorandum to escape being copied when the epitome is prepared.

Although the vendor bears the expense, if any, of producing the deeds for preparation of the abstract and for handing over on completion, the purchaser bears the expense of producing the deeds for verification of the abstract, unless they are in the possession of the vendor or his mortgagee or trustee.[14] This latter will in fact normally be the case but nevertheless it is common practice to leave verification until completion.[15] Whilst this can be seen as convenient in that the purchaser's solicitor or his agent need only make one visit to the vendor's solicitors – on completion – instead of having also to make another earlier visit for verification, it would be most inconvenient if some defect should be revealed on verification. There would inevitably be a delay on completion, which would probably have been avoided had verification taken place earlier. The objection to the title will clearly be outside the time limit for raising requisitions, but as the defect is presumably not discoverable from the abstract alone, this will not prejudice the purchaser.[16]

It is doubly important to verify the abstract against the originals if the vendor is retaining some or all of the original deeds, because he is only selling part of the property to which they relate. This would probably happen, for example, on the sale of a new house on a building estate. As we shall see, the purchaser will have a right to production of the original deeds but the only actual evidence of his title which he will have in his possession will be the verified abstract or epitome, together of course with the conveyance to him. In such a situation the purchaser's solicitor will on verification mark the abstract or epitome to the effect that he has examined it against the original

14 Law of Property Act 1925, s. 45(4).

15 NC 12(3) provides that the vendor shall not be required to procure the production of any document not in his possession nor in the possession of his trustees or mortgagees and of which the vendor cannot obtain production.

16 See section 22 ii, below.

deeds. When the purchaser himself comes to sell, he will not have in his possession the original documents, but only the abstract of them that was marked when he bought. One might think that a subsequent purchaser's solicitor ought to demand that the original deeds be produced so that he can check them, although this would be at the expense of the subsequent purchaser. Common practice seems to be not to do this and to rely on the accuracy of the marked abstract. One wonders whether this practice would protect a solicitor from an action for negligence, if he relied on a marked abstract which was in fact incorrect. Indeed in practice verification seems to not be accorded the importance it perhaps deserves.

21 Investigating title – registered land

i Examination of office copy entries

As we have already seen, title to land which is registered is deduced by supplying the purchaser's solicitor with copies of the register entries, normally in the form of office copy entries, but possibly photocopies of the entries in the vendor's Land or Charge Certificate. It is these which the purchaser's solicitor must examine against the contract to ensure that the vendor does own, and can convey, that which he has contracted to convey. If, as is common, the contract refers to the Property Register and the Charges Register in the particulars and conditions of the contract then there will clearly be no difficulty and indeed the office copies will normally have been sent with the draft contract. However even in this situation the purchaser's solicitor must be on the lookout, for example, for restrictions in the Proprietorship Register which restrict the vendor's powers of disposal.

There is really no equivalent, in respect of registered land, to the process of verification as both the office copy entries and the Land Certificate are admissible evidence of the state of the register at the appropriate time.[17] However, if photocopies of the entries in the certificate are provided they would have to be checked against the originals.

Even though title to the land is registered, an abstract or epitome would still be provided in respect of matters upon which the register was not conclusive, if any. The requirements would be just the same as if the land were unregistered. Overriding interests would fall into this category. If the purchaser is buying leasehold land then he will also want a copy of the lease as this does not form part of the register.[18]

ii Searches

The investigation of title is continued by pre-completion searches, principally a search at the Land Registry and an inspection of the property. The object of the Land Registry search is to bring up to date the information on the state of the register which the purchaser has acquired from the office copy entries (or photocopies of the vendor's Land or Charge Certificate). There is no need

17 Land Registration Act 1925, ss. 68, 113.

18 The purchaser's solicitor may also be examining the superior title(s), registered or unregistered.

to make a search at the Central Land Charges Registry except in relation to matters on which the register is not conclusive. For example, if the purchaser were buying a property held on a good leasehold title, then if the freehold title was unregistered and the purchaser was entitled by virtue of the contract to examine it, he would be provided with an abstract and would wish to do a land charges search in connection with the examination of the unregistered freehold title.

22 Requisitions on title

i Raising requisitions

We have already seen that if there is any aspect of the title which is unsatisfactory to the purchaser's solicitor he can raise it with the vendor's solicitor by means of a requisition. A requisition is so called because the purchaser is pointing out the defect and 'requiring' the vendor to remedy it. This right to raise requisitions is subject to the restriction on pre-root requisitions in respect of unregistered land, and to any provision in the contract. If a defect in the title is properly disclosed in the contract then the purchaser cannot object to it at this stage and raise a requisition about it. If the vendor has provided that the purchaser accept the title offered and raise no requisitions, this will not prevent the purchaser raising a requisition and objecting to a defect if the vendor did not make full disclosure of the defects of which he knew. In *Becker v Partridge*[19] the vendor provided in a contract for the assignment on sale of an *underlease* that the purchaser should raise no requisitions on his title. The purchaser discovered that there were breaches of covenant which gave grounds for forfeiture of the *lease*. The vendor had constructive notice of these defects but did not disclose them and the purchaser was entitled to rescind. Similarly, although the purchaser cannot raise requisitions on matters prior to the root of title, he can object if he becomes aware that there is a pre-root defect in title.[20]

When submitting requisitions the purchaser's solicitor will normally use a standard form.[1] This may seem surprising as by definition requisitions will be peculiar to a particular title and it would not seem possible to standardise such a form. In fact most if not all of the questions on the standard form are of a procedural nature rather than being requisitions on title. Any requisitions arising out of a particular title must be added at the end of the form. The following are examples of the sort of questions which may be found on a standard form of requisitions.

(a) A request for a completion statement showing the amount due on completion, including any appointment, eg of rates or rent.
(b) Confirmation as to how and where completion is to take place and how the money is to be paid.
(c) Confirmation that in the case of leasehold property the last receipt for

19 [1966] 2 QB 155, [1966] 2 All ER 266, CA.
20 For example a covenant created before the root and not disclosed by the vendor. The purchaser will not be compelled to accept a title which is clearly a bad title.
1 See for example the form produced by Oyez.

rent will be produced for inspection on completion, along with the receipts for outgoings such as rates in respect of which the vendor is claiming an apportionment (see (a)).

(d) Confirmation that existing mortgages will be discharged on or before completion. This is not really a requisition on title as the purchaser is entitled to assume that existing mortgages will be paid off unless the sale has been made subject to them.

(e) If the receipted mortgage deed, or form 53 in the case of registered land, will not be handed over on completion, an enquiry as to the form of undertaking which will be given to pay off the mortgage and forward the receipted deed or form 53.

(f) In respect of unregistered land, an enquiry whether any abstracted documents will not be handed over on completion and confirmation that an acknowledgment and undertaking will be given in respect of any original documents retained.

(g) In respect of registered land, if the purchaser has merely been provided with photocopies of the vendor's Land or Charge Certificate, an enquiry as to when the Certificate was last examined with the register. This information will be needed for the pre-completion search at the Land Registry.

(h) On a sale of part of registered land, an enquiry whether the vendor's Land Certificate is on deposit with the Land Registry and if so, the deposit number.

(i) Again in respect of registered land, where the purchaser is buying a new house on a building estate, an enquiry whether there is an estate layout plan approved by the Land Registry so that on the purchaser's pre-completion search at the Land Registry the property can be identified by reference to its plot number.

(j) Confirmation of the arrangements for delivery of keys to the purchaser and/or an authority to tenants to pay their rent to the purchaser in the future.

(k) The form may include a question asking whether, if the preliminary enquiries of the vendor were repeated, the same replies would be given. It is difficult to see the point in asking this and the vendor is under no duty to answer it.

ii Time for raising requisitions

Under an open contract requisitions must be raised within a reasonable time of delivery of the abstract. Not surprisingly, standard conditions of sale will normally specify a precise time limit. The Law Society Conditions specify a time limit of six working days after receipt of the abstract or after the date of the contract if the abstract is supplied before the date of the contract.[2] The National Conditions are more generous to the purchaser and give him eleven working days after delivery of the abstract in which to deliver his requisitions.[3] Both sets of conditions provide that time is of the essence for raising requisitions, with the effect that if a requisition is not raised within the time limit it is

2 LSC 15(2).
3 NC 9(3).

deemed to be waived and the title accepted. However, this rule must be subject to two exceptions. Firstly, the purchaser can still object to a fundamental defect in title, even after the time for raising requisitions has expired. This occurred in *Re Cox and Neve's Contract*[4] where the defect was an undisclosed restrictive covenant and in *Re Brine and Davies' Contract*[5] where under an open contract for sale of registered land the vendor had not got absolute title. Secondly, the purchaser is not subject to the time limit in respect of defects which are not discoverable from the abstract, for example defects which only show up on pre-completion searches or on verification of the abstract. If the abstract is for some reason delivered in separate parts at different times, the Law Society Conditions provide that the time limits for requisitions on each part run separately.[6] The National Conditions contain a similar provision.[7]

The Law Society Conditions also provide that the vendor must deliver his replies to the requisitions within four working days of delivery of the requisitions and that the purchaser shall deliver any observations on the vendor's replies within a further four working days.[8] Again time is of the essence, so if the purchaser is not satisfied with the vendor's replies he must preserve his position by repeating the requisition within the time limit. Under the National Conditions there is no time limit laid down for the vendor to reply to requisitions. Presumably if the vendor fails to reply within a reasonable time the purchaser can serve a notice requiring a reply within a stated time and making time of the essence. There is a time limit for the purchaser to deliver observations on the vendor's replies when they are received; it is six working days after delivery of the replies.[9] Again, time is of the essence.

iii Vendor's duty

The vendor is bound to answer all specific questions related to the title. If the vendor does not answer a proper requisition then the purchaser can rescind, or compel the vendor to answer by issuing a vendor and purchaser summons. If the vendor's solicitor does answer requisitions which are raised out of time then he may wish to make it clear (if such be the case) that he is only answering as a matter of courtesy and is not waiving the contractual time limit.

iv The vendor's contractual right to rescind

Both the National and Law Society Conditions contain a provision permitting the vendor to rescind if the purchaser will not withdraw a requisition.[10] This may seem surprising in view of the statement in the previous paragraph that the vendor must reply to proper requisitions. At first sight it seems to offer the vendor a wide escape route where, for example, he has not complied with his duty of disclosure in the contract. However, the courts interpret these provisions

4 [1891] 2 Ch 109.
5 [1935] Ch 388.
6 LSC 15(4).
7 NC 9(5).
8 LSC 15(2), (3).
9 NC 9(3).
10 LSC 16(1), NC 10.

very restrictively. A vendor will only be allowed to take advantage of such a condition and rescind if all the following requirements are met.[11]

(a) The vendor must have at least some title to the property sold.
(b) The vendor must not have known about the defect at the date of the contract and that lack of knowledge must not be due to the vendor's recklessness.[12]
(c) The defect must be irremovable, or only removable at disproportionate expense to the vendor.[13]
(d) The vendor must rely on the contractual condition within a reasonable time.

The Law Society Condition provides that the vendor can give the purchaser notice to withdraw 'any requisition or objection' (not, apparently, just an objection to title) 'which the vendor is unable or unwilling, on reasonable grounds, to remove'; after which the purchaser has seven working days in which to do so. The National Condition provides that if the purchaser persists in 'any objection to the title which the vendor shall be unable or unwilling, on reasonable grounds, to remove', the vendor can require the purchaser to withdraw the requisition within ten working days. If the purchaser fails to withdraw the requisition the vendor – or either party under the Law Society Conditions – can rescind the contract by notice to the other party, 'notwithstanding any intermediate negotiation or litigation'. On rescission the vendor must return the deposit to the purchaser and the purchaser must return the abstract and any other documents he has received under the contract. On a purely practical note the vendor may still have to pay his estate agent, despite the aborted sale.

v Waiver of right to raise requisitions

It is possible that submission of the draft conveyance to the vendor's solicitor for approval might constitute an acceptance of the vendor's title, defects and all, and a waiver of any outstanding requisitions. The Law Society Conditions specifically provide that this shall not be the case.[14] Similarly, a purchaser who takes possession before completion may, in some circumstances, be deemed to have waived any objection to defects in the title. We have already seen that both the Law Society and National Conditions state that this shall not be the case.[15]

11 *Selkirk v Romar Investments Ltd* [1963] 3 All ER 994, [1963] 1 WLR 1415.
12 *Baines v Tweddle* [1959] Ch 679, [1959] 2 All ER 724, CA.
13 In *Leominster Properties Ltd v Broadway Finance Ltd* (1981) 42 P & CR 372, a vendor, who was a mortgagee exercising a power of sale, was held to be unable to rely on NC 10 in respect of a prior mortgage which the vendor thought had priority.
14 LSC 17(3).
15 LSC 18(3), NC 8(3).

11 Pre-completion searches

1 Unregistered land

i Search in Central Land Charges Register

It may be convenient here to dispel any confusion about the various charges registers and registries that are encountered in conveyancing. Firstly there is the Local Land Charges Register kept under the Local Land Charges Act 1975 by the Local Authority. This contains details of purely local matters and was described in chapter 6. It is searched in respect of both registered and unregistered land before exchange of contracts. Secondly there is the Central Land Charges Register which is only relevant to unregistered land and which is described in detail below. The system of registration *of title* is overseen by the Land Registry and there are District Land Registries for each area of the country. When title to land is registered, the register of that title is split into three parts, namely the Property Register, the Proprietorship Register and the Charges Register. The latter should not be confused with either the Central or Local Land Charges Register. Finally, the word 'charge' is often used in the sense of a legal charge or mortgage, for example in the case of a mortgage of registered land which is known as a registered charge and is protected by an entry in the Charges Register of the title.

Returning to the Central Land Charges Register, there are in fact five registers. We shall be concerned principally with the register of land charges, the register of pending actions and the register of writs and orders but there are also registers of deeds of arrangement and of annuities.

1 *Land Charges Register* There are a number of classes of land charge, as follows.

Class A[1] This is a financial charge arising out of some statutory provision which only comes into existence following an aplication by some person. An example would be a charge under the Landlord and Tenant Act 1927 in respect of compensation paid by the landlord to the tenant for improvements to business premises. Class A land charges are not very common in practice.

1 Land Charges Act 1972, s. 2(2).

Class B[2] This is a financial charge arising out of some statutory provision, but different from a Class A charge in that it is actually created by the statute and does not depend on an application by some person. An example would be the Law Society's charge over property preserved or recovered under a Legal Aid Certificate.[3]

Class Ci[4] A puisne mortgage, that is a legal mortgage not protected by deposit of title deeds with the mortgagee. This would normally be a second legal mortgage, the title deeds being held by the first legal mortgagee.

Class Cii[5] A limited owners charge. This is an equitable charge obtained by a tenant for life or statutory owner of settled land by virtue of having paid death duties (or capital transfer tax, now inheritance tax) on the land.

Class Ciii[6] A general equitable charge. This is something of a mixed bag but specifically *excluded* are:

(a) an equitable charge protected by deposit of title deeds;
(b) a charge included in any other class;
(c) a charge arising under a trust for sale or settlement.

A common example of a Ciii charge would be the vendor's lien for unpaid purchase money or the purchaser's lien for his deposit, or an equitable mortgage.

Class Civ[7] An estate contract. This is defined as a contract by an estate owner, or someone entitled to have the legal estate conveyed to him, to convey or create a legal estate. This class of charge is very common in practice. It includes the everyday contract between the vendor and purchaser for the sale of land and it also includes an option to purchase, a right of pre-emption,[8] an option to renew a lease, an agreement for a lease and also, strictly, an equitable mortgage which constitutes an agreement to create a legal mortgage.

Class Di[9] A charge for unpaid death duties (or capital transfer tax, now inheritance tax) registered by the Inland Revenue Commissioners. Again this is rare in practice.

Class Dii[10] A restrictive covenant made after 1925, but not including a restrictive covenant contained in a lease. The latter are not registrable nor are restrictive covenants affecting freehold land created before 1926. Dii registrations are very common in practice.

Class Diii[11] An equitable easement arising after 1925. An example would be a right of way for life. This category does not include legal easements which are of course binding on a purchaser quite irrespective of notice.

Class E[12] An annuity created before 1926 and not registered in the then

2 Ibid, s. 2(3).
3 Legal Aid Act 1974, s. 9(6).
4 Land Charges Act 1972, s. 2(4)(i).
5 Ibid, s. 2(4)(ii).
6 Ibid, s. 2(4)(iii).
7 Ibid, s. 2(4)(iv).
8 Subject to the dicta in *Pritchard v Briggs* [1980] Ch 338, [1980] 1 All ER 294, CA.
9 Ibid, s. 2(5)(i).
10 Ibid, s. 2(5)(ii).
11 Ibid, s. 2(5)(iii).
12 Ibid, s. 2(6).

existing register of annuities. This class will eventually become obsolete and registrations are rare in practice.

Class F[13] This is a spouse's statutory right of occupation under the Matrimonial Homes Act 1983. By virtue of that Act a spouse who has no legal estate in the matrimonial home, or in other words who is not the sole or a joint legal owner, has a registrable statutory right of occupation. Registrations are quite common in practice.

2 *Register of Pending Actions*[14] A pending action is defined as any action or proceedings pending in court relating to land or any interest in or charge over land.[15] An obvious example would be a dispute about the ownership of a piece of land. Also included would be a spouse's claim in divorce proceedings for a transfer of property order. Most importantly, a bankruptcy petition is also registrable as a pending action. Registration of a pending action is only valid for five years and must then be renewed.[16]

3 *Register of Writs and Orders*[17] This includes not only writs and orders affecting land made by a court for the purpose of enforcing a judgement, but also bankruptcy orders. Again registration is only effective for five years unless renewed.

4 *Register of Deeds of Arrangement*[18] A deed of arrangement is a document whereby a debtor agrees to hand over control of his property to his creditors in an attempt to avoid bankruptcy proceedings. Again registration is only effective for five years unless renewed.

5 *Register of annuities*[19] This is a Register of Annuities created before 1926 and registered in the then existing Register of Annuities. There can be no new registrations and the Register will in due course become obsolete. Registrations are rare in practice.

6 *Effect of Registration and Non-Registration* Registration in any of the Registers constitutes actual notice of the matter registered to all persons, for all purposes connected with the land affected.[20] This is of course the reason why a search of the Registers is necessary. The effect of non-registration of an interest which should be registered varies according to the Register. Land charges of Classes A, B, Ci, Cii, Ciii and F are void as against a purchaser (including a lessee and a mortgagee) for valuable consideration of the land or any interest in it

13 Ibid, s. 2(7).
14 Ibid, s. 5
15 The exact scope of a pending land action is difficult to define; see *Selim Ltd v Bickenhall Engineering Ltd* [1981] 2 All ER 210, [1981] 1 WLR 1318; *Regan & Blackburn Ltd v Rogers* [1985] 2 All ER 180, [1985] 1 WLR 870.
16 Ibid, s 8.
17 Ibid, s. 6.
18 Ibid, s. 7.
19 Ibid, s. 1(4), Schedule 1.
20 Law of Property Act 1925, s. 198(1).

unless registered before completion of the purchase.[1] Land charges of classes Civ and D are void against a purchaser *of a legal estate* in the land for money or money's worth unless registered before completion.[2] A purchaser's actual knowledge of an interest which is registrable but which is not in fact registered is immaterial. As we shall see, an official certificate of search is conclusive in favour of a purchaser.

Once an interest which should have been protected by registration as a land charge has become void for non-registration, it cannot normally be revived against a future purchaser by later registration. To allow this would be to devalue the property in the hands of the purchaser against whom the interest is void.[3] However a land charge such as a restrictive covenant might revive against successors in title such as squatters. By examining the date of registration of the charge and the dates of previous purchases, a purchaser's solicitor will be able to ascertain whether a land charge has become void for non-registration. He may be able to see this quite easily by examining old search certificates.

As regards the other registers, a pending action will not bind a purchaser for valuable consideration without express notice of it unless it is registered.[4] As we have seen earlier, a bankruptcy petition will not bind a purchaser of a legal estate in good faith for money or money's worth unless it is registered. A writ or order will be void against a purchaser for valuable consideration unless it is registered.[5] Again, as we have seen earlier, there is a special rule for a bankruptcy order which is similar to the rule relating to the bankruptcy petition; that is, the title of the trustee in bankruptcy will be void against a purchaser of a legal estate in good faith for money or money's worth unless the bankruptcy order is registered.[6] A deed of arrangement will be void against a purchaser for valuable consideration of any land affected by it unless it is registered.[7]

7 *Manner of registration* It would be difficult to deal with searches for existing registrations without first examining how those registrations are made. A registration to be valid must be made against the name of the owner, at the time of registration, of the legal estate affected.[8] We have already noticed the complications caused on a sub-sale, where the sub-vendor does not have the legal estate at the time of the registration of the sub-sale contract by the sub-purchaser; registration must be against the name of the vendor.

There will sometimes be problems over the correct version of a person's name. In *Diligent Finance Co Ltd v Alleyne*[9] it was held that in the absence of evidence to the contrary, the correct name of the estate owner would be the

1 Land Charges Act 1972, ss. 4(2), (5).
2 Ibid, s. 4(6).
3 See for example *Wilkes v Spooner* [1911] 2 KB 473, CA.
4 Ibid, s. 5(7).
5 Ibid, s. 6(4).
6 Ibid; s. 6(5).
7 Ibid, s. 7(2).
8 Ibid, s. 3(1).
9 (1972) 23 P & CR 346.

name appearing in the conveyance to him. In that case a wife had registered a Class F charge against her husband in the name of Erskine Alleyne, which she believed to be his name. However his full name, which appeared in the deeds, was Erskine Owen Alleyne. The Class F charge was therefore void against a later mortgagee who had searched the name of Erskine Owen Alleyne,[10] because the registration had not been made against the correct name. Difficulties of this sort are inevitable in a system which relies on registration against name rather than against the land affected.

8 *Against which names should a search be made?* As registrations are possible against the names of estate owners for the time being, the search ought to be against the names of all the owners of the legal estate since 1925 (the date when the register in its present form was brought into existence) in respect of the period of ownership of each estate owner. If there is more than one estate owner at any one time, for example where there are joint tenants, a search should be made against each name. At the risk of stating the obvious, if a registration is made against the name of estate owner A in say 1930, the registration stays against A's name and is not transferred into B's name when A eventually sells to B. Ideally therefore the purchaser will want to know the names of all estate owners since 1925.

How does the purchaser discover the names of the estate owners? The answer of course is from the abstract of title. This illustrates another of the disadvantages of a system of registration by name. It is possible, indeed very probable, that the abstract will not go back as far as 1925, or in other words that the root of title will be dated some time after 1925. The purchaser will be unable to discover the names of the estate owners since 1925 but prior to the date of the root and thus will not be able to search against those names and discover any registrations made against them. Yet if there are such registrations, the purchaser will be bound by them, because they are registered as land charges. In these circumstances the purchaser, if adversely affected by a registration which he could not discover, may be entitled to compensation.[11] Unfortunately this provision for compensation does not extend to the purchaser of leasehold land where there are undiscoverable land charges, such as restrictive covenants, registered against the superior freehold or leasehold title which the purchaser is precluded – by statute – from investigating.

The purchaser's solicitor may be faced with problems concerning the correct name of an estate owner. If the name appears in different forms in the abstract then the purchaser's solicitor can raise a requisition asking which is the correct version but it would be safer to search against all versions of the name. Even if a registration is in a slightly incorrect version of the name of the estate owner it will still be effective against someone who searches against the wrong name. This is illustrated by the case of *Oak Co-operative Building Society v Blackburn*.[12] A purchaser registered a Civ estate contract against his vendor in the name of Frank David Blackburn. The vendor's correct name was Francis David Blackburn. Blackburn was also in the process of mortgaging the property to a

10 And therefore not discovered the class F registration.

11 See further in ch 16, below.

12 [1968] Ch 730, [1968] 2 All ER 117, CA.

Building Society who made a search against the name of Francis Davis Blackburn which revealed no entries. At first instance it was held that the search was ineffective as it was in the wrong name but that in any event the registration was also ineffective as it was in the wrong name too. The result was that the estate contract was void against the Building Society and indeed it would not have mattered if the Building Society had not made a search at all. This decision was reversed in the Court of Appeal, which held that registration against a 'version' of the correct name will be effective against someone who searches against the wrong name. The Building Society were therefore bound by the estate contract because the estate contract had been registered against a version of the estate owner's correct name and the Building Society had not searched against the correct name. Exactly how close a name must be to the correct name to amount to such a version is unclear. Of course if the Building Society had searched against the correct name they would not have been bound by the estate contract.

The register is computerised. The computer has no intelligence and will only do what it is told. The importance of giving the correct names on registration and searching cannot be overemphasised. On searching, the computer is programmed to reveal entries against the precise name searched against and some, but not many, variations of it. For example a search against Arthur William Lee will reveal registrations against Arthur William Lee and also against A W Lee, but will not reveal registrations against Arthur Lee or Arthur W Lee or A William Lee. However certain groups of words are treated by computer as being the same. These include '&' and 'and'; Ltd, Limited, public limited company, plc and their Welsh equivalents; Co, Company and Companies; and Brother, Brothers and Bros. A search therefore against Arthur Lee & Co plc will also reveal registrations against Arthur Lee and Company Limited. The Companies Act 1980 caused some complications as certain companies had to change their names to a name ending in plc or public limited company or their Welsh equivalents. On the face of it this will cause no problems because of the interchangeability of Ltd, Limited, plc and public limited company as far as the computer is concerned. However, on the change of name a company might also have dropped the word company or any abbreviation of it, or the Welsh version or abbreviation, from its old name. Thus Arthur Lee and Company Limited may become Arthur Lee plc. A search against Arthur Lee plc, although it will reveal registrations against Arthur Lee Limited will not reveal registrations against Arthur Lee and Company Limited. Thus where the purchaser's solicitor sees that one of the previous estate owners is a company which has changed its name in this way he should make sure a search is made against both the old name and the new name. Quite apart from the provisions of the Companies Act 1980, if a company does change its name then a search must be made against both names for the respective periods of ownership, unless the changes are within the categories treated as equivalent by the computer.

9 *Mechanics of searching* The normal method of searching is by a written application for an official Search Certificate. There is a standard form of application, called a Form K15. The form contains space for up to six names to be searched against. The purchaser's solicitor will need a further form if he

wishes to search against more than six names. We have already seen the importance of giving the correct names. On the form, there is a separate line for the surname and forename. If there should be any doubt as to whether a middle name is a second forename or part of a hyphenated surname then a search should be made against both versions.

The purchaser's solicitor must also state on the form the appropriate period of ownership of the legal estate in respect of each name, in terms of years, eg 1967–1975. This is a means of excluding irrelevant registrations as a registration against the name supplied, made outside the period of ownership of the land being purchased, must have been made in respect of some other land which a person with that name owned at the time; if made in relation to the land being bought, is clearly ineffective, as registration must be against the name of the estate owner at the time of registration. Another means of filtering out irrelevant registrations is by requiring, on registration and searching, a statement of the county in which the land affected is situated. Thus a registration of a land charge in 1975 against a particular name in respect of land in Leicestershire will not be revealed on a search against the same name for the same year in respect of Nottinghamshire. On searching, care must be taken to state the county correctly. County boundaries were altered by the Local Government Act 1972, the changes taking place as from 1 April 1974. It may therefore be necessary to supply the name of any former county, either if the present county simply did not exist before 1974 (eg Avon, Tyne and Wear, South Yorkshire); or if the pre-1974 county has ceased to exist, meaning that the land is now in another county (eg Rutland, Huntingdonshire); or if because of a boundary change the land has moved from one county into another.

Space is also given on the form for a brief description of the land. Unlike the period of ownership and the county and former county, it is not essential that this information be supplied. It will act as a further filtering device, meaning that registrations obviously affecting land other than that which the purchaser is buying can be kept off the search certificate. However, if a description is given it must be correct and any former description must also be given. It will then be used when a large number of entries are disclosed against a particular name for a particular county and period of ownership. The certificate will state that entries that are clearly irrelevant have been excluded and will also include the description supplied on the application for the search and by reference to which the exclusion was made. It is not normal practice to give a description unless it is anticipated that there may be a large number of entries against a particular name as there may be, for example, against a firm of builders or a Local Authority.

It is possible to request the search by telephone, without using the written form of application. The necessary information, that is the name, county and period of ownership, is given to the Land Charges Department over the telephone and if there are less than five entries for a particular name, county and period of ownership these will be read out. In any event the search certificate is then posted to confirm the result of the search. It is also possible to apply for a search by telex, again without using the standard form; the result of the search will not be telexed back but a search certificate posted in the normal way. A personal search is also feasible if not very practicable. This involves submitting an application form and watching the entries as they are displayed on a visual display unit by the Land Charges computer operator. The maximum number of entries which can be displayed against one name is 25. Again, an official certificate is subsequently posted to the applicant.

Fees are payable on all three searches by cash (on a personal search), postal order, cheque or through a credit account. Telephone and telex searches can only be made by persons with such an account but this will include most firms of solicitors. The Land Charges Department is situated at Plymouth although telephone and personal searches can also be made at a branch office in Croydon.

10 *Official Search Certificate* The official search certificate will show the entries revealed by the search. It is conclusive in favour of a purchaser.[13] However, as well as informing the purchaser of the existing registrations it also confers some degree of protection on the purchaser. Any entry on the register made after the date of the search certificate will not bind the purchaser provided that completion of the purchase takes place within 15 working days of the date of the certificate. This period of 15 working days is called the priority period because if entries are made during it, but the purchaser completes before the end of it, the purchaser has priority over those entries and is not bound by them.[14] Of course the purchaser only gets the benefit of the protection if he has searched against the correct name. The priority period is extremely convenient in practice as if it were not available, a purchaser would have to delay his search until immediately before completion. The availability of the priority period means that the search can be done say a week before the contractual completion date, to allow time for the certificate to be posted back, and completion can then take place in reliance on the search. Even if completion is delayed by a week or so the purchaser will still be able to complete within the priority period. If he cannot, then a new search must be done which will of course provide a new period of priority. The date of the expiry of the priority period is given on the search certificate although strictly it should be checked by the purchaser's solicitor.

The search certificate will give brief details of all entries against the specified name in respect of land in the specified county registered during the specified period of ownership. For each land charge entry the certificate will show the type of registration ie the class of land charge, the district and county in which the land affected is situated often including a brief description of the land such as a postal address, and the date of registration and the registration number. If a description of the land affected has been provided on the application for the search then as already mentioned the list of entries may be edited to exclude those that are obviously irrelevant.

If an entry is revealed, the purchaser's solicitor may wish to obtain further details of it, either to find out what it is or to confirm that it is what he thinks it is. He can apply for an office copy of the registration which will give more details than those which appear on the certificate. This office copy should not be confused with the office copies of the register entries in respect of registered land.

13 Land Charges Act 1972, s. 10(4).
14 Ibid, s. 11(5).

The search, although commonly called a land charges search, is in fact a search of all five registers. Entries in the registers of writs and orders, pending actions and deeds of arrangement against the name specified will be revealed on the search certificate quite irrespective of the county or period of ownership specified in the search. This is to the purchaser's advantage as there may be occasions particularly in relation to bankruptcy when an entry, even though made outside the period of ownership of the legal estate, has important consequences for the purchaser. An example would be under the Insolvency Act 1986, section 339 where the estate owner has given the property away and then become bankrupt.

An official certificate of search protects the purchaser's solicitor in that the Land Charges Act 1972 provides that he shall not be answerable for any loss arising out of an error on it nor an error on an office copy.[15]

11 *Priority notice* The priority period, whilst of great advantage to the purchaser, can on the face of it be something of a disadvantage to other parties. It would seem to be impossible to register a land charge arising shortly before completion of a purchase, in order to bind the purchaser, because he will probably have already done his search. In fact this is not the case and there is a special priority notice procedure. A priority notice must be lodged at the Land Charges Registry at least 15 working days before creation of the charge, giving details of the proposed charge. This 15 day period gives time for the priority period on any current searches to expire. If the land charge is then registered within 30 working days of the date of the priority notice, the registration takes effect as if it had been made immediately at the time of creation of the charge.[16] A purchaser who does a search is not prejudiced because the priority notice will be disclosed on his search certificate. The priority notice procedure is often used in the following situation. The conveyance from the vendor to the purchaser is to contain a new restrictive covenant by the purchaser. The purchaser is financing his purchase by a contemporaneous mortgage to a Building Society. On completion there will be the conveyance from the vendor to the purchaser, including the new restrictive covenant and, notionally immediately afterwards, the purchaser mortgages the property to the Building Society by means of the mortgage deed. Even if the vendor registers the new covenant as a Dii land charge as soon as possible after completion it will still be void against the Building Society for non-registration, because at the date of the mortgage it is not registered. The vendor therefore, at least 15 working days before completion when the covenant will be created, enters a priority notice giving details of the proposed covenant. When land charges searches are done for the purchaser and the Building Society this priority notice will be revealed. The vendor must then apply for registration of the covenant after completion and within 30 working days of the priority notice. The effect of this will be that the covenant will be treated as having become registered as soon as it is created on completion of the purchase and it is thus already registered when the mortgage is entered into immediately thereafter. The Building Society is therefore bound by the

15 Ibid, s. 12.
16 Ibid, ss. 11(1), (2), (3).

restrictive covenant. In order to cater for just this situation, the National Conditions provide that where a conveyance of unregistered land is to contain restrictive covenants the purchaser must inform the vendor if, as would be usual, he intends to execute a mortgage contemporaneously with the conveyance.[17]

12 *Reliance on old searches* The purchaser's solicitor's duty is to search against all known owners of the legal estate since 1925. However, if the solicitors for the various previous owners have acted properly on their respective purchases there should be with the deeds the searches which were made when the previous owners bought. Although the vendor is under no duty to abstract these old searches he may do so, or otherwise make them available. There is no reason why the purchaser's solicitor should repeat a search which has been made properly in the past. For example if when A bought property in 1971, a search was made against the vendor B for his period of ownership of 1964 to 1971, there is no point in a purchaser from A in 1982 repeating that search. When the purchaser's solicitor does wish to rely on an old search in this way he should check that it was made against the correct name for the correct period of ownership and did specify the correct county. He should also check the date of the subsequent conveyance in order to confirm that completion did take place within the priority period of the search.

If the purchaser is buying property from someone who acquired it not by purchase but by gift, then it may be necessary to make a search against the donor even if such a search was made at the time of the gift. A donee is given no protection by an official search certificate and the purchaser would also be concerned about the effect of the Insolvency Act 1986, section 339.

Old search certificates are useful in that as well as saving the purchaser money in search fees, they may readily reveal whether any interests have become void for non-registration. This information could also be obtained by checking the date of registration of the interest to see whether there had been a disposition to a purchaser before the interest was registered.

13 *Procedure if an entry is revealed* The purpose of the search is to discover whether there are any matters of which the purchaser does not already know but which will be binding on him. There may be some entries which come as no surprise to the purchaser, for example a Dii registration in respect of a restrictive covenant which was disclosed in the contract and which is apparent from the abstract. Similary the purchaser himself may have protected his own contract by registering a Civ land charge. On the other hand if an entry is revealed which cannot be explained in this way the purchaser's solicitor will immediately raise a requisition to find out what the entry relates to and how the vendor proposes to deal with it. He can also obtain an office copy of the entry. For example, the vendor's solicitor may have forgotten to abstract a second legal mortgage which will show up on a search certificate as it will have been registered as a Ci land charge. The vendor's solicitor will then abstract the second mortgage and the purchaser's solicitor can ensure that it is discharged on or before completion. If a restrictive covenant is revealed as being

17 NC 19(4).

registered as a Dii land charge then if this has not been disclosed in the contract, prima facie the vendor will be in breach of contract as he will be unable to convey what he has contracted to; he can only convey the property subject to the restrictive covenant. If a Civ entry is revealed then again the purchaser's solicitor will want an explanation. The entry may simply relate to the vendor's contract when he bought, in which case it can be and indeed should have been cancelled. If a Class F land charge is revealed then the purchaser's solicitor will insist that it is cancelled before completion or possibly that a form of application for cancellation signed by the spouse who registered the charge is handed over on completion. If the vendor's solicitor is properly prepared then he will have anticipated the problem. Otherwise, if the charge cannot be cancelled, the vendor will be in breach of contract. If a bankruptcy petition or order against the vendor is revealed then the purchaser cannot complete but must wait and if needs be complete with the trustee in bankruptcy.

Of course it may be that there is a quite innocent explanation for some of the entries on the search certificate. They may relate to someone else with the same name or they may relate to land other than that which the purchaser is buying.

ii Search in the Companies Register

1 *Need for the search* Prior to 1 January 1970 if a company created a land charge for securing money (potentially registrable as a class Ci) this could be protected by registration in the Companies Register under the Companies Act 1948, section 95.[18] Since that date registration in the Companies Register on its own is insufficient to bind a purchaser for value and there must be registration in the Land Charges Register. This means that in respect of a company which owned the land being sold before 1970, it is not sufficient to make a search in the Land Charges Register but a search must also be done in the Companies Register. If a financial charge is revealed as affecting the property being sold then the same considerations apply as to any other mortgage or charge; the purchaser will want it to be discharged on or before completion or else the property to be released from the charge.

A floating charge whenever created is not registrable as a land charge but must be registered in the Companies Register. This, then, is a second reason for making a search of the Companies Register; not only to reveal pre-1970 charges but also to reveal floating charges, whenever created. If a floating charge is revealed, the purchaser will require some assurance, in the form of a letter or certificate from the chargee – often a bank – to the effect that the charge had not crystallised at the date of completion. If it has crystallised it has become a fixed charge and will be treated by the purchaser like any other charge or mortgage.

There are further matters about which the purchaser may be concerned. The purchaser may wish to ascertain that the company was incorporated at the date of the conveyance of the property to it. He may wish to confirm that the company has not been struck off the register, or that no winding up proceedings have started in respect of the company;[19] if a winding up has

18 Land Charges Act 1972, s. 3(7).

19 If this is suspected, the purchaser's solicitors should have a search made of the London Gazette for an advertisement of a petition.

commenced, then any disposition by the company is void unless the court orders otherwise.[20]

2 *Mechanics of search* There is no provision for an official search of the Companies Register, which can be searched either in London or Cardiff. The purchaser's solicitor will normally instruct a firm of agents, who advertise in the legal press, to do a personal search and report the result. A letter of instruction to the agents should cover all points on which the solicitor wants information. The agent's fee is reasonably modest. As there is no official search so there is no protection for a purchaser. The search should therefore be timed to be as close as possible to completion; the search can even be made on the day of the completion and the result telephoned by the agents.

3 *Reliance on old searches* For the reasons mentioned in section 1, above, it may be necessary to make this search not only when the vendor is a company but also if a company appears on the title as an owner of the property in the past. If a search was made when the company disposed of the property and this is made available to the purchaser's solicitor by the vendor then there may be no need to make a further search if the old search appears adequate and there are no other reasons why a fresh search should be made.

iii Inspection of the property

We have already seen how occupation of the property can fix the purchaser with constructive notice of an occupier's rights.[1] A typical situation is where a spouse or some other person has an equitable interest in the property (but does not hold the legal estate); his or her occupation gives notice of the equitable interest to the purchaser. The purchaser should thus arrange for an inspection, if not already done prior to exchange (and possibly even if already done prior to exchange, depending on what is 'reasonable' under section 199 of the Law of Property Act 1925), to see if there are any such interests discoverable by resonable enquiries. This is rather more easily said than done. An appropriate question could be added to the requisitions although this will not prevent the occupier's rights being binding on the purchaser if they are not revealed by the vendor.

What though if an equitable interest *is* known to the purchaser, either as a result of inspection or otherwise? If the person with the equitable interest is the vendor's spouse and is willing to co-operate, it may be possible to transfer the property into the joint names of the vendor and his/her spouse before completion and both spouses can then convey to the purchaser. Alternatively, the person with the interest could sign some form of consent or join in the conveyance, to release or convey his or her rights vis à vis the purchaser. In this situation the person with the equitable interest should receive independent advice before signing the form.[2] Another way of dealing with the problem

20 Companies Act 1985, s. 522.
1 See ch 6, section 8 iii.
2 This point is discussed further in ch 13 in relation to a prospective mortgagee requiring a consent form from a prospective occupier with an equitable interest (eg the purchaser's spouse).

would be for the vendor to appoint someone other than the owner of the interest to be a second trustee and thereby overreach the interest,[3] although leave the problem of disposal of the proceeds of sale. The onus is on the vendor to devise a way in which the property can be conveyed to the purchaser free of the equitable interest as otherwise the vendor will very probably be in breach of contract; he will be unable to give vacant possession, and he may also be in breach of the covenants for title implied into the purchase deed after completion. However this will be of little consolation to the purchaser, who wants the property rather than an action against the vendor. From the purchaser's point of view it is preferable to investigate this situation, so far as possible, before exchange of contracts, to prevent the problem ever arising.

Despite the foregoing, there is some comfort for the purchaser in the cases of *Bristol and West Building Society v Henning*[4] and *Paddington Building Society v Mendelsohn*,[5] which concern the position of a mortgagee who may be bound by the interest of someone who moves into the property with the purchaser/mortgagor, and are discussed in that context in chapter 13. Applying the cases by analogy to the vendor/purchaser situation, they suggest that if the occupier knows of and supports the vendor's sale, he or she may then be unable to enforce the interest against the purchaser.

iv Further search of the Local Land Charges Register and enquiries of the Local Authority

It may in certain circumstances be necessary to do these searches again, particularly if a relatively long time has elapsed since such searches were made before exchange of contracts. They are rarely done again in practice and the registration of a local land charge or the advent of some new local authority proposals affecting the property would not normally affect the relationship between the vendor and the purchaser, the risk thereof being assumed by the purchaser on exchange of contracts.

2 Registered land

i Search of the Register

1 *Purpose of the search* This is the main search which needs to be done on a purchase of registered land. Its purpose is to bring up to date the information which the purchaser has concerning the state of the entries in the register which will have been derived from the copy entries by means of which title was deduced. The purchaser must have this up to date information as not only does the register describe what he is buying but he will also be affected by any entries such as notices or cautions appearing on the register.

2 *Mechanics of search* There is a standard form of application for a search of the register, for use by prospective purchasers, lessees and mortgagees. This is Form 94A under the Land Registration (Official Searches) Rules 1981. The

3 *City of London Building Society v Flegg* [1986] Ch 605, [1986] 1 All ER 989, CA, (1987) Independant, 15 May, HL.
4 [1985] 2 All ER 606, [1986] 1 WLR 778, CA.
5 (1985) 50 P & CR 244, CA.

form is sent to the District Land Registry for the area in which the land is situated. On the form the purchaser or his solicitor must certify that the purchaser intends to purchase (or lease or lend money on a mortgage of) the land. As the register is private an authority to inspect from the vendor is necessary.[6] This is provided as part of the process of deducing title under the Land Registration Act 1925, section 110. However, if the person making the search is a solicitor the authority to inspect does not actually need to be sent to the District Land Registry with the form but the solicitor can merely certify on the form that he does hold an authority to inspect. The form must also specify the date after which details of any changes in the entries on the register are required. If the purchaser has received office copy entries this will be the date the copies were taken, which is stated on the copies. If the purchaser has only received photocopies of the entries in the vendor's Land or Charge Certificate then the relevant date will be the date on which the Certificate was last brought up to date, which can be ascertained by raising a requisition. The form is submitted in duplicate and the reverse of one part of the form is the basis of the official certificate of the result of the search.

The search can also be done by telephone or telex.[7] The purchaser's solicitor will have to give an undertaking to submit an application form for a search forthwith. The reply, by telephone or telex, has none of the advantages of an official certificate but an official certificate will be forwarded in due course as a result of the application form. A personal search can be made at the District Land Registry but again this does not have any of the advantages of an official certificate.

3 *Search of part* If the purchaser is only buying part of the land comprised in the vendor's title then he will only wish to know the up to date state of the register as it affects the part which he is buying. There is a standard form of application 94B to be used by such a purchaser. This is similar to the form 94A but must contain a reference to the part which the purchaser is buying and in respect of which the search is to be done. A plan in duplicate would have to be sent, showing this part, unless either it can be clearly identified by reference to the filed plan or it is a numbered plot on a new building estate of which the estate layout plan has already been deposited with the Registry. In the latter case the date of approval of the plan must also be given on the form.

4 *Official Search Certificate* The certificate despatched as a result of the application for a search shows all entries made since the date specified in the application. It is not conclusive but if the purchaser suffers loss as a result of an error in the certificate he will be entitled to an indemnity under the Land Registration Act 1925, section 83(3). In the first part of this chapter we saw that an official Land Charges search certificate gave the purchaser of unregistered land some protection in that if he completed within a certain period of the date of the search he was not bound by entries made in the meantime. The same principle applies to the search of the register in respect of registered land. The purchaser will obtain priority over any entry made on

6 On the Law Society contract form, the authority is included as part of Special Condition E.
7 Land Registration (Official Searches) Rules 1986, rr. 7, 8.

the register between the date of the search and the date the purchaser applies for registration of his purchase, but only if the purchaser's application for registration is in order and is deemed to have been delivered to the District Land Registry before 9.30 a.m. on the thirtieth working day after the application for the search is deemed to have been delivered;[8] an application for a search or an application for registration which is delivered after 9.30 a.m. on one working day and before 9.30 a.m. on the next working day is deemed to have been delivered immediately before 9.30 a.m. on the second day.[9] The date of expiry of the priority period is shown on the search certificate but this should be checked by the purchaser's solicitor.

In effect, then, the period is 30 working days from the date of the search but within this period the purchaser must not only complete but also *apply for registration of his purchase*. The purchaser's solicitor will send off the application for the search shortly before completion is due so as to receive the search certificate before completion but also to allow sufficient time to complete and apply for registration within the priority period even if completion is delayed. If completion cannot take place within the priority period then a new search must be done; this will give a new period of priority and not an extension of the priority period under the original search.

5 *Procedure if an entry is revealed* If the purchaser's information about the register is obtained from recently obtained office copies then it is unlikely that any new entry will be revealed by the search. However, if some adverse entry is disclosed then the comments made in section 13 above in relation to land charges apply with equal force. For example a registered charge may be revealed which the purchaser will want to see discharged. A notice in respect of a spouse's statutory right of occupation under the Matrimonial Homes Act 1983 may have been entered. A creditor's notice in respect of a bankruptcy petition or a bankruptcy inhibition following a bankruptcy order may have been entered. If the vendor is selling part of a larger piece of land, he might have recently sold another part and granted an easement over the part which the present purchaser is buying; this will be revealed by the search as having been noted on the register (although it is an overriding interest) and the vendor will be in breach of contract unless he disclosed it in the contract.

6 *Sub-sales* On a sub-sale, the position is that the vendor has contracted to sell to the purchaser (P1) who has in turn contracted to sell to the sub-purchaser (P2) before completion of his own purchase. Completion of the two transactions will normally be co-ordinated so that there will be just the one purchase deed direct from the vendor to P2. P1 will only be able to supply P2 with office copies showing the vendor as the registered proprietor. If P1 also supplies P2 with an authority to inspect from the vendor, P2 can still make a search based on these office copies, but the contract between the vendor and P1 would also have to be abstracted. In such a situation P1 would have to ensure that in his contract with the vendor there was a provision allowing him a further authority to inspect for P2. The Law Society Conditions provide that

8 Ibid, rr. 2(1), 5.
9 Ibid, r. 2(3).

the vendor must provide the purchaser with additional authorities to inspect for any sub-purchasers or prospective mortgagees.[10]

ii Search in the Companies Register

In accordance with the basic principles of registration of title, charges created by a company for securing money would have to be noted in some way on the register of title if a purchaser for value is to be bound. There is no need therefore to search the Companies Register to discover pre-1970 charges or floating charges, as there is in the case of unregistered land. Similarly there would seem to be no other need for a search of the Companies Register as the purchaser will be able to rely on the guaranteed accuracy of the register of title showing a company as registered proprietor. However, the register may be subject to rectification, and so it may be thought advisable to do a search to discover the existence of, for example, winding-up proceedings or whether the company has been struck off the Register.

iii Inspection of the property

This is of obvious importance in relation to registered land. A purchaser takes subject to overriding interests whether he knows of them or not and one category of overriding interest is the rights of a person in possession or in receipt of rents or profits. We have already seen the consequence of this, particularly in the case of a spouse or other occupier with an equitable interest in the property. The purchaser would take subject to the spouse's equitable interest which would constitute not only a financial burden on the property but also give the spouse a right to possession. As in the case of unregistered land, the purchaser's solicitor should arrange for an inspection of the property. There is no requirement that the occupation must be discoverable on reasonable inspection and we have already considered the extreme difficulties involved in making such an inspection. Again, the purchaser cannot rely on the vendor's reply to a requisition asking whether there is anyone in occupation and if so what their rights are, because if the vendor fails to disclose the information the purchaser will still be bound. However, there is one significant difference from the position as it applies to unregistered land. The time at which one must assess whether a person with an interest in the property is in possession and therefore has an overriding interest which will bind the purchaser is the time of the purchaser's subsequent application for registration of his purchase.[11] However if the property is vacant at completion it is reasonable to assume that it will be vacant, in the sense of not being occupied by the vendor's spouse or whoever, at the time of the purchaser's subsequent registration. Thus the problems are avoided if the property is vacant on completion, a matter considered further in chapter 14, section 3ii.

If an investigation should reveal someone who may have an equitable interest, then if enquiry is made of that person and the interest is not revealed, there will be no overriding interest. Otherwise, the purchaser's course of action will be the same as if the land were unregistered, discussed at section iii above.

10 LSC 12(1) (b) (ii), but cf LSC 17(6).

11 *Re Boyle's Claim* [1961] 1 All ER 620, [1961] 1 WLR 339.

iv Search in the Local Land Charges Register

The comments made above in section iv apply equally here.

v Search in the Central Land Charges Register

If the purchaser is buying an absolute freehold or an absolute leasehold title then there will be no need to do a search in the Central Land Charges Register. If the title he is buying is less than absolute then he may need to do a search in respect of that part of the title on which the register is not conclusive. For example if the purchaser is buying a good leasehold title, the superior freehold title being unregistered, then if the freehold title is deduced to him he will wish to do land charges searches in respect of it as part of the process of investigating that title. For the same reason there may be a need to do a search at the Companies Register if the freehold abstract reveals that the freehold has been owned by a company.

Whether the freehold title is deduced depends on whether the purchaser has been able to negotiate for the inclusion of an appropriate condition in the contract; under open contract rules superior title need not be deduced. As we have seen earlier the purchaser would be well advised to try and have such a condition included in the contract.

3 Searches made by the solicitor for a prospective mortgagee

These are discussed in chapter 13, below.

12 Drafting the deed

1 Introduction

It is the purchaser's solicitor's task to draft the purchase deed. With a few exceptions, a deed is needed to transfer a legal estate[1] – one of the exceptions is an assent by personal representatives. We shall consider in this chapter three basic forms of deed; the conveyance, used for unregistered freehold land; the assignment, used for unregistered leasehold land; and the transfer, used for registered land, leasehold or freehold. We shall not discuss here the form and contents of a lease or underlease; a discussion of the contents of a lease or underlease raises substantive questions of law, concerning the respective obligations of the parties, which are rather different to those questions raised by the contents of a conveyance, assignment or transfer. The contents of a lease or underlease will therefore be discussed in a subsequent chapter, which will also reiterate the conveyancing procedure as it applies to the grant of a lease or underlease.[2]

Let us assume that the purchaser's solicitor has already examined the title and satisfied himself that the vendor can convey what he has contracted to. This means that the investigation of title, including the searches, has not revealed any defect in title. The contents of the deed will thus reflect the contract, and those matters, if any, which did not need to be disclosed in the contract.[3] If on the other hand the investigation of title does reveal some undisclosed defect of title, such as a restrictive covenant, the purchaser has certain remedies against the vendor. If the purchaser does not rescind but completion does eventually take place, the deed will necessarily refer to the covenant as clearly the vendor can only convey the property subject to it.

The deed, particularly in the case of unregistered land, may be fairly lengthy as the land must be fully described and the interests such as easements and covenants of which it either has the benefit or subject to which it is held must also be mentioned. A transfer of registered land can be much shorter as it can

1 Law of Property Act 1925, s. 52(1).

2 See ch 17, below.

3 It will be remembered that under an open contract the vendor need not disclose patent defects in title or defects in title of which the purchaser is aware; see ch 5, above.

refer quite simply to the entries in the register; it is only the property comprised in the register that the vendor can sell! There is a temptation for the purchaser's solicitor when drafting a conveyance or assignment to merely repeat the most recent conveyance or assignment in the abstract, changing matters such as the names of the parties and the consideration. This temptation is to be resisted. The previous deed may have been incorrectly drafted, as the solicitor may have discovered on his investigation of title. Also, the contract may impose some new obligations on the parties which must be incorporated in the conveyance or assignment. The preferable procedure is for the purchaser's solicitor to work from the contract when drafting the deed but of course he may then find that reference is made in the contract to earlier deeds for the exact wording of the description of the land and covenants and easements affecting it. Indeed, the new conveyance or assignment itself may follow this same practice; it will certainly shorten the deed although it may not be appropriate in every case. The purchaser's solicitor will often also use a standard precedent, either of his own or obtained from a book of precedents, to guide him on the form and wording of the deed. There is also obviously scope for using a word-processor when drafting the deed. There are a number of different forms the deed could take, but the overriding consideration is that the deed must be precise and accurate in all respects.

2 The conveyance

i Commencement

The opening words are normally 'This Conveyance is made the day of 19 between ....' followed by the names of the parties. The date would not of course be inserted at this stage; this is normally done on completion. In fact the effective date of a deed is the date it is delivered, which as we shall see may be before the date of completion. However the date stated in the deed is presumed to be correct until the contrary is shown.

ii Parties

Who will the parties to the deed be? Obviously the vendor and the purchaser. If the vendors are trustees for sale or personal representatives then they must all be parties to the deed. If the purchase money is to be paid to someone other than the vendor then that person should join in the deed in order to give a receipt for the purchase money. The obvious example is on a sale by the tenant for life of settled land where all the trustees (being at least two in number) would join in the deed to give a receipt and thereby over-reach the equitable interests under the settlement. Another example is where the vendor is a company which is in liquidation. The company will convey the property but the liquidator will join in as a party to give a receipt for the purchase money. If an order has been made under the Companies Act 1985, section 538, the property vests in the liquidator who would also convey the property and the company need not be a party to the deed. If a vendor has become bankrupt, his trustee in bankruptcy will convey and again the vendor need not be made a party. There will be other situations in which another party joins in the deed, to release the property from some interest or to vest some interest in the purchaser. So where property is held under a mortgage and part of it is to be sold, the mortgage may not be discharged but instead the mortgagee may agree to join in the deed to release the property sold from the mortgage. Similarly, on a divorce or separation property previously held in the spouses' joint names may be conveyed into one spouse's sole name; if the property is mortgaged to a Building Society, it may join in to release the conveying party from his or her obligations under the mortgage. A person with an equitable interest in the property being sold may join in to convey his interest to the purchaser, although normally this would not happen because a sale by the trustees would over-reach the equitable interest.

On a sub-sale, where the vendor has sold to the purchaser (P1) who has resold to the sub-purchaser (P2), the deed may be directly from the vendor to P2. However, there are a number of reasons why P1 might also join in the deed. Firstly if the resale was at a higher price than the initial sale he would join in to give a receipt for the balance paid to him. Secondly the effect of him joining in the deed would be to convey his equitable interest to P2, although this would not seem to be necessary. Thirdly he can give implied covenants for title to P2.[4] The Law Society Conditions do contain a restriction on the power of the purchaser to sub-sell, as the vendor can on reasonable grounds decline to convey the property to any person other than his purchaser.[5] This leaves room for argument about whether the vendor's grounds are reasonable or not.

The purchaser's solicitor should also check with his client who is to take the conveyance ie who the purchaser(s) is to be. It may be that all the solicitor's instructions have come from one spouse and the contract is in the name of that spouse but that the property is in fact to be conveyed to the spouses jointly. If so, the solicitor will also need to know whether the property is to be held by them as beneficial joint tenants or beneficial tenants or beneficial tenants in common. If on the other hand one spouse wants the property to be conveyed into his or her sole name, the solicitor should perhaps warn him or her that this does not mean that he or she can do as he or she pleases with the property; the other spouse would have a statutory right of occupation under the Matrimonial Homes Act 1983[6] and may well have an equitable interest in the property as a result of contributing to the purchase price.

As well as the names of the parties, their addresses must also be given to further identify them. In days gone by their occupations were also given but there would now seem little point in this unless perhaps there are two people with the same name living at the same address. The addresses given are those at the time of execution of the deed and so the vendor's address will commonly be the address of the property, unless the purchasers have taken possession before completion. For a company, the address of its registered office would be given.

By way of illustration, a typical conveyance between two vendors as joint

4 The conveyance may state that the vendor conveys to P2 by the direction of P1. If P1 is described as a beneficial owner he then impliedly gives the appropriate covenants for title to P2.

5 LSC 17(6).

6 If it is to be the matrimonial home.

owners and the purchaser might read as follows: 'Between David Jones and Angela Jones both of 5 Meadow Lane Derby in the County of Derbyshire (hereinafter called the vendors) of the one part and John French of 10 Arkwright Street Worksop in the County of Nottinghamshire (hereinafter called the purchaser) of the other part'. This could be shortened to '(1) the vendors David Jones and Angela Jones both of 5 Meadow Lane Derby Derbyshire and (2) the purchaser John French of 10 Arkwright Street Worksop Nottinghamshire'.

If there were another party to the deed, for example a Building Society joining in to release property from a mortgage, the parties would be the vendor of the first part, the Building Society of the second part and the purchaser of the third part.

Traditionally punctuation is not used in deeds. The theory is that if punctuation was used it would be simple to alter it fraudulently and thereby change the meaning of the deed. The sense of the deed must be made clear without the use of punctuation. Unfortunately practice does not always accord with theory and one can encounter very long and apparently incomprehensible sentences. In the case of the parties, if there are three or more people who together form one party – for example four trustees for sale – it could be difficult at first sight to tell how many there are. For example if the vendors are described as 'Dylan Richard Thomas David Herbert Lawrence and Henry James' it would be difficult to tell whether there were three or four vendors unless commas were inserted after their names. One would look at the execution at the end of the deed to discover how many there were.

iii Recitals

The recitals are the introductory part of the conveyance which precedes the main operative part. As such, they are normally not essential and in more modern and shorter forms of conveyance they may be left out altogether. If they are used then they have three main consequences. Firstly a recital in a deed 20 years old is sufficient evidence of the truth of what is recited.[7] So if the death of a joint tenant is recited in a conveyance over 20 years old which is included in an abstract of title, this is sufficient proof of the death for the purchaser in the absence of any evidence to the contrary. Secondly, a party to a conveyance may be estopped from denying the accuracy of a statement in the recitals. An illustration of this is provided by the case of *Cumberland Court (Brighton) Ltd v Taylor*[8] where there was a recital that the vendor owned the property free from encumbrances; he was thereby estopped from setting up a mortgage which had not in fact been discharged but had been transferred to him because it was paid off after the date of the conveyance. The estoppel operates against the party making the statement and his successors in title in favour of the other party and his successors in title. Thirdly, a clear unambiguous recital may be used to assist in the interpretation of an ambiguity in the actual operative part of the deed. However even if recitals are used, it is unlikely nowadays that they would contain anything which could be of such assistance.

7 Law of Property Act 1925, s. 45(6).
8 [1964] Ch 29, [1963] 2 All ER 536.

The function of recitals is really twofold; to explain how the vendor came to own the property sold and to state that he does indeed own it, and to explain the reason for this particular conveyance. The first sort of recital in its simplest traditional form would read:

> The vendor is seised of the property hereinafter described for an estate in fee simple in possession free from encumbances save as hereinafter mentioned.

It is largely a matter of the purchaser's solicitor's personal preference as to how much detail is included. If the sale is by the survivor of two joint tenants there could be a recital of the conveyance to the joint tenants followed by a recital of the death of one of them. If the sale is by a personal representative then there may be a recital that the deceased was seised of the property at the date of his death, a recital of the death and the grant of probate to the vendor. If one of two beneficial tenants in common has died, a subsequent conveyance might recite the conveyance to the tenants in common, the death, and the appointment of another trustee. None of this is essential but it does explain the background to the conveyance and can be useful to a future purchaser looking through the title. As to the second sort of recital, explaining the reason for the conveyance, this will normally be because the vendor has just agreed to sell the property to the purchaser. A standard recital would read:

> The vendor has agreed with the purchaser for the sale to him of the said property for a like estate at the price of.........

If there was some other party joining in the deed, for example a mortgagee releasing the property from a mortgage of that and other property, this could also be explained in the recitals. It may be that the conveyance is resulting not from a contract for sale but from a compulsory purchase order or from an agreement to exchange land in order to settle a boundary dispute between neighbours. Again this can be explained in a recital.

It is thus largely a matter of personal choice for the purchaser's solicitor whether to include recitals and if so in what form. The one potential disadvantage of a recital is that it will give a future purchaser notice of what is recited if the conveyance forms part of a future abstract of title. This can have inconvenient results as is shown by the cases of *Re Duce and Boots Cash Chemists (Southern) Ltd's Contract*[9] and *MEPC Ltd v Christian-Edwards*.[10] There are however two situations in which a recital will normally be essential. On the sale by the survivor of beneficial joint tenants we have already seen that for the protection of the purchaser the vendor should make a statement that he is solely and beneficially entitled.[11] Similarly on a sale by personal representatives they should make a statement that they have not made any previous assent or conveyance in respect of the property now sold.[12] These statements are normally made in the recitals to the conveyance. If there are no recitals as such the statements will still have to be included in the conveyance.

9 [1937] Ch 642, [1937] 3 All ER 788.

10 [1981] AC 205, [1979] 3 All ER 752, HL.

11 Law of Property (Joint Tenants) Act 1964.

12 Administration of Estates Act 1925, s. 36(6).

After the recitals comes the operative part to the deed introduced by the testatum.

iv Testatum

This merely says 'Now this deed witnesseth as follows'. In a modern form of deed where there are no recitals the testatum can be dispensed with.

v Consideration and receipt clause

The operative part of the conveyance normally begins with a statement of the consideration and the vendor's receipt of it. In the traditional conveyance this is the beginning of a long first clause which will go on to deal with the conveyance of the property and its description. Typically this would read 'In consideration of the sum of   thousand pounds (£   ) paid by the purchasers (the receipt whereof the vendor hereby acknowledges) the vendor hereby conveys ....'. In a more modern form of conveyance the consideration and receipt clause can be separated from this long first clause; the more the deed can be broken up in this way the easier it is to read.

The Stamp Act 1891, section 5 provides that any consideration must be stated. On the other hand the receipt clause is not essential but there are three reasons why it is invariably included. Firstly by the Law of Property Act 1925, section 67, it is a sufficient discharge to the purchaser and no further receipt is necessary. This is quite important if the money is paid to trustees for sale or the trustees of a Settled Land Act settlement because it is only if the money is paid to the trustees that the equitable interests are over-reached. In the latter case the receipt clause would state that the money had been paid to the trustees rather than the vendor tenant for life. Secondly by the Law of Property Act 1925, section 68, the receipt will be sufficient evidence of payment in favour of a subsequent purchaser without notice that payment was not in fact made. If the purchase money or part of it *is* unpaid, the vendor, who has a lien over the property in respect of the unpaid money, should either retain the deeds or register the lien as a Ciii land charge in order to protect it against a subsequent purchaser. Thirdly, by the Law of Property Act 1925, section 69, the inclusion of the receipt clause in the conveyance is a sufficient authority to the purchaser to pay the money to the vendor's solicitor rather than to the vendor personally.

vi The operative words and statement of the vendor's capacity

1 *Operative words* The crucial part of the conveyance is the phrase that states that the legal estate in the property is passing from the vendor to the purchaser. In the traditional form of conveyance this will follow the consideration and receipt in the first clause. In a more modern conveyance it will be included in a second clause, after the consideration and receipt clause. The usual wording is 'the vendor hereby conveys' but any words showing the vendor's intention to pass the legal estate to the purchaser will suffice.

2 *Statement of the vendor's capacity* It was mentioned in chapter 5 that the vendor conveying and being expressed to convey in a certain capacity will mean that certain covenants for title by the vendor will be implied into the conveyance. The nature and extent of these covenants are dealt with in chapter

16, but there are only certain expressed capacities which have this effect. As mentioned in chapter 5, they are beneficial owner, trustee, settlor, personal representative, mortgagee and under an order of the court. So if the vendor was a beneficial owner, the clause would read 'the vendor as beneficial owner hereby conveys ....'.

vii Parcels clause

1 *Introduction* Having stated that the vendor is conveying, the conveyance must next state *what* the vendor is conveying, by describing the property. This part of the conveyance is often called the parcels clause and it will follow immediately after the operative words; alternatively the description could be given in a schedule at the end of the deed, referred to in the body of the deed.

2 *Physical Description* The parcels clause is a physical description of the property sold. The legal description of the estate in that property (in the case of a conveyance, the freehold) comes later in the habendum. The physical description must be clear, complete and accurate. Assuming that the investigation of title has not revealed anything untoward, the description in the particulars in the contract will be the basis of the description in the conveyance. Indeed the purchaser must accept the description in the contract for inclusion in the conveyance unless it is in some way inadequate. The description in the contract may well be identical with the description in the previous conveyances of the property and may or may not refer to a plan. What though, if the description in the contract is inadequate and does not accurately identify the property sold? The purchaser is entitled to a fresh description which does correctly describe the property. But is the purchaser entitled to have not only a verbal description but also a plan? The case law is somewhat contradictory but it seems that if a purely verbal description will afford a sufficient description the purchaser cannot insist on a plan;[13] otherwise he can.[14]

3 *Plan* If a plan is used it should be referred to in the verbal description. The property will normally be referred to as being either 'more particularly delineated' on the plan or else 'shown by way of identification only' on it. If the former words are used then, as the words suggest, if there should be any discrepancy between the plan and the verbal description the plan will prevail. Conversely if the plan is referred to as being for identification only, the verbal description will prevail. To use both formulae – to say that the property is more particularly delineated for the purpose of identification only on the plan – is quite meaningless,[15] but it is an expression sometimes found in conveyances. Even if a plan is expressed to be for identification only, it can still be of use; although it cannot prevail over a clear contrary verbal description it can be used to settle points which are not resolved by the verbal description because

13 *Re Sharman's Contract* [1936] Ch 755, [1936] 2 All ER 1547.
14 *Re Sansom and Narbeth's Contract* [1910] 1 Ch 741.
15 *Neilson v Poole* (1969) 20 P & CR 909.

the latter is either ambiguous or totally silent on the particular point.[16] Even if the plan is, by mistake, not referred to at all in the conveyance it could still be consulted if the verbal description was unclear provided that it was either drawn on or bound up with the conveyance.[17] A plan is normally taken as showing the boundaries at ground level only. In *Truckell v Stock*[18] the footings of the property projected beyond the boundary shown on the plan and although in any case of conflict between the verbal description and the plan would have prevailed, the Court of Appeal held that there was no conflict as the plan merely showed the boundaries at ground level and the verbal description included the footings which were of course below ground level.

Descriptions in conveyances, and in particular the use of plans, is an area where conveyancers in the past have perhaps been somewhat remiss. It is all too easy to keep repeating a description and a reference to a plan contained in a conveyance of some years ago, even though it no longer in fact represents the current position. There is for example little point in repeating in 1987 that the property sold is bounded on the East by property that in 1924 was in the possession of various named individuals, and that it is shown for identification on a fairly rough and ready sketch plan on a 1924 conveyance. Caution in abandoning old descriptions is understandable, but it does lead ultimately to sloppy and inaccurate conveyancing. It is surely far better to introduce an up to date plan whenever necessary. Indeed one of the recommendations of the Royal Commission on Legal Services in 1979 was that all conveyances should normally contain a reference to an up-to-date plan. This was underlined in the case of *Scarfe v Adams*[19]. It will be doubly important, on a sale of part only of the land comprised in the conveyance to the vendor, to have an accurate description and plan of the part which is being sold off. In *Scarfe v Adams*, the Court of Appeal made it clear that on a sale of part it was essential that the description was such that there was no room for doubt about the boundaries, and that the plan should be sufficiently large scale to do this.[20] In *Jackson v Bishop*,[1] the Court of Appeal decided that a vendor/developer owed a duty of care to purchasers to prepare a site plan that was not misleading.

Perhaps an illustration of the care which is needed in drafting the parcels clause is afforded by the case of *Eastwood v Ashton*.[2] The description was of 'all that farm called ...... Bank Hey Farm .... containing 84 acres, 3 roods and 4 perches or thereabouts, and in the occupation of (names of two tenants) all of which premises are more particularly described on the plan endorsed on these presents and are delineated and coloured red on such plan'. The question was whether a particular small piece of land was included in the property. The court rejected the first description by the name of the farm because there was in fact no longer any farm with this name; they rejected the second

16 *Wigginton v Milner Ltd v Winster Engineering Ltd* [1978] 3 All ER 436, [1978] 1 WLR 1462, CA.

17 *Leachman v L & K Richardson Ltd* [1969] 3 All ER 20, [1969] 1 WLR 1129.

18 [1957] 1 All ER 74, [1957] 1 WLR 161, CA.

19 [1981] 1 All ER 843, CA; *Spall v Owen* (1982) 44 P & CR 36.

20 Above, at 845.

1 (1979) 48 P & CR 57, CA.

2 [1915] AC 900, HL.

description, the area, because it was only expressed to be approximate; and they rejected the third description because the tenants were no longer in possession and had in fact sub-let. The only part of the description which was helpful was the plan.

4 *Rules of construction* There are a number of rules of construction which should be borne in mind when drafting the parcels clause. Firstly, if a boundary is formed by a ditch and a bank there is a presumption that the boundary runs along the side of the ditch which is further from the bank. The reasoning is apparently that the person who dug the ditch would have dug it on the extremity of his own land and thrown the earth back on to his own land to form the bank. The same rule applies to a ditch and hedge. Secondly, where land adjoins a road there is a presumption that the adjoining landowner owns the land up to the mid point of the road. The same presumption applies to a non-tidal river. Finally an obvious inaccuracy will not vitiate the description. If land in Nottinghamshire is referred to by mistake as being in Derbyshire the mistake will be ignored.

viii Rights for the benefit of the property

After the physical description, there will be a statement of the rights that will exist for the benefit of the purchaser, such as easements or the benefit of covenants. This will normally be introduced by the words 'together with'. It will include both already existing rights and new rights which the vendor is granting to the purchaser, for example on a sale of part of the vendor's land. The latter in particular depend for their inclusion on some corresponding provision in the contract; the purchaser cannot have a right of way granted to him in a conveyance unless the contract gives him that right. However, the purchaser's solicitor should bear in mind that the rule of implied grant on a sale of part contained in *Wheeldon v Burrows*[3] does apply to a contract so if the contract is silent, the purchaser may be entitled to the grant of rights in the conveyance under *Wheeldon v Burrows*. The rule also applies to a conveyance so if the conveyance in its turn is silent it will impliedly grant rights under *Wheeldon v Burrows* to the purchaser. If under the contract the rule of implied grant has been expressly excluded or restricted, the conveyance should make this clear by containing a clause also expressly excluding or restricting the implied grant.

As regards any new easements which the contract expressly provides should be granted to the purchaser, the contract should have provided for the precise scope of the easement, the land affected by the easement and the persons to have the benefit of the easement. The conveyance must do likewise to ensure that the easement is validly granted.

There is a further manner in which the conveyance can impliedly grant rights to the purchaser. The Law of Property Act 1925, section 62(1) states that

3 (1879) 12 Ch D 31, CA.

> a conveyance of land shall be deemed to include and shall by virtue of this Act operate to convey with the land all buildings, erections, fixtures, commons, hedges, ditches, fences, ways, waters, watercourses, liberties, privileges, easements, rights and advantages whatsoever, appertaining or reputed to appertain to the land or any part thereof, or, at the time of conveyance, demised, occupied, or enjoyed with, or reputed or known as part or parcel of or appurtenant to the land or any part thereof.

A fairly comprehensive list, which is wider than the *Wheeldon v Burrows* category of implied rights (and also includes quasi-easements) and is applicable to all conveyances and not just sales of part. It follows that there is strictly no need to enumerate all the rights that already exist for the benefit of the land (as opposed to newly created rights). The implication only arises in the absence of any express stipulation to the contrary and does not affect the contractual position between the parties. If the purchaser under the terms of the contract is not entitled to all the rights which would impliedly pass to him under section 62 the conveyance should contain a clause excluding or restricting the effect of section 62. For the avoidance of doubt, and to prevent the purchaser getting more than the vendor intended, the contract on a sale of part should stipulate what rights are (and are not) to be granted to the purchaser; the conveyance will then expressly include such rights and if necessary a clause excluding or restricting section 62 (and/or *Wheeldon v Burrows, supra*).

ix Exceptions and reservations

An exception is a right adversely affecting the property which is already in existence and subject to which the property is sold to the purchaser. A straightforward example would be a right of way over the property for the benefit of adjoining property, created at some time in the past. A reservation on the other hand is some new right to be created by the conveyance in favour of the vendor and subject to which the purchaser will take the property. An example would be the reservation, on a sale of part, of a right of way over the land sold for the benefit of the land retained by the vendor. Both exceptions and reservations must be disclosed by the vendor in the contract (unless of course the exceptions are apparent on inspection or already known to the purchaser). The vendor cannot in the conveyance reserve a right unless he has provided for it in the contract. As we have seen when drafting the contract, this is of particular importance on the sale of part because although there may be implied grants of easements there will be no implied reservations. As with the express grant of an easement, care must be taken that when an easement is expressly reserved it is validly created with the scope of the easement and the dominant and servient lands being identified. Again, as with the grant of an easement, the contract should have given the full wording, to be incorporated in the conveyance.

In the conveyance, the exceptions and reservations are usually stated immediately after the parcels clause and the easements existing for the benefit of the property, and before the habendum, introduced by the words 'except and reserving'. Sometimes the reservations are stated before the habendum and the exceptions listed after the habendum, together with the other matters subject to which the purchaser is taking the property such as existing covenants and declarations. The conveyance should make clear that the exceptions are already existing rights; merely repeating the wording used when the right was originally reserved may give rise to the misunderstanding that the conveyance is reserving a new right rather than simply stating that the property is subject to an already existing one. To avoid any confusion there would seem to be some merit in separating the exceptions and reservations.

x Habendum

This is the clause which follows the parcels clause and describes the estate which is conveyed to the purchaser, which in the case of a conveyance is the freehold. The normal wording is 'to hold unto the purchaser in fee simple'. In fact, the inclusion of such words is not essential in a conveyance of the freehold. The Law of Property Act 1925, section 60 states that a conveyance of freehold land without words of limitation shall pass a fee simple or other interest of the vendor or donor which he has power to convey unless a contrary intention appears from the conveyence. Although a more modern form of conveyance may omit a habendum in the form suggested above, there will normally be some indication, perhaps in the parcels clause, that the freehold is being conveyed. If there is no mention at all of the freehold estate, it appears possible that the statutory covenants for title may not be implied.[4]

xi Statement of existing encumbrances

It has already been suggested that the exceptions could be stated after the habendum. There will also be mention of other existing encumbrances and adverse interests subject to which the property is conveyed. These will have been disclosed in the contract. Existing covenants will be mentioned here. If the property is terraced, and there has in the past been a declaration in a conveyance that the common walls are party walls and jointly maintained, then this too will be mentioned here. The statement of these encumbrances is often introduced by the words 'subject to'.

xii Reference to earlier conveyances

There are a number of areas where the purchaser's solicitor, in drafting the conveyance, may wish to make some reference to the contents of an earlier conveyance. The description, both in the contract and in the proposed parcels clause, may be by reference to a more lengthy description in an earlier conveyance or to a plan attached to an earlier conveyance. The statement of existing covenants, exceptions, declarations and other encumbrances is almost bound to refer back to the conveyances which created those encumbrances. The reason is that if the purchaser's solicitor is to reproduce in full the wording of the description or the easement or covenant or whatever, then although this will have the advantage that earlier conveyances need not be referred to and the conveyance will be complete in itself, it will make the conveyance extremely long. If the purchaser's solicitor merely makes brief mention of the description or covenant or easement and then refers to the earlier conveyance as containing the full details, this will result in the present conveyance being much shorter but of course there is the disadvantage that the earlier conveyance must be read with the present conveyance in order for the latter to make any real sense.

4 See *May v Platt* [1900] 1 Ch 616.

Perhaps a compromise can be reached by the intelligent use of schedules. Instead of giving full details of the description or the existing covenants or easements in the body of the present conveyance, reference can be made to a schedule at the end of the conveyance in which the full details are set out. This avoids the need to refer back to the earlier deeds because the full wording will be incorporated in the schedule, but it will make the present conveyance rather easier to read, although it will still be quite long.

xiii Conveyance to co-owners

1 *Statement of beneficial interest* If the conveyance is to co-owners, for example a husband and wife, the purchaser's solicitor in drafting the conveyance will want to know whether they wish to take the property as beneficial joint tenants or beneficial tenants in common. The legal estate must of course be held by them as joint tenants. The purchaser's solicitor will have to explain to them the differences between the two capacities. He will explain that the survivor of beneficial joint tenants takes the whole of the property whereas on the death of a beneficial tenant in common his equitable share passes under his will or intestacy. He may also mention that it is always possible to sever a beneficial joint tenancy to form a beneficial tenancy in common. Normally spouses take as beneficial joint tenants, but if, for example, the property is being purchased by an engaged couple who intend to get married some time after the conveyance, they may wish to hold the property initially, whilst they are still unmarried, as beneficial tenants in common.

The briefest way of stating the beneficial interests is as part of the habendum, which would then read 'to hold unto the purchasers as beneficial joint tenants' or '...... as beneficial tenants in common in equal shares'. There will then be an implied statutory trust for sale.[5] The alternative is to include a clause declaring an express trust for sale. This could be in the form:

> The purchasers shall hold the property hereby coveyed upon trust to sell the same or any part thereof with power to postpone the sale and shall hold the net proceeds of sale and the net rents and profits until sale upon trust for themselves as joint tenants (or ... as tenants in common in equal shares).

The only advantage of including such an express declaration is that it does put totally beyond doubt what the equitable interests are. The entirely practical disadvantage is that the purchasers will quite logically point out that they wish to live in the property rather than sell it and the purchaser's solicitor will be left to explain an area of land law which even he may find rather unrealistic.

The need for the conveyance to state where the equitable interests do lie has been stressed in recent cases such as *Bernard v Josephs*[6] and *Walker v Hall*.[7] This is particularly important where the co-owners are not a married couple and there is therefore no power for the court to make an order transferring property on divorce. The court can simply declare what the existing interests are: if the

5 Law of Property Act 1925, ss. 34–36.
6 [1982] Ch 391, [1982] 3 All ER 162, CA.
7 [1984] FLR 126, [1984] Fam Law 21, CA.

conveyance deals expressly with them this will be conclusive, but otherwise there may need to be a lengthy and expensive action to establish the interests.[8]

If co-owners expressly hold as beneficial joint tenants, this is conclusive of their entitlement on severance as tenants in common in equal shares.[9]

2 *Extension of the powers of the trustees for sale* Joint purchasers such as spouses will as we have seen be trustees for sale, and a secondary question is whether their powers as trustees should be extended in the conveyance. Powers of trustees for sale under the Law of Property Act 1925, section 28 are all the powers of the tenant for life and trustees of settled land. These powers are not all-embracing. Although they do include a power of sale, there is no power for the trustees to give the property away; indeed this would offend the fundamental principles of a trust. The power of mortgaging is limited and does not include a power to mortgage to raise the initial purchase price. Of course if the trustees are also the persons who hold the whole of the legal estate and the equitable interests in the property – as almost inevitably joint purchasers will – then they are in fact beneficial owners, simply because they do hold the whole of the legal estate and the equitable interests. They can therefore deal with the property as beneficial owners, the restriction on their powers as trustees being immaterial. However, there may be circumstances where the trustees are not beneficial owners. If one of two beneficial tenants in common died and the new trustee who was appointed was not the person who took the deceased's share under his will or intestacy, the trustees would not own the whole of the equitable interests and would have to deal with the property as trustees.

It is common to include in the conveyance an extension of the trustees' powers to include all the powers of an absolute owner. A typical clause would read:

> The purchasers or other trustees for the time being of this deed shall have power to sell mortgage charge lease or otherwise dispose of all or any part of the property hereby conveyed with all the powers in that behalf of an absolute owner.

It is doubtful whether since the Perpetuities and Accumulations Act 1964 there is any need to restrict the extension of the powers to the perpetuity period. To be absolutely safe, there is no harm in adding at the commencement of the clause extending the powers 'until the expiration of the period of 80 years from the date hereof'.

xiv Imposition of new covenants

Particularly on the sale of part of land the vendor owns, the conveyance may contain new covenants entered into by the purchaser and possibly by the vendor. Again these will have been provided for in the contract where the full wording of the proposed covenants should appear. In chapter 5 the rules governing the enforceability of covenants and the running of the benefit and the burden were considered; these will influence the language of the covenant. The proper place for consideration of this is at the time of drafting and

8 See for example *Grant v Edwards* [1986] Ch 638, [1986] 2 All ER 426, CA, where the property was (effectively) in the sole name of one of two cohabitees.

9 *Goodman v Gallant* [1986] Fam 106, [1986] 1 All ER 311, CA.

approving the contract, when the wording of the covenant is settled. In particular, care should be taken over the wording of the covenant in relation to the annexation of the benefit of the covenant to the whole of the land retained by the vendor, and to the continuing liability of the covenantor even after he has disposed of the land affected by the covenant if there is to be a chain of indemnity covenants in the future.

One situation in which there will inevitably be a large number of new covenants will be on the sale of a new house on a building estate. They may well be separated off into a schedule at the end of the conveyance. In drafting these covenants consideration should have been given at the contract stage to the special position of a building estate under *Elliston v Reacher*[10] and the potential mutual enforceability of the covenants.

xv Indemnity covenants

The vendor may remain liable on a covenant even after he has parted with the property which is subject to the covenant. This would be the case if he was the original covenantor and on the wording of the original covenant, he did remain so liable. Of course after he has parted with the property he has no control over whether the covenant is observed or not and will therefore want an indemnity, in respect of his continuing liability for a breach of the covenant, to be given by the purchaser. The indemnity is in the form of an indemnity covenant by the purchaser and is only necessary if the vendor does remain liable on the original covenant after he has sold the property. The purchaser, and subsequent purchasers, will also take an indemnity covenant when they in turn sell the property and as a result a chain of indemnity covenants will be built up. The present vendor, if he gave an indemnity covenant when he bought, will require in turn an indemnity covenant to be given by the purchaser, to indemnify him against his continuing liability under the indemnity covenant.

Even under an open contract, if the vendor will remain liable after the conveyance, he can require the purchaser to give an indemnity covenant in the conveyance to indemnify the vendor against the conveyances of a breach of the covenant.[11] A typical indemnity covenant would read as follows:

> With the object of affording the vendor a full and sufficient indemnity in respect of the said covenants but not further or otherwise, the purchaser hereby covenants with the vendor that he will at all times hereafter perform and observe the said covenants and keep the vendor indemnified against all actions, claims, demands and liability in respect thereof so far as the same affect the property hereby conveyed and are still subsisting and capable of being enforced.

If there are joint purchasers the indemnity covenant will be given by them jointly and severally. The Law Society Conditions specifically provide that the purchaser must give the vendor an indemnity covenant if the vendor will remain liable after the conveyance on any 'covenant stipulation, provision or other matter' subject to which the property is sold.[12] The corresponding

10 [1908] 2 Ch 665, CA.
11 *Re Poole and Clarke's Contract* [1904] 2 Ch 173, CA.
12 LSC 17(4).

provision in the National Conditions additionally provides for the purchaser to covenant to perform and observe the existing covenants as well as giving an indemnity.[13] Under this sort of covenant the vendor might be able to obtain an injunction restraining the purchaser from breaching the original covenants.

It must be emphasised that if the original covenant does not impose liability on the covenantor after he has disposed of the property, but limits his liability to his period of ownership, there is no need for any indemnity covenant.

xvi Acknowledgment and undertaking

1 *Terms of acknowledgment and undertaking* On completion the purchaser may not be receiving the title deeds, or at least not all of them. The most likely reason for this is that the deeds relate to other land which the vendor is retaining.

The Law of Property Act 1925, section 45(9) provides that the vendor is entitled to keep documents of title which relate to any part of land which the vendor is retaining, or which are subsisting trust instruments, or which relate to the appointment or discharge of trustees of an existing trust. Thus a personal representative will retain the grant of probate or administration, which will be needed for other purposes in the future. It has been held that a vendor is entitled to keep a deed which shows the extinguishment of a right of way over land retained by him,[14] but not a mortgage of both the land sold and a life policy, as the latter is not 'land' within the meaning of section 45(9).[15]

A purchaser, though, will need to be able to produce the original deeds if he ever needs to prove his title. All that he will have in his actual possession will be the abstract of title which was examined against the originals when it was verified. He will want, in the conveyance, an acknowledgment of his right to the production of the originals. The effect of such an acknowledgment is set out in the Law of Property Act 1925, section 64(4). It gives the purchaser a right to production of the documents of title for inspection and for the purpose of any court hearing, and the right to delivery of copies of them. Any costs involved are to be paid by the person requiring production, that is by the purchaser. It will be seen that the terms of the acknowledgment do not in fact give the purchaser the right to make copies of the documents himself, merely to have copies made and delivered by the person with possession, that is the vendor. In addition and complementary to this acknowledgment, the purchaser may want an undertaking that the retained documents of title will be kept safe. The terms of such an undertaking are contained in the Law of Property Act 1925, sections 64(9) and (10). The person with custody of the documents must keep them 'safe, whole, uncancelled and undefaced unless prevented from so doing by fire or other inevitable accident'. If the deeds are lost or damaged, the purchaser will be entitled to damages from the person with custody of them for a breach of the undertaking.

13 NC 19(6).
14 *Re Lehmann and Walker's Contract* [1906] 2 Ch 640.
15 *Re Williams and Duchess of Newcastle's Contract* [1897] 2 Ch 144.

2 *The purchaser's entitlement* The purchaser will want an acknowledgment and undertaking in every case where deeds are retained. Will he get this? Under an open contract, the purchaser is entitled to the statutory acknowledgment and undertaking in respect of documents he is not to receive. This will extend not only to previous conveyances, mortgages etc. but also to grants of probate and administration, although not to such documents as old search certificates since these are not documents of title. Nor apparently will it extend to pre-root documents of title even though in normal circumstances the vendor would be under a duty to hand them over on completion. Neither the Law Society nor the National Conditions make any alterations to this basic principle.

There are further complications for the purchaser. Firstly, the statutory acknowledgment (and undertaking) must be given 'to another'. Where a personal representative assents to the vesting of property in himself, he cannot give an acknowledgment in the assent. A subsequent purchaser from him should try and obtain an acknowledgment in the conveyance. Secondly, the acknowledgment (and undertaking) must be given by the person with possession of the documents. If the vendor's property is in mortgage, and the mortgage is not being discharged but the property sold, being part of the mortgaged property, is being released from the mortgage, the person with possession of the documents is the mortgagee. He is therefore the proper person to give the acknowledgment. The Law Society Conditions do provide specifically that the vendor will procure an acknowledgment from the mortgagee.[16] The purchaser is not necessarily prejudiced if he fails to obtain an acknowledgment as it appears that a person does have an equitable right to production of the documents necessary to prove his title.

A third complication for the purchaser is that it is usual for fiduciary owners (that is mortgagees personal representatives and trustees) to give only the acknowledgment for production and not the undertaking for safe custody. There seems little authority for this rule but in practice it is well established. The position is slightly improved for a purchaser under the Law Society Conditions, for they provide that where the documents of title are retained by the vendor's mortgagee in the situation described in the previous paragraph, then unless the vendor holds the property in a fiduciary capacity himself, he will covenant to give an undertaking for safe custody (at the purchaser's expense) as and when he does receive the documents of title back from the mortgagee.[17]

3 *Running of the benefit and the burden of the acknowledgment and undertaking* The acknowledgment and undertaking are enforceable by the purchaser and his successors in title (excluding lessees), whether they hold the whole or part of the land. The burden runs with the deeds and thus the person with the custody of the deeds for the time being is bound.

4 *Form* The normal wording of the acknowledgment and undertaking is as follows:

16 LSC 17(5).
17 LSC 17(5).

> The vendor hereby acknowledges the right of the purchaser to production of the documents specified in the schedule hereto (the possession of which is retained by the vendor) and to delivery of copies thereof and hereby undertakes with the purchaser for the safe custody thereof.

xvii Certificate of value

Conveyances on sale bear ad valorem stamp duty. This will be examined in more detail in chapter 15, but it means that the duty payable is proportionate to the value of the property, which in the case of a sale is the purchase price. The basic rate of duty is 1 per cent but there is exemption if the consideration does not exceed £30,000 and if a certificate of value is included in the conveyance. It is the last clause in the conveyance and reads as follows:

> It is hereby certified that the transaction hereby effected does not form part of a larger transaction or of a series of transactions in which the amount or value or the aggregate amount or value of the consideration exceeds £30,000.

Stamp duty is not payable on chattels. Any chattels which are sold with the property should not be made the subject of the conveyance but should be allowed to pass in the normal way by delivery. The consideration stated in the conveyance should be the consideration for the property alone without the chattels. This may result in some saving of stamp duty, particularly if the aggregate price of the property and the chattels is just above the £30,000 limit, and the price of the property alone just below the limit. Any such apportionment of the price between the property and the chattels should be stated in the contract and should be absolutely genuine otherwise it would amount to a fraud on the Inland Revenue to whom stamp duty is payable.

xviii Testimonium

This is the clause which introduces the execution by the parties. For a deed to be executed by individuals, the clause will normally read:

> In witness whereof the parties hereto have hereunto set their hands and seals the day and year first hereinbefore written.

If one of the parties is executing the conveyance under a power of attorney then mention of this will be incorporated into the testimonium. If the conveyance is to be executed by a corporation, the testimonium will refer to the corporation having 'caused its common seal to be hereto affixed'. In a shorter more modern form of conveyance the testimonium is sometimes omitted altogether.

xix Schedules

If there are to be any schedules to the conveyance, referred to in the body of the conveyance, these are incorporated after the testimonium but before the execution and attestation. Matters commonly included in schedules are a description of the property, rights of which it has the benefit and to which it is subject, covenants, and lists of documents in respect of which an acknowledgment and undertaking have been given.

xx Execution and attestation

The last part of the deed will be the execution by the parties; signing and sealing in the case of an individual. It is standard practice for the signature to be witnessed (or 'attested'), with the witness adding his or her name and address. However the lack of such attestation does not affect the validity of the execution. In practice the execution and attestation will appear as follows:

Signed sealed and delivered by the said .... in the presence of:	(Signature of party) (Seal)
(signature and address of witness)	

There will be a similar clause for each executing party. If a party is executing under a power of attorney this may be referred to in the attestation clause. A corporation will execute a deed by having its common seal affixed, normally in the presence of a director and secretary who will also add their signatures. The actual manner of execution, both by an individual and by a corporation, will be dealt with in detail in chapter 14, below.

xxi The conveyance and the contract

It will be obvious that there are many similarities between the contents of the contract and the conveyance. Indeed, this is to be expected as the contract contains the agreement to buy and sell the property on certain conditions and the conveyance puts this into effect, actually transferring the property. So whereas in the contract there is a description in the particulars, there is a parcels clause in the conveyance. Both will contain details of existing easements and covenants both for the benefit of the property and subject to which it is held. The contract will also contain details of any new easements and covenants to be incorporated in the conveyance.

3 Assignment of lease

The form and much of the contents of the assignment of a lease are the same as in the conveyance of the freehold dealt with in the previous section. The differences between the two are mentioned below.

i Commencement

Obviously the opening words will be 'The assignment is made ....'.

ii Parties

See section 2 ii, above.

iii Recitals

The function and effect of recitals have been discussed at section 2 iii, above. In respect of the brief statement of the vendor's title there will be a difference from the conveyance. There would normally be a recital dealing with the grant of the lease and, as this is the first time that the lease will have been mentioned in the assignment, this will include the date of the lease, the parties, the term, the rent and a description of the property comprised in the lease, the latter probably by reference either to the lease or to a schedule. The recitals will then show how the present vendor came to own the leasehold estate. If he is the assignee from the original lessee then that assignment can be recited. If not, then the following recital is often used.

> By virtue of divers mesne assignments acts and events and ultimately by (the assignment to the vendor can then be recited) the said property became and is now vested in the vendor for all the unexpired residue of the said term subject to the rent reserved by and the performance and observance of the covenants on the part of the lessee and the conditions contained in the lease but otherwise free from encumbrances.

The initial phrase of this clause is rather over-blown and could perhaps be omitted. If the assignment is of an underlease then the grant of the headlease (if known) could be recited as well as the grant of the underlease and the assignment of the underlease to the vendor. None of these recitals is of course absolutely essential. Other recitals, for example on a sale by personal representatives, would be included as mentioned in section 2 iii above. If a licence to assign in respect of the present assignment was necessary then this also can be recited.

iv Testatum

See section 2 iv, above.

v Consideration and receipt clause

See section 2 v, above.

vi Operative words and statement of vendor's capacity

The operative words of an assignment are 'the vendor assigns'. Covenants for title are implied by the use of the various expressions mentioned at section 2 vi, above. As will be seen in chapter 16, extra covenants for title are implied on a sale of leasehold land, in addition to those implied on a sale of freehold land.[18]

vii Parcels clause

In a way the question of a description of the property which is being sold is less of a problem in an assignment than in a conveyance. This is because the property that the vendor owns is that comprised in the lease and the property will of course be described in the lease. Usually all that is necessary is either reference to the description in the lease or to a schedule to the assignment where that description can be reproduced. There may of course have been changes since the grant of the lease – for example if the lease is of a plot of land on which a house has now been built – and the description will then need to be brought up to date.

If the assignment is of only part of the property comprised in the lease then

18 It may be necessary to modify the implied covenants for title to ensure that the vendor is not impliedly covenanting that the property is in a good state of repair – see ch 16, section 4 i.

the comments made at section 2 vii, above apply equally here and a plan will probably be necessary.

viii Rights for the benefit of the property

The lease will normally have included the grant of rights for the benefit of the property. Again, reference can be made to the lease or to a schedule to the assignment setting out these rights. If the property being sold is only part of the property comprised in the lease, ie there has been an assignment of part *in the past*, then there may be further rights granted in the assignment by which the part was sold off. If, on the other hand, the vendor is *now* assigning part of the property comprised in the lease, the question of new rights to be granted in favour of the part sold off will have been considered at the contract stage and the wording of the assignment will follow that of the appropriate contractual provision. The rule in *Wheeldon v Burrows*[19] applies to a contract for sale of leasehold property and an assignment in the same way that it applies to freehold land.

ix Exceptions and reservations

The rights adversely affecting the property will again be found in the lease or in an assignment of part if this has occurred. If the present assignment is an assignment of part then any new reservations will be dealt with in the contract and will then be incorporated in the assignment.

x Habendum

As the estate being sold is leasehold, the habendum will read 'to hold unto the purchaser for all the residue now unexpired of the term created by the lease'.

xi Statement of existing encumbrances

The lease will impose an obligation to pay rent, to perform covenants and possibly to comply with other conditions. After the habendum there will normally be a clause such as 'subject henceforth to the payment of the rent reserved by and the performance and observance of the covenants on the part of the lessee and the conditions contained in the lease'. If there has been an assignment in the past of part on which fresh covenants have been imposed then these will be mentioned too.

xii Assignment to co-owners

See section 2 xiii, above.

xiii Imposition of new covenants

On an assignment of part of the property comprised in the lease the vendor may wish to impose new covenants, in just the same way as he may wish to do so on a sale of part of freehold land. There should be a provision in the contract stating what new covenants will be imposed. Not being covenants between lessor and lessee, they will need to be registered as Dii land charges to be enforceable against future purchasers.

19 (1879) 12 Ch D 31, CA.

xiv Indemnity covenants

The Law of Property Act 1925, section 77(1)(c) provides that on an assignment for valuable consideration of a lease, the assignee impliedly covenants that in the future he will pay the rent and perform and observe all the covenants (positive or restrictive) and other conditions in the lease. He also covenants to indemnify the vendor in respect of non-payment of rent or breach of any of the covenants or conditions. This is different from the position under a conveyance of the freehold where although the right to an indemnity covenant may be implied in the contract an express covenant must still be inserted in the conveyance. Section 77(1)(d) of the Act contains a similar provision in relation to the assignment for value of part of the property comprised in the lease.[20] The assignee impliedly covenants to pay an apportioned rent and to observe and perform the covenants in the lease so far as they affect his part; he also gives a covenant for indemnity. The vendor, who is retaining part, also gives an implied covenant to pay the balance of the rent, to observe and perform the covenants and conditions and for indemnity. However this covenant is only implied if the vendor assigns and is expressed to assign as beneficial owner; in that respect it is similar to a covenant for a title.

The assignee may of course be directly liable to the lessor for breach of covenant. Provided the covenants touch and concern the land the burden of them will run with the leasehold interest under the doctrine of privity of estate.

xv Acknowledgment and undertaking, Certificate of value, Testimonium, Schedules, Execution and attestation

See sections 2 xvi–xx, above.

4 Transfer of registered land

The deed necessary on the sale of land title to which is registered, freehold or leasehold, is called a transfer. Its form is prescribed by the Land Registration Rules 1925; it is form 19 in the Schedule to the Rules for a transfer of the whole of the land comprised in a title and form 20 for a transfer of part.

i Heading

The form is headed by a statement of the county and district in which the property is situated; the title number; and a brief description of the property, normally just the postal address. All this will be apparent from the office copy entries. There is then a space for the date. On the printed forms available from law stationers there is no space for recitals and indeed the Land Registry discourages the use of recitals in transfers. There is no reason why the purchaser's solicitor should not dispense with the ready-printed form and draft his own transfer. He could include recitals but one practical problem is that the transfer does not form part of the register but is the means by which a purchaser obtains a change of the register, to show his name on the proprietorship register in place of the vendor's name. The transfer is filed away

20 This applies when the lessor's consent has not been obtained to the apportionment of the rent. If it has, there is an implied covenant under s. 77(1)(c) relating to the part assigned.

at the District Land Registry and it would then be difficult to ascertain what statements, if any, had been made in recitals unless a copy of the transfer was made and kept with the Land or Charge Certificate.

ii Consideration and receipt clause

The transfer continues: 'In consideration of pounds (£) the receipt whereof is hereby acknowledged ....'. In fact the receipt clause does not appear in the prescribed form but is invariably inserted on a transfer on sale and will appear in the standard law stationers printed form, for the reasons already explained in section 2 v, above.

iii Vendor's name, Operative words, Statement of vendor's capacity

The transfer continues: 'I/We .... as .... hereby transfer to ....'. There is space for the insertion of the vendor/registered proprietor's name and address and the capacity in which he is expressed to convey in order to imply the appropriate covenants for title by him. A printed form of transfer may already have the words 'beneficial owner' filled in and these may need to be amended or deleted. The operative word in a transfer is, logically, 'transfer'.

iv Purchaser's name

There is then a space for the insertion of the purchaser's name(s) and address. It is vital that the accurate name(s) and address is given as any error may be reproduced in the proprietorship register causing difficulties in the future.

If the transfer is to joint proprietors, for example a husband and wife, then the comments made in section 2 xiii, above are equally applicable. There must at least be a statement of the beneficial interest (eg 'as beneficial joint tenants') which would normally be included after the reference to the property being transferred. Instead of this reliance on the implied statutory trust for sale there could be an express trust for sale, and there could also be an extension of the trustee's powers. The Land Registry are really only interested in whether the survivor of joint proprietors can give a valid receipt for capital money. If the proprietors are beneficial joint tenants then the survivor can give a valid receipt and there is no need for a restriction on the register. If they are beneficial tenants in common then the survivor cannot give a valid receipt and a restriction will be entered in the proprietorship register preventing the survivor from dealing with the property; he would have to appoint another trustee. A special form 19(JP) is published which incorporates a statement as to whether the survivor can or cannot give a valid receipt, but use of this form is not compulsory.

It was mentioned in the earlier part of this chapter that on a conveyance or assignment of part of mortgaged property, then if the mortgage is not being discharged, the mortgagee may join in the deed to release the part sold from the mortgage. This procedure is inappropriate on a transfer of part of mortgaged registered land. The correct procedure is for the mortgagee to provide a form of discharge, form 53, which relates just to the part to be released from the mortgage.[1]

1 See further in ch 13, below.

v Description of property

If the sale is of the whole of the property comprised in the title, the description is simple. Having stated that the vendor is transferring to the purchasers, the form continues 'the land comprised in the title abovementioned'. If the property is leasehold, the clause will continue 'for the residue of the term granted by the registered lease'. That is all that is needed. There is no need to mention existing easements either benefitting the property nor subject to which the property is held, nor existing covenants.

If the sale is of part of the property comprised in the title then the description will probably be in three parts. Firstly there will be a reference to a plan, which will normally be a modified version of the filed plan. Secondly there will be a brief description of the property, probably just the postal address and thirdly there will be a statement that the property sold does form part of the land comprised in the title 'abovementioned'.

vi New rights, reservations and covenants

On a sale of part, the vendor may be granting or reserving easements or imposing new covenants for exactly the same reasons as on a conveyance or assignment of unregistered land. This will be particularly appropriate on the sale of new houses on a building estate which is held under a registered title. There is a small space on the printed form of transfer available from law stationers for the inclusion of such clauses, or joint ownership clauses, but if the clauses are extensive it is clearly impracticable to use the printed form and the purchaser's solicitor will prepare his own form of transfer.

The same considerations apply as have been mentioned already in relation to unregistered land. For example, the rule in *Wheeldon v Burrows*[2] and the Law of Property Act 1925, section 62 are applicable, as is the problem of enforceability of positive covenants. New restrictive covenants will be protected by the entry of a notice in the charges register of the title to the part affected.

vii Indemnity covenants

The position on the sale of freehold registered land where the vendor will remain liable on covenants is similar to the position on the sale of freehold unregistered land. The vendor will want an indemnity covenant in the transfer and as we have seen the Law Society and National Conditions give him this right. The complicating factor in the case of registered land is that the covenant is contained in the transfer which is sent to the District Land Registry on registration but which as has already been mentioned does not form part of the register. The indemnity covenant is by its very nature a positive covenant and as a rule positive covenants are not noted on the register. There is a danger that the registered proprietor who gave an indemnity covenant when he purchased may forget that he has done so and his solicitor may then fail to require an indemnity covenant when the registered proprietor himself eventually sells the property. The Land Registry have therefore adopted the practice of entering details of the indemnity covenant in the proprietorship register. The problem does not arise in the case of an indemnity covenant given on a conveyance giving rise to first registration, because it is perfectly possible for

2 (1879) 12 ChD 31, CA.

the solicitor to look back at the pre-registration deeds when the first registered proprietor comes to sell, to see that an indemnity covenant was given. In this situation there will be no mention of the covenant in the register; the solicitor for a first registered proprietor who is selling should remember to check whether an indemnity covenant is needed.

In respect of a transfer of leasehold land, ie the assignment of a registered leasehold title, there is an implied covenant by the transferee to perform the covenants in the lease and indemnify the transferor.[3] On the sale of part of the land comprised in the lease then both the transferee and the transferor give a similar implied covenant, in relation to their respective parts.[4] The covenant by the transferor is implied whether or not the transfer is for valuable consideration and whether or not he transfers as beneficial owner.

viii Acknowledgment and undertaking

Because the register is the evidence of title there is normally no need to include an acknowledgment or undertaking in respect of previous documents, certainly if the title is absolute. However an acknowledgment (and undertaking) may be desirable in some circumstances, for example on the transfer of part of leasehold property, in respect of the lease; on the transfer of part of a possessory title, in respect of any retained pre-registration documents of title; and possibly on a transfer by personal representatives who have not been registered as registered proprietors in the place of the deceased, in respect of the grant of probate or administration.[5]

ix Certificate of value

A certificate of value will be included if the consideration is £30,000 or under, the position being the same as for unregistered land.

x Testimonium

The prescribed forms of transfer contain no testimonium.

xi Execution and attestation

Execution of a transfer is the same as execution of a conveyance or an assignment. In addition, if the transfer incorporates a plan, then the plan must be signed by the transferor personally and also by the transferee or his solicitor on his behalf. A corporation would affix its common seal to the plan which would be attested by its officers in the usual way.

As the prescribed forms contain provision for attestation of the parties' signatures by a witness, it would seem that this must be done even though it is not strictly a requirement in relation to unregistered conveyancing.

3 Land Registration Act 1925, s. 24(1)(b).
4 Ibid, s. 24(2).
5 It will need to be produced on the application for registration, although the Registry will accept a certified photocopy.

5 Other deeds

i Transfer under rule 72

Rule 72 of the Land Registration Rules 1925 provides in effect that if a disposition of unregistered land will give rise to first registration, the deed can be in the form of a transfer rather than a conveyance or assignment. It would still contain the same provisions as would be found in the conveyance or assignment. Once a compulsory registration order has come into force then both conveyances on sale and assignments on sale of leases with over 21 years left to run do give rise to first registration.

ii Deed of gift

If the property is being given away rather than sold, the appropriate deed will still be a conveyance, assignment or transfer, which will be in the same form as on a sale. Care should be taken in relation to implied covenants. On an assignment of a (unregistered) lease without valuable consideration, there will be no implied indemnity covenant,[6] whereas such a covenant is implied on the transfer of a registered lease without valuable consideration.[7] Similarly there are differences in the covenants for title which the vendor impliedly gives if the transaction is not for valuable consideration. This will be considered further in chapter 16.

iii Assent

An assent is the document which a personal representative will normally use to vest the property in the beneficiary entitled to it under the will or intestacy. In the case of unregistered land, the assent will have the same broad structure as the conveyance or assignment; for registered land, the form of assent is prescribed by the Land Registration Rules 1925. The operative word is of course 'assent'. Recitals are not normally included but there would usually be an acknowledgment of the right of the assentee to production of the grant of probate or administration unless of course the personal representative is assenting to the vesting of the property in himself. Again, the question of indemnity covenants must be considered; an assent is not a dealing for valuable consideration. An assent need not be a deed, that is to say it can still take effect to transfer the legal estate if it is just signed and not sealed. A memorandum of the assent should be endorsed on the grant of probate or administration.

6 Procedure

Although it is the task of the purchaser's solicitor to draft the deed, the contract might make quite specific provision about the form and contents of the deed. This will often happen on the sale of a house on a new building estate where there may be a standard form of conveyance, assignment or transfer, containing details of new easements and covenants, which is referred to in the contract.

6 Law of Property Act 1925, s. 77(1)(c).
7 Land Registration Act 1925, s. 24(1)(b).

The appropriate time for agreeing alterations to this form is therefore before exchange of contracts.

Having drafted the deed, the purchaser's solicitor sends it, normally in duplicate, to the vendor's solicitor for approval. Once approved, the deed, as amended if necessary, will be 'engrossed' by the purchaser's solicitor, that is to say a final copy of it is prepared normally on thick, good quality paper reserved for deeds. Any new plan will be bound up with the deed. The Law Society Conditions provide that the draft deed must be delivered to the vendor's solicitor at least twelve working days before the contractual completion date and that within four working days the vendor will deliver it back approved or revised.[8] The purchaser's solicitor must then deliver the engrossment to the vendor's solicitor at least five working days before the contractual completion date.[9] The conditions specifically provide that the purchaser shall not be deemed to have waived his right to raise or maintain requisitions by delivering the draft or engrossment;[10] under an open contract an implication of acceptance of the vendor's title might possibly arise. Under the National Conditions the draft must be delivered at least six working days before the completion date and the engrossment within three working days of the return of the approved draft.[11]

8 LSC 17(1).
9 LSC 17(2).
10 LSC 17(3).
11 NC 19(3).

13 Mortgages

1 Redemption of the vendor's mortgage(s)

If the property which the vendor is selling is subject to a mortgage or mortgages then almost inevitably it will not be sold subject to the mortgages but they will be redeemed on or before completion of the sale. In practice, the proceeds of sale will be used to pay off the mortgages; the money will be paid to the mortgagees immediately after completion and the purchaser will be given, on completion, an undertaking by the vendor's solicitor that the mortgages will be so redeemed. This procedure is discussed in more detail in the next chapter. In many cases the first mortgagee, often a Building Society or a bank, will already have provided the vendor's solicitor with the deeds, or Charge Certificate in respect of registered land, on an undertaking given by the vendor's solicitors. The mortgage can then be redeemed after the completion by remitting the sum due on the mortgage to the mortgagee who will return the receipted mortgage deed (or form 53 for registered land),[1] which can then be forwarded to the purchaser's solicitor. The purchaser's solicitor will already have been given the deeds (or Charge Certificate) on completion. The same procedure is adopted in relation to any second mortgages; the money due being sent off and the receipted deed (or in the case of registered land form 53 and the further Charge Certificate if not already to hand) will be returned and then forwarded to the purchaser's solicitor. If the first mortgagee has *not* released the deeds (or Charge Certificate) to the vendor's solicitor then as the purchaser's solicitors will want to receive the deeds (or Charge Certificate) on completion, it may be necessary to complete at the office of the solicitor for the first mortgagee. Again, this procedure will be discussed in more detail in the next chapter.

The reason that not only first mortgages but also any second mortgages must be paid off and discharged is because, assuming they are protected in the appropriate way, they will be binding on the purchaser unless discharged. In addition in the case of unregistered land the first mortgagee might otherwise be failing in its duty if it released the deeds to the mortgagor (the vendor), who of course hands them on to the purchasers; if there are any second

1 See ch 10, section 13 above.

mortgages in existence then the deeds ought to be handed to the second mortgagee or if there are more than one, the one with best claim to priority.[2] In fact the first mortgagee is only obliged to hand the deeds to the second mortgagee in these circumstances if it has actual notice of the existence of the second mortgage. In practice the vendor's solicitors, who are in effect acting as the mortgagee's solicitors, might do a land charges search against the vendor to discover whether any second mortgages have been registered as land charges. This search may well be done before exchange of contracts to check that the vendor has not forgotten to tell his solicitor about any second mortgages and as part of the general investigation of title. Failing that, then assuming that the purchaser's solicitor does a land charges search against the vendor, as he should, this will reveal the existence of any second mortgages registered as land charges and the vendor's solicitor will very soon be made aware of their existence.

2 The purchaser's new mortgage

There is a general rule that a solicitor cannot normally act for both parties in a conveyancing transaction.[3] The reason is obvious; the likelihood of a conflict of interest between the parties. Nevertheless, it is quite normal for the solicitor for the purchaser to also act for the purchaser's mortgagee, normally a Building Society or a bank, on the mortgage being entered into by the purchaser to raise finance for the purchase. Indeed this was encouraged by the 1979 report of the Royal Commission on Legal Services. To understand why this is so, the nature of a mortgage must first be appreciated.

When property is mortgaged, it is really very similar to the property being sold. On a sale, the vendor sells the property to the purchaser. The purchaser acquires the property and in return gives the vendor the purchase price. The purchaser is obviously concerned to find out as much as he can about the property and to establish that title to the property is good, as otherwise it would not be worth what he was paying. On the mortgage, the mortgagor mortgages the property to the mortgagee. The mortgagee thus acquires not the property but a mortgage over it, including a number of rights perhaps the most important of which is a power of sale of the property. The mortgagor receives not the sale price but the mortgage advance. The advance is in due course paid off and the mortgage discharged. However, the mortgagee is concerned to find out as much as possible about the property and to establish that title to the property is good, because it represents the security for the loan and if the title is defective, the property may not be worth the amount lent; if the mortgagor defaults in paying off the mortgage and the property is sold, the amount recovered may not be sufficient to pay off the debt. There is therefore an identity of interest between the purchaser buying the property and the mortgagee to whom the purchaser is mortgaging the property. Both are concerned to establish exactly what the property is and that the vendor's

2 Priority of second mortgages is in order of registration as a land charge, or on the register of title, if title is registered. See further in section 4 ii, below.

3 Solicitors Practice Rules 1936–1972, r. 2.

title to it is a good one. This is why there is nothing untoward in the purchaser's solicitor acting for the Building Society or bank to whom the property is being mortgaged, as well as the purchaser. In fact, the solicitor will commonly have three roles. He will be acting for the purchaser on the purchase, for the purchaser on the mortgage and also for the Building Society or bank on the mortgage.

Nevertheless it will not be in every case that the purchaser's solicitor also acts for the mortgagee. Certain Building Societies and certain banks will want their own solicitors to act. This does mean that there will be a certain amount of duplication of work. The mortgagee's solicitor will want to investigate the property in the same manner as the purchaser's solicitor. The purchaser's solicitor will therefore have to supply the mortgagee's solicitor with copies of the purchaser's pre-contract searches and enquiries, the abstract or epitome of title (or office copies) and copies of the purchaser's requisitions and the vendor's replies thereto, copies of the pre-completion searches made for the purchaser and any other relevant information. It is clearly more convenient and more cost-effective for the purchaser's solicitor to do all this work for two clients, the purchaser and the mortgagee. In the rest of this chapter we shall assume that this is indeed the position. However the purchaser's solicitor must not lose sight of the fact that he is acting for two clients and that he must take instructions from them both. For example if the purchaser is buying a leasehold property, the mortgagee may insist that the superior title also be deduced, which would require a condition in the contract, whereas the purchaser might be quite happy to rely on the open contract rule and not see any of the superior title. Similarly if the property is shown to be affected by restrictive covenants but their exact nature is unknown, the purchaser may be quite happy to accept the risk whereas the mortgagee may insist at least on some sort of insurance and might even refuse to go ahead with making the advance. If a conflict of interest should arise between the purchaser and the mortgagee, the solicitor will have to cease to act for one or both.

The various types of mortgage and the institutions which offer them have been discussed in chapter 8. The mortgagee will commonly be either a Building Society or a bank. The purchaser will have had to pay an inspection fee on submitting his application for the mortgage in order for the mortgagee to have the property surveyed and valued. If his application is successful, the purchaser will in due course receive a formal written offer of mortgage. Before exchange of contracts, the purchaser's solicitor should ensure not only that the mortgage offer has been accepted and that the advance will be available by the completion date but that the purchaser will be able to comply with any conditions subject to which the offer of mortgage is made. If the purchaser wants to exchange contracts on his purchase before an offer of mortgage has been received, he is running the risk of not having the funds available when he needs them on completion.

i Mortgage offer

There are a number of matters which may be the subject of conditions in the mortgage offer. Further details are given in chapter 8.

1 *Mortgage guarantee premium* If the amount being lent is not much less than the value of the property, the mortgagee will be concerned lest the value of the property should fall below the amount owing. If that happened and the mortgagee sold the property under its power of sale, it would not recover the amount owing and would be left with an unsecured debt for the balance. To avoid this difficulty mortgagees will insure the excess of the loan above a certain percentage of the value of the property. There is a single premium payable for this insurance policy. It is payable by the borrower (the purchaser) and is often added on to the amount of the loan to avoid the borrower having to find it from his own savings.

2 *Endowment policy* If the mortgage is an endowment mortgage, that is a mortgage linked to a life assurance policy, it will be a condition of the mortgage offer that a policy in the appropriate form is issued and assigned to the mortgagee.

One advantage of an endowment mortgage is that funds are generated to pay off the mortgage on the death of the person who life is insured. In the case of a married couple with young children where the husband is the breadwinner, the wife would not be left saddled with the mortgage debt on the husband's death if the policy is on his life. Alternatively both lives could be insured. This effect can also be achieved in relation to a straightforward repayment mortgage by a mortgage protection policy. For a relatively modest premium, the insurance company will pay off the outstanding balance of the mortgage at the time of death of the life insured. The premium is modest because although the chance of death increases with age, the amount owing on the mortgage is at the same time decreasing.

3 *Retentions* The circumstances in which the mortgagee may wish to make a retention from the advance, and the effect on the purchaser, are discussed in chapter 8, section 1 iii, above.

ii Instructions to solicitors

Once the mortgage offer has been accepted by the purchaser, the solicitor will receive a set of instructions from the mortgagee, normally in a standard form. These should be perused carefully; they may contain, for example, an instruction that a leasehold title must either be absolute (if registered) or accompanied by an abstract of the superior title.

iii Investigation of title

The examination of the evidence of title, be it an abstract, an epitome or office copy entries, is being done both for the purchaser and the mortgagee. Instructions on any defect in title should therefore be obtained from both clients.

1 *Particular problems* As the purchaser can only mortgage what he has, the mortgagee will be particularly concerned to establish what if any rights affecting the property are being created as a result of the purchase. The most obvious examples of this are new easements and covenants created in the purchase deed when the vendor is selling part of what he owns. New restrictive covenants

over unregistered land must be registered to be binding on the mortgagee, which will only be the case if the priority notice procedure has been used. A further pitfall for the mortgagee is illustrated by the case of *Church of England Building Society v Piskor*.[4] The purchaser had been allowed into possession of the property before completion and had purported to grant a legal tenancy to a third party. At that time, having no legal estate himself, the purchaser could not pass a legal estate to the tenant. However on completion of the purchase, when the purchaser did acquire the legal estate, the tenant also received a legal estate by virtue of the doctrine of 'feeding the estoppel'. Thus at the time of completion of the mortgage, which must necessarily be immediately after completion of the purchase, the tenant did have a legal estate and the mortgagee was thus bound by the tenancy. Title to the land was unregistered; had title been registered then the mortgagee would also have been bound if the tenant was in occupation, because his interest would have been an overriding interest. One way in which the mortgagee can try and avoid this problem is by an inspection of the property which is dealt with below at section vi.

If the property mortgaged is leasehold, and the lease contains a forfeiture clause, this may be of concern to the mortgagee. The position is discussed in chapter 17 where the lessor's remedy of forfeiture is considered.

2 Searches The part of the process of investigation of title that involves searches is again being done for both the purchaser and the mortgagee. In the case of unregistered land the mortgagee will have the benefit of the land charges searches obtained for the purchaser. An additional search must be made for the mortgagee; as on completion the purchaser is becoming owner of the legal estate and immediately mortgaging it, the mortgagee will require a land charges search against the purchaser. In particular this will reveal any bankruptcy entries against the purchaser; if the purchaser were shown to be bankrupt then the mortgagee would not want to proceed with the mortgage. This, then, is a search which the solicitor is doing for his mortgagee client rather than for the purchaser.

In the case of registered land, the normal search effected for the purchaser is the official search at the District Land Registry which updates the office copy entries with any subsequent entries made on the register. If this search is done for the purchaser then the mortgagee gets no protection from it. If on the other hand the search is done for the mortgagee, the search certificate also protects the purchaser. If the same solicitor is acting for both the purchaser and the mortgagee only one search need be done, but the application form should state that it is being done for the mortgagee. It is possible that an additional authority to inspect might be needed, and the Law Society Conditions do contain a provision for additional authorities to inspect for mortgagees.[5] If the same solicitor is not acting for the mortgagee and the purchaser, the mortgagee's solicitor *will* require an authority to inspect in order to do a search and the purchaser's solicitor should ensure that the vendor is bound to supply such an authority by an appropriate provision in the contract.

Registrations in the Land Charges Registry are normally irrelevant when

4 [1954] Ch 553, [1954] 2 All ER 85, CA.
5 LSC 12(1)(b)(ii).

dealing with registered land as has already been mentioned in chapter 11. However most mortgagees adopt the practice of asking the solicitor to obtain for them a bankruptcy only search against the purchaser in the Land Charges Registry even though the title being mortgaged is registered. This is a search not in the register of Land Charges classes A–F but in the register of pending actions and writs and orders. It will thus reveal bankruptcy petitions and orders. The mortgagee will not wish to proceed with a mortgage to someone who is bankrupt.

The mortgagee will also be interested in the results of the pre-exchange searches such as the enquiries of the vendor and the local search and enquiries of the Local Authority. To take an example, if the property is to lose some of a garden for a road widening scheme then not only might this affect the purchaser's decision to buy but it will also affect the mortgagee's decision about the size of the loan or indeed even whether any loan will be made at all. If a long time has passed since the local search and local authority enquiries were made before exchange of contracts, it might be necessary to repeat them for the mortgagee.

iv Mortgage deed

The deed by which the property is mortgaged will normally be in a standard form supplied by the mortgagee. The purchaser has little choice but to agree to the terms of the deed if he wants a mortgage. Nevertheless it is important that the terms be explained to the purchaser. The following is a summary of the terms most likely to be found in a standard Building Society mortgage deed.

1 *Nature of the deed* The structure of the mortgage is rather complex and indeed artificial, due largely to the historical evolution of mortgages. Originally, the loan would have to be repaid on the date stated in the mortgage deed, a date thus called 'the legal date for redemption' of the mortgage. If payment was not made on that day, the mortgagee could foreclose, that is he could keep the property which was mortgaged. In the case of payment being only slightly late then this was clearly inequitable, particularly where the property was worth considerably more than the amount of the loan. Equity thus stepped in to alleviate the legal position and provided that after the legal date for redemption there would still be an (equitable) right to redeem the mortgage. This is still the position. The mortgage deed will still name a legal date for redemption commonly only a month or so after the date of the mortgage. The significance of this date is that once it has passed many of the mortgagee's powers arise, including the power of sale. In practice of course the mortgage will be intended to run over a perod of 15, 20 or 25 years. Assuming a constant rate of interest over that time then a monthly repayment figure can be inserted in the deed which, if paid over that period, will repay both the principal and interest over that period. In the case of an endowment mortgage when only payments of interest are made, the principal being repaid by the amount generated by a life insurance policy, the payment figure in the deed will nevertheless normally still be the figure which would be inserted in the normal repayment mortgage (including repayments of the principal) rather than a lower figure based purely on payment of interest. This protects

the mortgagee against the life policy lapsing for non-payment of the premiums. The mortgagee will of course agree to accept the lower figure so long as premium payments on the policy are kept up.

In practice most mortgages do not run for the full term of years; the property is sold and the mortgage redeemed out of the proceeds of sale. This could happen at any time but some mortgagees might require the purchaser to give a certain period of notice of redemption or to pay monthly repayments in lieu of such notice.

2 *Interest rate* The initial interest rate will be stated in the deed although it will be variable. The repayments necessary to repay the mortgage over the initially agreed term are therefore also variable.

3 *Exercise of mortgagee's powers* The main power of the mortgagee is its power of sale of the mortgaged property. A statutory power of sale arises on the legal date for redemption[6] but only becomes exercisable as against the mortgagor on certain default being made by the mortgagor. The circumstances in which the statutory power becomes exercisable are set out in the Law of Property Act 1925, section 103. The mortgage deed may add to the circumstances in which the power becomes exercisable; for example many mortgage deeds make the power exercisable in the event of the mortgagor's bankruptcy.

4 *Right to grant tenancies* The mortgagor has a statutory power to grant certain leases of the mortgaged property.[7] The mortgagee when exercising its power of sale may have great difficulty in finding a buyer for tenanted property and so most Building Society and bank mortgage deeds will exclude the mortgagor's power of leasing and provide that no leases or tenancies of the property are to be granted by the mortgagor without the mortgagee's consent. The most common situation in which the mortgagor may wish to let the property is if he is going abroad for a period in connection with his employment. He may therefore need the consent of the mortgagee before doing this.

5 *Insurance* It is clearly in the interests of the mortgagee to see that the property which is security for the loan is adequately insured. To this end the mortgage deed may provide that the mortgagee has power to effect insurance with the premiums being recoverable from the mortgagor. A mortgagee does have a statutory power to insure but this only relates to fire insurance and the premium is only recoverable from the mortgagor in the sense that it is added to the amount owing on the loan.[8] This explains the popularity of an express power to insure in the mortgage deed.

v Endowment mortgage – life policy

An endowment mortgage involves the assignment of a life insurance policy to the mortgagee. There will be a deed of assignment of the policy. The provisions

6 Law of Property Act 1925, s. 101(1)(i); see also ch 10, section 6, above and in particular note 14 thereto.

7 Ibid, s. 99.

8 Ibid, s. 101(1)(ii).

of this deed will tie it in to the mortgage deed, for example allowing the mortgagee to surrender the policy should its power of sale be exercised in respect of the mortgaged property. The solicitor in his role of acting for the mortgagee should examine the title to the policy although in fact a new policy is normally issued. If the policy is already in existence, the solicitor would need to enquire of the insurance company to check that they had not been given notice of any prior assignment of the policy, which would then mean that the policy could not be assigned to the mortgagee.

vi Report on title

Before completion the solicitor will report anything untoward in the title to the mortgagee and will otherwise state that the title is in order. This is commonly done on a standard form report on title supplied by Building Societies and banks which may incorporate a request for the cheque for the mortgage advance in readiness for completion.

There is one particular point on the title which may concern the solicitor. Dealing firstly with registered land, it has already been pointed out that the rights of an occupier of the land are overriding interests.[9] The difficulties thereby caused to the purchaser have already been examined in chapter 11. The typical problem would be where the property is in the sole name of the vendor, whose spouse has an equitable interest. If the spouse does not vacate the property then the purchaser is bound by that equitable interest. On the same theme, there are further difficulties for the purchaser's mortgagee. The time at which to judge whether anyone does have an overriding interest against the mortgagee is the time of registration of the mortgage, which is of course bound to be at some time after actual completion. In other words if anyone with an interest in the land is in possession at the time of registration of the mortgage then he or she will have an overriding interest as against the mortgagee. So if the purchaser takes the property in his sole name, and the *purchaser's* spouse has an equitable interest in the property, it is likely that the spouse will be in possession at the time of registration of the mortgage and the mortgagee will be bound by his or her interest. This will mean that if the mortgagee wishes to sell, it will not be able to recover possession against the spouse. Of course the rule is not restricted to spouses' equitable interests but covers any other interests in land of occupiers.[10] As regards spouses, Building Societies and banks far prefer them to buy (and thus mortgage) the property in their joint names as the problem is thereby completely avoided. If the mortgagee is faced with someone with a potential overriding interest, there are various methods of mitigating the danger of the overriding interest. As a precaution, many mortgagees will ask the purchaser to state who will be in possession of the property after completion. Anyone who may have an interest in the land can then be approached and asked to postpone their interest to that of the mortgagee, signing a declaration or consent form confirming this. This practice does have its problems. One is relying on the purchaser to be straightforward

9 Land Registration Act 1925, s. 70(1)(g).

10 For example, the vendor's parents or other relatives living with the vendor, if they have an equitable interest. The parents, for example, may have contributed to the cost of building a 'granny-flat'.

in disclosing who will be in possession of the property. Even if the purchaser does disclose the existence of such persons, it may place the solicitor in an awkward position. He is acting for the mortgagee and the purchaser, and he must now obtain a declaration from, say, the purchaser's wife postponing her interest to that of the mortgagee. On the face of it, this is a step which is detrimental to the interests of the wife, although if she refused to postpone her interest this would also be detrimental in that the mortgage (to her husband) might fall through. There is clearly a possible conflict of interest between the purchaser and the mortgagee on the one hand and the purchaser's wife on the other hand and it would seem that it is preferable to the purchaser's wife to have separate advice.[11] It might be better if possible to have the spouse join in the purchase deed and the mortgage, rather than rely on a declaration by the wife postponing her interest.

Broadly speaking the same difficulties apply to unregistered land, with the one difference, already commented upon in chapter 11, that the rationale by which the mortgagee is bound by the equitable interest is the doctrine of constructive notice. If someone with an equitable interest is in occupation then their presence may amount to constructive notice of their interest. On a purchase in a husband's sole name there is little chance that his wife, if she has an equitable interest, will be in occupation before completion of the mortgage, which is immediately after completion of the purchase: nevertheless, in practice, mortgagors will probably take the same precautions as have just been discussed in relation to registered land.

If no consent form is signed, the equitable interest may not necessarily be binding on the mortgagee. The cases of *Bristol and West Building Society v Henning*[12] and *Paddington Building Society v Mendelsohn*[13] suggest that if the occupier knows of and supports the mortgage, his or her equitable interest may be subject to the mortgage anyway.

If the mortgage is by (at least two) trustees for sale, it will overreach the equitable interest which will then not be binding on the mortgagee.[14]

11 *In Kingsnorth Trust Ltd v Bell* [1986] 1 All ER 423, [1986] 1 WLR 119, CA, a mortgagee wanted the mortgagor's wife, who had an equitable interest in the property, to execute the mortgage deed so as to ensure it was not bound by the interest. The wife's signature was obtained by the mortgagor, her husband, who misrepresented the purpose of the loan. The wife did not receive independent advice. The mortgage was not binding on the wife and the mortgagee could not recover possession against her. However, in *National Westminster Bank Ltd v Morgan* [1985] AC 636, [1985] 1 All ER 821, HL, where the property was in joint names, it was held that in the circumstances of that case there was no duty on the bank manager to ensure that the wife had independent advice before she executed the mortgage. The position appears to be that if the signature is obtained for the mortgagee by a third party who is not an agent of the mortgagee, the mortgagee's duty is simply to point out the desirability of independent advice, not to ensure that it is taken. In *Bell*, the husband was such an agent. See *Coldunell Ltd v Gallon* [1986] QB 1184, [1986] 1 All ER 429, CA, and [1986] Conv 212.

12 [1985] 2 All ER 606, [1985] 1 WLR 778, CA.

13 (1985) 50 P & CR 244, CA.

14 *City of London Building Society v Flegg* [1986] Ch 605, [1986] 1 All ER 989, CA, (1987) Independant, 15 May, HL.

vii Completion

Completion of the mortgage, which will take place at the same time as completion of the purchase, is discussed in the next chapter. The mortgage advance will have been received before completion, normally in the form of a cheque from the mortgagee. This will be paid into client account before completion. It really ought not to be paid into the purchaser's client account because at this stage he is not entitled to the money; it ought to be paid into a separate mortgagee client account. If completion is delayed, the mortgagee will be losing interest on the amount of the advance if the cheque for the advance has been presented and paid into client account.[15] The purchaser will certainly not wish to be liable to make payments under his mortgage before completion, but the mortgagee might conceivably start charging interest under the new mortgage from the time the cheque is presented. It might be better to leave the cheque on the file and only present it shortly before completion. If the delay is lengthy, it may be necessary to return the mortgage advance to the mortgagee.

viii After completion

There are certain steps necessary to perfect the purchaser's title such as stamping the purchase deed, applying for registration of title or applying for registration on a transfer of registered land. These will be discussed in chapter 15 but as the mortgagee's title is derived from the purchaser, the solicitor also has a duty to his mortgagee client to carry out these steps. Additionally there are certain steps after completion which are necessary purely from the mortgagee's point of view. It is not necessary to stamp the mortgage deed but it may be necessary to protect the mortgage in some way. In the case of unregistered land a first legal mortgage will be protected by deposit of title deeds. The solicitor will have to schedule the deeds and send them off to the mortgagee as soon as possible after completion. The procedure is different in the case of registered land, that is to say land which is already registered or in respect of which the purchaser's solicitor must apply for first registration. The appropriate method of protecting the mortgage is as a registered charge, registered in the charges register of the title. In his capacity as solicitor for the mortgagee, the solicitor will apply for registration of the registered charge at the same time as applying for registration of the purchase. A charge certificate will be issued by the Land Registry rather than the land certificate and this must be sent to the mortgagee once it has been checked. It is common for the old pre-registration title deeds also to be sent to the mortgagee; they have lost their significance as proof of the title but are not totally redundant.

ix Mortgages not contemporaneous with a purchase

It may be that a solicitor is acting on a mortgage which is not contemporaneous with a purchase, but where the mortgagor is already the owner of the property. The task of the solicitor here is nevertheless to find out information about the property which will concern the mortgagee and to check that the mortgagor's title is good. He will thus make the usual searches made for a purchaser before exchange of contracts, will investigate title in the normal way and will make the

15 The solicitor really ought to put the money on deposit, thus earning interest.

appropriate pre-completion searches. The problem of occupiers with equitable interests will be particularly acute where the mortgagor is already established in the property, and indeed most of the cases mentioned in the previous section, as well as the *Williams and Glyn's Bank Ltd v Boland* case itself,[16] involve non-contemporaneous mortgages. In relation to a registered title it will be important to try and ensure that there are no occupiers at the date of registration of the mortgage, the crucial date; this would mean making sure there were no occupiers on completion of the mortgage, and then immediately applying for registration.

Additionally, the case of *Kingsnorth Trust Ltd v Tizard*,[17] considered above in chapter 6 section 8, demonstrates the difficulty of inspecting the property in the case of unregistered title in order to satisfy section 199 of the Law of Property Act 1925. In that case, a wife was only sleeping intermittently in the property although she would return each morning. She was held to be in occupation and the mortgagee had not done enough in arranging a time with the husband to inspect the property, when of course her occupation was not discovered. The mortgagee was therefore unable to recover possession against her, but the fact that the mortgagee knew that the mortgagor was married but separated seems to have had some bearing on the level of inspection necessary.

3 Sale by mortgagee

i Power of sale

This is dealt with at chapter 10, section 6, above.

ii Proceeds of sale

Most sales in practice will be by the first mortgagee, for example a Building Society or a bank or a Local Authority. If a sale is by a second mortgagee than almost inevitably the sale will not have been subject to the prior mortgage(s) and the first step must therefore be to discharge the prior mortgage(s) out of the proceeds of sale in accordance with the undertaking which the vendor/mortgagee's solicitor will have had to give to the purchaser on completion. The procedure is the same as if the mortgagor were selling and redeeming a mortgage out of the proceeds of sale.

Apart from this, the proceeds of sale are held by the mortgagee on trust and the order of application of the proceeds, after discharge of any prior mortgages, is as follows:[18]

(a) payment of costs and expenses incidental to the sale, for example solicitor's costs and estate agent's and auctioneer's fees:

(b) payment of principal, interest and any other costs due under the mortgage.

The mortgagee having taken what he is owed, any residue must be paid to the

16 [1981] AC 487, [1980] 2 All ER 408, HL; see also *Winkworth v Edward Baron Development Co Ltd* [1987] 1 All ER 114, [1986] 1 WLR 1512, HL.

17 [1986] 2 All ER 54, [1986] 1 WLR 783.

18 Law of Property Act 1925 s. 105.

'person next entitled to the mortgaged property'. If there are any subsequent mortgages, this means the mortgagee with best claim to priority amongst them.

That person then holds the balance of the proceeds on a similar trust. His mortgage will have been 'over-reached' by the sale and he will pay himself the amount owed under his mortgage and hand any residue on to the person next entitled, as above. Ultimately, after the proceeds have passed through the hands of all the subsequent mortgagees (if any), the mortgagor will receive the residue.

In order for the mortgagee's solicitor to ensure that he is handing on the balance of the proceeds to the correct person, a search should be made of the Land Charges Register for unregistered land and at the Land Registry for registered land, to ascertain if there are any subsequent mortgages and if so who has the best claim to priority.

When a mortgagee exercises his power of sale the mortgage is 'discharged' by the sale and there is no need for a receipt on the mortgage.

4 Further advances and further charges

Further advances and further charges are alike in that neither normally takes place when the property is bought but at some later date when the mortgagor already owns the property and for some reason wants to increase the amount borrowed.

i Further advances

A further advance is made when a mortgagor wishes to borrow more money from an existing mortgagee, to be added to the existing debt. Many standard mortgage deeds are expressed to be security not only for the original loan but also for any further advances made in the future. This means that no further deed is necessary when the further advance is made, merely a receipt for the additional loan. A mortgagor might want a further advance to assist the building of an extension onto the mortgaged property or to install central heating. The mortgagor will make an application to the mortgagee and the money will be released after the appropriate work has been done or possibly merely on an undertaking by the mortgagor to have the work done within a specified time. A further inspection fee may be payable. A further advance will result in a revised repayment figure for the monthly instalments, calculated to pay off the whole sum borrowed, with interest, over the original term of the mortgage. In the case of an endowment mortgage it may be necessary to increase the premiums on the life policy so that the sum payable at the end of the term of the policy will be the whole sum now borrowed.

ii Further charges

A further charge can be a second legal mortgage or possibly an equitable mortgage. It will arise in practice when the mortgagor needs to borrow more money, probably for a relatively short period of time as compared to the term of the first legal mortgage to a Building Society or bank. The purpose of the loan may not be in connection with the improvement of the property; it might be to help buy a car for example. If so then the payment of interest will not qualify for income tax relief. There are a number of finance companies and other banks which are prepared to make such a loan on the security of a second mortgage. When acting for a prospective second mortgagee, title should be investigated in exactly the same way as when acting for a purchaser or first mortgagee.[19] An additional element will be a consideration of the first (and any other prior) mortgages. The first mortgage, to a Building Society or to a bank, may restrict the power of the mortgagor to enter into any subsequent mortgages. Also, the amount owing under prior mortgages is highly relevant. If property is worth £20,000 and there is a first mortgage with £18,000 owing, a second mortgagee would be extremely foolish to lend a sum approaching or exceeding the balance or 'equity' as it is called of £2,000 in the property. Thirdly, the prospective second mortgagee will be concerned about any right to 'tack' which the prior mortgagee may have. Tacking occurs when a mortgagee who makes a further advance can treat the further advance as having been made at the same time as the original mortgage for the purpose of priority of repayment; the further advance is tacked to the original advance and jumps the queue over any subsequent mortgagees. Tacking can only take place if made either with the consent of the intervening mortgagees (which would be unlikely); or without notice of the existence of intervening mortgagees; or under a binding obligation in the original mortgage deed.[20] The solicitor for the second mortgagee will therefore be careful to give notice to prior mortgagees of the new mortgage, as notice by registration is technically insufficient.[1] This will be enough to prevent tacking as standard mortgage deeds will not contain a binding obligation to make a further advance. Finally, the second mortgagee may be affected by a prior mortgagee having in his mortgage deed excluded the Law of Property Act 1925, section 93 and thereby reserved a right of consolidation. The prior mortgage deed(s) should be abstracted to enable the second mortgagee's solicitor to check these points.

In practice, the real security of a second mortgage lies in the second mortgagee's interest in the proceeds of sale, after that of prior mortgagees. A disadvantage is that the second mortgagee has no control over the exercise of the first mortgagee's power of sale. The second mortgagee will normally also have a power of sale although he can only sell subject to prior mortgages and in practice would have to sell free from them and discharge them out of the proceeds of sale.

A typical second mortgagee will be a finance company or a bank. Although the vast majority of these are reputable and indeed have to be so to comply with the terms of the Consumer Credit Act 1974,[2] the proposed content of the second mortgage deed should be carefully scrutinised by the mortgagor's solicitor. In particular the interest rate may often be quite high.

The priority of further charges will be in their order of registration, either

19 See section 2 ix, above.
20 Ibid, s. 94(1).
1 Ibid, s. 94(2).
2 The requirements of the Act concerning the provision of a copy of the mortgage and the right of the mortgagor to withdraw during a 'cooling off' period may well be applicable; Consumer Credit Act 1974, s. 58 and Consumer Credit (Exempt Agreement) Order 1980.

as land charges for unregistered land (Ci, Ciii or Civ) or as registered charges for registered land.[3]

3 As to the consequences of non-registration, see ch 11, section 1 i 6 above.

14 Completion

1 Preparation for completion

i Title investigated

It goes without saying that before completion both solicitors should ensure that all necessary steps in deducing and investigating title have been carried out. It is not unknown for the purchaser's solicitor to discover a day or so before the contractual completion date that he has forgotten to do his searches. As we have seen it is possible to request a search by telephone.

ii Conditional contracts

If the contract has been made conditional on the occurrence of some external event, such as the granting of planning permission, then again it hardly needs saying that before completing the contract the parties should see whether the condition is satisfied so as to establish whether there is indeed a contract and contractual duty to complete. Under the rule in *Aberfoyle Plantations Ltd v Cheng*[1] the date for satisfaction of the condition may be the contractual completion date. In addition, although there may not be a conditional contract, the purchaser may be able to rescind if certain 'conditions' are not fulfilled. An example would be if the requisite licence to assign leasehold property had not been obtained from the landlord. Similarly if the contract is subject to Law Society Condition 4 or National Condition 3; if any of the matters referred to in those conditions have come to light within the relevant time then the contract may have been rescinded by the purchaser.

iii Execution

1 *Who executes?* The deed, prepared by the purchaser's solicitor, must be executed by the parties in readiness for completion when it is handed over to the purchaser's solicitor. The vendor – or all of them if they are joint tenants – must always execute the deed, but the purchaser will only need to execute it if he is actually 'doing something' in it, for example entering into a covenant or declaring an express trust for sale. If the purchaser's execution is necessary

1 [1960] AC 115, [1959] 3 All ER 910, PC.

this should be done before the deed is sent to the vendor's solicitor for the vendor's execution in readiness for completion. The reason for this is that once the vendor has executed the deed, the vendor's solicitor will be unwilling to let the deed go back to the purchaser for him to add his execution. Nevertheless, the purchaser's execution might be quite important to the vendor; if the purchaser is entering into an indemnity covenant or a new restrictive covenant then the vendor will not want to complete before the purchaser has executed the deed. The purchaser's solicitor should not offer and the vendor's solicitor should not accept an undertaking given on completion by the purchaser's solicitor that he will have the deed executed by the purchaser as soon as possible. This is quite outside the purchaser's solicitor's control and should not be the subject of an undertaking.

In addition to the vendor, it may be necessary for some other party to the deed to execute it. For example on the sale by a tenant for life of settled land the trustees will join in the deed to give a receipt; on the sale of part of property subject to a mortgage the mortgagee may join in to release the part sold from the mortgage.

2 *Execution by an individual* To be properly executed a deed must be signed sealed and delivered. Firstly then, the party must sign or, if he cannot write, place his mark on the deed.[2] Secondly the deed must be sealed. In times gone by this would be achieved with the aid of molten sealing wax. Now a small circular piece of red self-adhesive paper or 'wafer' is used. The executing party will not normally affix this himself but just sign opposite a previously affixed seal. The justification for this procedure can be found in *Stromdale & Ball Ltd v Burden*,[3] where it was said that 'if a party signs a document bearing wax or wafer or other indication of a seal, with the intention of executing the document as a deed, that is sufficient adoption or recognition of the seal to amount to due execution as a deed.'[4] Some standard form deeds such as mortgages contain the letters L. S. inside a circle opposite the space for signature. This is an abbreviation for the Latin 'locus sigilli' and indicates the place where the seal should be stuck. In a case where no seal was in fact affixed but the party did sign (across the circle) the deed was held still to have been duly executed.[5] Signing after a testimonium and attestation clause referring to sealing can also raise an estoppel as to sealing.[6] The solicitor must be prepared to explain to his client what he is in fact doing in signing opposite the seal. Sealing a deed is one of the parts of a conveyancing transaction which the lay client could be excused for thinking deliberately mysterious and ritualistic. Certainly there must be some mechanism for distinguishing a deed from a document that is only signed, but the present procedure must seem rather unreal to the lay client.

2 Law of Property Act 1925, s. 73.
3 [1952] Ch 223, [1952] 1 All ER 59.
4 Ibid at 230.
5 *First National Securities Ltd v Jones* [1978] Ch 109 [1978] 2 All ER 221, CA.
6 Confirmed in *TCB Ltd v Gray* [1986] Ch 621, [1986] 1 All ER 587, where it was held that a party executing a deed after the normal clause referring to signing, sealing and delivery was estopped from denying it was sealed when another person relied on the deed to his detriment.

The final part of execution is delivery. This does not mean the handing over of the deed to the other party, for example handing over to the purchaser on completion, although this would certainly amount to delivery. There is a helpful dictum in *Vincent v Premo Enterprises (Voucher Sales) Ltd*[7] where it was said that 'delivery ... means an act done so as to evince an intention to be bound. Even though the deed remains in the possession of the maker, or of his solicitor, he is bound by it if he has done some act evincing an intention to be bound'.[8] In practice, delivery will most commonly be achieved by the client handing the signed and sealed deed to his own solicitor in readiness for completion. Delivery is the final formality of execution and the deed once delivered becomes fully effective; indeed the date of the deed is the date of delivery, the date on which the deed becomes effective. However it will be ridiculous if the deed becomes effective, and the purchaser thus acquires the legal estate, when the vendor hands the signed and sealed deed to his own solicitor, before completion and before the purchaser has paid the purchase price. The answer is that the delivery can be absolute or conditional. Most deliveries in practice will be conditional. A deed delivered conditionally is called an escrow. The most common condition of a delivery by the vendor will be payment of the purchase price by the purchaser. This condition will normally be implied even if the deed is not delivered with this express condition. So typically, the vendor will hand the signed and sealed deed to his solicitor sometime before completion. The deed is thereby delivered but conditionally on the purchaser paying the purchase price. The condition is satisfied on completion and the deed then becomes effective to pass the legal estate to the purchaser.

Even though delivery may be only conditional, it does have consequences for the vendor. The delivery is irrevocable. The vendor, having delivered the deed conditionally in the manner described above, cannot change his mind and tear the deed up. He has committed himself to wait and see whether the condition of the delivery is satisfied. If it is, the deed becomes effective and there is nothing the vendor can do about it. This is illustrated by the case of *Beesly v Hallwood Estates Ltd*.[9] A lease contained an option for the lessee to renew. The lessee exercised the option and the lessor executed a new lease. This was delivered by the lessor, conditionally on the lessee executing a counterpart lease. The lessee did so. The lessor then discovered that the option was unenforceable against him. The lessor refused to carry on with the transaction, but to no avail; the condition of the conditional delivery had been satisfied and the new lease had become effective. Even if the condition had not been satisfied at the time the lessor wanted to withdraw, he would not have been able to do so; he would have had to wait and see whether the condition was satisfied.

There appears to be no particular time limit for the satisfaction of the condition of delivery although clearly there must come a time when the vendor will be entitled to withdraw if the condition has not been satisfied.

Once the condition has been satisfied, the deed is treated as having been

7 [1969] 2 QB 609, [1969] 2 All ER 941, CA.
8 Ibid at 619.
9 [1961] Ch 105, [1961] 1 All ER 90, CA.

delivered on the date of the conditional delivery.[10] The correct date of the deed is therefore the date of the conditional delivery and not the date that the condition is satisfied. That is rather odd and presumably means that most purchase deeds, being dated as they are with the date of completion, are wrongly dated.

It might be thought better for the vendor not to deliver the deed before completion but to delegate his solicitor to deliver it on completion, by handing it over to the purchaser's solicitor. The difficulty is that the authority for the solicitor to do this would have to be given by deed – in effect a power of attorney. This might be almost as inconvenient as delivering the deed conditionally before completion!

Execution – that is the signature opposite the seal – is normally done in the presence of a witness who then adds his signature and address by way of attestation.

3 *Execution by corporations* A corporation – such as a limited company – clearly cannot sign the deed. The Law of Property Act 1925, section 74 provides that in favour of a purchaser, a deed is presumed to have been duly executed by a corporation aggregate if its seal is affixed in the presence of and attested by its secretary or clerk or other permanent officer or his deputy, and also by a member of the Board of Directors or other governing body. When a seal purporting to be the corporation's seal has been affixed, attested by persons purporting to be the requisite officers, the deed shall be deemed to have been executed in accordance with section 74 and thus duly executed. The rule applies to companies, Local Authorities, Building Societies and other corporations. The requirement of sealing from the *corporation's* point of view may be contained in a company's articles of association or a Building Society's rules. If section 74 is not complied with, a purchaser's solicitor would have to check that the deed had been properly executed by investigating such rules. As section 74 does not mention delivery but states that the deed shall be deemed executed if sealed and signed appropriately, it might be thought that delivery is not a requirement of execution for a corporation. It would follow that a corporation could not deliver a deed conditionally but this is clearly not the case and a corporation can execute an escrow.[11]

4 *Execution by attorneys* An individual who is the attorney for one of the executing parties can sign the deed in one of two ways. The attestation clause will contain some reference to the power of attorney. The attorney can either sign in his own name, adding underneath 'as attorney for . . .', or he can sign in the name of the donor of the power of attorney and add 'by . . . his attorney'.

5 *Registered land* There are two particular requirements in relation to the execution of a transfer of registered land. The first is that the execution *must* be attested. The second is that if the transfer is accompanied by a plan then the plan must be signed by the vendor and by or on behalf of the purchaser.[12]

10 *Alan Estates Ltd v W G Stores Ltd* [1982] Ch 511, [1981] 3 All ER 481, CA.
11 *Beesly v Hallwood Estates Ltd*, above.
12 See ch 12, above.

6 *Other deeds* So far we have considered execution of the purchase deed, be it a conveyance or assignment or transfer. However other deeds must be executed in readiness for completion. If the purchaser is buying with the aid of a mortgage then he will have to execute the mortgage deed and in the case of an endowment mortgage, a deed of assignment of the life policy. These mortgage deeds are not normally executed by the mortgagee.

7 *Alterations* There is a rebuttable presumption that any alteration to a deed was made before execution. It is good practice to ensure that any alterations are initialled by the parties on execution. Alterations should not be made after execution.

8 *Procedure* The purchase deed, in draft and final form, passes between the parties a number of times. As we have seen it is drafted by the purchaser's solicitor and then sent to the vendor's solicitor for approval. It will then be returned approved and possibly amended. It is then engrossed by the purchaser's solicitor, executed by the purchaser if this is necessary and then sent to the vendor's solicitor for execution by the vendor in readiness for completion, when it will be handed over to the purchaser's solicitor. This procedure is even longer if there is another party who must approve the draft and execute the deed, for example on a conveyance of the former matrimonial home following a divorce or separation, from the joint names of the spouses into one spouse's sole name; if, as is likely, the property is subject to a mortgage then the mortgagee will be made a party to release the other spouse from his or her obligations under the mortgage.

iv Finance

1 *Redemption of vendor's mortgage* If the property the vendor is selling is subject to a mortgage, then this will ordinarily be redeemed using the proceeds of the sale. Before completion the vendor's solicitor must contact the mortgagee and ask for a redemption figure, being the amount required to redeem the mortgage on the completion date. The mortgagee would normally also give an additional daily rate to be added to the figure so that if completion and thus redemption is delayed by a few days the solicitor can still calculate the amount required to redeem the mortgage. The solicitor ought to have already checked that the proceeds will be sufficient to both redeem the mortgage and pay his own costs and any other disbursements. If the proceeds are not sufficient to redeem the mortgage, the vendor's solicitor will be unable to give the purchaser on completion the usual undertaking to redeem the mortgage; in the absence of this the purchaser will refuse to complete and the vendor will be in breach of contract.

If the vendor has any second mortgages then redemption figures should be obtained for these also, as they will all need to be redeemed out of the proceeds of sale.

2 *Amount required to complete* The purchaser's solicitor will want to know the precise amount required on completion. The standard form of requisitions will contain a request for a completion statement giving this information. The bulk

of the sum will be the sale price less the deposit already paid. There are two other items which may be reflected in the completion statement; apportionment and interest.

There are certain sums which may be payable in respect of the property, either in advance or in arrear. Rates are an example. The vendor may have paid the general and water rates on the property and want to recoup from the purchaser the amount paid for the period in the future, of which the purchaser will have the benefit. Alternatively he might recoup that sum from the Rating Authority who would send a fresh demand to the purchaser. Similarly for a leasehold property the vendor may have paid the ground rent in advance and wish to recoup a proportion of this from the purchaser. If the rent is paid in arrear then the purchaser will wish to deduct from the purchase price the proportion which will be paid by him in respect of the time during which the property has been in the vendor's ownership. The date at which the apportionment of these outgoings is made is normally the contractual completion date; as was mentioned in chapter 8, the vendor is responsible for outgoings up to that date and the purchaser afterwards. This is the open contract rule, which may be altered in the contractual conditions. In particular, if completion is delayed then apportionment may be made at the date of actual completion rather than the contractual completion date. The Law Society Conditions provide that the apportionment date shall be the date of actual completion if the sale is with vacant possession.[13] (They also provide that if the delay between the contractual completion date and actual completion is the vendor's fault, the purchaser can claim compensation, and vice versa; this is dealt with in more detail later in this chapter.) Under the National Conditions the position is rather more complicated, but the basic rule is that the apportionment date is the contractual completion date unless the vendor remains in possession after the contractual date in which case the purchaser can elect to have the apportionment made at the date of actual completion.[14] Both sets of Conditions provide that if the purchaser has been given possession before completion, he is responsible for the actual outgoings from the date he took possession; he is also entitled to any income of the property for that period.[15] This reflects the open contract position.

The second adjustment which may have to be made on the completion statement is the payment of interest. In certain circumstances, if completion is delayed or if the purchaser has been given possession before completion, the purchaser may have to pay interest on the outstanding balance of the purchase money. This is discussed in detail later in this chapter.

Having ascertained the amount payable on completion, the purchaser's solicitor must take steps to ensure that this sum is available. If it is not, and the purchaser's solicitor, rather ill-advisedly, uses his own money to complete the purchase, he will have the benefit of what would otherwise be the vendor's lien over the property for unpaid purchase money; *Boodle Hatfield & Co v British*

13 LSC 19(1), LSC 19(6) also provides for provisional apportionment of estimates, if the precise figure is as yet unknown, eg the service charge in respect of one of a block of flats.

14 NC 6(3).

15 LSC 18(4), NC 8(1).

Films Ltd,[16] where the purchaser's solicitors completed on the strength of a cheque from the purchaser which was not cleared before completion and was subsequently dishonoured.

3 *Mortgage advance* If part of the purchase money is being provided by a mortgage advance, this must of course be to hand by completion. If there is to be any retention, this will not be included in the sum sent to the purchaser's solicitor. If for some reason the mortgage advance is not available on the completion date, the purchaser may have to arrange a bridging loan until the advance does become available. This might arise if the purchaser has unwisely exchanged contracts without waiting for a mortgage offer.

4 *Synchronisation* Part of the purchase money may be provided from the proceeds of a contemporaneous sale. If completion of that sale is delayed or for some other reason does not take place until after the time scheduled for completion of the purchase, the purchaser must either delay completion of the purchase, or again, arrange a bridging loan until the sale is completed.

5 *Bridging loans* Two examples in which the need for a bridging loan may arise have been mentioned above. Provided that in the first case a mortgage offer has been made and that in the second case contracts on the sale have been exchanged, the purchaser should not find it too difficult to arrange a bridging loan from a bank. As the loan is only required until either in the one case the mortgage advance or in the other case the sale money comes to hand, the period of the loan will be a finite term and the bank will be virtually certain that there will be no problem over the repayment of the loan. On the other hand if in the one case no mortage offer has yet been received or in the other case if contracts on the sale have not yet been exchanged, the bridging loan is an open ended commitment and the bank might be less likely to grant the loan.

A bank making a bridging loan will require an undertaking from the purchaser's solicitor to pay in the one case the mortgage advance, or in the other case the net proceeds of sale, to the credit of the loan account. The purchaser's solicitor should not undertake to actually repay the loan in case the mortgage advance or the net proceeds are not sufficient for that purpose. However, the bank will want some assurance as to the likely amount of the net proceeds, and also as to the deductions which will be made by the solicitor, such as the solicitor's own costs. In practice the bank may have its own standard form of undertaking; if so the purchaser's solicitor should ensure that he only undertakes to do what he can in fact do. As with all undertakings he must obtain his client's agreement to the undertaking.

6 *Payment of purchase price* The purchaser's solicitor must make preparations to pay the purchase price on completion. Depending on how and when completion is to take place, there are in practice two methods of payment. The first is by banker's draft. This is rather like a cheque drawn on a bank, rather than on a particular account at the bank, and is thus virtually as good

16 [1986] NLJ Rep 117.

as cash. It will be made out in favour of the vendor's solicitor. A banker's draft will be used if completion is by the purchaser's solicitor personally attending at the vendor's solicitor's office. It may also be used if completion is by the purchaser's solicitor's agent attending at the vendor's solicitor's office, if the latter is some distance from the purchaser's solicitor's office. It could also be used if completion takes place not by personal attendance but through the post. The disadvantage of using a banker's draft in any but the first of these three situations is that the draft must be obtained a day or two before completion so that it can be posted to the purchaser's solicitor's agent or the vendor's solicitor as the case may be.

If completion is taking place not at the vendor's solicitor's office but at the office of the solicitor for the vendor's mortgagee, because the vendor's mortgagee will not release the deeds or the charge certificate to the vendor's solicitor, then two banker's drafts may be needed, one payable to the vendor's solicitor and the other payable to the solicitor for the vendor's mortgagee. The latter would represent the redemption figure on the vendor's mortgage and the former the remaining balance of the purchase monies owed to the vendor. The mechanics of such a completion will be discussed in more detail later in this chapter.

Although it is clearly safer for a vendor's solicitor to insist on a banker's draft, he might in some situations be willing to accept the purchaser's solicitors client account cheque, particularly if accompanied by an undertaking that it will be honoured on first presentation.

The other method of payment is by bank telegraphic transfer, or credit transfer as it is sometimes called. This can be used to transmit the completion money to the vendor's solicitor (if completion is by post) or to the purchaser's solicitor's agent if completion is to be by the attendance, at the vendor's solicitor's office, of the agent. To take the former as an example, the vendor's solicitor will provide the purchaser's solicitor, before completion, with the name and address of his bank and the number of the client account. The purchaser's solicitor asks his own bank to transfer the completion money from his client account to the vendor's solicitor's client account. This can often be done very quickly, in a matter of an hour or so. The receiving bank can be asked to notify the vendor's solicitor as soon as the funds are received. Although most if not all banks offer this service, the Trustee Savings Bank has developed in conjunction with the Law Society a service specifically designed for solicitor's conveyancing and other transactions called 'Speedsend'. The credit transfer procedure is particularly useful on a contemporaneous sale and purchase where speed of the transfer of funds is very important.

The method of payment on completion may be prescribed by the conditions in the contract – see chapter 5, section 4 xix.

v Lodging a priority notice

This is a step which may be taken by the vendor's solicitor before completion, in particular where the purchaser is buying unregistered land with the aid of a mortgage, and the vendor is selling only part of what he owns and imposing new restrictive covenants on the part sold to the purchaser. The priority notice procedure is considered in chapter 11, section 1 i 11, above.

vi Placing Land Certificate on deposit

If the vendor is only selling part of the land comprised in his registered title, he will not wish to hand over his Land Certificate to the purchaser as it relates to land that he is keeping. However the general rule is that on an application for registration the Certificate must be produced.[17] The problem is solved by a compromise. The vendor's solicitor will send the Land Certificate directly to the District Land Registry, where it is then available when the purchaser's application for registration is dealt with. Afterwards, it will be returned to the vendor, suitably amended to reflect the up to date position of the register, with the part of the land sold having been removed from the title. When the Land Certificate is sent to the registry by the vendor's solicitor, he will be given a deposit number. This can be communicated to the purchaser's solicitor on or before completion and can then be quoted on the purchaser's application for registration. If the vendor's property is in mortgage the Land Certificate is held at the Registry anyway. If the mortgage is only being discharged as to the part sold, a similar procedure is adopted in respect of the Charge Certificate; it is sent by the vendor's mortgagee's solicitor to the Registry to await the purchaser's application for registration, which will include an application for the discharge of the mortgage in relation to the part sold on which application of course the Charge Certificate is needed.

It is the vendor's duty to ensure that the certificate is deposited at the Registry for use on the purchaser's application for registration.[18]

2 Delayed completion

i Delayed completion

As time is not normally of the essence of completion, if one party does not complete on the contractual date for completion the other party cannot treat the contract as discharged by the breach but must give the first party time in which to complete. However, the delay may result in some adjustment of the purchase price. The open contract approach is to treat the parties as if they had completed on the contractual completion date. The purchaser therefore becomes entitled to any income received after the contractual completion date and must also bear the outgoings.[19] If the vendor has remained in occupation then he must also pay a fair occupation rent to the purchaser for the period between the contractual completion date and the actual completion date, unless the delay is due to the purchaser's default.[20] Under an open contract, the vendor is entitled to receive interest on the balance of the purchase money for the period of the delay. Again this accords with the principle of treating the parties as if they had completed on the contractual completion date. If the delay is due to the wilful default of the vendor, and if the interest payable to the vendor would exceed the net income (if any) of the property for the period of the delay, then the purchaser can keep the interest and the vendor can keep

17 Land Registration Act 1925, s. 64(1).
18 Ibid, s. 110(6).
19 See section 2, above.
20 *Metropolitan Rly Co v Defries* (1877) 2 QBD 387, CA.

the income, as otherwise the vendor would be profiting from his default.[1] Additionally, if the purchaser is liable to pay any interest, he can put the balance of the purchase money on deposit and the vendor will then only be entitled to the interest actually accruing.[2] In practice the purchaser will probably not have the balance of the purchase money available to put on deposit, as some of it may be coming by way of mortgage advance which will not be available until completion. Similarly some of it may be coming from the proceeds of sale of the purchaser's present property, completion of which may also be delayed to coincide with completion of the purchase.

As well as these adjustments to the purchase price, the innocent party may be entitled to some compensation for loss caused by the delay. Although time is not of the essence and a failure to complete on the contractual completion date does not entitle the other party immediately to rescind, it is nevertheless a breach of contract giving rise to a liability to pay damages. This was confirmed in *Raineri v Miles*,[3] where a purchaser claimed the cost of temporary accommodation necessary as a result of a delay in completion. The normal contractual rules of the measure and remoteness of damages will apply.

This, then, is the open contract position, but what of contracts which are subject to the Law Society or National Conditions? The question of apportionment of income and outgoings has already been dealt with in section 2 above, but what of the payment of interest and compensation for late completion? The open contract interest rate used to be 4 per cent although it is now acknowledged that this is ludicrously low and it would be increased.[4] In practice the interest rate will normally be specified in the special conditions. Failing this the National Conditions prescribe the interest rate under the Land Compensation Act 1961, section 32 – the rate payable by a local authority after entry under a compulsory purchase order.[5] The National Conditions provide that the purchaser must pay interest at this rate unless the delay is due to the vendor's default, or unless the vendor elects to take the net income for the period of the delay instead of the interest.[6] The purchaser's open contract right to put the balance of purchaser money on deposit is preserved.[7] Presumably the innocent party would still have the right to damages under *Raineri v Miles*[8] in respect of any loss caused by the delay in completion.

The Law Society Conditions approach the problem in rather a different way, combining the rule in *Raineri v Miles*[9] with the provisions as to payment of interest. If the rate of interest is not specified in the special conditions, the Law Society Conditions, like the National Conditions, refer to the rate under section 32 of the Land Compensation Act 1961.[10]

1 *North v Percival* [1898] 2 Ch 128.
2 See for example, *Bennett v Stone* [1903] 1 Ch 509, CA.
3 [1981] AC 1050, [1980] 2 All ER 145, HL.
4 See *Wallersteiner v Moir (No 2)* [1975] QB 373, [1975] 1 All ER 849, CA: *Bartlett v Barclays Bank Trust Co Ltd (No 2)* [1980] Ch 515, [1980] 2 All ER 92, CA.
5 NC preliminary note 4.
6 NC 7(2)(i), 7(1)(i).
7 NC 7(1)(ii).
8 Above.
9 Above.
10 LSC 1(b).

The general principle, stated in Law Society Condition 22, is that the party in default should compensate the other party for the loss caused by the default. A party is defined as being in default if he has delayed for a period in excess of the period of delay (if any) of the other party, and the period of the default is the length of the excess (or the delay in completion, if shorter). A party has delayed if he has failed or been late to perform some contractual obligation which contributes to the lateness of completion. The condition then gives two optional methods of calculating the compensation payable as a result of the late completion. Firstly, *either* party can elect, by notice given before actual completion, or within five working days thereafter, to be paid interest at the contractual rate on the outstanding purchase money, as liquidated damages. However, the interest is only payable for the period of the default, as defined above. Secondly, the vendor can elect before completion to take the net income of the property for the period of default in lieu of compensation.

ii Forcing a party to complete

The preceding section has examined the compensation payable, and other financial consequences, of late completion. This assumes of course that completion does eventually take place. How can a party compel the other party to complete? He has two alternatives; he can either apply for a decree of specific performance or he can make time of the essence of completion by serving a notice to complete. The latter will not in itself force the other party to complete but will make the consequences of non-completion more serious; if a party does not complete within the period of a notice to complete which has made time of the essence, then the other party is entitled to rescind and sue for damages for breach of contract. Specific performance, notices to complete and damages for breach of contract are all considered in more detail in chapter 16.

iii Practical consequences of delay

If a client is both buying and selling, and one of these transactions is delayed, he faces the prospect of either delaying the other transaction (and making himself liable for interest – and/or compensation – if he does so) or completing the other transaction, which would doubtless cause inconvenience. If he completed his sale before his purchase he would need somewhere to live and to store his furniture; if he completed his purchase before his sale, he would need a bridging loan until the proceeds of sale became available. Assuming that the delay was not caused by his default, he could attempt to recover his loss from the party who caused the delay.

If completion of a purchase is delayed and the purchaser's solicitor is also acting for the mortgagee from whom the purchaser is receiving a loan, then the mortgagee client should be informed of the delay and it may be necessary to return the advance to the mortgagee pending a resolution of the delay.

3 Completion

i Method of completion

There are two principal ways in which a transaction can be completed; by personal attendance or through the post. Attendance could be by the party's solicitor or the solicitor may appoint an agent. The purchaser money may be paid by banker's draft or by bank telegraphic transfer. The venue for a completion by personal attendance will normally be the vendor's solicitor's office. If the vendor's solicitor is not acting for the vendor's mortgagee, and thus has not got the deeds or charge certificate, completion may take place at the offices of the solicitor for the vendor's mortgagee. We shall deal firstly with a completion where the vendor's solicitors do act for the vendor's mortgagee (if any), which does take place at the vendor's solicitor's office and where the purchaser's solicitor also acts for the purchaser's new mortgagee (if any). We shall then deal with the other possibilities including completing through the post.

ii Procedure on a typical completion

1 *Verification* This has been discussed already in chapter 10, when it was noted that although there are advantages in verifying the abstract or epitome on a sale of unregistered land before completion, common practice is to leave verification until completion. The vendor is then under a duty to produce the documents of title which are to be handed over and the abstract or epitome can be verified as the first step on completion. Verification is doubly important if the sale is a sale of part, because the vendor will be retaining the original deeds (although the purchaser will be receiving an acknowledgment and possibly an undertaking in respect of them). The purchaser's solicitor will mark on his abstract that he has verified it against the originals and give the date and name of his firm. This marked abstract is the only evidence of title (apart from the purchase deed) which the purchaser will have, although of course he will have the right to production of the originals.

Again as we saw in chapter 10, problems can occur if the property sold is property which was the subject of a sale of part sometime in the past. The vendor will not have the original deeds but only the marked abstract that was obtained when the sale of part took place. The purchaser's solicitor might rely on this marked abstract when verifying his own abstract, and not insist on production of the originals; the purchaser could insist on production of the originals, albeit at his own expense, under the Law of Property Act 1925, section 45(4). Reliance on a marked abstract is a potentially risky practice, convenient though it is, and the purchaser's solicitor should at the very least check the date of examination of the marked abstract when checking for the existence of memoranda etc. If the abstract was marked against the originals *before* completion of the sale off, then it clearly offers no sort of evidence that such memoranda were not endorsed on the originals at the time of the sale off.

The general conditions in the contract may contain some limitation on the vendor's duty to produce documents. The National Conditions limit the vendor's duty to production of documents of which he can actually obtain production.[11] The Law Society Conditions provide that the vendor must produce at his own expense the original documents of title or marked abstracts thereof.[12] Whilst this relieves the purchaser of his obligation under the Law of Property Act 1925, section 45(4) to pay for production of documents not in the vendor's possession (or the possession of the vendor's mortgagee or trustee), it leaves open the question of whether the purchaser *ought* to be satisfied with seeing marked abstracts.

If an original document should be lost or destroyed, the vendor can comply with his obligation of production by providing secondary evidence of the contents of the document, including execution;[13] this might include a draft of the document and/or a statutory declaration as to its contents.

2 *Vendor's solicitor* There are a number of documents and items which the vendor's solicitor will need on completion, either for handing over to the purchaser's solicitor or for examination by him.

(a) The vendor's solicitor will hand over all the deeds and other documents of title except where they relate to land which the vendor is retaining. As mentioned in the previous paragraph, the vendor must bear the expense of obtaining these documents for the purpose of handing over on completion.[14] In addition to the original deeds, the vendor's solicitor will be handing over any other documents relating to the property, including abstracts and epitomes prepared in the past, old search certificates, and other documents which are not documents of title at all, such as planning consents and NHBC agreements, certificates or policies.

If the land being sold is registered land not subject to a registered charge, the vendor's solicitor will hand over the Land Certificate. If the property *is* subject to a registered charge, the vendor's solicitor will hand over the Charge Certificate, the Land Certificate having been retained at the Land Registry. On a sale of part of registered land the Certificate will not be handed over but instead put on deposit at the Land Registry as described earlier in this chapter. Even though title to the land is registered there will still be the old pre-registration title deeds which will also be handed over on completion.

(b) In certain circumstances the purchaser may require a memorandum of his conveyance or assignment to be endorsed on a document of title that the vendor is retaining. This would happen if the vendor of unregistered land was only selling part of the land comprised in the deeds in which case the purchaser would want a memorandum of the sale off to be endorsed on the conveyance or assignment to the vendor. Similarly if the vendor was a personal representative and thus retaining the grant of probate or administration, the purchaser would want a memorandum of the sale to be endorsed on the grant. The vendor's solicitor will write or type an undated memorandum on the appropriate document of title in readiness for completion and then on completion he will date it and hand the purchaser's solicitor a copy which can

11 NC 12(3).
12 LSC 12(2).
13 *Re Halifax Commercial Banking Co Ltd and Wood* (1898) 79 LT 536. Proof of loss must also be given although due stamping will be presumed.
14 Law of Property Act 1925, s. 45(4).

be kept with the purchaser's deeds. In neither of these circumstances is a memorandum essential; the object is to warn any future purchaser of the land that part of it has already been sold off. However if the vendor does sell the same land again to another purchaser, that purchaser cannot acquire a legal estate because the vendor no longer has a legal estate to sell; in the case of a sale by a personal representative, the first purchaser is protected by the provisions of the Administration of Estates Act 1925, section 36(6). Nevertheless, some inconvenience would occur if the vendor did either mistakenly or fraudulently purport to sell the same property again and the effect of the memorandum is to ensure that this will not happen.

(c) The purchase deed itself will be handed over on completion. The purchaser's solicitor will check that it has been duly executed by the vendor. The deed will de dated with the date of completion and will therefore only be dated actually on completion. Apparently insertion of the date after execution by the parties does not invalidate the deed. A solicitor may be tempted to back-date the deed, that is to date it with a date before the actual completion date; if the priority period of a search has expired at the time of completion, the deed might be back-dated to within the priority period in order to try and obtain the priority conferred by the search. Such back-dating is totally ineffective. In the case of a Land Charges search, the purchase must be *completed* within the period of the search to take priority. For registered land, to gain priority the purchaser's solicitor must not only complete but must also apply for registration within the priority period and the latter obviously cannot be back-dated. The proper course for the purchaser's solicitor in such a position is to do another search and to delay completion until the result is received. As we have seen, searches can be effected quite quickly by telephone.

(d) The purchaser's solicitor will wish to inspect the most recent receipt for rates and water rates to ensure that they have been paid, particularly if part of this payment has been apportioned to the purchaser in the completion statement.

(e) If the property sold is leasehold, the vendor's solicitor will produce for inspection the most recent receipt for ground rent. The Law of Property Act 1925, section 45(2) provides that on the sale of leasehold land the purchaser shall assume unless the contrary appears that the lease was duly granted and, on production of the last receipt for rent due, that the covenants and other provisions of the lease have been performed and observed. Section 45(3) contains a similar rule in relation to superior leases on the sale of an underlease. The rule is the corollary of the open contract rules in the Law of Property Act 1925 which restrict the purchaser's right to investigate title. If the receipt does contain reference to a breach of covenant then the purchaser would not be able to rely on the statutory assumptions. In addition, the receipt of course provides evidence that the rent has been paid up to date. Similarly if a leasehold property is subject to a service charge which is being apportioned, the purchaser's solicitor will wish to see evidence of the charge.

On the sale of leasehold property any requisite licence to assign would also be handed over, unless already supplied.

(f) On a sale of part by the vendor, thc title of which is not registered, the vendor will wish to keep some record both of precisely what land has been sold off and of any covenants or easements imposed. The vendor's solicitor will therefore keep a copy of the purchase deed which can be placed with the vendor's deeds. On a transfer of part of registered land, the land sold off will be removed from the register of the vendor's title and any easements or covenants contained in the transfer will be incorporated in the register of the vendor's title.

(g) As on completion the purchaser becomes entitled to possession of the property, keys may be handed over. If the keys are held by the vendor's estate agent then he should be authorised to hand them over to the purchaser. It may be better for the vendor's solicitor to telephone the estate agent in the presence of the purchaser's solicitor on completion, to ensure that there will be no problems. On the other hand the keys may be handed over by the parties as they move in and out respectively. The danger of this is that the actual removal out of and into the property becomes divorced from legal completion. It would not be impossible for the vendor to move out and the purchaser to move in only to discover that completion had not in fact taken place; or for completion to take place only to discover that the vendor, or some member of his family, was refusing to move out. At the very least, the vendor should be asked not to hand over the keys to the purchaser and let him into possession until his solicitor has confirmed that completion has taken place. A further refinement would be for completion to take place at the property itself. This happens very rarely, if ever, in practice but it would also have the advantage of avoiding to some extent (and particularly in relation to registered titles where it is the lack of occupiers at the date of registration of the purchase after completion which is significant) the problem of there being occupiers of the property whose interests would, by virtue of their occupation, be binding on the purchaser.[15] It might be extremely inconvenient to have both solicitors present at the property, but they could then ensure that it was vacant.

The National Conditions attempt to solve the problem of ensuring that the property is vacant on completion by providing that if the purchase deed will not over-reach the interests of persons in occupation, the purchaser may by giving reasonable notice require that on or immediately before the time of completion, possession of the property must be handed over to the purchaser or his representative at the property.[16] Whilst the idea behind this condition is admirable, it might be difficult to put into effect in practice. Indeed, the vendor might baulk at the idea of handing over possession before completion. What if completion then does not take place?

(h) What if the property is subject to a mortgage? To deal firstly with unregistered land, if the vendor's solicitor also acts for the mortgagee, he will have the deeds and can hand them over to the purchaser on completion. How is the purchaser to see that the mortgage has been discharged? A mortgage is discharged by receipt under either the Law of Property Act 1925, section 115 or the Building Societies Act 1986, Schedule 4. This is normally endorsed on the mortgage. The purchaser's solicitor will wish to see the mortgage discharged before he parts with the purchase money. However, if the funds to pay off the mortgage are being provided by the purchase money then obviously the mortgage cannot be paid off before completion! If the vendor has, on

15 See ch 11, sections 1 iii and 2 iii, above.
16 NC 5(4).

completion, the receipted mortgage deed in relation to not only the first mortgage but any other second mortgages, he will be able to hand these over on completion and there is no problem. This depends on the mortgagee(s) being willing to receipt the mortgage deed *before* the money necessary to redeem the mortgage is paid, on the understanding that when the solicitor hands the receipted deed over on completion he will immediately send off the redemption figure due on the mortgage. Not many Building Societies or banks are willing to do this, although at least one Building Society will receipt the mortgage deed in escrow, which means that the receipted deed can then be handed over on completion. It is likely, though, that the mortgagee will not receipt the deed until after completion when it receives the money required to pay off the mortgage. The problem of how the purchaser's solicitor is then to be satisfied that the mortgage(s) will indeed be discharged is solved by the use of the solicitor's undertaking. The vendor's solicitor will provide the purchaser's solicitor on completion with a written undertaking to send off the redemption money to the mortgagee and to forward the receipted mortgage deed to the purchaser's solicitor as soon as it is received from the mortgagee. In practice the purchaser's solicitor will normally be satisfied with this sort of undertaking, provided of course that it relates to all outstanding mortgages. It should be noted that the vendor's solicitor is only undertaking to do that which is actually within his control, that is to send off the money (which he knows he will be receiving on completion) and to forward the receipted mortgage deed when it is received. He is not undertaking to actually obtain the receipted deed and if there is some hold-up on the part of the mortgagee this would not amount to a breach of the undertaking. If the mortgagee is a Building Society or bank then the purchaser's solicitor will usually be happy to take this very slight risk, knowing that he can rely on the Building Society or bank to perform its functions properly. If on the other hand the mortgagee is a private individual or company (which is quite rare), the purchaser's solicitor may not be happy with an undertaking and may insist that completion take place at the mortgagee's solicitor's offices so that the receipted mortgage deed can be actually handed over on completion.[17] The receipt should be dated at the latest with the completion date, to avoid the receipt impliedly operating as a transfer.[18]

In theory the vendor's solicitors, in their role of acting for the mortgagee on discharge of the mortgage, should hand the deeds over to any subsequent mortgagee of whom the mortgagee has notice. In practice any second mortgages will also be discharged out of the proceeds of sale and so the deeds can be handed on to the purchaser's solicitors.

In the case of registered land, the basic problem is the same. Assuming that the mortgage is protected as a registered charge, it is discharged by the mortgagee signing, or in the case of a corporation, sealing, a form 53 application for discharge of the registered charge; this is then sent to the District Land Registry along with the Charge Certificate. If the vendor's solicitor has on completion the Charge Certificate and form 53 in relation to the first and any other mortgages, he can hand them over and there is no problem. Again, this

17 See section v, below.

18 See Law of Property Act 1925, s. 115(2) and *Cumberland Court (Brighton) Ltd v Taylor* [1964] Ch 29, [1963] 2 All ER 536.

is unlikely and an undertaking will be offered to the purchaser's solicitor, to pay off the mortgage and forward the form 53 when it is received.

Instead of being protected as a registered charge, an informal mortgage of registered land can be protected by a notice of deposit of the land certificate being entered on the register.[19] The appropriate method of discharge is by notice of withdrawal signed by the mortgagee.[20] This is a form 86 which is the equivalent of form 53.

If the vendor is a company and the investigation of title has revealed a floating charge over its assets including the property being sold, the purchaser's solicitor will require a letter of non-crystallisation from the chargee or its solicitors, confirming that at the date of completion the floating charge had not crystallised.

(i) The vendor's solicitor may prepare a schedule of the deeds and other documents of title which he is handing over, which the purchaser's solicitor will sign on completion; this avoids any argument later about any missing deeds or documents.

(j) If in order to save stamp duty, the consideration in the purchase deed only reflects the amount paid for the property and not any additional sum for chattels such as carpets or curtains, the purchaser's solicitor may require a further receipt in respect of the amount paid for the chattels.

3 *Purchaser's solicitor* As well as examining and receiving the various documents already referred to in the previous section, the purchaser's solicitor will have other matters to attend to on completion.

(a) Payment of the purchase price: this will normally be by means of a banker's draft if completion is taking place by the purchaser's solicitor attending at the vendor's solicitor's office.

(b) Land Charges searches: as a precise description of the property need not be given on the application for the land charges search, the search certificate may reveal certain entries which do not in fact relate to the property sold. The purchaser's solicitor may ask the vendor's solicitor to certify on the search certificate that the entries do not affect the property. In fact, rather better practice would be for the purchaser's solicitor to obtain office copy entries of the registrations to check for himself that they do not affect the land which the purchaser is buying.

(c) Authority to release the deposit: if a deposit is held by a stake-holder, he cannot release it unless one party becomes entitled to it under the terms of the contract. Obviously on completion the vendor does become entitled to keep the deposit and indeed it forms part of the purchase money. If it is held by the vendor's solicitor, it can be released to the vendor. However, a preliminary deposit may he held by the vendor's estate agent and before releasing the money to the vendor, the estate agent might require some proof that completion has taken place and that the vendor has become entitled to the money. On completion, the purchaser's solicitor may have to provide a brief written authorisation to the estate agent acknowledging the vendor's

19 Land Registration Rules 1925, r. 239.
20 Ibid, r. 246.

right to the deposit. In practice the estate agent may set the deposit against his fee and send a bill to the vendor for the balance.

iii Agency completion

If the purchaser's solicitor does not wish to attend on completion because the vendor's solicitor's office is too far away, he can appoint a local solicitor as his agent to attend on completion. The agent should be given full instructions in line with the matters considered in this chapter, not forgetting verification for which the agent will need the abstract or epitome. The agent will charge for his services, but this may be very much cheaper than the purchaser's solicitor travelling to attend on completion personally.

The agent may be sent a banker's draft for the completion money with his other instructions through the post, but this depends on the finance being available a day or two before completion. Alternatively the money could be telegraphed to him and he could then obtain a banker's draft from his own bank. The purchaser's solicitor may even decide to telegraph the money direct to the vendor's solicitor on his undertaking not to release the money to his client until completion and to return the money if completion does not take place, although this does involve some slight element of risk and it is better to send the money to the agent.

iv Postal completion

On a postal completion instead of the two solicitors being present and exchanging inter alia the purchase deed and other documents of title, and the money, the exchange is made through the post or the money sent by telegraphic transfer. The purchaser's solicitor sends the purchase money and the vendor's solicitor in return sends the purchase deed, other title deeds, Land Certificate or Charge Certificate etc. Whilst this arrangement has the advantage of convenience, it has the disadvantage that no-one appears to be looking after the purchaser's interests on completion. Who will check that the purchase deed is properly executed? Who will verify and mark the abstract? The answer is that if completion is to take place by post, the vendor's solicitor must be instructed to act as agent for the purchaser's solicitor, to attend to these matters. It might be thought that there would necessarily be a conflict of interest in the same solicitor acting for both vendor and purchaser on completion. However it is the Law Society's view that this is not necessarily so. Postal completions are indeed very common in practice.

The problems were highlighted by the case of *Edward Wong Finance Co Ltd v Johnson, Stokes and Masters*.[1] In that case, a firm of solicitors in Hong Kong acting for a purchaser had sent the purchase money, including the mortgage advance, to the vendor's solicitor on the basis of the vendor's solicitor undertaking to forward the documents of title including the discharge of the vendor's mortgage. However, the vendor's solicitor absconded with the purchase money and the Privy Council held that the loss had to be borne by the purchaser's solicitors for failing to take appropriate steps to protect their client's interests. The case caused some concern in this country as the procedure resembled that followed on postal completions in this country. As a result, the Law Society in

1 [1984] AC 296, [1984] 2 WLR 1, PC.

1984 issued a code for completion by post.[2] Adoption of the code must be specifically agreed by the solicitors concerned and there will normally be a question on the form of pre-contract preliminary enquiries to this end. The code provides that the vendor's solicitor will act as agent on completion for the purchaser's solicitor without any fee. The vendor's solicitor undertakes that on completion he will have the vendor's authority to receive the purchase money and that he will be the duly authorised agent of any existing mortgagee to receive the part of the money paid to him which is needed to discharge such mortgage. Building Societies have indicated that it is not yet universal for a building society to automatically appoint the vendor's solicitors as such agent when sending him the title documents prior to the sale.[3] The vendor's solicitor (and the purchaser's solicitor too) should therefore confirm that such agency does exist.

The code further provides that the purchaser's solicitor will send the vendor's solicitor instructions as to what to do on completion, including verification and marking of documents, memoranda to be endorsed on deeds, the position in relation to keys, etc. In the absence of such instructions the vendor's solicitor is not under any duty to examine, mark or endorse any documents. Completion is actually effected by the purchaser's solicitor sending (normally by telegraphic transfer) the balance due to the vendor's solicitor. The vendor's solicitor will ask his bank to let him know when the funds are received and the vendor's solicitor holds the funds to the purchaser's solicitor's order pending completion taking place. The vendor's solicitor will then complete in accordance with the agreed instructions and thereafter he holds all title documents and other items to be sent to the purchaser's solicitor as agent for the purchaser's solicitor. He should immediately confirm to the purchaser's solicitor that he has completed and send confirmation together with the title documents and any other items to the purchaser's solicitor.

It will be seen that the basis of the code is that the vendor's solicitor acts as agent for the purchaser's solicitor so the purchaser's interests are being looked after on completion. Even prior to the publication of the code, postal completions should have been conducted on the basis of such an agency but it is fair to say that this was not always the case. The code has met with some criticism; it has been claimed that its provisions do not go far enough and that it does not meet the problem actually posed by the *Wong*[4] decision. In particular, it has been suggested that the purchaser's solicitor should seek confirmation from the vendor's mortgagee (rather than just the vendor's solicitor) that the vendor's solicitor has the authority to receive the money to discharge the mortgage.[5] Indeed, this point would seem to be equally applicable to a completion by personal attendance where an undertaking is given in the usual terms in respect of the discharge of the vendor's mortgage.

There is no obligation on the vendor to agree to adopt the code and to act as the purchaser's solicitor's agent on completion. If the vendor's solicitor does not co-operate then completion would have to take place by personal

2 [1984] LS Gaz 858.
3 Building Societies Association Circular 30 August 1985.
4 See footnote 1 above.
5 See (1984) Conv 158.

attendance or attendance of an agent. Clearly the vendor's solicitor would not agree to adopt the code if he thought there was any chance of a conflict of interest. If the code does apply then the specific instructions given by the purchaser's solicitor should include some agreement about the time of completion. This could be important not only from the point of view of synchronising two transactions but also because of the effect of there being occupiers in the property at the time of completion with interests potentially binding on the purchaser. Both the Law Society and National Conditions do contemplate completion taking place through the post.[6] Law Society Condition 21(3) defines completion as taking place when the money due is paid to the vendor's solicitors and when the vendor's solicitors hold the title documents to the order of the purchaser. Law Society Condition 21(4) further provides that the money is paid to the vendor's solicitors if it is paid to the vendor's solicitors' bank by telegraphic transfer, the vendor's solicitors having agreed to this method of payment.

v Completion at the office of the solicitor for the vendor's mortgagee

It may be that the vendor's solicitor is not also acting for the vendor's mortgagee. If the vendor's mortgagee is a Building Society, the vendor's solicitor may not be on the Building Society's panel of approved solicitors. In this case the vendor's solicitor will not have received the original deeds or Charge Certificate from the Building Society but merely, in the case of unregistered land, an abstract or epitome prepared by the Building Society's solicitor. Nevertheless on completion the purchaser will wish to examine and take away the original deeds, or the Charge Certificate in the case of registered land. The vendor's solicitor will not have them. Unless the mortgagee is prepared to release them to the vendor's solicitor, the answer is to complete at the office of the mortgagee or more likely its solicitor. The Law Society Conditions make specific provision for this.[7] This situation often occurs when the mortgagee is a Local Authority. It is normal for the purchaser to pay the purchase money by means of two banker's drafts. One will represent the amount outstanding on the vendor's mortgage. This will be made payable to the mortgagee's solicitor. The other will be for the remainder of the balance of the purchase money, made payable to the vendor's solicitor. On completion the first draft is paid direct to the mortgagee's solicitor who will then release the receipted mortgage deed (or form 53) along with the rest of the deeds (or Charge Certificate) to the vendor's solicitor who can then pass them on to the purchaser's solicitor. The mortgagee will normally receipt the mortgage deed or seal the form 53 in readiness for completion but if this is not done the purchaser's solicitor might accept an undertaking, which could be given by the mortgagee's solicitor instead of the vendor's solicitor.

If there are second mortgages, the vendor's solicitor may give an undertaking to discharge them in the normal way. An undertaking might also be given to the mortgagee's solicitor because unless the second mortgages are discharged, the mortgagee's solicitor ought to hand the deeds not to the mortgagor/vendor but to the second mortgagee with best claim to priority.

6 LSC 21(3); NC 5(4).
7 LSC 21(1).

vi Completion of the purchaser's new mortgage

The mortgage is completed immediately after the purchase; it cannot be completed before, because it is only when the purchaser has the legal estate that he can mortgage it. In practice if the same solicitor is acting for both purchaser and mortgagee it is difficult to actually detect completion taking place, but one *can* say that after completion, the documents of title are held by the solicitor on behalf of the mortgagee and not the purchaser. The mortgage advance would of course have been used to pay the purchase price. The mortgage deed itself would have been executed before completion and be already in the solicitor's possession.

If the purchaser's solicitor does not act for the purchaser's mortgagee, completion of the mortgage will be more apparent. The mortgagee's solicitor may attend on completion as well, to hand over the mortgage advance and to take away the documents of title including the new mortgage deed.

15 Post-completion

1 Vendor's solicitor

i Report to the client

Immediately after completion the vendor's solicitor should report to the vendor that completion has taken place.

ii Compliance with undertaking to discharge vendor's mortgage

The vendor's solicitor must attend to this immediately. On the day of completion, he must send to the mortgagee(s) the amount required to redeem the mortgage. The mortgagee will then return the receipted mortgage deed or in the case of registered land, form 53. In the case of unregistered land, if the mortgage deed was sent to the vendor's solicitor with the rest of the title deeds then it must of course be returned with the redemption money for it to be receipted. Having received the receipted mortgage or form 53, the vendor's solicitor should check it and then promptly forward it to the purchaser's solicitor in accordance with the undertaking.

iii Protection by registration

The sale deed may have created an interest which, if the land is unregistered, requires protection by registration as a land charge. A common example is a new restrictive covenant on a sale of part. Additionally, if some purchase money is left unpaid on completion, the vendor has a lien over the property to the extent of it and may protect this by registration as a Ciii land charge. The application for registration should be submitted as soon as possible to avoid the interest becoming void for non-registration should the purchaser dispose of the property. If the vendor has already registered a priority notice prior to completion, the application must be submitted within thirty days of the priority notice to gain the advantage of the priority notice procedure. There are standard forms of application for registration.

If new interests are created on a transfer of part of registered land, they will normally be protected automatically on the purchaser's application for registration. For example although a new covenant on a transfer of part of registered land is a minor interest and requires protection on the register, this will be effected when the purchaser applies for registration. However if the vendor has a lien as mentioned above, an application will need to be made for this to be protected as a caution.

iv Cancellation of registration

The vendor's solicitor will also attend to the cancellation of land charges registrations. So for example if the vendor had a second legal mortgage which was protected as a Ci land charge, on redeeming the mortgage the vendor's solicitor will also request the second mortgagee to cancel the registration. If the vendor has after completion registered a Ciii land charge (or caution) to protect his lien for some unpaid purchase money, then when he is paid the registration should be cancelled. If the vendor's spouse had registered a class F land charge (or Matrimonial Homes Act 1983 notice) then the purchaser would have only completed on provision of a form of application for cancellation signed by the spouse who registered it. If this is handed over on completion, the purchaser's solicitor will effect the cancellation by sending it off. It is an implied term of the contract that if there is a Matrimonial Homes Act 1983 registration, the vendor must procure its cancellation.[1]

The mere existence of a registration does not necessarily mean that the interest so protected is binding. If the interest is not binding on the purchaser under ordinary principles, the mere fact that it has been registered is neither here nor there. So if a restrictive covenant has become void for non-registration at some time in the past, the fact that it is now registered as a Dii land charge is immaterial. Similarly if a second mortgage has been discharged, the fact that the Ci land charge has not been cancelled is also irrelevant. Nevertheless it is proper practice to remove such redundant registrations as they will only lead to requisitions in the future.

In a registered land context, the cancellation of entries relating to registered charges such as second mortgages, and notices, will be dealt with on the purchaser's application for registration.

v Account to client for proceeds

As soon as possible after completion, the vendor's solicitor should account to the vendor for any balance of the proceeds of sale. The vendor should be sent a statement showing amounts received, payments, and a balance due to (or from) the vendor. This raises a number of subsidiary points.

1 *Estate agent's fee* If the vendor has used an estate agent, the latter will often send his account to the vendor's solicitor in the expectation that it will be paid out of the balance of the proceeds of sale. Before he pays it, the vendor's solicitor should check with the vendor that this is what the vendor intends and also check the amount of the account. If the estate agent holds a preliminary deposit from the purchaser, he might retain this on account of the fee.

2 *Solicitor's costs* The vendor's solicitor will wish to submit and agree a figure for his own costs and disbursements so that he can deduct these from the net proceeds. The solicitor's costs will probably be made up of two elements. Firstly there is a 'time costing' element calculated by multiplying the hours spent on

1 Matrimonial Homes Act 1983, s. 4.

the transaction by the hourly charging rate of the solicitor. Then there may be a second element reflecting the value of the property involved. It is quite in order to charge more on a £100,000 sale than on a £20,000 sale, to take account of the increased risks involved. There used to be a scale of charges for conveyancing transactions, calculated as a proportion of the sale price. This was abolished in the early 1970s. The Royal Commission on Legal Services in 1979 recommended that a scale charge be reintroduced but at the time of writing this has not yet happened. With increased competition for conveyancing, the solicitor may have been asked for a preliminary estimate of the costs or even a firm quotation; the Law Society produces a standard form for preliminary estimates.

3 *Capital gains tax* Although capital gains tax is payable on the gain accruing from the disposal of a house, as is the case with other assets, there is an exemption which will cover the vast majority of conveyancing transactions. The gain is exempt from capital gains tax if it arises on the sale of a dwelling house – including grounds up to one acre[2] – which has been occupied by the vendor as his only or main residence during his period of ownership.[3] There are detailed provisions to cover specific situations. For example, it is not necessary for the vendor to have been in occupation for the last two years before the sale, to cover the situation of a vendor who moves out of his house some time before he sells it. If the vendor has more than one house, he can elect which is to be his main residence and thereby qualify for the exemption. If the tax is payable, the vendor's solicitor should at the very least advise the vendor of this, and at an early stage in the transaction. It may be that the vendor's solicitor will also be instructed to deal with the assessment of the tax and payment out of the proceeds.

4 *Investment of proceeds* If the proceeds are substantial, particularly if the vendor is selling his house but not buying another, the solicitor may be asked to advise and deal with the investment of the proceeds.

5 *Position if vendor is a mortgagee exercising a power of sale* If the vendor is a mortgagee, for example a Building Society, exercising its power of sale, then it is not a simple matter of accounting to the client for the proceeds. The mortgagee is a trustee of the proceeds of sale and they must be applied in a particular order. This is considered at chapter 13, section 3ii, above.

6 *Reassignment of life policy* If the vendor's mortgage was an endowment mortgage, it will be necessary to reassign the life policy to the vendor.

2 And possibly larger grounds.
3 Capital Gains Tax Act 1979, ss. 101, 102.

2 Purchaser's solicitor

i Report to client

Immediately after completion the purchaser's solicitor should inform the purchaser that completion has taken place and that the purchaser is entitled to possession. If the purchaser's solicitor has also acted for the purchaser's mortgagee, then that client should also be informed of completion. Most Building Societies have a standard form which is completed and returned to the Building Society after completion.

ii Protection by registration

The purchase deed may create an interest in unregistered land which requires protection by registration as a land charge and which it is in the purchaser's interest to so protect. On a sale of part, the vendor may have entered into a new restrictive covenant affecting the land which he is retaining which would require registration as a Dii land charge. Similarly a new lease may contain an option, requiring registration as a Civ land charge. If title to land is registered, such matters are dealt with on the purchaser's application for registration.[4]

iii Cancellation of registrations

There are two registrations which the purchaser's solicitor may have made which he will wish to cancel after completion. These are registration of the purchaser's contract – as a Civ land charge for unregistered land or a notice or caution for registered land – and registration of the purchaser's lien for the deposit (if held by the vendor's solicitor as agent for the vendor) – as a Ciii land charge for unregistered land or a notice or caution for registered land.

iv Registration at the Land Registry

There are two circumstances in which the purchaser's solicitor will be obliged to register the purchaser's title at the Land Registry. Firstly, if title to the land is already registered, the purchaser having taken a transfer (or a lease for over 21 years) of whole or part. Secondly, if title to the land is not registered but there is a compulsory registration order in force which means that as a result of the purchase, the purchaser must now apply for first registration of title.

1 *Registration of a dealing in registered land* Following completion of a purchase of registered land, unless and until the purchaser applies for registration as proprietor of the land, the vendor's name will remain on the register and the vendor will therefore retain the legal estate. In addition, as was seen in chapter 2, a lease also counts as such a dealing and if the lease is registrable, ie for over 21 years, it must be registered with separate title to vest the legal estate in the lessee/purchaser. Registration is thus vital. Registration of a transfer will be dealt with here, and registration of a new lease will be dealt with in chapter 17.

Application for registration must be made within the priority period of the search done before completion, which is 30 working days. If not, priority over

4 As to registration of leases, see chapter 2, section 3, above.

intervening entries on the register which might affect the title is lost. Therefore the purchaser's solicitor must not only complete but also apply for registration within the 30 day period. There are standard forms of application provided, which vary according to whether the application is for registration of a transfer of the whole of the land in the vendor's title, or of part. If the vendor had a mortgage and if the purchaser has bought with the aid of a mortgage, the purchaser's solicitor also acting for the mortgagee, then the purchaser's solicitor is in fact making three applications.

(a) He is applying for the discharge of the vendor's mortgage(s). This application is supported by the form 53 and the Charge Certificate.
(b) He is applying for the registration of the transfer from the vendor to the purchaser. This application is supported by the deed of transfer and by the Land Certificate, which will already be at the Land Registry if the vendor had a mortgage.
(c) He is applying for the registration of the new mortgage as a registered charge in the Charges Register. This application is being made on behalf of the mortgagee and is supported by the new mortgage deed.

It can already be seen that the application must be accompanied by certain documents; the form(s) 53, the Charge Certificate(s), the transfer and the new mortgage deed. If the vendor had no mortgage, then the Land Certificate must be sent with the application.[5] The Land Certificate or Charge Certificate will have been handed over on completion to the purchaser's solicitor. As the original of the mortgage deed will be incorporated in the new Charge Certificate, a copy certified by the purchaser's solicitor as being a true copy must also be sent with the application. Should there be any delay in any document being available, the application should still be submitted within the priority period and the missing document forwarded as soon as possible. For example there might be some delay in the purchaser's solicitor receiving the form 53, or there might be some delay in the transfer being returned from the Inland Revenue where it will have been sent for stamping.

The application is sent to the appropriate District Land Registry. It must be accompanied by a fee, which is based on the value of the land, ie the consideration on a sale.[6] There is no fee payable on applying for the registration of a new mortgage made at the same time as registration of a transfer. If there is more than one purchaser, the application must state whether the survivor of them can give a valid receipt, which will only be the case if they are beneficial joint tenants rather than beneficial tenants in common. In the latter case, a restriction will be entered on the proprietorship register preventing a sole survivor dealing with the property. If the transfer contains new restrictive covenants, as it might well do on a sale of part, a certified copy must also be sent with the application.

In due course the Land Certificate (if there is no new mortgage) or a Charge Certificate (if there is a new mortgage which will be protected as a registered charge) will be issued to the purchaser's solicitor. Following a sale of part, a new title will be opened with a new title number for the part sold off and a new Land or Charge Certificate issued. The register of the vendor's title will

5 Land Registration Act 1925, s. 64(1).
6 Land Registration Fee Order 1986.

be amended to show that part of the property has been sold off and any provisions in the transfer which affect the vendor's title, for example if the vendor enters into new covenants or easements, will be noted on the register of the vendor's title.

On receiving the new Certificate the purchaser's solicitor should check it to ensure its accuracy. If it is a Charge Certificate it will then be sent to the mortgagee. If it is a Land Certificate the solicitor will require instructions from the purchaser as to its custody.

2 *First registration of title* As mentioned in chapter 2, where the purchaser is buying unregistered land and a compulsory registration order is in force for the area in which the land is situated, the purchaser must apply for first registration of his title if his purchase is either a conveyance on sale or an assignment on sale of a lease with over 21 years left to run or the grant of a lease for over 21 years. Thus it is highly likely that following a purchase of unregistered land in a compulsory registration order area, the purchaser will indeed have to apply for first registration. Registration following a conveyance or assignment will be dealt with here and registration following the grant of a lease will be dealt with in chapter 17.

The application must be made within two months of completion or the purchaser will lose the legal estate that he acquired on completion. However, late applications for registration are invariably accepted and by this means the legal estate is restored to the purchaser. There are a number of application forms to cover the various types of title which could be applied for, for example freehold or leasehold. On the forms, the purchaser's solicitor must certify that the title has been properly investigated, must disclose any incumbrances and explain any land charges registrations. The registry will also wish to examine the title themselves and to this end the application must be accompanied by all the title deeds and other documents of title including abstracts, epitomes, requisitions and replies thereto and land charges search certificates. The application is also accompanied by the purchase deed and a certified copy. If the purchaser has bought with the aid of a mortgage there will also be an application on behalf of the mortgagee for registration of the mortgage as a registered charge, and the mortgage and a certified copy of it must also be sent. The original mortgage is bound up with the charge certificate, but the original purchase deed is returned to the purchaser's solicitor after registration along with the rest of the pre-registration title deeds. There is a form of schedule which can be used for listing the documents sent with the application. If the applicants are joint purchasers there will be a question on the application form asking whether a survivor can give a valid receipt, similar to the question on the application form for registration of a dealing with registered land.[7]

The application form and accompanying documents together with the fee, which is proportionate to the sale price,[8] are sent to the District Land Registry for the area in which the land is situated. If the Land Registry have any queries on their investigation of the title they will raise a requisition of the purchaser's solicitor. Assuming that any such requisitions are satisfactorily answered, the

7 See section 1, above.

8 Land Registration Fee Order 1986.

title will be registered and a Land or Charge Certificate returned to the purchaser's solicitor along with the title deeds. Again, the Certificate should be checked carefully for accuracy. The title deeds will not normally be needed in the future; when the property is sold title will be deduced under the Land Registration Act 1925, section 110. However the pre-registration deeds are not totally redundant. They may contain more precise details of the boundaries of the property than the register and the filed plan. Also, any indemnity covenant included in the conveyance giving rise to first registration will not be noted in the register and thus when the first registered proprietor sells, it will be necessary to check the conveyance to him.

v Stamping

The purchase deed may require stamping. There are two forms of stamping; actual stamp duty itself and production to the Inland Revenue for the 'particulars delivered' or P.D. stamp. A purchase deed may require one or both or neither.

1 *Stamp duty*[9] Stamps to the value of the amount of duty payable are impressed on the deed. Stamp duty may be either ad valorem or at a fixed rate, ie 50p. Ad valorem duty is proportionate to the value of the property involved. Mention is made below not only of stamping purchase deeds but also the stamping requirements for other common conveyancing documents. This is important not only from the point of view of the purchaser's solicitor after completion but also from the point of view of the purchaser's solicitor in examining the abstract of title of unregistered land, to ensure that the abstracted documents have all been correctly stamped.

(a) *Conveyance on sale; assignment on sale; transfer on sale* Under this heading are the normal purchase deeds. They all bear ad valorem duty. The current rate is one per cent of the consideration. Provided that the deed contains the appropriate certificate of value, there is a total exemption if the consideration is £30,000 or less. If there are a number of connected transactions, duty is charged on the total consideration, so it is not possible to avoid duty by selling the property in a number of parts! The figures given are the current rates at the time of writing but they are changed periodically. In order to check the duties paid on deeds in the abstract it is necessary to know the rates applicable in the past; there are tables available from which this information can be ascertained.

On the sale of a new house, the stamp duty position can be rather complicated, because the actual conveyance may be just of the land, with the majority of the purchase price being payable under a separate contract for the erection of the house. The Inland Revenue work to a set of detailed rules which take into account in certain circumstances the contract price of the house.

(b) *Deed of gift ie voluntary conveyance, assignment or transfer; or any conveyance, assignment or transfer at an under value* Prior to 25 March 1985, ad valorem duty was payable on the value of the property. Now voluntary conveyances bear only the fixed 50p duty. At present, however, they must still be adjudicated by the Inland Revenue, although this requirement will be removed eventually,

9 See Stamp Act 1891 as amended.

provided the appropriate certificate is given.[10] (Adjudication is not in fact confined to such cases and any person interested can have a document adjudicated, that is have the Inland Revenue decide whether it bears duty and if so how much.) Since 25 March 1985, ad valorem duty is payable in respect of a conveyance at an undervalue on the actual consideration.

(c) *Leases* The rules regarding stamp duty are rather complicated. Briefly, ad valorem duty is payable on the premium, as if it were the consideration for a straightforward sale deed, as in paragraph (a), with the exemption if the lease contains the appropriate certificate of value. Ad valorem duty is also payable on the amount of the rent, the rate being dependent on the length of the term of the lease. A counterpart lease – that is the duplicate copy of the lease which is executed by the lessee and retained by the lessor – bears a fixed duty of 50p. See further at chapter 17, section 2 vii.

(d) *Assents* If an assent is not sealed but just signed, it bears no duty. An assent which is sealed bore the fixed duty of 50p prior to 25 March 1985, but now bears no duty.

(e) *Mortgages* Mortgages used to be liable to stamp duty but this rule was abolished as from 1 August 1971.[11] Similarly since that date, vacating receipts and deeds of discharge have not attracted duty. Building Society receipts were already exempt under the Building Societies Act 1962, section 117.

(f) *Deeds of appointment of new trustees, powers of attorney* These are both deeds which bore a fixed duty of 50p prior to 25 March 1985, but now bear no duty.

2 *Particulars Delivered Stamp* By the Finance Act 1931, section 28, whether or not stamp duty is payable certain documents must be produced to the Inland Revenue, together with a statement of the particulars of the document, whereupon a stamp – the P.D. stamp – will be impressed on the document. The documents which must be produced are:

(a) conveyances on sale, and transfers of registered freehold land:
(b) leases granted for terms of seven years or more:
(c) assignments on sale of such leases (and transfers on sale if the title to the lease is registered).

Some documents will require a P.D. stamp but not attract stamp duty, for example a conveyance on sale for under £30,000. Some documents on the other hand will attract stamp duty but not need a P.D. stamp, for example a deed of gift of property (fixed 50p duty). Some documents will require both stamp duty and a P.D. stamp, for example a conveyance on sale for over £30,000.

The statement of particulars is in a standard form, often called a P.D. form, and contains information as to the identity of the parties and the property and the amount of the consideration.

3 *Procedure* The stamp duty due, if any, and the P.D. form, if necessary, must be sent to the Inland Revenue with the deed within 30 days of the date of the deed. Late stamping is possible although a penalty could be charged. Under

10 Finance Act 1985, s. 87. (Fixed duty and adjudication requirement removed from 1 May 1987.)

11 Finance Act 1971, s. 64.

a procedure introduced in 1986, if a deed needs to be produced for a P.D. stamp, but does not bear stamp duty because the consideration does not exceed £30,000 and the deed contains a certificate of value, the P.D. stamping will be done at the District Land Registry, provided that registration is necessary either because title is already registered or because of compulsory first registration.

4 *Failure to stamp* The effect of failing to stamp either with the appropriate stamp duty or a P.D. stamp is that the document cannot be produced in court as evidence and thus cannot be used to prove title to the property.[12] An unstamped or insufficiently stamped document is clearly not a good link in the abstract of title to unregistered land and the importance of checking stamping on examining the abstract has already been mentioned. In the case of registered land, the Land Registry will not accept an application for registration which is supported by a document which is not duly stamped. The deed of transfer on a sale must therefore be stamped before the application for registration is made which, it should be remembered, must be within the priority period of the pre-completion search. If there is any delay the application for registration should be made without the deed, which should be forwarded as soon as possible.

5 *Stamp duty avoidance schemes* There was a vogue in the late 1970s and early 1980s for avoiding stamp duty on conveyances by an artificial scheme based on an agreement for a lease. Such schemes have been held to be ineffective and are now caught by Finance Act 1984, s. 11; if on examination of unregistered title it appears that such a scheme was used in the past, the purchaser's solicitor should raise a requisition based on the improper stamping of the conveyance unless it bears either an adjudication stamp or ad valorem duty.

vi Custody of title deeds, Land Certificate or Charge Certificate

If the purchaser has bought unregistered land with the aid of a mortgage, the purchaser's solicitor will have the title deeds, including the purchase deed and, assuming he also acted for the mortgagee, the new mortgage. The protection of a first legal mortgagee is to take custody of the title deeds rather than to register a Ci land charge. The deeds must therefore be sent as soon as possible to the mortgagee, probably a Building Society or bank. They should be listed on a schedule which the mortgagee should return receipted. If the purchaser's solicitor has not acted for the mortgagee, the mortgagee's own solicitor may have collected the deeds on completion.

If the land is registered then there will be a Charge Certificate and also the pre-registration title deeds. The mortgagee will want custody of the Charge Certificate and probably also the old title deeds.

If the property is not subject to a mortgage then the purchaser's solicitor will have the title deeds or if the title is registered, the Land Certificate and the old pre-registration title deeds. In each case the purchaser's solicitor should obtain instructions as to the custody of these documents. They might be left with the purchaser's solicitor for safe keeping; the might be sent to the pur-

12 Stamp Act 1891, s. 14(4).

chaser's bank for safe keeping; the purchaser might even want to keep them himself although he should be advised of their importance and the need to protect them from damage, destruction or theft.

vii Notice of assignment of leasehold land

If a lease contains a provision making the lessor's consent necessary to any assignment, that consent will have been obtained before exchange or certainly before completion. However the lease may merely provide that the lessor (or his solicitor) is to be given notice of any assignment, and any mortgage, or receipted mortgage, a certain time after the event. If so, the requisite notice must be given; it is normally sent in duplicate with a request that one copy be returned receipted. This can then be put with the deeds or the Land or Charge Certificate and is evidence that the requirement has been complied with. Even if there is no covenant requiring notice to be given, a mortgagee will want notice of the mortgage to be given to the lessor so that the mortgagee might be informed of any forfeiture proceedings.

viii Notice of assignment of life policy

If the purchaser has bought with the aid of an endowment mortgage, a life assurance policy will be assigned to the mortgagee. In his role of acting for the mortgagee, the solicitor must give notice of this assignment to the life assurance company. Building Societies will often provide a standard form of notice to ensure that the solicitor does not forget! Again, notice is normally given in duplicate and a copy returned receipted.

The life policy itself, the deed of assignment and the receipted notice will then be sent to the mortgagee along with the title deeds or the Charge Certificate; the life policy is security for the loan just as the property is, and the mortgagee will want custody of the policy and the assignment of it.

ix Registration at Companies Registry

If the purchaser is a company which has bought with the aid of a new mortgage, it will be necessary to lodge particulars of the mortgage at the Companies Registry within the prescribed period of 21 days from the date of the mortgage.[13]

x Rates

It is good practice to inform the Local Authority of the change of the rateable occupier of the property as a result of the purchase. A form is often sent with the Local Authority's replies to enquiries, which can be completed and returned to the Local Authority after completion. Similar notice can be given in respect of water rates.

xi Account to client

The same principles apply to the question of the solicitor's costs as have already been discussed in the previous section.[14] If the solicitor has been acting not only for the purchaser but also the mortgagee, then he will be submitting two

13 Companies Act 1985, s. 395.

14 Disbursements may include stamp duty, search fees and registration fee.

bills, although they may be combined. There is the bill for acting for the purchaser on his purchase (and also on his mortgage) and the bill for acting for the mortgagee on the mortgage, which is payable by the purchaser. In respect of the latter, there are guideline charges agreed between the Building Societies Association and the Law Society, based on the size of the mortgage advance.

3 Mortgagee's solicitor

In the previous section, we have assumed that the purchaser's solicitor is also acting for the mortgagee, and we have mentioned a number of steps which are taken after completion for the mortgagee rather than the purchaser. If there is a separate solicitor acting for the mortgagee, then these steps, such as giving notice to the lessor of the mortgage if the property is leasehold, and giving notice of assignment of the life policy in the case of an endowment mortgage, may be taken by the mortgagee's solicitor. However, the mortgagee's title is naturally dependant on the purchaser's title; for example, the mortgagee of a registered title will not be in a position to register the mortgage as a registered charge until the purchaser has registered the transfer; similarly if the necessary stamp duty is not paid on the purchase deed, this affects the mortgagee's title too. In practice therefore, the mortgagee's solicitor may take over such steps as registration and stamping, having been provided with the appropriate documentation and fees by the purchaser's solicitor.

16 Remedies

In the typical transaction the parties enter into a contract, which is then performed, and their remedies are largely the usual contractual remedies, set in the context of a conveyancing transaction. There are a number of different areas to consider. Firstly, there are situations in which a party is entitled to refuse to complete the transaction. Secondly, we must examine the ways by which one party can attempt to force the other party to complete if he is unwilling to do so, and the consequences of completion not taking place. Thirdly, the compensation which may be payable even though completion does take place must be considered. Fourthly, we must look at the remedies that exist after completion.

1 Situations in which a party can refuse to complete the contract

i Misrepresentation

An actionable misrepresentation is a statement of fact made by a party, which is untrue, on which the other party relies and which induces the other party to enter into the contract. One is normally dealing with misrepresentation by the vendor rather than by the purchaser. Misrepresentation can be categorised as fraudulent, negligent or innocent.

1 *Fraudulent misrepresentation* A fraudulent misrepresentation is one made knowing it is false or reckless as to whether it is false or true. The purchaser can rescind and also claim damages in the tort of deceit.[1]

2 *Negligent misrepresentation* A negligent misrepresentation is one which is not fraudulent, but where the vendor cannot prove that he had reasonable grounds for believing in the truth of the statement and did so believe right up to the time the contract was made. The purchaser can rescind, and/or claim damages under the Misrepresentation Act 1967, section 2(1). However the court has a power under the Misrepresentation Act 1967, section 2(2) to refuse to award rescission and to award damages in lieu. A negligent misrepresentation might

1 See for example *Derry v Peek* (1889) 14 App Cas 337, HL.

also amount to the tort of negligent mis-statement under *Hedley Byrne & Co Ltd v Heller & Partners Ltd.*[2]

3 *Innocent misrepresentation* An innocent misrepresentation is one which is neither fraudulent nor negligent. Again, rescission is available but there is no right to damages, although as with negligent misrepresentation the court has a power to award damages in lieu of rescission.

Rescission is an equitable remedy and thus the right to rescind can be lost even through no fault of the plaintiff.[3] This is particularly important in the case of innocent misrepresentation where the only method by which damages can be obtained is in lieu of rescission; if the right to rescind is lost then of course there can be no damages either.

The right to rescission is not lost merely because the mis-statement has become a term of the contract.[4]

4 *General conditions* It is likely that the purchaser's remedies for misrepresentation will be in some way curtailed in the general conditions in the contract. Both the Law Society Conditions and the National Conditions do contain such a provision. Briefly, the Law Society Conditions say that 'no error omission or misstatement ... in ... any statement made in the course of the negotiations leading to the contract shall annul the sale or entitle the purchaser to be discharged from the purchase'.[5] The purchaser is thus deprived of his right to rescind although the conditions do also provide that if compensation cannot be assessed or if the misstatement is such as to make the property substantially different from that agreed to be sold, the purchaser can still rescind.[6] The Law Society Conditions also provide that compensation will only be paid for 'material' as opposed to immaterial statements[7] and finally, and perhaps rather more controversially, that the purchaser acknowledges that he has not relied on any statements not made or confirmed in writing.[8] The National Conditions are of similar effect. They provide that unless either the misstatement was made fraudulently or recklessly or it is such as to prevent the purchaser getting substantially what he has contracted to buy,[9] the purchaser cannot rescind, and no compensation is payable unless the misstatement materially affects the description or value of the property.[10]

In addition to these conditions, the standard form of answers by the vendor to preliminary enquiries, which may be thought to be a potential source of misrepresentations by the vendor, may state that the answers are 'believed to

2 [1964] AC 465, [1963] 2 All ER 575, HL.
3 For example, if a third party would be prejudiced by the rescission.
4 Misrepresentation Act 1967, s. 1. Neither is the right lost merely because the contract has been completed, although if a third party such as a mortgagee would be prejudiced, rescission will not be granted.
5 LSC 7(1).
6 LSC 7(4).
7 LSC 7(2), 7(3).
8 LSC 7(5).
9 NC 17(2).
10 NC 17(1).

be correct' but that their accuracy is not guaranteed and they do not obviate the need to make appropriate searches and enquiries.[11]

The Misrepresentation Act 1967, section 3 regulates terms in contracts which restrict or exclude a party's liability for misrepresentation or the other party's remedies for misrepresentation. Both the Law Society condition and the National condition fall into this category. The effect of section 3 is that the term is of no effect except in so far as it satisfies the test of reasonableness laid down in section 11 of the Unfair Contract Terms Act 1977, the burden of proof being on the party relying on the term, ie the vendor. The test referred to is that the term must be a fair and reasonable one to be included in the contract having regard to the circumstances which were or ought to have been known by the parties at the time the contract was made. The question therefore arises whether the general conditions and the disclaimer on the form of preliminary enquiries are going to deprive the purchaser of his remedies for misrepresentation. There are cases which do give some comfort to the purchaser. In *Cremdean Properties Ltd v Nash*,[12] it was suggested that a disclaimer such as that on the standard form of preliminary enquiries would not necessarily exclude the vendor's liability although it might make it more difficult to show reliance on the statements made by the vendor. However in *Walker v Boyle*[13] it was held that the disclaimer on the standard form of enquiries was totally ineffective and also that the condition under review, which was the equivalent condition in the nineteenth edition of the National Conditions of Sale, did not meet the reasonableness test. That condition has now been modified in the current twentieth edition but it is significant that the court held that the condition did fall foul of section 3 despite its apparent acceptance in practice in being incorporated into a set of widely used general conditions.

ii Breach of contract

If a breach of contract is sufficiently serious, it may entitle the other party to withdraw from the contract. This will happen in practice in two main situations. Firstly, the vendor may be in default in being unable to convey that which he has contracted to convey, perhaps because he has misdescribed the property to the purchaser's detriment or failed to disclose a defect of title or cannot give vacant possession. Secondly, a party may be entitled to withdraw where the other party fails to complete and time is or has been made of the essence.[14]

1 *Misdescription and non-disclosure* Typically a misdescription might involve a misstatement of the area of the property,[15] or a description of land as simply

11 See for example the Oyez standard form. Such a disclaimer may also purport to exclude the liability of the vendor's *solicitor* to the purchaser in negligence – see *Wilson v Bloomfield* (1979) 123 Sol Jo 860, CA.

12 (1977) 244 Estates Gazette 547, CA.

13 [1982] 1 All ER 634, [1982] 1 WLR 495.

14 These are not the only situations in which a party can withdraw, but they are the most common in practice. So for example, if the purchaser fails to pay a deposit, the vendor can withdraw, always assuming there is a contract in existence.

15 For example *Watson v Burton* [1956] 3 All ER 929, [1957] 1 WLR 19.

'registered' when the title is not in fact absolute,[16] or the description of land as being held under a lease when it is in fact held on an underlease.[17] Non-disclosure will occur where some defect such as a restrictive covenant or a right of way is not disclosed. Under an open contract if the misdescription or non-disclosure is substantial, the vendor cannot force the purchaser to complete and the purchaser can recover his deposit.[18] If the misdescription or non-disclosure is *not* substantial then the purchaser must complete although with compensation by way of a reduction in the purchase price. Whether the misdescription or non-disclosure is substantial or not, the purchaser can always insist on completing, with an appropriate reduction in the purchase price. If the misdescription operates in the purchaser's favour, the vendor cannot claim an increase in the purchase price and will be forced to complete unless the court refuses the purchaser specific performance on the ground of hardship to the vendor; the purchaser could instead claim damages for breach of contract.

The general conditions mentioned in the preceding section as relevant to a claim for misrepresentation are wide enough to cover misdescription also. The Law Society Conditions state that 'no error omission or mis-statement' in the contract or any plan shall entitle the purchaser to rescind unless compensation cannot be assessed or the error results in the property being substantially different from that agreed to be sold.[19] Again, compensation is only payable in respect of a material error although it appears that if the error is in the purchaser's favour the vendor may be able to claim compensation![20] The National Conditions similarly refer to errors mis-statements and omissions in 'preliminary answers' or the sale plan or the special conditions;[1] the latter expression is defined in the preliminary note to the Conditions to include the particulars of the contract. Rescission is not allowed in respect of errors to which the National Conditions refer, with the saving that this restriction does not apply to an error made fraudulently or recklessly, or where the purchaser would not get substantially what he contracted to buy.[2] Compensation is only payable if such errors materially affect the description or value of the property.

2 *Failure by the vendor to show good title* We have seen that there are in essence two sorts of defect of title.[3] If the vendor cannot show good title because of the existence of some defect such as a right of way or restrictive covenant which he has failed to disclose then as mentioned in the preceding section, if the defect does substantially affect the property the purchaser will be able to withdraw from the contract and, on the face of it, sue the vendor for damages for breach. If the defect is a Matrimonial Homes Act 1983 registration then it becomes an implied term of the contract that the vendor will procure its

16 *Re Brine and Davies' Contract* [1935] Ch 388.
17 *Re Russ and Brown's Contract* [1934] Ch 34, CA.
18 *Flight v Booth* (1834) 1 Bing NC 370.
19 LSC 7(1), 7(4).
20 LSC 7(2), 7(3).
1 NC 17(1), 17(3).
2 NC 17(1), 17(2).
3 See ch. 5, section 4 ii, above.

removal;[4] if it is not removed then again the vendor is in breach of contract and the purchaser can withdraw and sue for damages.[5] Likewise if the vendor is unable to give vacant possession as a result of some undisclosed tenancy of the property.

The other sort of defect of title is the more 'technical' type, such as a flaw in the abstract of unregistered title. This again means that the vendor cannot show a good title and that the vendor is in breach of contract; the purchaser can 'rescind' and sue for damages. However the vendor's duty to show good title is not an absolute duty and there are degrees of 'goodness', as is shown by the case of *MEPC Ltd v Christian-Edwards*[6] where an investigation of title in 1973 revealed a contract for sale in 1912 not shown as having been discharged; the House of Lords held that good title had nevertheless been shown. The refusal by the vendor to answer a properly raised requisition will similarly entitle the purchaser to rescind.

3 *Failure to complete* Time is not normally of the essence of completion of a conveyancing transaction but it can be made of the essence by service of a notice to complete. This procedure is dealt with later in this chapter. Once time has become of the essence of completion by virtue of the notice, then if a party fails to complete this will amount to a breach of the contract entitling the other party to withdraw and claim damages for breach of contract.

iii Rescission under a specific contractual right

The contract may specifically provide that a party can in certain circumstances rescind the contract. An example of this is Law Society Condition 4 which provides that a purchaser can rescind within twenty working days of exchange if he becomes aware of some matter which would reduce the value of the property in that time. National Condition 3 is of similar effect. Under Law Society Condition 16 and National Condition 10, dealt with in chapter 10, section 22 iv, the vendor can in certain circumstances rescind if he is unable to comply with a requisition made by the purchaser. The contract will normally state the consequences of such rescission; under both sets of conditions the vendor repays the deposit and the purchaser returns all documents that have been sent to him.

iv Rescission for fraud, undue influence or mistake

Under ordinary contractual principles it may be possible to rescind in such cases.

v Damages

The word 'rescission' can bear a number of meanings. On rescission in the sense of setting the contract aside for misrepresentation or mistake, no damages may be claimed but merely an indemnity, the object of which is to compensate

4 Matrimonial Homes Act 1983, s. 4.
5 *Wroth v Tyler* [1974] Ch 30, [1973] 1 All ER 897.
6 [1981] AC 205, [1979] 3 All ER 752, HL.

the party in respect of obligations already incurred under the contract.[7] In a conveyancing context rescission by the purchaser may therefore be accompanied by a claim for return of the deposit and payment of any costs so far incurred in investigating the title. Rescission, though, in the sense of one party being entitled to withdraw from the contract as a result of a breach by the other party, can be accompanied by a claim for damages.[8] This will cover the situations mentioned in section ii, above. The amount of damages is discussed below.[9]

2 Forcing completion on an unwilling party

If a party is unwilling to complete, and does not fall within any of the categories which permit him to withdraw from the contract, then the other party has two main remedies; he can apply for a decree of specific performance or else he can serve a notice to complete.

i Specific performance

This is merely an ordinary contractual remedy in a conveyancing context. It is an equitable remedy and will only be granted if damages are not an adequate remedy. On a contract for the sale of land this is almost invariably the case. Similarly it is also subject to the other equitable bars such as undue delay.[10] In the unusual case of *Patel v Ali*,[11] specific performance was refused to a purchaser on the basis of hardship to the vendor, who since the date of the contract had been hit by many misfortunes, including serious illness.

A party is entitled to apply for a decree of specific performance when there is reason to believe that the other party will not perform the contract and complete. Thus in *Hasham v Zenab*[12] the purchaser applied for specific performance before the completion date where the vendor, having signed the contract, tore it up. Normally however the application will be made after the completion date has passed or after a notice to complete has expired and completion has still not taken place. It should be emphasised that there is no need to serve a notice to complete before applying for specific performance, but a party may wish to try that remedy first and if it fails then proceeed to apply for specific performance; alternatively, he could then claim damages. If a decree of specific performance is obtained but not carried out then damages can be awarded for breach of contract either at common law or under statute.[13]

7 Such rescission essentially restores the pre-contract position. Damages may of course be payable under the Misrepresentation Act 1967; see section i, above.

8 See *Buckland v Farmer and Moody* [1978] 3 All ER 929, [1979] 1 WLR 221, CA, confirmed in *Johnson v Agnew* [1980] AC 367, [1979] 1 All ER 883, HL.

9 See section 2 iii.

10 But see *Lazard Bros & Co Ltd v Fairfield Properties Co (Mayfair) Ltd* (1977) 121 Sol Jo 793.

11 [1984] Ch 283, [1984] 1 All ER 978.

12 [1960] AC 316, [1960] 2 WLR 374, PC.

13 Chancery Amendment Act 1858, s. 2; Supreme Court Act 1981, s. 50.

ii Notice to complete

Where a party has not been willing to complete on the completion date given in the contract, the other party clearly requires some process whereby he can make time of the essence of completion, so that if completion still does not take place he can treat the contract as at an end, sue for damages and, if the vendor, resell the property, or if the purchaser, look for another property to buy. This procedure is the service of a notice to complete. Under an open contract the party serving the notice must first of all wait until there has been an unreasonable delay after the contractual completion date, and then serve a notice requiring the other party to complete within a further period which in itself must be reasonable. This procedure is hazardous for the party serving the notice as he has to decide that two separate periods are sufficient to validate the notice – the period of delay and the period of the notice itself. Not surprisingly both sets of standard conditions contain a condition providing for a procedure which eliminates these difficulties.[14] The Law Society Conditions provide that the notice can be served at any time after the contractual completion date; the National Conditions provide that it can be served on or after that date. The period of a Law Society notice is fifteen working days; the conditions provide that the effect of the notice is that it becomes a term of the contract that the contract shall be completed within fifteen working days of service, time being of the essence. Under the National Conditions the period is 16 working days excluding the day of service.[15] The reasonableness or otherwise of these periods is immaterial. Under an open contract and also expressly under the Law Society Conditions, the notice is only valid if the party serving it is ready, willing and able to complete.[16] The Law Society Conditions specifically provide that a vendor is not unable to complete merely because there is an outstanding mortgage on the property, if that mortgage could (and would) be redeemed out of the proceeds of sale on completion.[17] Otherwise, if the vendor is not in a position to pass good title, he cannot serve a valid notice to complete.

Once a valid notice to complete has been served, it binds both parties, so that if the party serving the notice himself defaults and does not complete in time, the consequences are just the same as if the party on whom the notice is served is in default. So in *Oakdown Ltd v Bernstein & Co (a firm)*,[18] the vendor was in breach when it served a notice to complete which expired on a public holiday and then refused to complete on the previous day on religious grounds. (The problem could be avoided under current Law Society and National Conditions by specifying non-working days in the contract.) If after service of

14 LSC 23, NC 22.

15 In *Dimsdale Developments (South East) Ltd v De Haan* (1984) 47 P & CR 1, it was held that a notice which did not satisfy the general conditions (because it was too short) could nevertheless still be regarded as an effective common law notice.

16 NC 22(1) says 'ready and willing', which probably means the same.

17 This overcomes the problem in *Cole v Rose* [1978] 3 All ER 1121, which had indicated that if the parties had not agreed how the mortgage was to be discharged (the vendor's solicitors were unable to give the usual undertaking), the vendor might not be in a position to serve a notice; however, in a normal situation, the existence of the vendor's mortgage will not affect the validity of his notice to complete.

18 (1985) 49 P & CR 282.

the notice time is then extended by agreement, time can again be made of the essence by a further notice. The Law Society Conditions provide this need only be a seven instead of a fifteen day notice. If after expiry of the notice a party still refuses to complete, the other party may further attempt to enforce the contract by applying for a decree of specific performance or may rescind and sue for damages for breach of contract.

iii Damages if completion does not take place

We have mentioned a number of situations in which a party may rescind the contract and sue for damages, for example if the vendor cannot give vacant possession in accordance with the contract or if a party fails to comply with a notice to complete. The damages are those recoverable under the ordinary contractual rule in *Hadley v Baxendale*,[19] that is, the plaintiff can recover the loss which arises in the normal course of events from the breach or which may reasonably be supposed to have been in the contemplation of the parties at the time of the contract as the probable result of the breach. The loss is normally assessed at the date of the breach. The damages payable to a vendor will ordinarily be the contract price of the property (which he would have received under the contract but has not) less the current market value of the property and allowing for the additional expense of reselling the property. The Law Society Conditions specifically provide that if the purchaser does not comply with a completion notice and if the vendor then resells within a year of the contractual completion date, the vendor can claim as liquidated damages any loss incurred on the resale, and the costs of the resale (and any attempted resale). He can also claim interest at the contract rate on the outstanding balance of the purchase money from the contractual completion date.[20] That outstanding balance will presumably be the full ninety per cent of the purchase price, assuming a ten per cent deposit is paid, although it will be reduced eventually by the payment of the purchase price under the resale contract. None the less the figure for interest could be quite large. The National Conditions include a similar provision though without the reference to interest.[1] The Law Society Conditions further provide that the purchaser must cancel any registration relating to the contract.[2]

Even if the vendor suffers no loss he can forfeit the deposit although if he does claim damages he must give credit for the deposit. However, by the Law of Property Act 1925, section 49(2), the court is given a discretion to order repayment of the deposit to the purchaser even where the vendor would normally expect to be able to forfeit the deposit, for example, if the purchaser had refused to complete. The factors relevant to the exercise of this wide discretion include the conduct of the parties, the gravity of the matters in

19 (1854) 9 Exch 341.
20 LSC 23(5).
1 NC 22(3). This has led to some uncertainty as to whether interest can be claimed; see *Bruce v Waziri* (1982) 46 P & CR 81; *Wallace-Turner v Cole* (1982) 46 P & CR 164, and *Sakkas v Donford Ltd* (1982) 46 P & CR 290.
2 LSC 23(4)(a).

question and the amount of the deposit.[3] Thus if the deposit is very large, being 10 per cent of a very large purchase price, the court may feel it is fairer to let the purchaser have the deposit back, leaving the vendor with a claim in damages for his actual loss (if any). This jurisdiction is not to be confused with equitable relief against penalties – the court will not regard forfeiture of a 10 per cent deposit as a penalty. There was an interesting application of section 49(2) in *Dimsdale Developments (South East) Ltd v De Haan*,[4] where the court ordered return of the deposit on condition that the purchaser paid the vendor's expenses of the sale.

The damages payable to a purchaser will normally be the market value of the property at the date of the breach, less the contract price which the purchaser would have paid, but there may be other elements of loss recoverable as well. For example, the purchaser may have intended to redevelop the land and thereby make a profit which has now been lost. In such a case, as a result of the rule in *Hadley v Baxendale*, the purchaser's prospect of recovering his loss of profit will depend largely on whether the vendor was aware of the purchaser's plans. In *Diamond v Campbell-Jones*[5] the vendor was unaware and the purchaser could not recover his loss of profit whereas in *Cottrill v Steyning and Littlehampton Building Society*[6] the vendor was aware of the purchaser's intention to develop and damages did include an element of loss of profit.

In *Lake v Bayliss*,[7] the vendor, in breach of contract, resold the property to a second purchaser. Because the first purchaser had not protected his contract by registration, the sale to the second purchaser went ahead and the second purchaser did acquire the legal estate. However the first purchaser was able to recover from the vendor the excess of the price received by the vendor from the second purchaser over the price agreed for the first purchase. In effect, the first purchaser was being given the increase in the value of the property.

There is an old established and rather archaic rule that if the vendor is in breach of contract only because he cannot show good title, the purchaser can only recover his deposit and expenses of investigating title and not ordinary contractual damages for loss of bargain.[8] Thus although damages are in theory available from the vendor as a result of non-disclosure, this rule may effectively preclude such damages being payable. The rule is applied restrictively by the courts and the vendor must have used his best endeavours to perform the contract and to show good title, and must not have fraudulently misrepresented that he had a good title. In *Day v Singleton*[9] the vendor had failed to obtain a licence to assign leasehold property to the purchaser. As the vendor had in fact encouraged the lessor to refuse the licence, the vendor could not rely on

3 *Universal Corpn v Five Ways Properties Ltd* [1979] 1 All ER 552, CA; see also *Schindler v Pigault* (1975) 30 P & CR 328 and *Maktoum v South Lodge Flats Ltd* (1980) Times, 22 April.

4 Above.

5 [1961] Ch 22, [1960] 1 All ER 583.

6 [1966] 2 All ER 295, [1966] 1 WLR 753.

7 [1974] 2 All ER 114, [1974] 1 WLR 1073.

8 *Bain v Fothergill* (1874) LR 7 HL 158.

9 [1899] 2 Ch 320, CA.

this rule and had to pay full contractual damages. Similarly in *Re Daniel*[10] the vendor was unable to persuade his mortgagee to release the property sold from the mortgage, yet he could not rely on the rule. He should have obtained the mortgagee's concurrence before even entering into the contract of sale, or failing that, redeemed the mortgage, and he had to pay full contractual damages. More recently in *Malhotra v Choudhury*[11] one joint tenant failed to attempt to gain the other joint tenant's concurrence to a sale and was held liable in full damages. In *Wroth v Tyler*[12] it was held that a Matrimonial Homes Act 1983 charge is not within the scope of this rule and so a spouse who cannot obtain the cancellation of the other spouse's registration is liable in full damages to the disappointed purchaser. However, the rule was applied in the recent case of *Ray v Druce*[13] where the vendor could not convey because of a dispute about the extent of land which the vendor had previously sold off. In *Sharneyford Supplies Ltd v Edge* (*Barrington Black & Co, Third Party*),[14] the defect in title was a tenancy protected under Part II of the Landlord and Tenant Act 1954. The vendor could not rely on the rule because he had not served notice on the tenants (although even if he had, it is most likely that the tenants would have applied for a new tenancy under the provisions of the Act). The rule seems archaic in origin and somewhat illogical in operation, and the Law Commission has suggested that it be abolished.[15]

The Law Society Conditions specifically provide that if the vendor fails to comply with a notice to complete, the purchaser can demand repayment of his deposit. Having received this, the purchaser would be unable to obtain a decree of specific performance but would be entitled to sue for damages if he so wished.[16]

3 Damages payable even though completion does take place

Firstly, there will be many situations in which completion does take place as planned but one party, particularly the purchaser, may be entitled to some compensation. These have been mentioned in the first section of this chapter. For example the vendor may be guilty of misrepresentation but rescission may be refused or not sought by the purchaser, who may instead seek damages. A misdescription in the contract may be minor and the purchaser may still be bound to complete, but with a reduction in the purchase price. Despite the existence of an undisclosed defect in title, or the vendor's inability to give vacant possession, the purchaser may still complete in which case again his damages will be assessed under the ordinary contractual principles. So for example in *Beard v Porter*[17] the vendor could not give vacant possession in

10 [1917] 2 Ch 405.
11 [1980] Ch 52, [1979] 1 All ER 186, CA.
12 [1974] Ch 30, [1973] 1 All ER 897.
13 [1985] Ch 437, [1985] 2 All ER 482.
14 [1987] 1 All ER 588, [1987] 2 WLR 363, CA.
15 Working Paper 198 (1986). However, LSC 16 and NC 10 contain a similar rule.
16 LSC 23(6).
17 [1948] 1 KB 321, [1947] 2 All ER 407, CA.

accordance with the contract. The purchaser recovered the difference between the value of the property with vacant possession (ie the contract price) and the value with the sitting tenant. As he was buying the house to live in, he could also recover the costs incurred on the purchase of another house in which he could live, and the cost of his lodgings until he could move into this second house.

Another rather different situation in which compensation may be payable even though completion does take place is if completion takes place late. This is a breach of contract and the party in default is liable in damages, as was confirmed in *Raineri v Miles*.[18] (Assuming any notice to complete is complied with, it is not of course a breach which gives rise to a right to rescind but merely damages.) Compensation in these circumstances is discussed in chapter 14, section 2.

If completion takes place after a specified time on the completion date, this may entitle the vendor to compensation.[19]

4 Other post-completion remedies

Mention has already been made of some remedies which may be claimed after completion. Thus rescission for misrepresentation is still available after completion. In general, the terms of the contract merge into the deed on completion, although some do survive and can be sued on after completion, such as a term that vacant possession be given on completion.[20]

There are other remedies, against the vendor and others, which specifically relate to the post completion period.

i Covenants for title

In certain situations, the vendor will, in the conveyance or assignment, impliedly give certain covenants for title. The vendor's implied covenants for title to some extent replace the vendor's obligations under the contract, which merges into the deed. They can be extended or modified in the deed. The scope of the implied covenants depends on the capacity in which the vendor conveys and is expressed to convey in the deed. On a conveyance of freehold land for value by a vendor as beneficial owner, four covenants are implied.[1]

(a) Covenant that the vendor has a good right to convey. If the property is subject to some incumbrance such as a mortgage or easement or covenant not mentioned in the deed, this covenant will be broken.
(b) Covenant for quiet enjoyment.
(c) Covenant for indemnity in relation to any incumbrances. This covenant and the one above cover the situation where the purchaser's 'quiet enjoyment' of the property is affected, for example by the exercise of an undisclosed right of way.

18 [1981] AC 1050, [1980] 2 All ER 145, HL.
19 See ch. 5, section 4 xix.
20 *Hissett v Reading Roofing Co Ltd* [1970] 1 All ER 122, [1969] 1 WLR 1757.
1 Law of Property Act 1925, s. 76(1)(a).

(d) Covenant that the vendor will do anything else necessary to vest the property in the purchaser or a covenant for 'further assurance' as it is called. Thus if at the time of the conveyance to the purchaser, the vendor did not in fact own the land but did acquire title at some later date, he can be compelled to execute another conveyance in favour of the purchaser.

On an assignment for value of leasehold land by a beneficial owner, there are two further covenants implied.[2]

(a) Covenant that the lease is valid and subsisting.
(b) Covenant that the rent has been paid and all covenants and other obligations in the lease have been performed. If the lease contains a covenant to keep the property in good repair, the vendor is by his implied covenant in effect covenanting with the purchaser that the property is in good repair. The vendor will be unwilling to do this as he will wish to rely on the caveat emptor rule, that the purchaser must satisfy himself about the physical condition of the property. The vendor will therefore wish to modify his implied covenant in the deed of assignment. Both the Law Society Conditions and the National Conditions make specific provision for this.[3]

On a conveyance or assignment by a trustee or a mortgagee or personal representative, whether the transaction is for value or not, there is just one covenant implied, which is that the vendor himself has not created any incumbrance over the land.

The position on the transfer for value of freehold registered land by a beneficial owner is similar to the unregistered position. However rule 77 of the Land Registration Rules 1925 provides in effect that nothing appearing on the register, and no over-riding interest of which the purchaser has notice, can amount to a breach of the implied covenants. The first part of the rule is unremarkable but the second part does lead to problems. It introduces a doctrine of notice into registered land covenants for title which is not to be found in unregistered conveyancing. Furthermore it is by no means clear that the covenants do extend to over-riding interests of which the purchaser has *no* notice. Apart from rule 77, there is a further difference in relation to the covenants implied on the transfer of registered leasehold land. By the Land Registration Act 1925, section 24, the vendor does not covenant that the lease is valid and subsisting but merely that all covenants in the lease have been performed and the rent paid.[4] However this implied covenant is not dependent on the transfer being for value nor on the vendor transferring as beneficial owner. Again, the vendor may wish to expressly modify this covenant in the transfer in so far as it will relate to a repairing covenant in the lease.

Normally the vendor will only give the implied covenants in respect of acts by himself and persons through whom he claims otherwise than for value. Thus if a purchaser does have an action under the covenants for title it may not be against the vendor but one of the vendor's predecessors in title. The

2 Ibid, s. 76(1)(b).
3 LSC 8(5), NC 11(7).
4 However, s. 76(1)(b) above may apply.

covenants once given do run with the land although in practice it may be quite difficult to find the predecessor in title who gave the covenant in order to sue him.

The covenants are implied on a mortgage by a beneficial owner as well as on a conveyance, assignment and transfer. On a mortgage of leasehold land, there is an additional covenant by the mortgagor to pay the rent and perform the covenants in the lease for the duration of the mortgage.[5]

ii Compensation for undiscoverable Land Charges

As land charges registration is only relevant to unregistered titles, so is this compensation. Land charges are registered against the name of the estate owner at the time of registration. Thus to be sure of discovering all registrations, the purchaser should search against the names of all estate owners right back to 1925. It is very likely that he will not know all these names; he will only know the names of estate owners mentioned in the abstract or epitome which will probably commence after 1925. Yet by virtue of the Law of Property Act 1925, section 198, the purchaser will still be deemed to have notice of the matters so protected as a result of registrations. If the registrations do only come to light after completion of his purchase, he may be somewhat aggrieved. He could have an action against the vendor under the covenants for title, but rather better from his point of view he may be eligible for compensation from central funds under the Law of Property Act 1969, section 25. In order to qualify for this compensation, two conditions must be met. Firstly the purchaser must have had no actual knowledge of the charge at the time of completion (excluding of course notice by virtue of the Law of Property Act 1925, section 198). Secondly the charge must be registered against the name of an estate owner who was not revealed as such by the 'relevant title'. The latter phrase means the title to which the purchaser would have been entitled under an open contract (for example for a freehold, at least 15 years), or any longer title to which the purchaser was in fact entitled under the terms of his contract. This means that if the purchaser contracts for a title shorter than the statutory period and a title of statutory length would have revealed the name of the estate owner against whom the charge was registered, the purchaser will not get compensation. By sections 25(9) and 25(10), compensation is not payable in respect of charges registered against titles which the purchaser is precluded by statute from investigating on the grant or assignment of leases and underleases; the purchaser will nevertheless be bound by such charges.

iii Rectification of the register and indemnity

The remedies of rectification of the register and indemnity apply only in the case of registered land, and are discussed in chapter 2. They are remedies against the 'state' rather than the vendor and are available to persons other than the parties to the conveyancing transaction.

5 Law of Property Act 1925, ss. 77(1)(c), 77(1)(d).

iv Liens

The vendor has a lien over the property in respect of any unpaid purchase money following completion. He will protect this lien by retaining the deeds (of unregistered land), or registering a Ciii land charge (for unregistered land) or a notice or caution (for registered land). In the latter case, the lien could be an over-riding interest under the Land Registration Act 1925, section 70(1)(g) if the vendor did remain in possession.[6] Once the money has been paid, the registration should be cancelled.

If the purchaser has paid his deposit to the vendor's solicitor as agent for the vendor, he will have a lien over the property to the extent of his deposit which should be protected by the appropriate registration. This would be done after exchange of contracts.

6 *London and Cheshire Insurance Co Ltd v Laplagrene Property Co Ltd* [1971] Ch 499, [1971] 1 All ER 766.

Part two
Landlord and Tenant

17 Leasehold conveyancing

1 Introduction

The first part of the book has dealt with sales of both freehold and leasehold property. However, we indicated at the beginning of the book that in this chapter the particular features of a leasehold transaction would be reiterated. When talking of the sale of leasehold property we normally mean the assignment of a lease and it is, of course, this transaction which has been considered in the first part of the book. However, for that lease to exist in the first place it must have been granted at some time in the past, normally when the house was built and the first 'purchaser' was granted a lease by the builder or developer. When the first purchaser (strictly the tenant) sells he assigns the lease as does that second purchaser when he in turn sells, and so on.

The grant of a lease is a transaction which we have not, so far, considered in all its detail although we have mentioned in the first part of the book certain aspects of it; for example, the open contract rule as to the title deduced on the grant of a lease was considered in chapter 5. The grant of a lease is different from both the sale of a freehold or the assignment of a lease in that a legal interest is not just being transferred but a new legal estate created.

In this chapter we shall look first of all at the grant of such a lease, both where the lease is granted out of the freehold (a head lease) and where it is granted out of a leasehold interest (an underlease). We shall also look briefly at the particular problems posed by the lease of a flat in a block of flats, as opposed to a house. We shall then reiterate those features of the typical conveyancing transaction considered in the first part of this book which are peculiar to the assignment of a lease as opposed to the sale of the freehold.

2 Grant of lease

i Introduction

The obvious question which must first be answered is why a lease should be granted rather than the freehold being sold. The answer may be that the builder or developer of a new estate who granted leases of the houses on the estate may not have owned the freehold of the land on which the houses were built, but merely a leasehold interest in it, in which case he would probably grant a lease (in fact, an underlease) of part of the property comprised in the original lease rather than assign part of the original lease. However, this does not explain why the builder of a new housing estate who does own the freehold should decide not to sell the freehold of the individual houses but to grant long leases of them. The reasons are probably three-fold. Firstly, the builder will be able to receive some income in the form of rents, although the rents of the individual houses will not be very great. Secondly, he or his successors in title will hope in due course to be able to take over the houses again when the leases do eventually expire, although the longer the lease the less important this consideration will be. Thirdly, and most importantly, certainly to the lawyer, the creation of a landlord/tenant relationship means that there are normally no problems over the running of the benefit and burden of covenants contained in the lease, even if they are positive covenants. This contrasts with the position on the sale of freeholds where we have already seen that the burden of positive covenants does not run. Thus by granting a lease the builder or developer can keep more control over the property and can ensure that an estate development retains its character by the use of covenants. This is of even more importance when one is dealing with a block of flats. Because of their very nature, it is crucially important that the flat owners' various maintenance and repairing obligations are enforceable, as well as restrictions on the use of the flats, and other regulations concerning activities of people living in close proximity. This may be difficult to achieve if the freehold of the individual flats is sold, so much so that many building societies and other mortgagees are unwilling to lend money on the security of a freehold flat.

There are, of course, many different types of lease; formal and informal, short and long, fixed term and periodic, of houses, flats, business premises or agricultural land. The typical lease with which we shall be dealing in this chapter will be the relatively long term – 75, 99, 200 or even 1,000 years is not unknown – lease of a house or a flat, which, as we have seen, will normally have been granted when the house or flat was built or converted. The length of the term will be such that the buyer will think of himself as a purchaser and owner rather than a tenant or assignee of the lease. The term is also such that the capital sum or premium paid on the grant of the lease will be broadly equivalent to the freehold value of the property and this will also be the case on subsequent assignments of the lease, at least until the end of the term is approached.

ii Contents of the lease

The lease will normally be drafted by the landlord's/vendor's solicitor and sent with and referred to in the draft contract. There is obvious scope for negotiation over the terms of the draft lease, which the eventual contract will commit the parties to enter into, although on the development of an estate the lease will normally be in a standard form and the builder or developer may be very resistant to any amendments.

1 *Parties* The parties will be named and described as in a conveyance. The power of a party to grant a lease may vary according to the capacity in which he holds the freehold or leasehold estate out of which the lease is to be granted.

Obviously the leasing powers of a beneficial owner are unlimited. The powers of other estate owners can be limited. A charity is subject to the general restriction on dealing with property set out in the Charities Act 1960, section 29, but with an exception for leases of not more than 22 years where no fine is taken. A company's powers will be regulated by its memorandum of association. A tenant for life (or statutory owner) of settled land has certain leasing powers under the Settled Land Act 1925, sections 41–48. Trustees for sale and personal representatives have all the powers of the tenant for life and trustees of settled land. Mortgagees and mortgagors have certain statutory powers of leasing although these are often modified or excluded in the mortgage deed. A lease made by or to a person suffering from mental disorder will be valid if the other party was in good faith and unaware of the disability. However if a receiver has been appointed then no disposition by the patient can be valid. Minors cannot hold a legal estate. For further details of the capacity of estate owners reference should be made to chapter 10.

2 *Date* As with any other deed, the date of the lease is the date of delivery although the date expressed in the lease will be presumed to be the date of delivery in the absence of any evidence to the contrary. The date of the lease should be distinguished from the date of commencement of the term which will be given in the lease, and which may be different from, and is often earlier than, the date of the lease itself.

Recitals are not often included in a lease but they can be inserted if desired.

3 *Consideration* It may be that there is no capital sum, or premium, changing hands on the grant of a lease and that the consideration is merely the rent and the covenants given by the tenant. If there is a premium, it must be mentioned, not least for stamp duty purposes. There will normally be a receipt clause as well, as in a conveyance. Whether there is a premium will depend on the sort of lease being granted. On a long lease of a house granted by the developer of a new building estate then there will always be a premium which will be much the same as the price for which the developer would have sold the freehold. (On the other hand, on the grant of a monthly tenancy of a furnished flat, protected by the Rent Act 1977, there will be no premium and indeed to impose one would be unlawful.[1])

4 *Operative words* In a lease the landlord is normally expressed to 'demise' or 'lease' to the tenant although any words indicating the intention of the parties will be sufficient.

5 *Parcels* There must be a physical description of the property comprised in the lease. All that was said about the parcels in a conveyance, and the need for precise description, is equally applicable here. This is all the more important in the case of a lease of part only of a building, for example a flat.

6 *Easements* On the grant of a lease, particularly a lease of part of a building or part of a plot of land owned by the landlord, consideration must be given

1 Rent Act 1977, s. 119.

to the easements which the tenant will require and the easements which the landlord will wish to reserve. Again all that was said in relation to a conveyance of freehold land is equally applicable, including the rules contained in *Wheeldon v Burrows*[2] and the Law of Property Act 1925, section 62.

7 *Habendum* The habendum in a lease will indicate the length of the term and its commencement date, assuming it is a lease for a fixed term. In the case of a lease of a house or flat the term would normally be at least 75 or 99 years, and often much longer.

The habendum will also state the commencement date of the term. This may be the date of the lease or it could be before or after the date of the lease. However it must not be more than 21 years after the date of the lease otherwise the lease falls foul of the rule against perpetuities and is void.[3]

8 *Reddendum* The reddendum follows the habendum. It indicates that rent is payable and states the amount and how often it is to be paid. It normally starts with the words 'yielding and paying'. The question of payment of rent is dealt with in detail in the next section.

9 *Payment of rent* The amount of rent payable will depend on the type and size of the property and the length of the lease. The rent of a new house on a building estate on a long lease will be quite low.[4]

The amount of rent will normally be specifically stated. In a long lease, the parties may wish to include some provision by which the rent can be increased although this is unlikely in a long term residential lease. This could be an increase to a predetermined level after a particular period of time, for example half way through the term. Alternatively there might be a provision for 'rent review' after a certain length of time with specific machinery by which the new rent can be calculated.

In the absence of any provision to the contrary, rent under a fixed term tenancy is payable at the end of each year. However the lease will normally specify not only the periods for which rent is payable – for example quarterly or yearly – but the date on which such payments must be made. The lease will normally make rent payable in advance rather than in arrear. Typically rent under a fixed term tenancy may be made payable quarterly in advance, payment being made on the 'usual quarter days'. These are Lady Day (25 March), Mid-summer Day (24 June), Michaelmas Day (29 September) and Christmas Day (25 December). The tenant does not lose his obligation to pay rent by assigning the lease. If a subsequent assignee does not pay the rent then the landlord can recover it from the original tenant. The tenant is of course entitled to be indemnified, but that is not necessarily much consolation if the assignee has no funds.

10 *Covenants* The lease will invariably contain covenants detailing the obli-

2 (1879) 12 Ch D 31, CA; see ch 12, section 2viii, ix.

3 Law of Property Act 1925, s. 149(3).

4 This will also avoid Rent Act 1977 protection for the tenant – see ch 19.

gations of the parties in various areas. Covenants are dealt with in detail in the next section.

11 *Certificate of value* This will be included in the lease for the same reasons as warrant its inclusion in a conveyance, that is to take advantage of the stamp duty exemption.

iii Covenants

1 *Covenant by tenant to pay rent, rates and taxes* As well as a reservation of the rent there will also normally be an express covenant by the tenant to pay; if not it will be implied. The tenant also impliedly covenants to pay rates and certain other charges and taxes imposed on the property. The lease will normally contain express provision as to who is to pay such rates and taxes. A tenant remains liable to pay rent even after the premises are destroyed, for example by fire. However the lease may contain express provision for abatement of the rent in these circumstances. If the landlord has failed to comply with his covenant for repair, the tenant can have the repairs done and deduct the cost from his rent.[5] He should not however withhold rent to try and persuade the landlord to comply with his repairing obligations.

2 *Covenant by tenant not to repudiate the landlord's title* There is an implied covenant by the tenant not to do anything which could prejudice the landlord's title, such as assisting someone else to set up a title adverse to the landlord.

3 *Covenant by tenant to permit the landlord to enter and view the state of repair* If the landlord is under an obligation to repair as a result of either an express covenant in the lease or a statutory obligation, the tenant impliedly covenants to allow the landlord to enter and view the state of the premises. However, as mentioned in section 10 below, the landlord is unlikely to be liable for repairs on a long term residential lease.

4 *Covenant by tenant to pay a service charge* Particularly if the lease is of one of a number of units, such as a flat in a block of flats, the landlord may perform certain services for the tenants, such as maintenance of stairs and lifts and of the gardens of a block of flats. The landlord will covenant to perform these services and all the tenants will covenant in their leases to pay an annual service charge to reimburse the landlord. This could be expressed to be paid as additional rent. The amount of this service charge will vary from year to year. The Landlord and Tenant Act 1985 imposes restrictions on service charges for flats.[6] In the Act, a service charge is defined as an amount payable for services, repairs, maintenance or insurance or the landlord's costs of management. The landlord can only recover the costs he incurs to the extent that they are reasonable, and if the costs are incurred on the provision of services or the carrying out of works, they can only be recovered if the services or works are of a reasonable standard. If the service charge is payable in advance of the

5 *Lee-Parker v Izzet* [1971] 3 All ER 1099, [1971] 1 WLR 1688.
6 Landlord and Tenant Act 1985, ss. 18–30.

costs being incurred then the landlord can only recover an amount that is reasonable. Where costs incurred on the carrying out of works exceed a prescribed amount the landlord must obtain at least two estimates for the works, one of them from a person wholly unconnected with the landlord, and a notice accompanied by a copy of the estimates must be given to each of the tenants, inviting observations. The landlord must then pay regard to any observations. At present the prescribed amount is £25 multiplied by the number of flats in the building, or £500, whichever is the greater.

The tenant is also entitled to a summary of costs incurred by the landlord, certified by a qualified accountant who is not connected with the landlord.

5 *Covenant by tenant not to assign or sublet* The lease may include a provision against the tenant assigning the lease or granting a sub-lease or both. The purpose is to protect the landlord's interest by ensuring that no-one apart from the original tenant can have an interest in the property. No such covenant is to be implied. If the covenant is absolute, that is if it is not qualified by any reference to the landlord's consent, the landlord will be perfectly entitled to refuse to give the tenant consent to assign or sub-let as the case may be. Any such assignment or sub-letting would be a breach of covenant and the lease would be liable to forfeiture. Such an absolute covenant is clearly prejudicial to the tenant particularly if the lease is for a fixed term of any length, and the tenant must seriously consider the implications before accepting such a provision in his lease. However the covenant is not broken by an assignment by operation of law such as occurs on the death or bankruptcy of the tenant.

The covenant may not be absolute, but provide instead that there is to be no assignment (or sub-letting) without the licence or consent of the landlord. In this case it will be implied, even if the lease does not expressly so provide, that such consent must not be unreasonably withheld.[7] Nor can the landlord demand payment of a 'fine' for his consent[8] although he does have the right to demand payment of a reasonable sum for expenses incurred in connection with the consent, for example legal expenses.[9] (If the lease is a building lease of over 40 years then no consent is needed to assign or underlet at any time more than seven years before the end of the term, although notice does have to be given to the landlord. A building lease is a lease made in consideration of the erection or improvement of buildings.[10])

Assuming that there is a qualified covenant, in what circumstances would the landlord's refusal be held to be reasonable? The burden of proof is on the tenant to show that the landlord's refusal is unreasonable, and all relevant circumstances will be taken into account. If the refusal is made on grounds that do not concern the personality of the proposed assignee or the effect of the proposed assignment then it is probable that it will be held to be unreasonable.[11] In particular, any licence will be *unlawfully* withheld in so far as it is

7 Landlord and Tenant Act 1927, s. 19(1)(a).

8 Unless there is express provision for it in the lease; Law of Property Act 1925, s. 144.

9 Landlord and Tenant Act 1927, s. 19(1)(a).

10 Landlord and Tenant Act 1927, s. 19(1)(b).

11 *Re Gibbs and Houlder Bros & Co Ltd's Lease* [1925] Ch 575, CA; *Tredgar v Harwood* [1929] AC 72, HL. See also *Bromley Park Garden Estates Ltd v Moss* [1982] 2 All ER 890, [1982] 1 WLR

withheld on grounds of colour, race, ethnic or national origins[12] or sex;[13] there is, though, an exception for 'small premises' where the accommodation is shared with the landlord or a near relative.[14]

In all cases where consent is necessary, the tenant should apply for the consent even if he is sure that it will be refused. If it is refused then he can either go ahead and assign (or sub-let) or seek a declaration from the court that the refusal was unreasonable. The latter, although it takes time, might be preferable and indeed the proposed assignee or sub-lessee may insist on it. The danger in the former course is that the tenant and the proposed assignee or sub-lessee are gambling that if the landlord brings proceedings for breach of the covenant, probably by way of forfeiture, the court will agree that the refusal was unreasonable. There can be no guarantee of that. The express covenant in the lease may further limit the landlord's grounds for refusal, by providing for example that consent will not be refused in the case of assignment to a 'respectable responsible person'.[15]

When a licence or consent is given it is normally in writing and may also be recited in the assignment or sub-lease; the lease might in fact require the consent to be in writing, in which case an oral consent would be insufficient unless the landlord could be shown to have waived the requirement of writing.

It is unlikely that there will be an absolute or even a qualified covenant in a long term residental lease: there may, however, be a covenant to give notice of assignments (and mortgages) after the event, together with a small fee.

6 *Covenant by tenant not to make improvements or alterations* Again there is no implied covenant that the tenant is not to make improvements or alterations to the property, but there may be an express covenant which again may be either absolute or subject to the landlord's consent. The purpose is to protect the landlord both from any unwelcome changes to the property and from any potential liability to compensate the tenant for improvements at the end of the tenancy. If there is a qualified covenant, there is a statutory implication that the consent must not be unreasonably withheld, in the case of improvements.[16] Although the statutory provision refers merely to improvements, most alterations will be improvements. The statutory provision does not preclude the right of the landlord to require the payment of a reasonable sum in respect of any decrease in the value of the premises (or any adjoining premises of the landlord) and in respect of legal and other expenses incurred in connection with the consent, nor does it preclude the right to require an undertaking from the tenant to reinstate the premise to their original condition if the improvement does not add to the letting value of the premises.

1019, CA and *International Drilling Fluids Ltd v Louisville Investment (Uxbridge) Ltd* [1986] Ch 513, [1986] 1 All ER 321, CA.

12 Race Relations Act 1976, s. 24.

13 Sex Discrimination Act 1975, s. 31.

14 Race Relations Act 1976, s. 22(2); Sex Discrimination Act 1975, s. 32(2).

15 *Moat v Martin* [1950] 1 KB 175, [1949] 2 All ER 646, CA.

16 Landlord and Tenant Act 1927, s. 19(2).

7 *Covenant by tenant restricting his use of the property* There are a number of reasons why the landlord should want to restrict the use to which the property can be put. Most commonly in the case of business premises such as a shop, the landlord will own other shops in the vicinity and will want to control the use of the shop so as to prevent any duplication and to enable him to plan the development and make other units attractive to potential tenants. Similarly on the lease of a new house on a building estate the landlord may wish to restrict the use of the house to residential use only, to preserve the character of the development. The restriction, particularly on business premises, may affect the rent which the landlord can expect to negotiate under the lease. If there is an express covenant then again it may either be absolute or qualified by reference to the landlord's consent, but in the latter case there is no implication that the consent must not be unreasonably withheld. This could of course be inserted as an express provision in the covenant. However, the landlord cannot as a condition of giving the consent demand any sum of money other than in respect of any decrease in the value of the premises (or adjoining premises of the landlord) or in respect of legal and other expenses incurred in connection with the consent.[17]

A common covenant on a similar theme is that the tenant must not do or permit or suffer to be done on the premises anything which may become a nuisance or annoyance to the landlord or neighbouring owners and occupiers.

The provisions of the Law of Property Act 1925, section 84 concerning application to the Lands Tribunal for the discharge or modification of restrictive covenants are also applicable to restrictive covenants in leases for terms of more than 40 years of which at least 25 years have expired.[18]

8 *Landlord's covenant for quiet enjoyment* If there is no express covenant by the landlord for quiet enjoyment such a covenant will be implied. The covenant can be restricted in which case the landlord covenants that the tenant's possession will not be interrupted by acts of the landlord or of persons claiming lawfully through or under him. Alternatively the covenant can be absolute in which case the landlord also covenants that the tenant's possession will not be disturbed by lawful acts of anyone through whom the landlord claims title, ie the landlord's predecessors in title. An express covenant can be either absolute or restricted. In the absence of an express covenant the implied covenant will be in the restricted form.

9 *Landlord's covenant not to derogate from his grant* The landlord impliedly covenants not to derogate from his grant, that is not to do anything which will interfere with the use for which the premises were let. So in *Aldin v Latimer Clark, Muirhead & Co*[19] the landlord let part of his land to the tenant for the purpose of drying timber. The landlord erected on his adjoining land a building interfering with the flow of air to the tenant's land and thus preventing timber from drying. This constituted a breach of covenant. In these circumstances a

17 Ibid, s. 19(3); this provision only applies if the change of use does not involve structural alteration.

18 Law of Property Act 1925, s. 84(12).

19 [1894] 2 Ch 437.

landlord would be well advised to try and include in the lease a specific provision allowing him to use his adjoining land in any way he thinks fit whether or not it prejudices the tenant's enjoyment of the property comprised in the lease. It should be noted that there is in general no implied covenant by the landlord that the property leased is suitable for the tenant's needs. There is no implied covenant even that the use specified in the lease is lawful.[20]

10 *Covenant to repair* The lease may contain express provision as to the repairing obligations of either or both parties. The tenant under a long term residential lease would normally be liable for all repairs, subject to the builder's contractual liability in building the house, and the NHBC provisions.[1]

If the lease makes the tenant liable for repairs then he might have to rebuild a subsidiary part of the property if it is past ordinary repair.[2] If the property is destroyed, for example by fire, the tenant must rebuild it. If the covenant by the tenant is to *put the premises in repair* then, if they are not in repair at the beginning of the term, the tenant will have to do the necessary repairs. If the tenant has covenanted to repair, the landlord may wish to reserve the right to enter the premises to view the state of repair.

There are two statutory provisions which may affect the duty to repair. Firstly under the Occupiers' Liability Act 1957, section 2, where the landlord retains part of a building under his control, such as a common stair-case, he owes a duty of care to the tenant and the tenant's visitors. Secondly under the Defective Premises Act 1972, section 4, where the landlord has an obligation or right to repair, then he has a duty of care to anyone who might reasonably be affected by the lack of repair.

11 *Covenant to insure* There will normally be an express covenant in the lease dealing with insurance. In the absence of any express provision the tenant, if liable for repairs and to rebuild after destruction of the property, might feel the need to insure. The landlord might also wish to insure to preserve his interest in the premises. An express term might impose the obligation to insure on the landlord, and then provide that the premiums can be recovered from the tenant. If the landlord covenants to insure, there may be an additional covenant by the tenant not to do anything by which the premiums may be increased. If the lease imposes an obligation to insure on the tenant, he will naturally bear the expense of the premiums. The covenant might provide that the tenant must insure with a named insurance company or with an insurance company to be approved by the landlord. (This can cause problems if the tenant or his assignees are purchasing with the aid of a mortgage and the mortgagee wants insurance to be with a different company.) An express covenant will often provide that the insurance money is to be spent on reinstating the premises.

20 See for example *Hill v Harris* [1965] 2 QB 601, [1965] 2 All ER 358, CA.

1 See ch 5, section 4 xxi.

2 See for example *Ravenseft Properties Ltd v Davstone (Holdings) Ltd* [1980] QB 12, [1979] 1 All ER 929.

12 *Usual covenants* A lease may be expressed to be subject to the 'usual' covenants, without detailing what they are. Also, an agreement for a lease, in the absence of express provision as to the covenants to be inserted in the lease, contains an implied term that the lease will be subject to the usual covenants. These usual covenants are:

(a) covenant by the tenant to pay rent, rates and taxes;
(b) covenant by the tenant to keep and deliver up the premises in repair and allow the landlord to enter and view the state of repair;
(c) restricted covenant by the landlord for quiet enjoyment;
(d) a proviso for re-entry on non-payment of rent;
(e) any other covenants which are usual bearing in mind the nature of the property and the area in which it is situated.

13 *Enforceability of covenants* Implied covenants run with the land. However the person liable is only liable whilst he holds the estate, that is the leasehold interest or the reversion, and he is not liable for subsequent breaches, that is breaches committed after he has parted with the leasehold interest or reversion. There is therefore no need for an indemnity covenant in relation to the implied covenants.

Under the rule in *Spencer's* case,[3] provided that the covenant 'touches and concerns' the land, the successors in title of the tenant will be able to claim its benefit. This is so whether the covenant is positive or restrictive. A covenant touches and concerns the land if it affects the landlord *qua* landlord and the tenant *qua* tenant, rather than merely personally. All the covenants likely to be found in a typical lease will touch and concern the land except a covenant by the landlord giving the tenant the option to purchase the reversion.

By the Law of Property Act 1925, section 142, provided that the covenant has 'reference to the subject matter of the lease', it will bind successors in title to the landlord's interest, ie the reversion. The expression 'reference to the subject matter of the lease' means much the same as 'touches and concerns' mentioned in the previous paragraph.

By the Law of Property Act 1925, section 141, provided that the covenant has reference to the subject matter of the lease, successors in title of the landlord will be able to claim its benefit.

Under the rule in *Spencer's* case, provided that the covenant touches and concerns the land, it will bind successors in title of the tenant, ie assignees of the lease. As with the previous paragraphs, it does not matter whether the covenant is positive or restrictive.

The original tenant remains liable on his covenants in privity of contract, even though he has assigned the lease. He will therefore require an indemnity covenant from the assignee when he sells.

There may be mutual enforceability of covenants between tenants if there is a letting scheme, analogous to a building scheme – see chapter 5, section 4vi.

14 *Options* An option is normally in the form of a covenant by the landlord to allow the tenant the particular option. There are two main types of options

3 (1583) 5 Co Rep 16a.

which may be given to the tenant, an option to renew the lease and an option to purchase the reversion, that is the landlord's interest. However, neither is likely to be found in the typical long residential lease.

An option to renew is obviously very welcome from the tenant's point of view, if it can be negotiated. An option to renew runs with both the reversion and the leasehold interest, so successors in title of the tenant – assignees of the lease – can take the benefit and exercise the option, and successors in title of the landlord are bound by it. Such an option creates an estate contract and if the reversionary title is unregistered, the option must be registered as a Civ land change otherwise it will be void against a purchaser of the reversionary title for money or money's worth. If the reversionary title is registered, the option can be protected by a notice or caution although it is likely that even if this is not done a purchaser of the reversion will still take subject to it as it will be over-riding interest under the Land Registration Act 1925, section 70(1)(g) if the tenant or his successor in title is in possession. It is in the original landlord's interest to see that the option is registered, because even though the option may be void for non-registration, the original landlord is still bound by it in privity of contract. Having disposed of the reversion he cannot of course grant a new lease and is therefore liable to pay damages to the tenant.[4] He may be able to recover these damages from the person to whom he disposed of the reversion, under an indemnity covenant.

If the option is expressed in the lease to be exercisable only within a particular time limit, or if all other covenants in the lease have been observed and performed by the tenant, then these requirements will be interpreted by the courts quite strictly.[5]

In drafting the option, care should be taken over one matter in particular. If the lease is renewable on exactly the same terms, including the option to renew, there is in effect a perpetually renewable lease, which takes effect under the Law of Property Act 1922, section 145 as a lease for two thousand years. A properly drafted option will provide for the lease to be renewed on the same terms (except perhaps as to the length of the term and rent) but excluding the option itself.

The landlord may give the tenant an option to purchase the reversion, particularly if the reversion is the freehold. As with the option to renew, the option to purchase must be sufficiently certain. This means that there should be a fixed price or some means by which the price can be ascertained. Again as with the option to renew, it is an estate contract and will only bind the purchaser of the reversion if registered in the appropriate way or if it is an overriding interest. However the benefit and burden of the option do not run in the same manner as an option to renew. There is no privity of estate as there is with an option to renew, because the subject matter of the option is not the subject matter of the lease. Indeed although the option is in the context of a lease, there is no reason why it cannot exist quite independently of the lease. The burden of it will pass to the landlord's successors in title if it is registered, or it is an overriding interest. The benefit can be assigned to anyone,

4 *Wright v Dean* [1948] Ch 686, [1948] 2 All ER 415.

5 *West Country Cleaners (Falmouth) Ltd v Saly* [1966] 3 All ER 210, [1966] 1 WLR 1485, CA.

including of course an assignee of the lease.[6] If the tenant, to whom the option is granted, is defined in the lease as including the tenant's successors in title, then on an assignment of the lease the benefit of the option will be impliedly assigned to the assignee.[7] In this case the option is probably not assignable to anyone else.

Additionally, the option may be subject to the rule against perpetuities. If it is granted after 15 July 1964 and contained in a lease, the perpetuity rule does not apply provided that the option is only exerciable by the tenant or his successors in title and is not exercisable later than one year after the end of the lease.[8] Whether these conditions are satisfied depends on the precise wording of the option in the lease. If they are not satisfied and the option is granted after 15 July 1964 the option must be only exercisable within, or actually exercised within, a period of 21 years from the date of grant of the option, normally the date of grant of the lease.[9] Thus if the option is exercisable throughout the term of a 50 year lease and it is not actually exercised within the first 21 years, it falls foul of the rule against perpetuities and it is void. If the option was granted before 16 July 1964, the pre-1964 perpetuity rule applies except as between the original parties.

iv Determination of the tenancy

It is convenient here to consider the ways in which a tenancy may be terminated. A fixed term tenancy may expire by effluxion of time, ie by the term running out. It may come to an end by surrender. Surrender may be express or implied. An express surrender is agreed between the parties. A surrender can also be implied for surrounding circumstances, such as the tenant accepting a new tenancy before the old one has expired or the landlord accepting possession of the premises with the intention of terminating the tenancy. A fixed term tenancy can also be determined by merger or by the operation of a break clause. Merger occurs when the same person, usually the tenant, acquires the leasehold interest and the reversion. The leasehold interest merges into the reversion. A break clause is in effect an option to determine a lease before the end of the term and is unusual in a long term residential lease. It may be exercisable by the landlord or the tenant or either. A fixed term tenancy can also be determined by forfeiture. Forfeiture is a remedy of the landlord on breach of covenant by the tenant, which involves the landlord bringing the lease to an end. The landlord's right to forfeit must be contained in an express provision in the lease and it will not be implied. A typical forfeiture clause will state that if the rent is in arrear for 21 days, whether formally demanded or not, or if the tenant is in breach of any of his covenants, then the landlord can re-enter the property and the lease is thereby determined. Sometimes the landlord will be given the right to forfeit if the tenant becomes bankrupt or, being a company, goes into liquidation. If the tenant is in breach of covenant and the landlord has the right to forfeit, he must decide whether to forfeit or not. He can expressly waive his right to forfeit and it would be

6 *Griffith v Pelton* [1958] Ch 205, [1957] 3 All ER 75, CA.
7 *Re Button's Lease* [1964] Ch 263, [1963] 3 All ER 708.
8 Perpetuities and Accumulations Act 1964, s. 9(1).
9 Ibid, s. 9(2).

impliedly waived if he did something showing an intention to treat the lease as continuing, in the knowledge of the facts giving rise to the right to forfeit. Implied waiver will most commonly occur by the landlord accepting rent. However the waiver only relates to existing breaches of covenant and it does not extend to future breaches or continuing breaches (for example, breach of a covenant to repair or breach of a covenant relating to use of the property). The procedure on forfeiture depends on whether the landlord is forfeiting for non-payment of rent or breach of some other covenant.

1 *Forfeiture for non-payment of rent* Unless the lease dispenses with it (as does the typical forfeiture clause mentioned in the previous section) the landlord must make a formal demand for the rent, of the precise amount due and on the last day for payment. Even if the lease does not dispense with this requirement, there is no need for a formal demand if at least six months rent is in arrear and there is insufficient distress on the premises.[10] Although the landlord may re-enter peaceably, in practice he will bring an action for possession which will be heard in the High Court or the county court depending on the rateable value of the property. If the tenant pays the arrears and the landlord's costs before the court hearing or within a certain time thereafter (or after the landlord re-enters if he does so without a possession order), he may be granted relief against the forfeiture, which means that the lease is not forfeited but continues as before. The provisions for relief are in fact slightly different in the High Court and the county court.

2 *Forfeiture for breach of other covenants* The landlord must first of all serve a notice under the Law of Property Act 1925, section 146. This must:
(a) specify the breach of covenant;
(b) require the tenant to remedy the breach if it is capable of being remedied – some breaches, such as a breach of covenant against assignment or sub-letting, will be irremediable;
(c) require compensation if the landlord desires it.

If the breach is of a repairing covenant, then where the lease is for at least seven years of which at least three years are still to run, the section 146 notice must refer to the tenant's right under the Leasehold Property (Repairs) Act 1938 to serve a counter-notice within 28 days. If the tenant does so, the landlord needs the leave of the court to proceed with forfeiture and this leave will only be given on one of five specified grounds, for example if an immediate remedy would be cheap compared to the expense if repair were postponed. In specifying the breach of the repairing covenant in the notice, the landlord will normally prepare a schedule of dilapidations detailing the lack of repair.

After service of the notice, the landlord must allow reasonable time for the tenant to remedy the breach and to make compensation if requested, or to consider his position if the breach is irremediable. Failing the tenant remedying the breach and making compensation, the landlord can proceed with forfeiture, again normally by bringing a possession action in the High Court or the county court. The tenant is given the right by section 146(2) to apply to the court for relief whether the landlord re-enters peaceably or seeks a possession order. The

10 Common Law Procedure Act 1852, s. 210.

court has a wide discretion to grant relief but application must normally be made before the landlord actually re-enters the premises. If the breach relates to internal decorative repairs, the tenant can apply to the court under the Law of Property Act 1925, section 147 to be relieved from liability for such repairs on the grounds that the notice is unreasonable, although this does not apply to a breach of a covenant to put the property in repair at the beginning of the tenancy.

The landlord can recover the expense of preparing and serving a section 146 notice from the tenant where he does actually forfeit, where he waives forfeiture or where the tenant is granted relief. However if the tenant complies with the notice, the landlord cannot recover the cost of it under section 146 and so an express clause is often inserted in the lease giving the landlord the right to recover the costs of the notice from the tenant in these circumstances. If the Leasehold Property (Repairs) Act 1938 applies, the landlord can only recover costs with the leave of the court.

3 *Breach of condition against bankruptcy* The Law of Property Act 1925, section 146 does not apply to forfeiture for breach of a condition against bankruptcy in respect of certain property, including agricultural land and furnished dwelling houses. Even in respect of other leases, a section 146 notice is not needed after the first year following the tenant's bankruptcy.

4 *Position of under lessees* If a lease is forfeited and thereby terminates, any underleases granted out of that lease must also terminate. Thus forfeiture of a lease can be disastrous for any under lessees. Under lessees have a right to apply for relief against forfeiture of the superior lease quite independently of the tenant of the lease which is liable to forfeiture.[11] This becomes of importance if the tenant himself cannot apply for relief or else fails in his application. On an application by an under lessee, the court has discretion to grant relief, which is effected by the court ordering a new lease between the landlord and the under lessee. The conditions of the lease will be such as the court thinks fit although the term cannot be longer than the unexpired term of the under lessee's old lease. An under lessee in this context includes a mortgagee of a lease.

v Procedure

The procedure on the grant of a long lease of a house or flat is essentially similar to the conveyancing procedure already discussed in the earlier part of this book. There will be a contract in the same form as discussed in the first part of this book. Rather than setting out the detailed provisions of the lease, the contract will probably provide that the lease is to be in the form of a draft supplied with the contract. If the house is being newly built then there may be a separate term of a contract, or a separate contract, covering the erection of the house, as discussed in chapter 5. The landlord/vendor's solicitor will require instructions on the contents of the lease and the term, and will also have to advise on the clauses which are appropriate for inclusion, probably using a standard form precedent. He will also have to investigate title. In

11 Ibid, s. 146(4).

particular he may discover that there is a current mortgage, with the mortgagee's consent being necessary to the proposed lease. If there are covenants affecting the freehold title, the solicitor may wish to insert a condition in the contract providing for an indemnity covenant to be included in the lease.

The purchaser's solicitor (for the prospective lessee will regard himself as a purchaser) will make all the usual searches mentioned in chapter 6. He will also need to consider the terms of the draft contract and draft lease, and any incumbrances such as covenants affecting the freehold title which have been disclosed, in the same way as he would for a purchaser of freehold land; and if necessary try and negotiate some amendment. After exchange of contracts the vendor/landlord's solicitor will deduce title. Under an open contract the lessee is entitled to no title at all on the grant of a headlease and only a limited title on the grant of an underlease.[12] In particular, the lessee is not entitled to examine the freehold title. However the purchaser/lessee will *want* to examine the freehold and any other superior leasehold titles. The reasons for this have already been considered at chapter 5 section 4 xvii 2, above. It is thus essential that the purchaser's solicitor negotiates for the inclusion in the contract of some provision allowing the purchaser to examine the title including the freehold title. If he does not, then not only is the purchaser putting his money at some risk but he is much less likely to find a Building Society or other mortgagee willing to lend on the security of the property and he may find that when he comes to sell the property and assign the lease, he will have difficulty finding a purchaser; if the appropriate title was not deduced to him then he cannot in turn deduce it to his purchaser. If the superior leasehold and freehold titles are registered they will be deduced by use of office copy entries under the Land Registration Act 1925, section 110. If unregistered then an abstract or epitome will be used. The purchaser's solicitor can then examine the title and make the necessary searches as discussed in the first part of this book.

vi Completion

Both the lease, and an exact copy of it called a counterpart least, are prepared. The actual lease executed by the landlord will be handed over to the purchaser/tenant on completion but the purchaser will execute the counterpart lease, which is then retained by the landlord. Execution is effected in the same way as for any other deed. The landlord will normally be executing under an implied condition as to execution of the counterpart by the tenant and payment of the premium. The counterpart lease gives the landlord a record of the contents of the lease and as it is executed by the tenant, there is no problem over enforcement of the covenants in the lease. Obviously the purchaser will not receive any actual title deeds on a lease granted out of unregistered land but if the superior leasehold and freehold titles are unregistered, he will want to verify his abstract or epitome against the originals if possible. The balance of the purchase price, in effect a premium on the grant of the lease, will be handed over on completion. If rent is payable in advance, the purchaser/tenant may have to pay an apportioned sum on completion, and for his part will wish to receive any necessary consent of the vendor/landlord's mortgagee.

12 See ch 5, section 4xxii 2, 5.

vii Post-completion matters

1 *Stamping* The stamp duty position on the grant on a lease is considered in chapter 15 at section 2 v; if the lease contains a certificate of value, the premium does not exceed £30,000, and the rent does not exceed £300, then no stamp duty will be payable. Otherwise duty is payable on the premium (if over £30,000) and the rent, the latter being dependant on the amount of the rent and the length of the term of the lease. A lease for seven years or more does fall within the provisions for production in the Finance Act 1931. The counterpart lease bears a fixed duty of 50 pence.

2 *Registration under the Land Registration Act 1925* Application will have to be made for first registration of title to the lease at the appropriate District Land Registry if the lease is for a term of over 21 years in an area subject to a Compulsory Registration Order. If the reversionary title is registered then in any event title to the lease must be registered if the lease is for a term of over 21 years. Whether absolute leasehold or good leasehold title is registered will depend on whether the superior title(s) can be deduced. If the reversionary title is registered the lease will in addition need to be noted on the register of the reversionary title. To this end, the contract should include a condition that the lessor's Land Certificate be put on deposit at the Land Registry and the deposit number supplied to the purchaser on or before completion; this was dealt with in chapter 2 section 2 vi 3.

3 *Other matters* If the lease contains a provision requiring notice of any assignment or mortgage to be given to the lessor, and the purchaser/lessee has bought with the aid of a mortgage, then notice of the mortgage will have to be given. As in any other conveyancing transaction, the purchaser/lessee's solicitor would have to consider the question of custody of the deeds, which will comprise the lease, possibly an examined abstract or epitome of the superior title, the purchaser's mortgage if there is one, and if title is registered a Land Certificate or Charge Certificate. These deeds would, of course, be sent to the mortgagee if there was a mortgage.

viii Acting for the mortgagee

In the same way that on a purchase of freehold or leasehold land a purchaser's solicitor will normally also act for the purchaser's mortgagee, there is normally no problem and no conflict of interest in the solicitor for the purchaser/lessee also acting for the mortgagee who is providing the purchase price (the premium) on the grant of the lease. As in any other transaction the mortgagee will naturally be concerned about the title and the result of various searches; however, there are a number of matters of particular concern to the mortgagee of a grant of a lease. A mortgagee may wish to ensure that the freehold (and any other superior leasehold) titles are deduced. In the context of a registered title the mortgagee will wish to ensure that absolute as opposed to good leasehold title will be granted. For the reasons explained in section iii above the purchaser will also be concerned on the same account. Secondly, the mortgagee will wish to be aware of any provisions in the lease concerning insurance. Such a provision may conflict with the mortgagee's normal practice of insuring mortgaged property and charging the premiums to the borrower. Thirdly, the mortgagee will doubtless not accept as security a lease which contains a provision for forfeiture on the tenant's bankruptcy; it is in just such a situation that the mortgagee would want the loan to be secured and if the lease is forfeited the security in effect disappears. Finally, the mortgagee may be concerned about the possible forfeiture of the lease on other grounds, for example for non-payment of rent. We have already seen that relief will be available to the mortgagee, who will be in the position of under-lessee. However, such relief may depend on the mortgagee being aware of the forfeiture proceedings in time.[13] Ideally, the mortgagee would like a covenant in the lease to the effect that the landlord should inform the mortgagee of any proposed forfeiture but the mortgagee would want to ensure that the landlord was given notice of the mortgage because rules of court require a landlord to give notice of forfeiture proceedings to any mortgagee of whom he is aware.

ix Flats

We have already considered the advantages of an estate of houses being disposed of by granting long leases rather than selling the freehold. Many of these advantages apply with all the more force when the property is a block of flats with the individual flats being sold; such matters have been considered in section i and in chapter 5, section 4xxi. There will be a much greater need to identify accurately the property being sold which will be part of a building with, therefore, no immediately obviously delineated division between the various parts. For example, are the flat owners to own the outside walls of their flat? Is a flat owner at the top of the building to own the roof above his flat? There will be a corresponding greater need for easements to be accurately stated, both easements to be granted to flat owners and easements to be reserved. There will need to be easements relating to the use of the grounds, access to garages, etc. Similarly, it is vital that the flats are properly insured; this may be achieved by the landlord insuring all the flats under a block policy or there may possibly be a separate policy for the individual flats and the common parts of the building and grounds. The effect of a flat being destroyed by fire and not having been insured would be most unfortunate, not only for the owner of that particular flat but for the other flat owners in the block as well.

Because of the close proximity within which the flat owners are living there would probably be quite extensive covenants covering what can, and what cannot happen in the flats. There would also be provision for maintenance and repair of the various common parts, such as the main staircases, the external structure of the building and the grounds. There would probably therefore be a covenant to pay a service charge in relation to the expense of such matters to the landlord who would himself covenant in the leases to be responsible for repair and maintenance of the common parts. We have already noted the restriction and control over such service charges in section iii above. However, the builder or developer of the flats may not wish to be saddled with

13 See *Abbey National Building Society v Maybeech Ltd* [1985] Ch 190, [1984] 3 All ER 262 and *Smith v Metropolitan City Properties Ltd* [1986] 1 EGLR 52; and also Administration of Justice Act 1985, s. 55.

this maintenance and repair responsibility and may wish to have no further concern with the development once leases of all the individual flats have been granted. One way of achieving this and also giving the flat owners more control over their immediate environment would be for the common parts to be vested in a management company whose members would be the various flat owners from time to time. This management company would then be responsible for the repair and maintenance of the common parts and it would be to this management company that the flat owners paid their service charges; as members of the management company they would clearly have much more control than if the landlord were still in charge. If this scheme were adopted, then on the sale of each flat there would also be sold a share in the management company. It would be necessary for a purchaser's solicitor to examine the memorandum and articles of the management company.

x Under-Leases

If the landlord only has a leasehold interest himself, then the lease which he grants will be an underlease. From the under-lessee's point of view this means that there will be a superior leasehold title as well as the freehold title. On investigating title, therefore, the under-lessee/purchaser's solicitor will wish to be able to investigate the superior leasehold title as well as the freehold title. When we considered the open contract rule in chapter 5 section 4xvii, we saw that in relation to unregistered title the purchaser could examine the immediately superior leasehold title – out of which the underlease was being granted – but not the freehold title nor any other intermediate leasehold title. In relation to registered title, section 110 of the Land Registration Act 1925 is inapplicable. From the purchaser's point of view, therefore, in both cases a special condition is needed in the contract entitling the purchaser to examine the freehold and superior leasehold titles whether by means of abstract and epitome or office copy entries.

The purchaser's solicitor will also be concerned about the contents of the superior lease(s). It may reveal that the superior landlord's consent is necessary to any under-lease. Additionally, the purchaser/under-lessee will normally be subject to the covenants contained in the superior lease. If there is any breach of those covenants then this could, as we have seen, lead to forfeiture of the superior lease although, again, we have seen that the lessee does have the right to apply for relief against forfeiture of the superior lease. The vendor/underlessor would require an indemnity in the underlease against breach of the covenants in his own (the superior lease).

3 Assignment of lease

i Introduction

We have now seen how a lease (or under lease) is granted. We have already dealt with the assignment of such a lease in the conveyancing section forming the first part of this book. The object of this section is to reiterate the main differences between the freehold transaction and the assignment of a lease.

ii Drafting the contract

As part of the process of investigating title prior to the drafting of the contract the vendor's solicitor may discover that the landlord's consent is necessary to the proposed assignment to the purchaser. The vendor's solicitor would therefore have to request such consent and there may well be conditions in the contract covering the point. Law Society Condition 8 and National Condition 11 are discussed in chapter 5 section 4viii. However, in purely practical terms the purchaser may wish to ensure that the landlord's consent is forthcoming before exchange of contracts as otherwise, if the consent is not forthcoming, then although the purchaser will be able to rescind the contract, there would be difficulties if he has a synchronised sale proceeding at the same time. The written consent from the landlord would be handed over on completion, if not before.

When drafting the particulars and special conditions of the contract, the vendor's solicitor will normally make reference to the provisions of the lease, both for the description of the property (assuming the description in the lease is still up to date), for the remaining term of the lease and for the covenants and easements which the property is subject to. If the vendor is only selling part of the property comprised in the lease there may well, of course, be new covenants and easements in addition to those in the lease.

When we considered the open contract rule in relation to the title which would be deduced to the purchaser in chapter 5 section 4xvii, we saw that the open contract rule for unregistered title did not entitle the purchaser to examine the freehold (or any superior leasehold) title, but just an abstract of the leasehold title being sold going back at least 15 years (but not before the grant of the lease). The purchaser's solicitor would therefore wish to include a condition in the contract entitling the purchaser to examine such title. If the title to the lease is registered section 110 of the Land Registration Act 1925 applies and the vendor will have to deduce title in accordance with that section providing, inter alia, copies of the register entries and an authority to inspect the register. If the title is absolute there will be no need to examine the superior title, but if only good leasehold, the position is as for unregistered title. Law Society condition 8(2) does give the purchaser rather more than the open contract rule and may involve the vendor in deducing some superior leasehold or freehold title; it applies to unregistered titles and good leasehold titles.

The purchaser's solicitor will make the usual searches and enquiries. One additional point may be that the purchaser's solicitor might wish to try and establish that all the covenants in the lease have been duly performed and observed; for example, if the lease contains a covenant against making any extension to the property without the landlord's consent the purchaser's solicitor may want to establish where there has been any such extension and if so, whether consent has been given. As on the sale of the freehold the purchaser's solicitor would have to consider whether the property is appropriate for the purchaser in terms of the various covenants and easements which it is subject to, and of which it has the benefit.

iii The deed of assignment/transfer

Having exchanged contracts in the usual way, title will be investigated either by means of abstract or epitome for unregistered title or copy entries of the register for registered title. If the purchaser is given the right by the contract to examine superior leasehold and freehold title then this will also be deduced. The usual searches will be made depending whether the title is registered or unregistered. The purchase deed will either be a deed of assignment if the title is unregistered or a transfer if the title is registered. The particular features of these deeds were considered in chapter 12, sections 3 and 4. The main differences between an assignment and a conveyance are that the estate being sold will be referred to as the remainder of the term granted by the lease; that additional covenants for title are implied on a sale of leasehold title by a beneficial owner (and there will probably be a need to exclude the implied covenant for title which would otherwise involve the vendor in giving an assurance that a covenant to repair in the lease has been duly performed); and that an indemnity covenant on the part of the purchaser will be implied on an assignment of a lease for value.

If the title is registered the deed of transfer will follow the form of a freehold transfer, save that there may again be reference to the remainder of the term of the lease being vested in the purchaser. There will be a similar need to modify the implied covenants for title but an indemnity covenant on the part of the purchaser will be implied whether or not value is given by the purchaser, ie whether it is a sale or a gift.

iv Completion

In preparing for completion the vendor's solicitor may have to deal with apportionments of the rent and any service charge, and on completion the purchaser will wish to inspect the last receipt for rent on completion for the reasons set out in chapter 14, section 3ii 2e. The deeds handed over on completion will include the lease and if the title is unregistered the various assignments, mortgages, grants of probate and other documents under which the property has passed. There may also be a marked abstract of the freehold and any superior leasehold titles, if these are being deduced. If title is registered, then in addition to the lease there will be the Land Certificate or Charge Certificate and in the case of a good leasehold title there may again be a marked abstract of the superior leasehold and freehold title. This would, of course, be unnecessary if the lease were registered with absolute leasehold title. In both cases, there would be the assignment or transfer and if the development is managed by a management company whose members are the owners for the time being of the houses or flats there will be a share certificate in that company and a transfer of that share.

v Post-completion matters

Ad valorem stamp duty is payable on an assignment or transfer in the same way as on a conveyance of the freehold. The provisions of the Finance Act 1931 relating to production also apply to any assignment on sale of a lease granted for a term of seven years or more and thus a P.D. form will need to be filled in and sent with the assignment or transfer to the Inland Revenue (or in some cases, the District Land Registry) whether or not stamp duty is payable. If title to the lease is already registered then it will be necessary to apply for registration of the purchase within the priority period of the search which will have been done before completion. If title is not registered, but the land is situated in a compulsory registration area and the lease has more than 21 years left to run, first registration is compulsory. The process of registration is considered in chapter 15, section 2iv and the process of stamping in chapter 15, section 2v.

If the lease contains a covenant requiring that notice be given to the landlord of any assignment or mortgage or receipt of a mortgage, then notice will be given; such notice is normally given in duplicate and the landlord is requested to return one copy of the notice receipted which is then placed with the deeds. Even if there is no such covenant a mortgagee may wish to make the landlord aware of his interest in order to be informed should the landlord commence forfeiture proceedings in respect of the lease in future.

If the vendor has only sold part of what he owns, ie part of the property comprised in the lease, then if the title is unregistered any new covenants imposed should be registered as Dii land charges. (It is only covenants contained in a lease which are excepted from registration as Dii land charges.)

vi Under-leases

We saw in section 1(x) above the effect on examination of title of the lease being granted being an underlease rather than a headlease. Similar considerations will apply if the lease being assigned is an underlease rather than a headlease. The open contract rule as to the title to be deduced, mentioned in section ii above, does not entitle the purchaser to examine the freehold or superior leasehold title. Therefore if the title is unregistered or if the lease is registered with only good leasehold as opposed to absolute leasehold title, the purchaser will want in the contract a condition allowing him to investigate the freehold and superior leasehold titles. As on the grant of a lease, the purchaser's solicitor will be concerned about the contents of the superior lease and in particular the covenants contained therein. The contract should disclose that the lease being sold is an underlease rather than a head-lease.

18 Statutory provisions protecting long term residential tenancies

There are two statutes which give tenants under long residential leases certain rights both during and at the end of the lease.

1 Landlord and Tenant Act 1954, Part I

For the Act to be applicable, the tenancy must be a 'long tenancy', that is a tenancy granted for a term exceeding 21 years.[1] The rent must be a 'low rent' which means that it must be less than two-thirds of the rateable value of the property[2]. The appropriate rateable value is the rateable value on 23 March 1965 or when first rated if later. In addition, the tenancy must be a tenancy which would, apart from its low rent, be otherwise a protected tenancy under the Rent Act 1977. This means inter alia that the rateable value of the property must be within certain limits and the tenant must occupy the property as his home.

The effect of the Act is that the tenancy does not expire on its termination date but continues. This continuation can be brought to an end by notice by the tenant or the landlord. If the landlord gives notice he must include either proposals for a new statutory tenancy for the tenant under the Rent Act 1977 or state his grounds for wanting possession. The grounds on which he can obtain possession are set out in the Act and correspond with cases 1–9 of the grounds for possession under the Rent Act 1977.

2 Leasehold Reform Act 1967

1 *Application of the Act* The Act applies to a 'long tenancy' that is a tenancy granted for a term exceeding 21 years.[3] A tenancy will qualify if the tenant could at some point have said that he was entitled to remain as tenant for the next 21 years. Thus if there is a tenancy for 14 years renewable at the tenant's

1 Landlord and Tenant Act 1954, ss. 2(1), (4).
2 Ibid, s. 2(5).
3 Leasehold Reform Act 1967, s. 3.

option this would qualify, but not a tenancy of 14 years followed by another tenancy of 14 years where the tenant could not insist on renewal, because although the total period of the two tenancies is 28 years, at no point could the tenant have said that he was entitled to a further 21 years. A tenancy which is continuing under the Landlord and Tenant Act 1954, Part I can still be regarded as a long tenancy.

The tenancy must be at a 'low rent' which, as under the Landlord and Tenant Act 1954, Part I, means a rent less than two-thirds of the rateable value of the property.[4] The appropriate rateable value is the rateable value on the 23 March 1965 or when first rated if later, or on the first day of the term of the tenancy if later.[5] This will normally mean that the tenancy is not a protected tenancy under the Rent Act 1977. The property comprised in the tenancy must be a 'house'; this includes any building designed or adapted for living in, notwithstanding that it is not structurally detached.[6] If a building is divided horizontally, ie into separate flats, then the separate flats cannot be houses and do not get the benefit of the Act although the whole building could be a house. If a building is divided vertically, the separate units can be houses but the building as a whole cannot. If the property is used partly for residence and partly for business purposes – such as a shop with a flat above – then it could be a house depending on the precise circumstances.[7]

The Act only applies if the rateable value of the property falls within certain limits.[8] The appropriate rateable value is that on 23 March 1965 or when first rated if later, or in certain circumstances on 1 April 1973.

A tenant can claim the benefit of the Act if, when he gives notice to the landlord of his claim, he has been the tenant of the house under a long tenancy at a low rent and occupying it as his residence for the last three years or for three out of the last ten years.[9] Thus the qualifying conditions have to be fulfilled throughout this three year period. There are provisions whereby certain close relatives of a deceased tenant who have succeeded to the tenancy can add to their own residence as tenant the period of time when they were resident in the property with the deceased tenant.[10] The relatives so entitled include the deceased tenant's spouse, parents and children. There are also provisions covering occupation by beneficiaries under trusts or settlements.[11]

In *Duke of Westminster v Oddy*,[12] the tenant was a bare trustee, holding the leasehold interest in trust for a company and occupying the house under a licence from the company: he was not entitled under the Act, as he was not occupying 'in right of the tenancy'.[13]

4 Ibid, s. 4.

5 There is an exception for properties let between the end of August 1939 and the beginning of April 1963, where the tenancy is not at a low rent if the rent exceeded two-thirds of the *letting* value of the property at the commencement of the tenancy. For the calculation of the letting value, see *Johnston v Duke of Westminster* [1986] AC 839, [1986] 2 All ER 613, HL.

6 Leasehold Reform Act 1967, s. 2.

7 *Tandon v Trustees of Spurgeon's Homes* [1982] AC 755, [1982] 1 All ER 1086, HL.

8 Leasehold Reform Act 1967, s. 1.

9 Ibid, s. 1(1)(b).

10 Ibid, s. 7.

11 Ibid, s. 6.

12 (1984) 270 Estates Gazette 945.

13 Leasehold Reform Act 1967, s. 1(2).

2 *Effect of the Act* The Act gives a tenant the right either to purchase the freehold of the property (or 'enfranchise' as it is called) or to have an extended lease for a period of fifty years more than the original term. Most tenants in practice will enfranchise rather than claim an extended lease.

3 *Enfranchisement* The tenant must first of all give notice to the landlord that he wants to buy the freehold, called a desire notice. This creates a contract between landlord and tenant and if the house is then sold (ie the lease assigned) before the purchase is completed the benefit of the desire notice can be assigned with the tenancy.[14] The contract created by the notice can and should be protected as a Civ land charge if the title to the freehold is unregistered and by notice or caution if it is registered.[15] If the landlord had entered into a contract to sell the freehold prior to service of the notice, that contract will be discharged by the notice unless it actually provided for the eventuality of the notice.[16] The notice cannot be given more than two months after a notice by the landlord under the Landlord and Tenant Act 1954, Part I.[17] Within two months of the service of the desire notice the landlord must serve a notice on the tenant admitting or denying the tenant's claim.[18]

The price to be paid by the tenant is the open market value of the house and premises on the assumption that the purchaser is not the tenant or a member of his family residing with him and that the property is sold subject to the remainder of the tenancy including the 50 year extension to which the tenant is entitled under the Act.[19] This means that assuming that the tenancy is not too near the end of its term, the purchase price will be relatively low. It is normally agreed by the parties and is in practice sometimes fixed at a certain number of years rent eg ten or fifteen years. However, if the rateable value is above £1,000 in London (or £500 elsewhere), different assumptions apply[20] – for example the 50 year extension is ignored (unless the tenancy has already been extended[1]). In default of agreement the price will be fixed by the Leasehold Valuation Tribunal[2] with appeal to the Land Tribunal[3]. If a landlord does not own the freehold but only a superior leasehold interest, the tenant is still entitled to enfranchise but a separate price will be fixed for the superior leasehold interest and the freehold interest *both* of which the tenant will be buying.

In addition to the price the tenant must also pay the landlord's reasonable costs of investigating the tenant's title, of deducing title, of the conveyance and of valuing the property.[4] After the price has been ascertained the tenant can

14 Ibid, s. 5(2).
15 It cannot be an overriding interest; ibid, s. 5(5),
16 Ibid, s. 5(7).
17 Ibid, Sch 3, para 2.
18 Ibid, Sch 3, para 7.
19 Ibid, s. 9(1).
20 Ibid, s. 9(1A).
1 *Hickman v Phillimore Kensington Estate Trustees* [1985] 1 EGLR 205.
2 Ibid, s. 21.
3 Housing Act 1980, Sch 22, para 2.
4 Leasehold Reform Act 1967, s. 9(4).

withdraw his claim within one month.[5] The procedure for deducing title, raising requisitions, drafting the conveyance and completion is dealt with in regulations made under the Act.[6] The conveyance will be drafted by the tenant's solicitor and the Act makes provision for the contents.[7] Briefly, it will contain such restrictive covenants, easements and other provisions as are necessary to keep the parties in the same position as they were under the lease. The landlord need only give the limited covenant for title which would be implied on a conveyance by a trustee. The landlord must give an acknowledgment for the production of any document of title he retains but need not give an undertaking for safe custody. If the freehold is subject to a mortgage then unless it is discharged before completion in the usual way, the tenant should pay the purchase money to the mortgagee and this will discharge the mortgage so far as the property sold is concerned.[8] From a mortgagee's point of view it is necessary to bear in mind that a tenant does have a right to enfranchise and that therefore the property is only really worth what the tenant would have to pay on enfranchisement.

The landlord as vendor has a lien over the property not only for any unpaid purchase money but also for the costs mentioned above and any arrears of rent.[9]

4 *Extended lease* The procedure for service of a notice set out in the previous section applies equally to a notice to take an extended lease. A tenant cannot have more than one extension (but can still enfranchise provided the enfranchisement desire notice is served before the end of the term of the original lease).[10] Again the procedure is laid down in regulations under the Act.[11] The lease – for the remainder of the original term plus 50 years[12] – is drafted by the landlord's solicitor and will contain the same terms as the original lease. The rent will be the same as under the original lease until the end of the term of the original lease and thereafter it will be a ground rent representing the letting value of the site without buildings.[13] The rent can be reviewed halfway through the 50 year extension period. In default of agreement the rent is fixed by the Leasehold Valuation Tribunal.[14] The tenant must also pay the landlord's reasonable costs for investigating the tenant's title, of the lease and of a valuation of the property.[15]

5 *Landlord's overriding rights* The landlord can defeat the tenant's claim to an extended lease or to enfranchise in certain circumstances. He can obtain possession, thereby overriding an extension already granted or claimed, if he

5 Ibid, s. 9(3).
6 Leasehold Reform (Enfranchisement and Extension) Regulations 1967.
7 Leasehold Reform Act 1967, s. 10.
8 Ibid, s. 12.
9 Ibid, s. 9(5).
10 Ibid, s. 16(1).
11 See fn. 5, above.
12 Ibid, s. 14(1).
13 Ibid, s. 15(2).
14 Ibid, s. 21.
15 Ibid, s. 14(2).

can show within 12 months before the termination of the original lease, that he wishes to demolish or substantially reconstruct the property for the purposes of redevelopment.[16] He may be able to defeat a claim to an extended lease or enfranchisement if he can show that he wants the property as a residence for himself or an adult member of his family.[17] However this provision does not apply if the landlord's interest was purchased or created after 18 February 1966. In both cases the tenant is entitled to compensation.[18]

16 Ibid, s. 17. This does not affect a tenant who has enfranchised.
17 Ibid, s. 18.
18 Ibid, Sch 2.

19 'Short term' residential tenancies

1 Introduction

Although the expression 'short term' is used in the title to this chapter, there is nothing to prevent a tenancy with a long fixed term from being protected by the provisions discussed in this chapter. Having said that, the typical tenancy to which these provisions apply will be a weekly or monthly tenancy or a tenancy of a short fixed term such as six months or a year. However although the term is short in that sense, it may well be that the tenant actually remains in possession for an extremely long time; as we shall see, one of the protections given to such tenancies is that despite the ending of the contractual tenancy the tenant may be able to remain in possession unless the landlord can show certain grounds for recovery of possession. If the tenant dies, his wife or children may also similarly be able to remain in possession. In this sense, the tenancy can be quite long.

The procedure for the granting of such tenancies is normally quite informal. There is often, although not always, a written tenancy agreement. This will cover such matters as the length of the tenancy if it is a fixed term and the amount and payment of rent. It may be that the premises are let furnished in which case there will often be a schedule of the fixtures and fittings included in the tenancy, to enable the landlord to check at the end of the tenancy that nothing is missing or broken. There is normally no investigation of the landlord's title. Before discussing such tenancies in detail, it is worth mentioning the obligations of landlord and tenant in two areas. Firstly, in relation to repair. The tenancy agreement may make provision as to liability for repairs, but in certain circumstances the landlord will be under an implied *statutory* obligation to repair. The Landlord and Tenant Act 1985, sections 11 to 14, applies to leases of dwellings for less than seven years. A lease is treated as a lease of less than seven years if it is determinable by the landlord within seven years. Similarly a lease is not covered by the section if the tenant has a right to renew it, making the total period of the lease seven years or more. In the leases to which the section does apply, there is an implied covenant by the landlord to repair the structure and exterior of the dwelling, including drains, gutters and external pipes; to repair and keep in working order installations for the supply of water, gas and electricity and for sanitation (including sinks, baths and toilets but not appliances for using gas and electricity, such as cookers); and to repair and keep in working order installations for water heating and space heating (for example gas fires, central heating). The landlord is not liable to repair tenant's fixtures, that is fixtures which the tenant is entitled to remove when he leaves, nor is he liable for repairs as a result of failure by the tenant to use the property in a tenant-like manner. The Act does not make the landlord liable to rebuild after destruction or damage by fire, flood or other inevitable accident. There is an implied covenant by the tenant to allow the landlord to enter on 24 hours written notice to see the state of repair of the property. With the consent of the county court, it is possible for the parties to contract out of the provisions of the Act. Otherwise the statutory obligation overrides any express covenant in the lease or tenancy agreement.

Secondly we should look at the common law position regarding determination of the tenancy. A fixed term tenancy will expire by effluxion of time, or forfeiture, or even by a break clause, or merger or surrender, though the latter are unlikely in practice. These methods of determination are discussed in chapter 17, section 2 iv.

A periodic tenancy could in theory be determined by merger but is most likely to be determined by notice to quit; the essence of a periodic tenancy is that it will continue until an appropriate notice to quit is served and expires. At common law, in the absence of any express provision to the contrary, the period of notice required to determine a yearly tenancy is at least six months; for a quarterly tenancy it is a quarter; for a monthly tenancy, one month; and for a weekly tenancy, one week. The minimum period of the notice to quit can be extended by various statutory provisions applicable to certain types of tenancy. The notice must expire at the end of a period of the tenancy, that is on an anniversary of its commencement. This may be difficult to ascertain. If a monthly tenancy has been in existence for some years, it might be doubtful whether either party can remember on what precise date of the month it started and thus on what date the notice to quit should expire. The prudent landlord, or his solicitor, may therefore serve a notice to quit stating the day on which he believes the notice should expire, but adding in the alternative that the notice takes effect at the expiration of the quarter, month, week etc. of the tenancy which expires next after the expiration of a quarter, month, week etc. from service of the notice.

2 Basic protection for residential tenancies

It is a criminal offence for any person to unlawfully evict a 'residential occupier', that is to unlawfully deprive him of his occupation of premises, unless that person can show that he reasonably believed that the residential occupier had ceased to reside in the premises.[1] A 'residential occupier' is a person occupying premises as a residence, including both a tenant and a licensee during the

1 Protection from Eviction Act 1977, s. 1(2).

currency of his licence.[2] As we shall see, when a tenancy is protected by the Rent Act 1977 the landlord needs a court order to bring to an end the tenant's right to possession. Even when a tenancy is not so statutorily protected, if it is a tenancy of a dwelling and the 'occupier' continues to reside in the premises after the end of the tenancy, it is not lawful for the landlord to enforce his right to possession otherwise than by court proceedings.[3] An 'occupier' is anyone lawfully residing in the premises at the end of the tenancy.[4] This provision would not normally apply to licences but it does apply to restricted contracts[5] under the Rent Act 1977 which are licences not tenancies, provided they are created after the 28th November 1980.[6] It is also unlawful for the landlord to enforce a right of forfeiture of a lease of premises let as a dwelling except by court proceedings, while any person is lawfully residing in them.[7]

It is also a criminal offence for any person to do acts calculated to interfere with the peace or comfort of a residential occupier or member of his household or to persistently withdraw services, with the intent to cause the residential occupier to give up occupation of the whole or part of the premises or to refrain from exercising any right or pursuing any remedy in respect of the premises.[8]

The tenant's rights in respect of unlawful eviction and harassment can be protected by injunction and action for damages, possibly exemplary damages. These would be actions based on breach of a covenant for quiet enjoyment or trespass.

A rather different sort of protection is provided by the Protection from Eviction Act 1977, section 5, which states that the minimum period of notice to quit in respect of a periodic tenancy of a dwelling shall be four weeks and that the notice must be in writing and contain certain prescribed information. The current regulations under the section provide that the notice must inform the tenant that if he does not leave the dwelling the landlord must get a court order for possession before the tenant can be lawfully evicted.[9]

By section 4 of the Landlord and Tenant Act 1985, tenants who pay rent weekly have to be provided with a rent book (or equivalent), and by section 1 of the same Act, a tenant of a dwelling must be told the landlord's name and address within 21 days of a request to the landlord's agent (or anyone receiving the rent). Where the landlord's interest changes hands, section 3 of the Act requires the new landlord to give the tenant written notice of the change, and his name and address, within two months (or by the time rent is next due, if later).

These fundamental principles, then, apply to residential tenancies and some also apply to residential licences. However, many tenancies have a far greater and more sophisticated degree of protection controlling not just the manner

2 Ibid, s. 1(1). The distinction between a tenancy and a licence is discussed in the next section, 3 i.
3 Ibid, s. 3(1).
4 Ibid, s. 3(2).
5 See section 4, below.
6 Ibid, s. 3(2A). The provision also applies to service occupancies; ibid, s. 8(2).
7 Ibid, s. 2.
8 Ibid, s. 1(3).
9 Notices to Quit (Prescribed Information) Regulations 1980.

in which the landlord can regain possession but the circumstances in which he is actually entitled to possession and the rent that he can charge.

3 Protected tenancies under the Rent Act 1977

i What is a protected tenancy?

A protected tenancy is one under which a dwelling house (which may be a house or part of a house) is let as a separate dwelling.[10] Thus there must be a tenancy and not just a licence. The distinction between the two has not always been clear-cut, and there is an obvious opportunity for landlords who wish to avoid creating protected tenancies to grant licences instead. The essential characteristic of a tenancy, as opposed to a licence, is that the tenant has exclusive possession of at least part of the property. The courts have not been deceived by an agreement which calls itself a licence but is in fact a tenancy and have looked at the reality of the situation.[11] Nevertheless, there have in the past been cases in whch the courts have been satisfied that a licence did exist. In *Somma v Hazlehurst*,[12] an unmarried couple signed two identical licence agreements which inter alia stipulated that the licensees were not to have exclusive possession of the premises, which comprised a bedsit, and that the landlord could introduce other licensees into the bedsit. The Court of Appeal decided that this was a genuine licence. However the House of Lords has subsequently decided, in *Street v Mountford*,[13] that this case was wrongly decided. In *Street*, the House of Lords held that the test was whether the agreement, even though described as a licence, did in fact grant the occupier exclusive possession. This approach will presumably halt the spread of such licence agreements and ensure that occupiers are not deprived of the considerable protection of the Rent Act.

The tenancy must be of a house or part of a house thus including not only dwelling houses and flats but bedsits and possibly even static caravans.[14] The premises must be let as a dwelling, so if let for business or other non-residential purposes there will be no protected tenancy. If there is mixed business and residential use, the tenancy is normally treated as a business tenancy and is protected under the Landlord and Tenant Act 1954, Part II not the Rent Act 1977.[15] However, the premises must be let not just as a dwelling but as a 'separate' dwelling. If a tenant shares some essential accommodation (such as a kitchen, although just sharing a bathroom would probably not be sufficient) then on the face of it there can be no protected tenancy because there is no separate dwelling. However if the tenant is sharing with another tenant there

10 Rent Act 1977, s. 1.
11 *Walsh v Griffith-Jones* [1978] 2 All ER 1002.
12 [1978] 2 All ER 1011, [1978] 1 WLR 1014, CA.
13 [1985] AC 809, [1985] 2 All ER 289, HL.
14 *Rent Officer of Nottinghamshire Registration Area, ex p Allen* (1985) 2 EGLR 153.
15 Rent Act 1977, s. 24(3).

will still be a protected tenancy[16] and if he is sharing with the landlord he will have a restricted contract, a lesser form of protection.[17]

ii Exceptions

A tenancy will not be a protected tenancy if it falls within a series of exceptions.

(a) Premises above certain rateable values. For a protected tenancy, the rateable value must be below certain limits.[18] The relevant rateable value is the rateable value on 23 March 1965 or when first rated if later.[19]

(b) Tenancies at a low rent. The rent must not be less than two-thirds of the rateable value mentioned above.[20]

(c) Tenancies with board or attendance. A tenancy is not protected if the dwelling is let bona fide at a rent which includes payment in respect of board or attendance.[1] Board means provision of some form of food. Any board is sufficient to exclude the tenancy from protection subject to there being sufficient to demonstrate that it is not a sham to avoid protection. Attendance means services personal to the tenant performed by an attendant provided by the landlord. It would not include services common to all tenants such as cleaning communal areas or heating a communal water supply in a building with a number of tenants, but it might include cleaning a tenant's room or providing laundered linen. The amount of the rent attributable to attendance must form a substantial part of the whole rent for the tenancy to be excluded from protection.[2]

(d) Holiday lettings. A tenancy is not protected if the purpose is to give the tenant the right to occupy the dwelling for a holiday.[3] Again the court will be 'astute to detect a sham'.[4]

(e) Lettings to students. If a 'specified educational institution' grants a tenancy to a student pursuing a course of study, it will not be a protected tenancy.[5] This will cover rooms in halls of residence but not lettings by private landlords to tenants who happen to be students.

(f) Licensed premises. A tenancy of a dwelling with a licence for consumption of liquor on the premises is excluded.[6] A dwelling with an off-licence is not excluded *per se* but will be dealt with in the same way as any other premises with a business use.

(g) Parsonage houses of the Church of England.[7]

(h) Agricultural holdings. A tenancy is not protected if the dwelling house

16 Ibid, s. 22.
17 Ibid, s. 21 – see section 4, below.
18 Ibid, s. 4.
19 Ibid, s. 25(3).
20 Ibid, s. 5. In some cases the relevant rateable value is that on 22 March 1973.
1 Ibid, s. 7(1).
2 Ibid, s. 7(2).
3 Ibid, s. 9.
4 *Buchmann v May* [1978] 2 All ER 993, CA.
5 Rent Act 1977, s. 8.
6 Ibid, s. 11.
7 *Bishop of Gloucester v Cunningham* [1943] KB 101, [1943] 1 All ER 61, CA.

is comprised in an agricultural holding and is occupied by the person responsible for the control of the farming of the holding.[8]

(i) Business tenancies. If a tenancy is protected as a business tenancy under the Landlord and Tenant Act 1954, Part II it cannot also be protected under the Rent Act 1977.[9] As noted above if there is a mixed business and residential use, the tenancy will normally be protected as a business tenancy.

(j) Overcrowded dwelling house. If the dwelling house is overcrowded within the meaning of the Housing Act 1985 then although it can still be a protected tenancy the security of tenure provisions in the Rent Act 1977 do not apply.[10]

(k) Houses let with other land. The Rent Act 1977 provides that a tenancy is not protected if the dwelling is let with land other than the site of the dwelling.[11] To avoid an obvious absurdity, in that all houses will have some land let with them even if only a garden or a back yard, the Act further provides that any land or premises let 'together with' a dwelling house will be treated as part of the dwelling house unless it is agricultural land exceeding two acres.[12] Thus protection is only excluded if either the land, of whatever area, is not let together with the dwelling, taking into account the nature and purpose of the dwelling; or if it is agricultural land of over two acres.

(l) Lettings by a resident landlord. Protection is excluded in respect of a tenancy granted on or after 14 August 1974 of a dwelling which forms part of a building, by a landlord who resided in another dwelling in the same building and has continued to reside[13] (although certain gaps in the continuity of residence will not prevent the exception operating).[14] However the exception does not cover the letting by a landlord of a flat in a purpose-built block of flats, even though the landlord's residence is another flat in the same block. Neither does the exception apply to a tenancy granted to a person who immediately before the grant of the tenancy had a protected tenancy in any other dwelling in the same building; so a landlord cannot benefit by, after 1974, moving a tenant from one bedsit or flat to another one in the same building. If a tenancy is excluded from protection only by reason of this exception it will be a restricted contract.[15]

(m) Status of landlord. A tenancy is not protected if the landlord is the Crown, a Government Department,[16] a Local Authority,[17] a registered Housing

8 Rent Act 1977, s. 10; see Agricultural Holdings Act 1986, s. 1.
9 Ibid, s. 24.
10 Ibid, s. 101.
11 Ibid, s. 6.
12 Ibid, s. 26.
13 Ibid, s. 12(1). If there are joint landlords, not all need be resident for the exception to apply; *Cooper v Tait* (1984) 271 Estates Gazette 105, CA.
14 Ibid, Sch 2. It includes a period of 2 years following the death of the resident landlord, to allow the personal representatives to take advantage of the exception.
15 See section 4, below.
16 Ibid, s. 13.
17 Ibid, s. 14.

Association,[18] or a Housing Co-operative.[19] However a letting of a council house and a letting by a Housing Association or Co-operative may be a 'secure tenancy' and have some measure of protection under the Housing Act 1985.[20]

(n) Assured tenancies. Assured tenants are tenants of approved landlords whose dwellings were constructed since the coming into force of the Housing Act 1980 and then occupied under the assured tenancy. The object is to promote the building of property for residential letting and a number of landlords have been approved.

iii Scheme of protection

On the termination of the protected, ie contractual, tenancy – either by expiry of a fixed term or by notice to quit in respect of a periodic tenancy – a statutory tenancy arises. This gives the tenant the right to continue to occupy the dwelling as a resident unless and until the landlord can prove a specified ground for possession.[1] The terms of the statutory tenancy are discussed in the next section. The Rent Act 1977 also imposes a system of rent control on protected and statutory tenancies, regulating the amount that the landlord can charge. This is discussed later in this chapter.

Under the original legislation there were two sorts of protected tenancy, controlled and regulated. Controlled tenancies had to have been in existence in 1957 and all tenancies which were not controlled were regulated. By the Housing Act 1980 and earlier provisions, controlled tenancies have all been converted to regulated tenancies. Strictly one should talk therefore of regulated protected tenancies to differentiate them from controlled protected tenancies but as the latter have ceased to exist we shall refer simply to protected tenancies.

iv Statutory tenancy

The statutory tenancy is not really a tenancy as such but the personal right of the tenant to remain in possession of the dwelling. It arises when the (contractual) protected tenancy is terminated whether by effluxion of time or notice to quit or forfeiture, and the tenant continues to occupy the dwelling as a residence. It cannot be assigned or sub-let as a whole and does not vest in the tenant's trustee in bankruptcy if the tenant goes bankrupt. (This is rather anomalous because the protected tenancy *would* vest in the tenant's trustee in bankruptcy and the tenant would not then get a statutory tenancy on the eventual termination of the protected tenancy.) The terms of the statutory tenancy are those of the original protected tenancy so far as they are not inconsistent with the provisions of the Rent Act 1977.[2] The statutory tenancy will come to an end if the tenant ceases to occupy the dwelling as a residence, although he should give the landlord notice to quit in accordance with the original protected tenancy or, if no notice was required thereunder,

18 Ibid, s. 15.
19 Ibid, s. 16.
20 See section 6, below.
1 Ibid, s. 2(1)(a).
2 Ibid, s. 3(1).

at least three months notice.[3] The question of whether the tenant is occupying the dwelling as a residence may be one of degree. In *Hampstead Way Investments Ltd v Lewis-Weare*[4] the tenant married and went to live with his wife. However, he slept in the rented property five nights a week and had his mail directed there. There was held to be no statutory tenancy. Similarly, in *Kavanagh v Lyroudias*,[5] where the tenant slept in the rented property but did not eat there or use the living accommodation, and in *Regalian Securities Ltd v Scheur*,[6] where occasional occupation was not sufficient. The statutory tenancy will also come to an end when the landlord obtains an order for possession which is put into effect. The grounds on which the landlord can obtain a possession order are set out in the next section. The statutory tenancy does not necessarily come to an end on the death of a tenant. Although it does not pass to the tenant's personal representatives, the Rent Act 1977 does provide for succession to the tenancy.[7] If the tenant leaves a spouse who was resident in the property immediately before the tenant's death, then he or she can succeed to the statutory tenancy so long as he or she occupies the dwelling as a residence. If the tenant leaves no surviving spouse, a member of the tenant's family who was residing with him at the time of and for six months prior to his death can succeed to the statutory tenancy so long as he occupies the dwelling as his residence. If there is more than one such person then in default of agreement the county court will decide who shall succeed. There can be a second succession on the death of the first successor to the statutory tenancy; again first preference is given to the surviving spouse of the first successor and if none, then a member of the first successor's family can succeed on the same conditions as on a first succession. The expression 'family' in the Act is not a technical term and is used in its popular sense. It seems that a 'common law' wife or husband could be included as a member of the tenant's family.[8]

If, on the death of the tenant, the tenancy has not been terminated and is still therefore a protected tenancy rather than a statutory tenancy, then for the purposes of succession the statutory tenancy is deemed to have arisen just before the death and it can then be transmitted to the appropriate first successor.[9] The contractual protected tenancy remains in existence and will pass under the deceased's will or intestacy but it is in abeyance[10] and can presumably be terminated by notice to quit anyway if it is a periodic tenancy.

If on the death of the tenant or the first successor there is no successor, the statutory tenancy terminates. A statutory tenancy will also terminate on the termination of a superior tenancy unless the statutory tenant was a lawful sub-tenant and the superior tenancy was a protected or statutory tenancy itself.[11]

3 Ibid, s. 3(3).
4 [1985] 1 All ER 564, [1985] 1 WLR 164, HL.
5 [1985] 1 All ER 560, CA.
6 (1982) 263 Estates Gazette 973, CA. See further, comment on these three cases at (1985) Conv 224.
7 Ibid, Sch 1, Part 1.
8 *Dyson Holdings Ltd v Fox* [1976] QB 503, [1975] 3 All ER 1030, CA.
9 This is the effect of Rent Act 1977, Sch 1, para 1.
10 *Moodie v Hosegood* [1952] AC 61, [1951] 2 All ER 582, HL.
11 Rent Act 1977, s. 137(3) makes specific provision for a sub-tenancy of part of the property comprised in a tenancy which is not itself protected nor statutory.

v Possession orders

In order to obtain possession of a dwelling let on a protected/statutory tenancy, the landlord must be able to show the court that:

(a) the protected ie contractual tenancy has been terminated, (by expiry of a fixed term or notice to quit a periodic tenancy), and
(b) one of the specified grounds for possession applies, and
(c) if the ground for possession is a discretionary rather than mandatory ground, that it is reasonable for the court to order possession.[12]

The discretionary grounds are those set out in cases 1–10 of Schedule 15 to the Rent Act 1977, and there is also a further discretionary ground if the landlord can show the existence of alternative accommodation. The mandatory grounds are those set out in cases 11–20 of the Schedule.

1 *Alternative accommodation* The court may make an order for possession if satisfied that alternative accommodation is available for the tenant.[13] The accommodation must be suitable. The landlord can either produce a certificate from the Housing Authority confirming that it will provide suitable alternative accommodation by a specified date (which is conclusive) or the landlord can provide suitable alternative accommodation himself, which will give the tenant full Rent Act security or the equivalent and which satisfies the requirements set out in Part IV to Schedule 15 of the Act (which specify, inter alia, that the accommodation is reasonably suitable to the needs and means of the tenant).[14]

2 *Case 1* Where rent has not been paid or some other obligation under the tenancy has been broken.

3 *Case 2* Where the tenant or any person residing with him has committed an act constituting a nuisance or annoyance to neighbours or has been convicted of using the dwelling for illegal or immoral purposes.

4 *Case 3* Where the condition of the property has deteriorated due to the tenant's default.

5 *Case 4* Where the condition of furniture in a furnished tenancy has deteriorated due to the tenant's default.

6 *Case 5* Where the tenant has given notice to quit and the landlord has taken steps as a result of which he would be seriously prejudiced if he could not obtain possession, for example where the landlord has contracted to sell the property with vacant possession or to re-let it.

7 *Case 6* Where the tenant has after a certain date, normally 8 December 1965, or 14 August 1974 if the tenancy is furnished, assigned or sub-let the

12 Rent Act 1977, ss. 98(1), 98(2).
13 Ibid, s. 98(1)(a), Sch 15, Part IV. See eg *Battlespring Ltd v Gates* (1983) 268 Estates Gazette 355, CA.
14 See eg *Hill v Rochard* [1983] 2 All ER 21, [1983] 1 WLR 478, CA and *Gladyrid Ltd v Collinson* (1983) 267 Estates Gazette 761, CA.

whole of the dwelling without the landlord's consent. As the tenant can in any event not assign or sub-let the whole of his statutory tenancy,[15] the case would only ever be needed in relation to an assignment or sub-letting by the protected contractual tenant.

8 *Case 7* This only related to controlled protected tenancies and is therefore redundant.

9 *Case 8* Where the dwelling is reasonably required by the landlord for an employee, the present tenant also being an employee whose employment has now ceased.

10 *Case 9* Where the dwelling is reasonably required by the landlord for the occupation of himself or his son or daughter over 18 or his father or mother or his father-in-law or mother-in-law. This is to be assessed at the date of the court hearing.[16,17] The ground is not available if the landlord became landlord by purchasing the property already tenanted after a certain date, normally 23 March 1965 (or 24 May 1974 if the tenancy is furnished). This latter provision is to prevent the house being bought over the head of a sitting tenant who could then otherwise be evicted on this ground.

The court will not order possession if the tenant can show that greater hardship would be caused to him by the order being granted than would be caused to the landlord by the order being refused.

11 *Case 10* Where the tenant has sub-let part of the dwelling and is charging more than the lawfully recoverable rent.

The mandatory grounds for possession, where the landlord does not have to show that it is reasonable for the order to be made, are as follows.

12 *Case 11* Where a person who occupies[18] a dwelling as his residence (an 'owner occupier') has let it on a regulated protected tenancy then he can recover possession in certain circumstances.[19] Firstly, the landlord must, not later than the commencement of the tenancy, have given the tenant written notice that possession might be recovered on this ground. Secondly, the dwelling must not since a certain date, normally 8 December 1965 (or 14 August 1974 for a furnished tenancy), have been let on a protected tenancy without this notice having been given. If these conditions are satisfied the court must order possession in any one of five situations. Even if either or both the

15 He would then cease to be occupying the premises as his residence, a condition of the continuance of the statutory tenancy.
16 *Alexander v Mohamadzadeh* [1985] 2 EGLR 161.
17 In *Kidder v Birch* (1982) 46 P & CR 362, CA, a suspended possession order was made where the landlord required the property in the near future.
18 Even if intermittently, *Naish v Curzon* (1984) 129 Sol Jo 222 (1985) 1 EGLR 17, CA.
19 An owner-occupier can grant successive tenancies and still rely on case 11; Rent (Amendment) Act 1985 overturning *Pocock v Steel* [1985] 1 All ER 434, [1985] 1 WLR 229, CA.

conditions are not satisfied the court can still order possession if it is just and equitable to do so.[20] The five situations in which the court must order possession are:

(a) the dwelling is required as a residence for the owner occupier or a member of his family who resided with him when he last lived there;
(b) the owner occupier has died and the dwelling is required as a residence for a member of his family who was residing with him at the time of his death;
(c) the owner occupier has died and the dwelling is required by his successors in title, ie his personal representatives or a beneficiary under the will or intestacy, as a residence or for the purpose of disposing of it with vacant possession;
(d) the dwelling is subject to a mortgage made before the tenancy was granted and the mortgagee wishes to sell with vacant possession in exercise of his power of sale;
(e) the dwelling is not reasonably suitable to the owner occupier's needs having regard to his place of work and he wants to sell it with vacant possession in order to use the proceeds to acquire a residence which is more suitable to those needs.

This case is often used by house-owners who have to leave their houses for short periods, for example to work abroad for a year or so. If the property is subject to a mortgage then the mortgagee's consent will doubtless be required for the letting.

If the owner-occupiers are, in fact, joint owners it is sufficient for one of them to require the property as a residence.[1]

13 *Case 12* Where an owner intending to occupy a dwelling as his residence on retirement has in the meantime let it on a regulated protected tenancy. As in case 11, there are two conditions to be satisfied which relate to service of a notice on the tenant that this ground is applicable, and not letting on a protected tenancy in respect of which no such notice was given since a certain date. In four situations the court must order possession and again as in case 11 the court can still order possession if either or both of the conditions mentioned above is not satisfied if it would be just and equitable to do so. Three of the situations in which the court must order possession correspond with situations (b), (c) and (d) set out above under case 11, reference being to the owner rather than the owner-occupier. The fourth situation is where the owner has retired from regular employment and requires the dwelling as a residence.

14 *Case 13* Where the dwelling is let for a fixed term of eight months or less, having been let as a holiday home within the previous 12 months. Holiday lettings are not protected under the Act and this case provides that there can be an 'out of season' letting for a fixed term at the end of which the landlord is entitled to possession.

20 See eg *Fernandes v Parvardin* (1982) 264 Estates Gazette 49, CA (where the tenant had been given informal non-written notice) and *Minay v Sentongo* (1983) 45 P & CR 190 (where the tenant did not receive the notice); cf *Bradshaw v Baldwin-Wiseman* (1985) 49 P & CR 382.

1 *Tilling v Whiteman* [1980] AC 1, [1979] 1 All ER 737, HL.

15 *Case 14* Where the dwelling is let for a fixed term of 12 months or less having been let to a student by a specified educational establishment at some time during the previous 12 months. This allows a university or polytechnic to let out rooms in their halls of residence during vacations and be assured of being able to recover possession.

16 *Case 15* Where a dwelling held for the purposes of being available for occupation by a minister of religion as a residence has been let, but is now required for that purpose.

17 *Case 16* Where a dwelling has been occupied by a person employed in agriculture and is again required for that purpose, the present tenant not being such a person nor the widow of such a person.

18 *Case 17* This relates to proposals for amalgamation for agricultural purposes.

19 *Case 18* Where the dwelling was last occupied by a person responsible for the control of farming of land and it is now required for the occupation of such a person.

20 *Case 19* This is a more important case, introduced by the Housing Act 1980[2] to try and increase the amount of privately rented accommodation available. A dwelling can be let on what is ingloriously called a protected 'shorthold' tenancy. This is a tenancy for a fixed term of not less than one year nor more than five years. In the past a fair rent had to be registered, but this is no longer necessary. The tenant must be given notice before the tenancy is granted that it is a protected shorthold tenancy.[3] The tenancy can be brought to an end by the tenant before the end of the fixed term, by notice. Otherwise, at the end of the fixed term the landlord is entitled to possession under case 19. The landlord must give notice in writing to the tenant of his intention to bring possession proceedings. This notice must be served within the three month period immediately preceding either the date on which the fixed term ends or any anniversary of that date. This means that, for example, following a two year protected shorthold tenancy the landlord is entitled to possession not only at the end of the second year but also at the end of the third, fourth and subsequent years. The notice itself must be of at least three months, ie it must not expire until three months after service. The landlord must then commence possession proceedings not later than three months after the date of expiry of the notice.

If protected shortholds became popular with landlords they would remove at a stroke the security of tenure afforded to residential tenants by the otherwise limited grounds for possession under the Rent Act 1977. However, landlords should approach them with some caution, because the Labour Party has in the past stated its intention to repeal the relevant legislation if it ever has the opportunity.

2 Ss. 52–55.

3 Again the court has a discretion to waive these two conditions.

21 *Case 20* Where the owner, being a member of the Armed Forces, has let his property, he can recover it in certain circumstances. These correspond to situations (b), (c), (d) amd (e) described under case 11 above.

vi Rent control

The Rent Act 1977 contains a mechanism for the registration of what is called a fair rent, for a dwelling the subject of a protected or statutory tenancy. Either landlord or tenant can apply to the local Rent Officer to determine a fair rent.[4] The Rent Officer will have regard to the character, state of repair and locality of the dwelling and the quantity, quality and condition of the furniture provided if the tenancy is furnished.[5] The Rent Officer will probably use as a starting point the fair rents already registered for comparable properties. He must however disregard the effect on rent of the scarcity of accommodation in the area.[6] If either party is dissatisfied with the rent registered he can appeal to a tribunal called a Rent Assessment Committee. There is further appeal on a point of law to the Divisional Court. Once a fair rent has been registered there can be no further application for a period of two years unless it is either made jointly by the landlord and tenant or else there has been a change in circumstances, for example in the condition of the property or the terms of the tenancy.[7]

If on the grant of a new tenancy there is no fair rent registered in respect of the property then the parties can agree on whatever rent they choose. It is of course open to either party at any time to apply for a fair rent to be registered. If, on the other hand, on the grant of a new tenancy there is already a fair rent registered then this represents the maximum that the landlord can charge on that or any future tenancy unless or until the fair rent registered is increased on an application to the Rent Officer. If the parties do in fact agree on a higher rent than the fair rent, the excess is irrecoverable from the tenant.[8] As and when the tenant discovers that he has been paying over the odds he can recover the over payment for up to two years past.[9]

Turning from the rent recoverable on the grant of a new tenancy to the possibility of increasing (or decreasing) the rent during a protected or statutory tenancy, there are two ways in which this can be done. Firstly, there can be an application for registration of a fair rent, or re-registration if there is already a fair rent registered, subject to the two year rule. If the fair rent registered should be *less* than the rent being charged under the tenancy, then the fair rent becomes the maximum rent recoverable and the landlord must decrease the rent to the level of the fair rent. If the fair rent registered is *greater* than that being charged under the tenancy agreement, then the rent can be increased to the level of the fair rent. However, this increase cannot be made all at once; it must be phased and half of the increase is payable straightaway,

4 Rent Act 1977, s. 67(1).

5 Ibid, s. 70.

6 Ie he must 'value out' any distorting effect of scarcity – see *Western Heritable Investment Co v Husband* [1983] 2 AC 849, [1983] 3 All ER 65, HL.

7 Ibid, s. 67(3).

8 Ibid, s. 44.

9 Ibid, s. 57(3). By s. 57(2) the tenant can deduct what he is owed from his rent.

the other half only becoming payable at the end of a delay of one year.[10] Additionally, on each occasion the landlord must serve a prescribed notice of increase on the tenant.[11] However, if the tenancy is still protected rather than statutory it will probably not allow for an increase in rent. This contractual restriction on the landlord's right to increase the rent must be removed by terminating the contractual protected tenancy, allowing the statutory tenancy to arise. If the protected tenancy is for a fixed term the landlord must wait for it to expire, but if it is a periodic tenancy he can determine it by serving the appropriate notice to quit. In fact to avoid the landlord having to serve two notices, a notice to quit and then a notice of an increase in rent, the Rent Act 1977 provides that the landlord can simply serve a notice of increase which will also operate to terminate the protected tenancy as if it were a notice to quit.[12]

The other method of increasing the rent during a protected or statutory tenancy is by what the Rent Act 1977 calls a 'rent agreement with a tenant having security of tenure'.[13] This can be made where there is no rent registered but the landlord and tenant are agreeable to an increase in the rent under the tenancy. The agreement must be in writing, signed by both parties, and contain a prescribed statement addressed to the tenant to the effect that the tenant's security of tenure will be unaltered if he refuses to agree to the increase. Either party can of course still apply for registration of a fair rent. It must be said that in practice the requirements of this agreement are probably ignored in many cases; the landlord may just verbally tell the tenant that the rent is being increased and the tenant may verbally acquiesce. In such cases the increase is irrecoverable from the tenant who can claim back the amount of the increase for the past year.[14]

Any agreement to increase the rent under a statutory tenancy, if there is no rent registered, must be in a similar form. However, it will in effect amount to the grant of a new protected tenancy which may not be in the landlord's best interests, particularly if the statutory tenant is a successor.[15]

There is also a procedure whereby on a joint application by both landlord and tenant, at least two years after the registration of a fair rent, the Rent Officer can cancel the registration if satisfied that the new rent agreed between the landlord and tenant does not exceed the level of a fair rent.[16] This procedure is probably not used much in practice.

A landlord can ascertain before he grants a tenancy what a fair rent will be. He applies for a certificate of fair rent from the Rent Officer.[17] The dwelling must either be newly built, improved or converted or must be a dwelling in respect of which there has been no registration of rent in the last two years.

10 Ibid, Sch 8. This phasing rule is abolished from 4 May 1987.
11 Ibid, s. 49.
12 Ibid, s. 49(4).
13 Ibid, s. 51.
14 Ibid, ss. 54(1), 57(3).
15 Ibid, s. 51(1)(b).
16 Ibid, s. 73. The registered rent can also be cancelled if the dwelling is not for the time being let.
17 Ibid, s. 69.

If a solicitor is acting for a purchaser of property that is already let to residential tenants or which is to be used for such purposes, a search should be made of the register of fair rents to see what rents are registered in respect of the property. The purchaser should also be advised of the consequences for him of the whole scheme of security of tenure and rent control.

vii Premiums

It is an offence for any person to require or receive a premium as a condition of a grant, renewal, continuance or assignment of a protected tenancy.[18] The tenant can recover the premium.[19] A premium includes any pecuniary sum in addition to rent and any deposit, unless it does not exceed one-sixth of the annual rent and is reasonable in relation to the liability in respect of which it is paid.[20] An excessive price required for the purchase of furniture will also be treated as a premium thus removing a possible device for avoiding the anti-premium rule.[1]

4 Restricted contracts

i Definition

The Rent Act 1977 gives a certain limited degree of protection to what are called restricted contracts. A restricted contract will arise in three situations.

(a) A tenancy which would be a protected tenancy apart from the existence of a resident landlord.[2]

(b) A 'tenancy' which would be a protected tenancy if the tenant were not sharing accommodation with the landlord, provided the tenant has exclusive occupation of some accommodation.[3]

(c) A contract whereby one person grants to another the right to occupy a dwelling as a residence at a rent which includes payment for the use of furniture or services.[4] This category is not confined to tenancies and could include licences. Although some furniture or services must be provided, it should be emphasised that payment for the use of furniture or services does not mean that a tenancy cannot be a protected tenancy. A large proportion of protected tenancies are furnished tenancies.

Services are defined as including attendance, the provision of heating or lighting and the supply of hot water.[5] The tenant will not have a restricted contract under (c) if

(i) the rent includes substantial payment for board;
(ii) the rateable value of the dwelling is above certain limits;
(iii) the landlord is the Crown or a Government Department;

18 Ibid, s. 119(1) s. 120(1), subject to the provisions of s. 127 relating to long tenancies.
19 Ibid, s. 125(1).
20 Ibid, s. 128(1).
1 Ibid, s. 123.
2 Ibid, ss. 12, 20.
3 Ibid, s. 21.
4 Ibid, s. 19.
5 Ibid, s. 19(8).

(iv) the dwelling is for occupation for a holiday;
(v) the tenancy is a protected tenancy.

ii Security of tenure

The Rent Act 1977 as amended by the Housing Act 1980 provides the tenant under a restricted contract with very limited security of tenure. The landlord can determine the restricted contract in the ordinary way; by effluxion of time for a fixed term, or by serving a notice to quit. The basic protection of the Protection from Eviction Act 1977 discussed at section 2, above will apply, so the landlord must then get an order for possession. If the restricted contract is granted after 28 November 1980 the only additional protection is that the court, when making a possession order, has the power to postpone it for a maximum of three months.[6] However if the restricted contract was granted before that date there is a rather greater measure of security. This only applies to periodic restricted contracts determinable by notice to quit. Firstly, if a notice to quit is served after a tenant has applied to the rent tribunal, it will not take effect until six months after the decision of the tribunal.[7] This period can be reduced by the tribunal. Secondly, if a notice to quit is served and the tenant has applied to the tribunal, whether before or after service of the notice, then on application by the tenant before the notice or any extension of it under the previous provision has expired, the tribunal can delay the operation of the notice for up to six months.[8] The application to the tribunal referred to in these two provisions is in theory an application for a rent to be registered[9] but in practice the tenant's prime reason for making the application may be to obtain security of tenure.

iii Rent control

Either the landlord or the tenant can refer the restricted contract to the rent tribunal for registration of a rent.[10] A rent tribunal is another name for the rent assessment committee.[11] The tribunal will either approve the rent being charged or reduce or increase it. The rent must be 'reasonable' but there are no statutory criteria for the assessment of a reasonable rent. Once a rent is registered it is the maximum that the landlord can charge,[12] under that or any future restricted contract. If the registered rent is more than the rent previously charged the tenant must pay the increase immediately and there are no provisions for phasing in the increase.

As with a fair rent, there can be no application for reconsideration of a registered rent within two years of the registration unless there has been a change in circumstances.[13] If the landlord charges in excess of the registered rent then not only can the tenant recover such over-payments but the landlord

6 Ibid, s. 106A.
7 Ibid, s. 103.
8 Ibid, s. 104.
9 Ibid, ss. 77, 78.
10 Ibid, s. 77.
11 Housing Act 1980, s. 72.
12 Rent Act 1977, s. 81(1).
13 Unless made by landlord and tenant jointly; ibid, s. 80(2).

also commits a criminal offence.[14] It is also an offence to require payment of a premium on the grant or assignment of a restricted contract if there is a rent registered.[15]

If there is no registered rent the parties are free to fix whatever rent they wish, subject to the right of either party to apply to the tribunal.

5 Agricutural tied houses

The Rent (Agriculture) Act 1976 makes provision for security of tenure and rent control in respect of dwellings occupied by agricultural employees. However, a detailed consideration of the Act is outside the scope of this book.

6 Secure tenancies

A tenancy under which a dwelling is let as a separate dwelling to a tenant who occupies it as his only or principal home will be a secure tenancy if the landlord is one of a number of bodies.[16] These include Local Authorities (so council house tenancies will be secure tenancies), and registered Housing Associations. A licence, which but for the fact that it is a licence would be a secure tenancy, will be treated as a secure tenancy.[17] If the secure tenancy is periodic it can only be brought to an end by the landlord obtaining a possession order from the court.[18] The landlord must first of all serve a notice on the tenant in a prescribed form. The court will only order possession on a number of specified grounds.[19] Some grounds also require the court to be satisfied that it is reasonable to order possession; others that alternative accommodation will be available to the tenant; and for the remainder of the grounds the court must be satisfied on both counts. If the secure tenancy is for a fixed term then when it terminates a periodic tenancy arises, but this is possibly not itself a secure tenancy. Nevertheless the tenant will still have the basic protection of the Protection from Eviction Act 1977.[20] On the death of a tenant of a secure periodic tenancy, there can be one succession, to the tenant's spouse or to another member of his family who resided with him throughout the period of twelve months ending with his death. The successor must have occupied the dwelling house as his only or principal home at the time of the tenant's death.[1]

14 Ibid, ss. 81(3), 81(4).
15 Ibid, s. 122.
16 Secure tenancies were introduced by the Housing Act 1980; see now the Housing Act 1985.
17 Housing Act 1985, s. 79(3).
18 Ibid, s. 83.
19 Ibid, Sch 2.
20 See section 2, above.
1 Ibid, ss. 87–89.

7 Service tenancies and occupancies

If an employee is permitted to occupy a dwelling belonging to his employer, for convenience and as part payment for his services, then this will probably be a service tenancy. If he is required to occupy it to carry out his duties efficiently it will be a service occupancy or licence, not a tenancy. Service tenancies can be protected tenancies under the Rent Act 1977 but service occupancies obviously cannot. If agricultural they may be protected by the Rent (Agriculture) Act 1976 but otherwise they would only have the basic protection of the Protection from Eviction Act 1977; for the purposes of unlawful eviction they would be treated as tenancies, not licences.[2]

2 Protection from Eviction Act 1977, s. 8(2).

20 Business tenancies

1 Introduction

A tenancy of business premises is likely to be a more formal arrangement then a residential tenancy. Even if there is no lease, there will probably be a written tenancy agreement. It is likely to be for a fixed term rather than periodic as this gives the tenant a time scale against which to plan his future business activities. It is likely that the tenancy, of perhaps a shop or an office, will be of merely part of a building. The lease or tenancy agreement will therefore contain provision for easements for the use of stairs, lifts, corridors etc. There may be a service charge to pay for maintenance of these common parts and possibly also for maintenance of the structure of the building itself. It is very likely that there will be a covenant restricting the use of the property and restricting assignment and sub-letting without the landlord's consent.

Before entering into a tenancy of business premises both parties should be advised by their solicitors of the effect of the security of tenure provisions outlined in the rest of this chapter. This is of particular importance to the landlord, who may find it difficult to recover possession of the property.

2 Definition

The Landlord and Tenant Act 1954, Part II covers a number of aspects of business tenancies. The security of tenure provisions apply to 'any tenancy where the property comprised in the tenancy is or includes premises which are occupied by the tenant and are so occupied for the purposes of a business carried on by him or for those and other purposes'.[1] Business 'includes a trade, profession or employment'.[2] As well as the usual forms of commercial activity, business has been held to include the activity of a members' tennis club[3] and

1 Landlord and Tenant Act 1954, s. 23(1).

2 Ibid, s. 23(2).

3 *Addiscombe Garden Estates Ltd v Crabbe* [1958] 1 QB 513, [1957] 3 All ER 563, CA.

the activities of hospital governors in administering the hospital premises.[4] However, the following are excluded:

(a) a tenancy of an agricultural holding;[5]

(b) a mining lease;[6]

(c) a tenancy of premises with an on-licence, except premises such as hotels, restaurants and theatres where the licence is ancillary to the main purpose;[7]

(d) a service tenancy;[8]

(e) a tenancy where the business carried on is in breach of a general prohibition under the tenancy against business use (as opposed to a provision for or against particular business use);[9]

(f) a fixed term tenancy where the parties agree to the exclusion of the Act and the court grants its approval before the lease takes effect;[10] apart from this any agreement whereby the parties attempt to exclude the security of tenancy provisions of the Act or impose a penalty on the tenant if he takes advantage of them will be void;[11]

(g) a fixed term tenancy not exceeding six months; the tenancy must not contain any term allowing renewal beyond the six month period.[12]

3 Security of tenure

There are two separate aspects to the security of tenure provided by the Act. Firstly, the tenancy will continue, irrespective of effluxion of time of a fixed term tenancy or notice to quit a periodic tenancy, unless and until the tenancy is terminated in one of the ways permitted by the Act.[13] Secondly, even when a tenancy is terminated, the tenant has a prima facie right to the grant of another tenancy.[14] To take the first point, a fixed term tenancy will not terminate at the end of the fixed term. It will continue unless and until it is terminated in a way allowed by the Act. It does not continue as a periodic tenancy, it just continues as an extension of the fixed term on the same terms including payment of rent. Similarly, a periodic tenancy is not terminated by an ordinary common law notice to quit by the landlord, but continues.

i Termination

The following are the methods by which the tenancy can be terminated under the Act, thus preventing any (further) continuation:

4 *Hills (Patents) Ltd v University College Hospital Board of Governors* [1956] 1 QB 90, [1955] 3 All ER 365, CA.
5 Landlord and Tenant Act 1954, s. 43(1).
6 Ibid.
7 Ibid.
8 Ibid, s. 43(2).
9 Ibid, s. 23(4).
10 Landlord and Tenant Act 1954, s. 38(4).
11 Ibid, s. 38(1).
12 Ibid, s. 43(3).
13 Ibid, s. 24(1).
14 Unless termination is by forfeiture or surrender.

(a) forfeiture, including forfeiture of a superior lease;[15]
(b) surrender;[16]
(c) tenant's notice;
(d) landlord's notice in statutory form;
(e) tenant's request in statutory form.

The last three of these will now be examined in more detail.

1 *Tenant's notice* If the tenancy is periodic it can be terminated by an ordinary common law notice to quit given by the tenant.[17] However, to avoid abuse of this procedure by landlords, the notice cannot be given (and indeed a surrender cannot be agreed) unless the tenant has been in occupation for at least a month. This is to prevent the landlord demanding that the tenant sign a notice to quit (or a surrender) as a condition of the tenancy being granted in the first place. If the tenancy is for a fixed term the tenant can give notice to terminate it, which must be not less than three months notice to expire either at the end of the term or on any subsequent quarter day.[18]

2 *Landlord's notice* Apart from forfeiture or surrender, a landlord must serve a notice under the Landlord and Tenant Act 1954, section 25 to terminate the tenancy. The landlord who can serve such a notice (and who receives a tenant's request described in the next section) is not necessarily the tenant's immediate landlord. He is defined in the Act as the owner of the reversion *or of the nearest superior reversion* which is *not* a lease which will terminate within fourteen months, either by effluxion of time or because a notice to terminate it has been served.[19] The landlord's notice under section 25 must be in writing and in a prescribed form. It must state the date on which the tenancy is to end. There are two requirements for this date. Firstly, it must not be earlier than the date on which the tenancy could otherwise be brought to an end. For a fixed term tenancy it must not be earlier than the end of the term, and for a periodic tenancy it must not be earlier than the earliest date for which a common law notice to quit could be given. It should be noted that it need not be the actual date for which the common law notice to quit could be given, ie the end of a period of the tenancy; it must just not be earlier than that date. Secondly, the termination date must be not less than six nor more than twelve months after the date of the notice.

If the landlord wishes to obtain possession of the property and would oppose an application by the tenant for a new tenancy, he must say so in the notice and state the ground or grounds of opposition on which he relies. There are seven statutory grounds of opposition and the landlord cannot later rely on a ground which he has not stated at this stage. The seven grounds will be examined in detail later. The landlord may of course not want possession of the property; his objective in serving the notice may merely be to end the old

15 Ibid, s. 24(2). The (sub-)tenant may be able to apply for relief.
16 Ibid.
17 Ibid.
18 Ibid, s. 27.
19 Ibid, s. 44.

tenancy so that the tenant applies for a new tenancy under which the rent can be brought in line with current market rents.

The notice must also tell the tenant that within two months he must notify the landlord in writing whether he is willing to give up possession on the specified termination date or not. The tenant on receiving the notice must then decide whether he will give up possession or whether he wishes to apply to the court for a new tenancy. The notice will of course tell him whether or not the landlord will oppose such an application and on what grounds. If a tenant is happy to give up possession and does not want a new tenancy he need not do anything. Otherwise he must notify the landlord in writing that he will not give up possession, within two months of the service of the notice.[20] This time limit is strictly enforced and if the tenant fails to give his counter notice in time he cannot apply to the court for a new tenancy but must give up possession on termination of the current tenancy unless he can negotiate a new tenancy with the landlord. If the tenant's solicitor is responsible for serving the counter-notice he should make a diary note to ensure that it is done in time.

If a counter-notice is served, then unless the landlord and tenant can agree on terms for a new tenancy the tenant must, if he still wants a new tenancy, apply to the court not earlier than two nor later than four months after service of the *landlord's notice*.[1] Again these time limits are strictly enforced and perhaps even greater care should be taken over the timing of the application to the court since it is possible to apply too early as well as too late.[2]

The effect of a landlord's notice in the proper form is to terminate the tenancy on the specified date. However, if the result of the notice is an application by the tenant to the court for a new tenancy then the old tenancy will only terminate three months after the tenant's application is finally disposed of.[3]

3 *Tenant's request* The tenant may be quite happy to allow the current tenancy to continue, particularly as he is paying rent at the amount set under that tenancy. However, he may wish to make long term future plans and establish whether he is going to get a new tenancy on termination of the current tenancy. If he merely waits for the landlord to serve a notice he will not be able to make any such long term plans because it will only be when the landlord does serve a notice that he will be able to apply for a new tenancy. There is therefore a procedure by which the tenant can bring matters to a head; he can bring the current tenancy to an end with the object of applying for a new tenancy. He does this by serving on the landlord a request for a new tenancy.[4] This is analogous to the landlord's notice in that it will specify a termination date for the current tenancy. What was said about the termination

20 Ibid, s. 29(2).
1 Ibid, s. 29(3).
2 The time limits can be waived by the landlord; *Kammins Ballrooms Co Ltd v Zenith Investments (Torquay) Ltd* [1971] AC 850, [1970] 2 All ER 871, HL; *EJ Riley Investments Ltd v Eurostile Holdings Ltd* [1985] 3 All ER 181, [1985] 1 WLR 1139, CA.
3 Landlord and Tenant Act 1954, s. 64.
4 Ibid, s. 26.

date in relation to the landlord's notice applies equally to the tenant's request, in that the date must not be earlier than the end of a fixed term tenancy nor the earliest date for which the tenant could have given a common law notice to quit a periodic tenancy; and it must also be not less than six nor more than twelve months after the date of the request. The request must be in writing and in a prescribed form. It must also propose terms for a new tenancy. The request must be served on the landlord, as defined in the previous section. The landlord must, within two months of the request, serve a counter-notice on the tenant otherwise he loses his right to oppose the tenant's application for a new tenancy.[5] The counter-notice must state that the landlord will oppose the application and also state the statutory ground or grounds on which the landlord relies. Thus far, the procedure has been the reverse of the procedure under a landlord's notice; the tenant instead of the landlord initiating the process and the landlord instead of the tenant giving a counter-notice within two months. However, unless agreement can be reached on a new tenancy, it is still the tenant who must apply to the court within two to four months of his request if he wishes to apply for a new tenancy, which presumably he does! This means that it is possible for the tenant to have terminated his tenancy and then have debarred himself from applying for a new tenancy by applying to the court too late.

The effect of the tenant's request is the same as the landlord's notice. It terminates the current tenancy on the termination date subject to the tenant's application to the court for a new tenancy. It is only certain tenants who can serve a request, principally tenants whose tenancy is a fixed term of over one year.[6] When the landlord has served a section 25 notice the tenant cannot serve a request and vice versa, the object of both being the same, to terminate the existing tenancy and to allow the tenant to set in motion the procedure for applying for a new tenancy.

ii Application to the court – grounds of opposition

The stage has now been reached either by a landlord's notice or a tenant's request where the tenant has made an application to the court for an order for a new tenancy. This is his prima facie right but the landlord can successfully oppose the application if he can show one or more of seven statutory grounds. These will have been pleaded by the landlord in his notice, or his counter-notice in reply to the tenant's request. If the landlord is seeking possession, the first stage of the court hearing will involve a decision as to whether or not any ground for possession has been made out. If the court is satisfied that one or more grounds have been proved then the tenant does not get a new tenancy. If the landlord fails to prove one or more grounds to the court's satisfaction or if the landlord is not in fact seeking possession and did not oppose the grant of a new tenancy, the court must, in the absence of agreement by the parties, determine the terms of the new tenancy.

The seven statutory grounds of opposition are set out below.

5 Ibid, s. 26(6).
6 Ibid, s. 26(1).

1 *Breach of repairing obligations by tenant* The landlord must show that the tenant ought not to be granted a new tenancy in view of the state of repair of the property.[7]

2 *Persistent delay in paying rent* The landlord has to show that the tenant ought not to be granted a new tenancy in view of his persistent delay in paying his rent.[8] The court will take into account the number of times there has been a delay and the length of the delay.

3 *Substantial breaches of other obligations* The landlord must show that the tenant ought not to be granted a new tenancy in view of other substantial breaches of his obligations under the tenancy.[9]

4 *Alternative accommodation* The landlord must have offered and be willing to provide alternative accommodation to the tenant on reasonable terms.[10] The accommodation must be suitable for the tenant's requirements, bearing in mind his business and the size and situation of the new accommodation. This ground, unlike the previous three grounds, is not discretionary: if suitable accommodation has been offered on suitable terms, the court must refuse the tenant's application.

5 *Possession of whole property required where tenant has a sub-tenancy* If the tenant's tenancy is a sub-tenancy of part only of the property comprised in a superior tenancy, and that superior tenancy is shortly to end, the relevant landlord will be the owner of the reversion of the superior tenancy. He may obtain possession from the tenant if he wants to re-let or otherwise dispose of the property as a whole, if the rent available on a letting of the property as a whole would be substantially more than the aggregate rents available on separate lettings of the premises included in the current tenancy and the remainder of the property[11] and if the court accepts that in view of this, the tenant ought not to be granted a new tenancy.

6 *Intention to demolish or reconstruct* The landlord must show that on the termination of the tenancy he intends to demolish or reconstruct the premises, or a substantial part of them, or to carry out substantial work of construction, and that he cannot reasonably do so without obtaining possession.[12] The landlord must have a firm and settled intention but this need only be shown at the date of the court hearing, rather that the date of service of his notice.[13] Again, the court has no discretion if the landlord can prove this ground. Evidence of the intention could include the preparation of plans, the granting of planning permission or the obtaining of quotations for the work. The

7 Ibid, s. 30(1)(a).
8 Ibid, s. 30(1)(b).
9 Ibid, s. 30(1)(c).
10 Ibid, s. 30(1)(d).
11 Ibid, s. 30(1)(e).
12 Ibid, s. 30(1)(f).
13 *Betty's Cafés Ltd v Phillips Furnishing Stores Ltd* [1959] AC 20, [1958] 1 All ER 607, HL.

landlord will not succeed on this ground if the tenant agrees to the inclusion in his new tenancy of terms giving the landlord access, and the landlord can then reasonably carry out the work without obtaining actual possession; or if the tenant is willing to accept a tenancy of part only of the property, if necessary with the landlord having access to it.[14]

7 *Intention to occupy premises* The landord must, on the termination of the tenancy, intend to occupy the premises himself either for the purpose or partly for the purpose of a business to be carried on by him at the premises, or as a residence.[15] What was said about intention in the previous paragraph applies equally here. If the landlord is a company then the ground is satisfied if possession is required for a subsidiary company or, if the landlord company is a subsidiary of another company, if possession is required for that company or another subsidiary company.[16] If the landlord is an individual it is sufficient if the premises are required for a company which he controls.[17] A landlord cannot rely on this ground if his interest was purchased by him within the five years preceding the termination date of the tenancy specified in the landlord's notice or the tenant's request.[18] So if the landlord owns the freehold and bought it within the last five years, subject to the tenancy, then he cannot rely on this ground. To take an example, if the landlord bought the freehold in 1980, subject to the tenancy, he cannot rely on this ground until 1985 at the earliest. If the tenancy is renewed under the Act in 1983, perhaps in consequence of the tenant's request, the landlord cannot rely on this ground to oppose the renewal at that time. He can only hope that the new tenancy granted in 1983 is relatively short! Of course, if the landlord *granted* the tenancy in question he is not a landlord by purchase and there is nothing to prevent him relying on this ground within five years.

The landlord cannot rely on this ground if his intention is to re-let the premises, even if he will occupy as a residence for a brief period whilst redecoration and conversion work is done.[19]

iii Terms of the new tenancy

If a new tenancy is ordered by the court then the court must, in the absence of agreement between the parties, determine its terms.[20] Even if all the terms of the tenancy have not been agreed, the parties may have reached agreement on some terms, such as the rent or the length of the new tenancy. In the absence of agreement the court has a wide discretion. The term of the new tenancy must be such as is reasonable in all the circumstances, with a maximum of fourteen years.[1] Obviously the duration of the old tenancy is a relevant factor. The property comprised in the new tenancy will normally be the same

14 Landlord and Tenant Act 1954, s. 31A.
15 Ibid, s. 30(1)(g).
16 Ibid, s. 42.
17 Ibid, s. 30(3).
18 Ibid, s. 30(2).
19 *Jones v Jenkins* (1985) Times, 14 December, CA.
20 Ibid, ss. 29(1), 35.
1 Ibid, s. 33.

as that comprised in the old tenancy but it may exclude a part not occupied by a tenant.[2] The rent must be an open market rent, disregarding certain factors including any goodwill attached to the premises by reason of the tenant's business and also the effect of improvements made by the tenant so long as they were not made in pursuance of an obligation to the landlord.[3] In practice both the landlord and the tenant will consult a professional surveyor and the figure determined by the court will probably be somewhere between the figures suggested by the two surveyors.

There is also a procedure whereby the landlord can apply for an interim rent. Once the landlord has given his section 25 notice or the tenant has served his request, the landlord can apply to the court to fix a rent which it is reasonable for the tenant to pay whilst the old tenancy continues.[4] The interim rent is payable from the date proceedings for its determination were commenced, or the termination date specified in the landlord's notice or the tenant's request, whichever is the later. It should be emphasised that this procedure is not available during the continuation of the tenancy until either the landlord has served a section 25 notice or the tenant has served a request.

The other terms of the tenancy will also be determined by the court in the absence of agreement and will probably closely follow the terms of the old tenancy; indeed it will in effect be for a party to persuade the court of the need for change. Once the terms of a new tenancy are decided the tenant has an option to withdraw; if for example he cannot afford the new rent, he can apply within fourteen days for the order for a new tenancy to be revoked, although he risks being ordered to pay costs if the court thinks fit.[5] If the tenant does withdraw, the old tenancy terminates on a date to be agreed or determined by the court to allow the landlord a reasonable chance to re-let or otherwise dispose of the premises. In the normal case where the tenant accepts the new tenancy, the old tenancy continues for three months after the date of the hearing, or the hearing of any appeal, and the new tenancy then commences.[6] Similarly if the landlord successfully opposes an application to the court by the tenant for a new tenancy, the old tenancy continues for a further three months after the hearing. The provisions of the Act will apply to the new tenancy and so it also will continue until determined in the appropriate way whereupon the tenant can apply for another new tenancy. And so it goes on.

iv Contracting out

With the exception already mentioned, where the court gives its prior approval, it is not possible by agreement to exclude the tenant from applying for a new tenancy.

2 Ibid, ss. 23(3), 32.
3 Ibid, s. 34.
4 Ibid, s. 24A. The application for an interim rent could be made in the landlord's answer to the tenant's application to the court for a new tenancy; *Thomas v Hammond-Lawrence* [1986] 2 All ER 214, [1986] 1 WLR 456, CA.
5 Ibid, s. 36(2), (3).
6 Ibid, s. 64.

4 Compensation

Compensation is payable in two situations, firstly for disturbance where the tenant fails to obtain a new tenancy and secondly for improvements at the end of the tenancy.

i Compensation for disturbance

This is payable when the landlord successfully opposes the grant of a new tenancy solely on one or more of the last three statutory grounds, that is where the property is held on a sub-tenancy and the landlord wishes to re-let or dispose of the property as a whole; where the landlord wishes to demolish or reconstruct; or where the landlord intends to occupy the premises himself.[7] If possession is ordered on any other ground then whether or not it is also ordered on any of the above three grounds, compensation is not payable. The tenant can ask the court to certify whether the landlord successfully opposed the application only on one or more of the above three grounds.[8] Compensation is also payable if the landlord's notice (or counternotice to the tenant's request) specifies only one or more of the above three grounds of opposition and the tenant then does not apply to the court for a new tenancy.[9] It will be noticed that all the other grounds, apart from the three mentioned above, include some aspect of fault on the part of the tenant, except where alternative accommodation is offered in which case although the current tenancy is ending it is being replaced by a tenancy of alternative premises.

Compensation is payable when the tenant leaves the premises. The amount of compensation is three times the rateable value of the premises. If during the fourteen years preceding the end of the tenancy, the premises have been occupied by the tenant or his predecessors in the same business, the compensation is doubled to six times the rateable value.[10] It is only possible to exclude or restrict the right to compensation where the tenant or his predecessors in the same business have been in occupation for less than five years on the date of termination of the tenancy.[11] Such an exclusion will often be incorporated into the tenancy agreement or lease.

ii Compensation for improvements

This is governed by the Landlord and Tenant Act 1927. Generally, if a tenancy is protected under the 1954 Act, Part II it will also be covered by the 1927 Act[12] but there are minor differences in the scope of the two statutes. On the termination of the tenancy, the tenant is entitled to compensation in respect of any improvements made by him or his predecessors in title. However, the improvement must add to the letting value of the property and must not be a fixture which the tenant is entitled to remove and take with him.[13] Before

7 Ibid, s. 37(1).
8 Ibid, s. 37(4).
9 Ibid, s. 37(1).
10 Ibid, s. 37(2), (3).
11 Ibid, s. 38(2), (3).
12 See Landlord and Tenant Act 1927, s. 17.
13 Landlord and Tenant Act 1927, s. 1(1).

making the improvement the tenant must have served the landlord with written notice of his intention to do so. The landlord has three months in which to serve a notice of objection. If he does so the tenant must apply to the court for a certificate.[14] This will only be granted if the court is satisfied firstly that the improvement will add to the letting value at the end of the tenancy; secondly that the improvement is reasonable and suitable to the character of the premises; and thirdly that it will not diminish the value of any other property belonging to the landlord or any superior landlord. If the landlord does not object, or objects but the court nevertheless grants the certificate, this displaces any prohibition in the lease or tenancy agreement against making improvements.[15]

The tenant must then serve a written notice of his claim for compensation, within certain time limits set out in section 47 of the Landlord and Tenant Act 1954; for example if the tenancy is ended by the landlord's notice under section 25, a claim must be made within three months of the notice. The compensation is only payable if the tenant does not obtain a new tenancy and does leave the premises. The amount of compensation will be fixed by the court in the absence of agreement. It will not exceed the addition to the letting value of the premises as a result of the improvement.[16] It is not possible to exclude or restrict the right to compensation.[17]

14 Ibid, s. 3.
15 Ibid, s. 3(4).
16 Ibid, s. 1(1).
17 Ibid, s. 9.

Appendix

Law Society's General Conditions of Sale (1984 revision)
National Conditions of Sale (20th edition, 1981)

Law Society's General Conditions of Sale (1984 revision)

Reproduced by kind permission of the Law Society

1 Definitions

In these conditions –
(a) 'completion notice' means a notice served under condition 23(2)
(b) 'the contract rate' means the rate specified in a special condition or, if none is so specified, the rate prescribed from time to time under section 32 of the Land Compensation Act 1961 for interest payable thereunder
(c) 'contractual completion date' has the meaning given in condition 21
(d) 'conveyance' includes an assignment and a transfer under the Land Registration Acts
(e) 'lease' includes underlease
(f) 'normal deposit' means the sum which, together with any preliminary deposit paid by the purchaser, amounts to ten per centum of the purchase money (excluding any separate price to be paid for any chattels, fixtures or fittings)
(g) 'working day' means any day from Monday to Friday (inclusive) other than –
  (i) Christmas Day, Good Friday and any statutory bank holiday, and
  (ii) any other day specified in a special condition as not a working day
(h) a reference to a statute includes any amendment or re-enactment thereof.

2 Service and delivery

(1) Section 196 of the Law of Property Act 1925 applies to any notice served under the contract, save that –
(a) a notice shall also be sufficiently served on a party if served on that party's solicitors
(b) a reference to a registered letter shall include a prepaid first class ordinary letter
(c) if the time at which a letter containing a notice would in the ordinary course be delivered is not on a working day, the notice shall be deemed to be served on the next following working day
(d) a notice shall also be sufficient served if –
  (i) sent by telex or by telegraphic facsimile transmission to the party to be served, and that service shall be deemed to be made on the day of transmission if transmitted before 4 p.m. on a working day, but otherwise on the next following working day
  (ii) when the addressee is a member of a document exchange (as to which the inclusion of a reference thereto in the solicitors' letterhead shall be conclusive evidence) delivered to that or any other affiliated exchange, and that service shall be deemed to have been made on the first working day after that on which the document would, in the ordinary course, be available for collection by the addressee.
(2) Sub-condition (1) applies to the delivery of documents as it applies to the service of notices.

3 Matters affecting the property

(1) In this condition –
(a) 'competent authority' means a local authority or other body exercising powers under statute or Royal Charter
(b) 'requirement' includes (whether or not subject to confirmation) any notice, order or proposal
(c) 'relevant matter' means any matter specified in sub-condition (2) whenever arising.
(2) The property is sold subject to –
(a) all matters registrable by any competent authority pursuant to statute
(b) all requirements of any competent authority
(c) all matters disclosed or reasonably to be expected to be disclosed by searches and as a result of enquiries formal or informal, and whether made in person, by writing or orally by or for the purchaser or which a prudent purchaser ought to make
(d) all notices served by or on behalf of a reversioner, a tenant or sub-tenant, or the owner or occupier of any adjoining or neighbouring property.
(3) (a) Notwithstanding sub-condition (2), the vendor warrants that he has informed the purchaser of the contents of any written communication received by, or known to, the vendor on or before the working day preceding the date of the contract relating to any relevant matter. Failure to give such information before the contract is made shall be deemed to be an omission in a statement in the course of the negotiations leading to the contract, but shall give rise to no right to compensation to the extent that the purchaser has a claim for damages against a competent authority
(b) In the event of any conflict or variation between information in fact received from any competent authority relating to any relevant matter and any statement made by the vendor in respect of the same matter, the purchaser shall rely on the information received from the competent authority to the exclusion of that given by the vendor
(c) The vendor shall forthwith inform the purchaser of the contents of any written communication received by him after the working day preceding the date of the contract and before the day of actual completion which if received on or before the former day would have fallen within paragraph (a).
(4) The purchaser (subject to any right or remedy arising under sub-condition (3)) will indemnify the vendor in respect of any liability under any requirement of a competent authority (whether made before or after the date of the contract), including the reasonable cost to the vendor of compliance after reasonable notice to the purchaser of the vendor's intention to comply, such sum to be payable on demand. The provisions of this subcondition shall prevail in the event of conflict with any other condition.

4 Opportunity to rescind

(1) This condition only applies if a special condition so provides.
(2) Within such period as is specified in a special condition or, if none is so specified, within twenty working days from the date of the contract (as to which, in either case, time shall be of the essence), the purchaser shall be entitled, notwithstanding condition 3(2), to rescind the contract by service of notice on the vendor specifying a matter to which this condition applies affecting the property.
(3) This condition applies to any of the following matters of which the purchaser had no knowledge on or before the working day preceding the date of the contract –
(a) a financial charge which the vendor cannot or has not at the purchaser's written request agreed to discharge on or before actual completion
(b) a statutory provision prohibiting, restricting or imposing adverse conditions upon the use or the continued use of the property for such purpose as is specified in a special condition or, if none is so specified, the purpose for which the vendor used it immediately before the date of the contract
(c) a matter which is likely materially to reduce the price which a willing purchaser

could otherwise reasonably be expected to pay for the relevant interest in the property in the open market at the date of the contract.
(4) For the purposes of this condition, the purchaser's knowledge –
(a) includes everything in writing received in the course of the transaction leading to the contract by a person acting on his behalf from the vendor, a person acting on the vendor's behalf, or a competent authority (as defined in condition 3(1)(a))
(b) does not include anything solely because a statute deems that registration of a matter constitutes notice of it.

5 Easements, reservations, rights and liabilities

(1) The vendor warrants that he has disclosed to the purchaser the existence of all easements, rights, privileges and liabilities affecting the property, of which the vendor knows or ought to know, other than the existence of those known to the purchaser at the date of the contract, or which a prudent purchaser would have discovered by that date.
(2) Without prejudice to the generality of sub-condition(1) –
(a) the purchaser shall purchase with full notice of the actual state and condition of the property and shall take it as it stands, save where it is to be constructed or converted by the vendor
(b) the property is sold, and will if the vendor so requires be conveyed, subject to all rights of way, water, light, drainage and other easements, rights, privileges and liabilities affecting the same.
(3) (a) In this sub-condition 'the retained land' means land retained by the vendor –
(i) adjoining the property, or
(ii) near to the property and designated as retained land in a special condition.
(b) The conveyance of the property shall contain such reservations in favour of the retained land and the grant of such rights over the retained land as would have been implied had the vendor conveyed both the property and the retained land by simultaneous conveyances to different purchasers.

6 Tenancies

(1) This condition applies if the property is sold subject to any lease or tenancy and shall have effect notwithstanding any partial, incomplete or inaccurate reference to any lease or tenancy in the special conditions or the particulars of the property.
(2) Copies or full particulars of all leases or tenancies not vested in the purchaser having been furnished to him, he shall be deemed to purchase with full knowledge thereof and shall take the property subject to the rights of the tenants thereunder or by reason thereof. The purchaser shall indemnify the vendor against all claims, demands and liability in respect of such rights, notwithstanding that they may be void against a purchaser for want of registration.
(3) The vendor gives no warranty as to the amount of rent lawfully recoverable from any tenant, as to the effect of any legislation in relation to any lease or tenancy or as to the compliance with any legislation affecting the same.
(4) The vendor shall inform the purchaser of any change in the disclosed terms and conditions of any lease or tenancy.
(5) If a lease or tenancy subject to which the property is sold terminates for any reason, the vendor shall inform the purchaser and, on being indemnified by the purchaser against all consequential loss, expenditure or liability, shall act as the purchaser may direct.

7 Errors, omissions and misstatements

(1) No error, omission or misstatement herein or in any plan furnished or any statement

made in the course of the negotiations leading to the contract shall annul the sale or entitle the purchaser to be discharged from the purchase.
(2) Any such error, omission or misstatement shown to be material shall entitle the purchaser or the vendor, as the case may be, to proper compensation, provided that the purchaser shall not in any event be entitled to compensation for matters falling within conditions 5(2) or 6(3).
(3) No immaterial error, omission or misstatement (including a mistake in any plan furnished for identification only) shall entitle either party to compensation.
(4) Sub-condition (1) shall not apply where compensation for any error, omission or misstatement shown to be material cannot be assessed nor enable either party to compel the other to accept or convey property differing substantially (in quantity, quality tenure or otherwise) from the property agreed to be sold if the other party would be prejudiced by the difference.
(5) The purchaser acknowledges that in making the contract he has not relied on any statement made to him save one made or confirmed in writing.

8 Leaseholds

(1) This condition applies if the property is leasehold.
(2) In all cases the immediate title to the property shall begin with the lease. Where the lease, unless registered with absolute title, is dated not more than fifteen years before the date of the contract and was granted for a term exceeding twenty-one years, the freehold title and all other titles superior to the lease shall be deduced for a period beginning not less than fifteen years prior to the date of the contract and ending on the date of the lease.
(3) A copy of the lease and a copy of, sufficient extract from, or abstract of, all superior leases, the contents of which are known to the vendor, having been supplied or made available to the purchaser, he shall be deemed to purchase with full notice of the contents thereof, whether or not he has inspected the same.
(4) Where any consent to assign is necessary –
(a) the vendor shall forthwith at his own cost apply for and use his best endeavours to obtain such consent
(b) the purchaser shall forthwith supply such information and references as may reasonably be required by the reversioner before granting such consent
(c) if any such consent is not granted at least five working days before contractual completion date, or is subject to any condition to which the purchaser reasonably objects, either party may rescind the contract by notice to the other.
(5) Any statutory implied covenant on the part of the vendor shall not extend to any breach of the terms of the lease as to the state and condition of the property and the assignment shall so provide. This sub-condition applies notwithstanding that a special condition provides for the vendor to convey as beneficial owner.
(6) Where the property is sold subject to an apportioned rent specified as such in a special condition, the purchaser shall not require the consent of the reversioner to be obtained, or the rent to be otherwise legally apportioned.
(7) The purchaser shall assume that any receipt for the last payment due for rent under the lease before actual completion was given by the person then entitled to such rent or his duly authorised agent.

9 Deposit

(1) The purchaser shall on or before the date of the contract pay by way of deposit to the vendor's solicitors as stakeholders the normal deposit, or such lesser sum as the vendor shall have agreed in writing. On a sale by private treaty, payment shall be made by banker's draft or by cheque drawn on a solicitors' bank account.
(2) Upon service by the vendor of a completion notice, the purchaser shall pay to the

vendor any difference between the normal deposit and any amount actually paid (if less).
(3) If any draft, cheque or other instrument tendered in or towards payment of any sum payable under this condition is dishonoured when first presented the vendor shall have the right by notice to the purchaser within seven working days thereafter to treat the contract as repudiated.

10 Optional methods of exchange

(1) Exchange of contracts may be effected by a method authorised by condition 2 for the service of notices. If so effected, the contract shall be made when the last part is, as the case may be, posted or delivered to a document exchange.
(2) Where contracts have not been exchanged, the parties' solicitors may agree by telephone or telex that the contract be immediately effective and thereupon the solicitors holding a part of the contract signed by their client shall hold it irrevocably to the order of the other party.

11 Insurance

(1) If the property is destroyed or damaged prior to actual completion and the proceeds of any insurance policy effected by or for the purchaser are reduced by reason of the existence of any policy effected by or for the vendor, the purchase price shall be abated by the amount of such reduction.
(2) Sub-condition (1) shall not apply where the proceeds of the vendor's policy are applied towards the reinstatement of the property pursuant to any statutory or contractual obligation.
(3) This condition takes effect in substitution for section 47 of the Law of Property Act 1925.
(4) The vendor shall be under no duty to the purchaser to maintain any insurance on the property, save where the property is leasehold and the vendor has an obligation to insure.

12 Abstract of title

(1) Forthwith upon exchange of contracts the vendor shall deliver to the purchaser –
(a) where the title is not registered, an abstract of the title to the property or an epitome of the title together with photocopies of the relevant documents
(b) where the title is registered –
  (i) the documents, particulars and information specified in sub-sections (1) and (2) of section 110 of the Land Registration Act 1925, save that copies of the entries on the register, the filed plan and any documents noted on the register and filed in the registry shall be office copies, and
  (ii) such additional authorities to inspect the register as the purchaser shall reasonably require for any sub-purchaser or prospective mortgagee or lessee.
(2) Where the title is not registered, the vendor shall at his own expense produce the relevant documents of title or an abstract, epitome of title or copy thereof (bearing in each case original markings of examination of all relevant documents of title or of examined abstracts thereof).
(3) Where before the date of the contract any abstract, epitome or document has been delivered to the purchaser, he shall not, save as provided by conditions 6(2) or 8(3), be deemed to have had notice before the date of the contract of any matter of title thereby disclosed.

13 Identity and boundaries

(1) The vendor shall produce such evidence as may be reasonably necessary to establish the identity and extent of the property, but shall not be required to define exact

boundaries, or the ownership of fences, ditches, hedges or walls, nor, beyond the evidence afforded by the information in his possession, separately to identify parts of the property held under different titles.

(2) If reasonably required by the purchaser because of the insufficiency of the evidence produced under sub-condition (1), the vendor shall at his own expense provide and hand over on completion a statutory declaration as to the relevant facts, in a form agreed by the purchaser, such agreement not to be unreasonably withheld.

14 Mortgages in favour of friendly and other societies

Where the title includes a mortgage or legal charge in favour of trustees on behalf of a friendly society, a building society registered under the Industrial and Provident Societies Acts, the purchaser shall assume that any receipt given on the discharge of any such mortgage or legal charge and apparently duly executed was in fact duly executed by all proper persons and is valid.

15 Requisitions

(1) In this condition 'abstract' means all the documents, particulars and information required to be delivered by the vendor under condition 12.

(2) Subject to sub-condition (4), the purchaser shall deliver any requisitions or objections relating to the title, evidence of title or the abstract, in writing within six working days of receipt of the abstract (or, in the case of an abstract delivered before the date of the contract, within six working days of the date of contract). Within four working days of such delivery the vendor shall deliver his replies in writing.

(3) The purchaser shall deliver any observations on any of the vendor's replies in writing within four working days of their receipt.

(4) Where some but not all parts of the abstract have been delivered, and defects in title are not disclosed by such parts of the abstract as have been delivered, then in respect only of the undelivered parts or undisclosed defects (as the case may be) the abstract shall be deemed to be received for the purpose of sub-condition (2) at the time or respective times when any previously undelivered part is delivered.

(5) Time shall be of the essence for the purposes of this condition.

16 Rescission

(1) If the vendor is unable, or on some reasonable ground unwilling, to satisfy any requisition or objection made by the purchaser, the vendor may give the purchaser notice (specifying the reason for his inability or the ground of his unwillingness) to withdraw the same. If the purchaser does not withdraw the same within seven working days of service, either party may thereafter, notwithstanding any intermediate negotiation or litigation, rescind the contract by notice to the other.

(2) Upon rescission under any power given by these conditions or any special condition –

(a) the vendor shall repay to the purchaser any sums paid by way of deposit or otherwise under the contract, with interest on such sums at the contract rate from four working days after rescission until payment

(b) the purchaser shall forthwith return all documents delivered to him by the vendor and at his own expense procure the cancellation of any entry relating to the contract in any register.

17 Preparation of conveyance

(1) The purchaser shall deliver the draft conveyance at least twelve working days before contractual completion date, and within four working days of such delivery the vendor shall deliver it back approved or revised.

(2) The purchaser shall deliver the engrossment of the conveyance (first executed by him, where requisite) at least five working days before contractual completion date.
(3) The purchaser shall not, by delivering the draft conveyance or the engrossment, be deemed to accept the vendor's title or to waive any right to raise or maintain requisitions.
(4) Save to the extent that a covenant for indemnity will be implied by statute, the purchaser shall in the conveyance covenant to indemnify the vendor and his estate (and any estate of which the vendor is personal representative or trustee) against all actions, claims and liability for any breach of any covenant, stipulation, provision or other matter subject to which the property is sold and in respect of which the vendor or any such estate will remain liable after completion.
(5) The vendor shall give an acknowledgement for production and, unless in a fiduciary capacity, an undertaking for safe custody of documents of title retained by him. Where any such document is retained by a mortgagee, trustee or personal representative, the vendor shall procure that such person shall give an acknowledgement for production, and the vendor, unless in a fiduciary capacity, shall covenant that if and when he receives any such document he will, at the cost of the person requiring it, give an undertaking for safe custody.
(6) The vendor shall be entitled on reasonable grounds to decline to convey the property to any person other than the purchaser, by more than one conveyance, at more than the contract price or at a price divided between different parts of the property.

18 Occupation before completion

(1) This condition applies if the vendor authorises the purchaser to occupy the property before actual completion, except –
(a) where the purchaser already lawfully occupies any part of the property, or
(b) where the property is a dwellinghouse and the authority for the occupation is only for the purpose of effecting works of decoration, repair or improvement agreed by the vendor.
(2) The purchaser occupies the property as licensee and not as tenant. The purchaser may not transfer his licence or authorise any other person save members of his immediate family to occupy any part of the property.
(3) The purchaser shall not, by taking such occupation, be deemed to accept the vendor's title or to waive any right to raise or maintain requisitions.
(4) While the purchaser is in occupation of the whole or any part of the property under this condition, he shall –
(a) pay and indemnify the vendor against all outgoings and any other expenses in respect of the property and pay to the vendor in respect of such occupation a sum calculated at the contract rate on the amount of the purchase money (less any deposit paid)
(b) be entitled to receive any rents and profits from any part of the property not occupied by him
(c) insure the property in a sum not less than the purchase price against all risks in respect of which premises of the like nature are normally insured.
(5) The purchaser's licence to occupy the property shall end –
(a) on contractual completion date, or
(b) upon termination of the contract, or
(c) upon the expiry of five working days' notice given by either party to the other, and thereupon the purchaser shall give up occupation of the property and leave the same in as good repair as it was in when he went into occupation.
(6) If the purchaser, after his licence has ended under sub-condition 5(a), remains in occupation with the express or implied consent of the vendor, he shall thereafter occupy

on the other terms of this condition and on the further term that the vendor's rights under condition 22 shall not thereby be affected.

19 Apportionments

(1) In this condition –
(a) 'the apportionment day' means –
(i) if the property is sold with vacant possession of the whole, the date of actual completion
(ii) in any other case, contractual completion date
(b) 'payment period' means one of the periods for which a sum payable periodically is payable, whether or not such periods are of equal length.
(2) This condition shall not apply to any sum if –
(a) the purchaser cannot, by virtue only of becoming the owner of the property, either enforce payment of it or be obliged to pay it, or
(b) it is an outgoing paid in advance, unless the vendor cannot obtain repayment and the purchaser benefits therefrom or is given credit therefor against a sum that would otherwise be his liability.
(3) On completion the income and outgoings of the property shall, subject to sub-condition (2) and conditions 3 and 22(4) and to any adjustment required by condition 18(4), be apportioned as at the apportionment day.
(4) For the purposes of apportionment only, it shall be assumed –
(a) that the vendor remains owner of the property until the end of the apportionment day, and
(b) that the sum to be apportioned –
(i) accrues from day to day
(ii) is payable throughout the relevant period at the same rate as on the apportionment day.
(5) Sums payable periodically shall be apportioned by charging or allowing –
(a) for any payment period entirely attributable to one party, the whole of the instalment payable therefor
(b) for any part of a payment period, a proportion on an annual basis.
(6) (a) This sub-condition applies to any sum payable in respect of any period falling wholly or partly prior to the apportionment day, the amount of which is not notified to either party before actual completion.
(b) A provisional apportionment shall be made on the best estimate available. Upon the amount being notified, a final apportionment shall be made and one party shall thereupon make to the other the appropriate balancing payment.

20 Endorsement of memorandum

Where the vendor does not hand over all the documents of his title, he shall at completion endorse a memorandum of the sale to the purchaser on the last such document in each relevant title and thereupon produce the endorsed documents for inspection.

21 Completion

(1) Contractual completion date shall be as stated in the special conditions but if not so stated shall be the twenty-fifth working day after the date of the contract. Completion shall take place in England or Wales either at the office of the vendor's solicitors or, if required by the vendor at least five working days prior to actual completion, at the office of the vendor's mortgagee or his solicitors.
(2) The vendor shall not be obliged to accept payment of the money due on completion otherwise than by one or more of the following methods –
(a) legal tender

(b) a banker's draft drawn by and upon a settlement bank for the purposes of the Clearing House Automated payments System or any other bank specified in a special condition
(c) an unconditional authority to release any deposit held by a stakeholder
(d) otherwise as the vendor shall have agreed before actual completion.
(3) If completion is effected otherwise than by personal attendance the time for completion is when on a working day
(a) the money due on completion is paid to the vendor or his solicitors, and
(b) the vendor's solicitors hold to the order of the purchaser all the documents to which he is entitled on completion.
(4) For the purposes of this condition money is paid when the vendor receives payment by a method specified in sub-condition (2). Where the parties have agreed upon a direct credit to a bank account at a named branch, payment is made when that branch receives the credit.
(5) (a) This sub-condition applies if the money due on completion is not paid by 2.30 p.m. on the day of actual completion or by such other time on that day as is specified in a special condition
(b) For the purposes of condition 22 only, completion shall be deemed to be postponed by reason of the purchaser's delay from the day of actual completion until the next working day
(c) The purchaser shall not as a result of the deemed postponement of completion be liable to make any payment to the vendor unless the vendor claims such payment by giving notice at completion or within five working days thereafter (as to which period time shall be of the essence). Payment shall be due five working days after receipt of such notice.

22 Compensation for late completion

(1) For the purposes of this condition –
(a) 'delay' means failure to perform or lateness in performing any obligation of the contract which causes or contributes to lateness in completion
(b) a party is 'in default' if and to the extent that the period, or the aggregate of the periods, of his delay exceeds the period, or the aggregate of the periods, of delay of the other party
(c) 'the period of default' means the length of the excess defined in paragraph (b) or, if shorter, the period from contractual completion date to the date of actual completion.
(2) If the sale shall be completed after contractual completion date, the party in default (if any) shall be liable to compensate the other for loss occasioned to him by reason of that default.
(3) Before actual completion, or within five working days thereafter (as to which period time shall be of the essence), the party entitled to compensation may, by notice to the other party, opt to be paid or allowed a sum calculated at the contract rate on the amount of the purchase money (less any deposit paid) for the period of default as liquidated damages in settlement of his claim for compensation.
(4) If the vendor is entitled to compensation, he may, before actual completion, by notice to the purchaser, opt to take the net income of the property for the period of default in lieu of such compensation.
(5) The right to recover any compensation under this condition shall not be prejudiced by completion of the sale, whether before or after the commencement of proceedings.

23 Completion notice

(1) This condition applies unless a special condition provides that time is of the essence in respect of contractual completion date.
(2) If the sale shall not be completed on contractual completion date, either party, being then himself ready able and willing to complete, may after that date serve on

the other party notice to complete the transaction in accordance with this condition. A party shall be deemed to be ready, able and willing to complete –
(a) if he could be so but for some default or omission of the other party
(b) notwithstanding that any mortgage on the property is unredeemed when the completion notice is served if the aggregate of all sums necessary to redeem all such mortgages (to the extent that they relate to the property) does not exceed the sum payable on completion.
(3) Upon service of a completion notice it shall become a term of the contract that the transaction shall be completed within fifteen working days of service and in respect of such period time shall be of the essence.
(4) If the purchaser does not comply with a completion notice –
(a) the purchaser shall forthwith return all documents delivered to him by the vendor and at his own expense procure the cancellation of any entry relating to the contract in any register
(b) without prejudice to any other rights or remedies available to him, the vendor may –
(i) forfeit and retain any deposit paid and/or
(ii) re-sell the property by auction, tender or private treaty.
(5) If on any such re-sale contracted within one year after contractual completion date the vendor incurs a loss and so elects by notice to the purchaser within one month after the contract for such re-sale, the purchaser shall pay to the vendor liquidated damages. The amount payable shall be the aggregate of such loss, all costs and expenses reasonably incurred in any such re-sale and any attempted re-sale and interest at the contract rate on such part of the purchase money as is from time to time outstanding (giving credit for all sums received under any re-sale contract on account of the re-sale price) after contractual completion date.
(6) If the vendor does not comply with a completion notice, the purchaser, without prejudice to any other rights or remedies available to him, may give notice to the vendor forthwith to pay to the purchaser any sums paid by way of deposit or otherwise under the contract and interest on such sums at the contract rate from four working days after service of the notice until payment. On compliance with such notice the purchaser shall not be entitled to specific performance of the contract, but shall forthwith return all documents delivered to him by the vendor and at the expense of the vendor procure the cancellation of any entry relating to the contract in any register.
(7) Where after service of a completion notice the time for completion shall have been extended by agreement or implication, either party may again invoke the provisions of this condition which shall then take effect with the substitution of 'seven working days' for 'fifteen working days' in sub-condition (3).

24 Chattels

The property in any chattels agreed to be sold shall pass to the purchaser on actual completion.

25 Auctions

(1) This condition applies if the property is sold by auction.
(2) The sale is subject to a reserve price for the property and, when the property is sold in lots, for each lot.
(3) The vendor reserves the right –
(a) to divide the property into lots and to sub-divide, re-arrange or consolidate any lots
(b) to bid personally or by his agent up to any reserve price
(c) without disclosing any reserve price, to withdraw from the sale any property or lot at any time before it has been sold, whether or not the sale has begun.

(4) The auctioneer may –
(a) refuse to accept a bid
(b) in the case of a dispute as to any bid, forthwith determine the dispute or again put up the property or lot at the last undisputed bid.
(5) The purchaser shall forthwith complete and sign the contract and pay, but not necessarily by the means specified in condition 9(1), the normal deposit.

National Conditions of Sale (20th edition, 1981)

Reproduced by kind permission of the Solicitors' Law Stationery Society plc

Construction of the conditions

In these conditions, where the context admits –

(1) The 'vendor' and the 'purchaser' include the persons deriving title under them respectively

(2) 'Purchase money' includes any sum to be paid for chattels, fittings or other separate items

(3) References to the 'Special Conditions' include references to the particulars of sale and to the provisions of the contract which is made by reference to the conditions

(4) The 'prescribed rate' means the agreed rate of interest or, if none, then the rate of interest prescribed from time to time under Land Compensation Act 1961, s. 32

(5) 'Solicitor' includes a barrister who is employed by a corporate body to carry out conveyancing on its behalf and is acting in the course of his employment

(6) 'Working day' means a day on which clearing banks in the City of London are (or would be but for a strike, lock-out, or other stoppage, affecting particular banks or banks generally) open during banking hours Except in condition 19(4), in which 'working day' means a day when the Land Registry is open to the public

(7) 'Designated Bank' means a bank designated by the Chief Registrar under Building Societies Act 1962, s. 59

(8) The 'Planning Acts' means the enactments from time to time in force relating to town and country planning

(9) On a sale by private treaty references to the 'auctioneer' shall be read as references to the vendor's agent

(10) On a sale in lots, the conditions apply to each lot

(11) 'Abstract of title' means in relation to registered land such documents as the vendor is required by Land Registration Act 1925, s. 110, to furnish.

The conditions

1 The Sale: by Auction: by Private Treaty

(1) Paragraphs (2) to (5) of this condition apply on a sale by auction and paragraphs (6) and (7) on a sale by private treaty

(2) Unless otherwise provided in the Special Conditions, the sale of the property and of each lot is subject to a reserve price and to a right for the vendor or any one person on behalf of the vendor to bid up to that price

(3) The auctioneer may refuse any bid and no person shall at any bid advance less than the amount fixed for that purpose by the auctioneer

(4) If any dispute arises respecting a bid, the auctioneer may determine the dispute

or the property may, at the vendor's option, either be put up again at the last undisputed bid, or be withdrawn

(5) Subject to the foregoing provisions of this condition, the highest bidder shall be the purchaser and shall forthwith complete and sign the contract, the date of which shall be the date of the auction

(6) Where there is a draft contract, or an arrangement subject to contract, or a negotiation in which there are one or more outstanding items or suspensory matters (which prevent there being yet a concluded agreement of a contractual nature), a solicitor, who holds a document signed by his client in the form of a contract of sale in writing and embodying this condition, shall (unless the other party or his solicitor is informed to the contrary) have the authority of his client to conclude, by formal exchange of contracts, or by post, or by telex or other telegraphic means, or by telephone, and in any case with or without involving solicitors' undertakings, a binding contract in the terms of the document which his client has signed

(7) The date of the contract shall be –

(i) the date, if any, which is agreed and put on the contract, but if none, then

(ii) on an exchange of contracts by post (unless the parties' solicitors otherwise agree), the date on which the last part of the contract is posted, or

(iii) in any other case, the date on which, consistently with this condition, a binding contract is concluded.

2 Deposit

(1) Unless the Special Conditions otherwise provide, the purchaser shall on the date of the contract pay a deposit of 10 per cent, of the purchase price, on a sale by auction, to the auctioneer, or on a sale by private treaty, to the vendor's solicitor and, in either case, as stakeholder

(2) In case a cheque taken for the deposit (having been presented, and whether or not it has been re-presented) has not been honoured, then and on that account the vendor may elect –

either (i) to treat the contract as discharged by breach thereof on the purchaser's part

or (ii) to enforce payment of the deposit as a deposit, by suing on the cheque or otherwise.

3 Purchaser's short right to rescind

(1) This condition shall have effect if the Special Conditions so provide, but not otherwise

(2) If the property is affected by any matter to which this condition applies, then the purchaser may by notice in writing (hereinafter referred to as a 'Condition 3 Notice') given to the vendor or his solicitor and expressly referring to this condition and the matter in question, and notwithstanding any intermediate negotiation, rescind the contract on the same terms as if the purchaser had persisted in an objection to the title which the vendor was unable to remove

(3) A Condition 3 Notice shall not be given after the expiration of 16 working days from the date of the contract, time being of the essence of this condition

(4) This condition applies to any matter materially affecting the value of the property, other than –

(i) a matter which was not yet in existence or subsisting at the date of the contract

(ii) a specific matter to which the sale was expressly made subject, or

(iii) a matter of which the purchaser had at the date of the contract express notice or actual knowledge, not being notice or knowledge imputed to the purchaser by statute solely by reason of a registration of such matter, or notice or knowledge which the purchaser is only deemed to have had by the conditions

(5) This condition and condition 15 are additional to each other.

4 Chattels, etc, and separate items

If the sale includes chattels, fittings or other separate items, the vendor warrants that he is entitled to sell the same free from any charge, lien, burden, or adverse claim.

5 Date and manner of completion

(1) The completion date shall be the date specified for the purpose in the contract or, if none, the 26th working day after the date of the contract or the date of delivery of the abstract of title, whichever be the later

(2) Unless the Special Conditions otherwise provide, in respect of the completion date time shall not be of the essence of the contract, but this provision shall operate subject and without prejudice to–

(i) The provisions of condition 22 and

(ii) the rights of either party to recover from the other damages for delay in fulfilling his obligations under the contract

(3) The purchaser's obligations to pay money due on completion shall be discharged by one or more of the following methods–

(i) authorisation in writing to release a deposit held for the purposes of the contract by a stakeholder

(ii) banker's draft issued by a designated bank

(iii) cheque drawn on and guaranteed by a designated bank

(iv) telegraphic or other direct transfer (as requested or agreed to by the vendor's solicitor) to a particular bank or branch for the credit of a specified account

(v) legal tender

(vi) any other method requested or agreed to by the vendor's solicitor

(4) Completion shall be carried out, either formally at such office or place as the vendor's solicitor shall reasonably require, or (if the parties' solicitors so arrange) by post, or by means of solicitors undertakings concerning the holding of documents or otherwise provided that on a sale with vacant possession of the whole or part of the property, if the conveyance or transfer will not, by overreaching or otherwise, discharge the property from interests (if any) of persons in, or who may be in, actual occupation of the property of such part of it, then (subject always to the rights of the purchaser under Law of Property Act 1925, s. 42(1)), the purchaser may, by giving reasonable notice, require that on, or immediately before the time of, completion possession of the property or part be handed over to the purchaser or his representative at the property

(5) The date of actual completion shall be the day on which, the contract being completed in other respects, the purchaser has discharged consistently with the provisions of this condition the obligations of the purchaser to pay the money due on completion Provided that–

(i) for the purposes only of conditions 6, 7 and 8, if but for this proviso the date of actual completion would be the last working day of a week (starting on Sunday) and the purchaser is unable or unwilling to complete before 2.15 pm on that day, then the actual completion shall be taken to be the first working day thereafter

(ii) a remittance sent by post or delivered by hand shall be treated as being made on the day on which it reaches the vendor's solicitor's office, unless that day is not a working day in which case the remittance shall be treated as being made on the first working day thereafter.

6 Rents, outgoings and apportionments

The purchase being completed (whether on the completion day or subsequently), the income and outgoings shall be apportioned as follows (the day itself in each case being apportioned to the vendor):–

(1) In a case to which proviso (i) to condition 7(1) applies apportionment shall be made as the date of actual completion
(2) In a case in which the purchaser is in possession of the whole of the property as lessee or tenant at a rent apportionment shall be made as at the date of actual completion unless proviso (ii) to condition 7(1) applies, when apportionment shall be made as at the date of the purchaser's notice under that proviso
(3) In any other case apportionment shall be made as from the completion date Provided nevertheless that, if delay is attributable to the vendor's failure to obtain the reversioner's licence, where necessary, or if the vendor remains in beneficial occupation of the property after the completion date, the purchaser may by notice in writing before actual completion elect that apportionment shall be made as at the date of actual completion
(4) Rates shall be apportioned according to the period for which they are intended to provide and rents (whether payable in advance or in arrear) according to the period in respect of which they have been paid or are payable; and apportionment of yearly items (whether or not the same are payable by equal quarterly, monthly or other instalments) shall be according to the relevant number of days relatively to the number of days in the full year
(5) Service charges under leases, in the absence of known or readily ascertainable amounts, shall be apportioned according to the best estimate available at the time of completion and, unless otherwise agreed, the vendor and the purchaser shall be and remain mutually bound after completion to account for and pay or allow to each other, within 15 working days after being informed of the actual amounts as ascertained, any balances or excesses due.

7 Interest

(1) If the purchase shall not be completed on the completion date then (subject to the provisions of paragraph (2) of this condition) the purchaser shall pay interest on the remainder of his purchase money at the prescribed rate from that date until the purchase shall actually be completed Provided nevertheless –

(i) That (without prejudice to the operation of proviso (ii) to this paragraph) the vendor may by notice in writing before actual completion elect to take the income of the property (less outgoings) up to the date of actual completion instead of interest as aforesaid

(ii) That, if the delay arises from any cause other than the neglect or default of the purchaser, and if the purchaser (not being in occupation of the property in circumstances to which condition 8 applies) places the remainder of his purchase money (at his own risk) at interest on a deposit account in England or Wales with any designated bank, and gives written notice thereof to the vendor or his solicitor, then in lieu of the interest or income payable to or receivable by the vendor as aforesaid, the vendor shall from the time of such notice be entitled to such interest only as is produced by such deposit

(iii) That the vendor shall in no case be or become entitled in respect of the same period of time both to be paid interest and to enjoy income of the property, or to be paid interest more than once on the same sum of money

(2) The purchaser shall not be liable to pay interest under paragraph (1) of this condition –

(i) so long as, or to the extent that, delay in completion is attributable to any act or default of the vendor or his mortgagee or Settled Land Act trustees

(ii) in case the property is to be constructed or converted by the vendor, so long as the construction or conversion is unfinished.

8 Occupation pending completion

(1) If the purchaser (not being already in occupation as lessee or tenant at a rent) is let into occupation of the property before the actual completion of the purchase, then, as from the date of his going into occupation and until actual completion, or until upon discharge or rescission of the contract he ceases to occupy the property, the purchaser shall –

(i) be the licensee and not the tenant of the vendor

(ii) pay interest on the remainder of the purchase money at the prescribed rate

(iii) keep the property in as good repair and condition as it was in when he went into occupation

(iv) pay, or otherwise indemnify the vendor against, all outgoings and expenses (including the cost of insurance) in respect of property, the purchaser at the same time taking or being credited with the income of the property (if any)

(v) not carry out any development within the meaning of the Planning Acts

(2) Upon discharge or rescission of the contract, or upon the expiration of 7 working days' or longer notice given by the vendor or his solicitor to the purchaser or his solicitor in that behalf, the purchaser shall forthwith give up the property in such repair and condition as aforesaid

(3) A purchaser going into occupation before completion shall not be deemed thereby to have accepted the vendor's title.

(4) Where the purchaser is allowed access to the property for the purpose only of carrying out works or installations, the purchaser shall not be treated as being let into occupation within the meaning of this condition.

9 Abstract, requisitions and observations

(1) The vendor shall deliver the abstract of title not later than 11 working days after the date of the contract but, subject and without prejudice as mentioned in condition 5(2), that time limit shall not be of the essence of the contract

(2) Subject always to the rights of the purchaser under Law of Property Act 1925, s. 42(1), the vendor may be required by the purchaser to deal with requisitions and observations concerning persons who are or may be in occupation or actual occupation of the property, so as to satisfy the purchaser that the title is not, and that the purchaser will not be, prejudicially affected by any interests or claims of such persons.

(3) The purchaser shall deliver in writing his requisitions within 11 working days after delivery of the abstract, and his observations on the replies to the requisitions within 6 working days after delivery of the replies

(4) In respect of the delivery of requisitions and observations, time shall be of the essence of the contract, notwithstanding that the abstract may not have been delivered within due time

(5) The purchaser shall deliver his requisitions and observations on the abstract as delivered, whether it is a perfect or an imperfect abstract, but for the purposes of any requisitions or observations which could not be raised or made on the information contained in an imperfect abstract, time under paragraph (3) of this condition shall not start to run against the purchaser, until the vendor has delivered the further abstract or information on which the requisitions or observations arise

(6) Subject to his requisitions and observations, the purchaser shall be deemed to have accepted the title.

10 Vendor's right to rescind

(1) If the purchaser shall persist in any objection to the title which the vendor shall be unable or unwilling, on reasonable grounds, to remove, and shall not withdraw the same within 10 working days of being required so to do, the vendor may, subject to the purchaser's rights under the Law of Property Act 1925, ss. 42 and 125, by notice

in writing to the purchaser or his solicitor, and notwithstanding any intermediate negotiation or litigation, rescind the contract
(2) Upon such rescission the vendor shall return the deposit, but without interest, costs on investigating title or other compensation or payment, and the purchaser shall return the abstract and other papers furnished to him

11 Existing leaseholds

(1) Where the interest sold is leasehold for the residue of an existing term the following provisions of this condition shall apply
(2) The lease or underlease or a copy thereof having been made available, the purchaser (whether he has inspected the same or not) shall be deemed to have bought with full notice of the contents thereof
(3) on production of a receipt for the last payment due for rent under the lease or underlease, the purchaser shall assume without proof that the person giving the receipt, though not the original lessor, is the reversioner expectant on the said lease or underlease or his duly authorised agent
(4) No objection shall be taken on account of the covenants in an underlease not corresponding with the covenants in any superior lease
(5) The sale is subject to the reversioner's licence being obtained, where necessary. The purchaser supplying such information and references, if any, as may reasonably be required of him, the vendor will use his best endeavours to obtain such licence and will pay the fee for the same. But if the licence cannot be obtained, the vendor may rescind the contract on the same terms as if the purchaser had persisted in an objection to the title which the vendor was unable to remove
(6) Where the property comprises part only of the property comprised in a lease or underlease, the rent, covenants and conditions shall, if the purchaser so requires, be legally apportioned at his expense, but completion shall not be delayed on that account and in the meantime the apportionment by the auctioneer shall be accepted, or the property may at the option of the vendor be sub-demised for the residue of the term, less one day, at a rent apportioned by the auctioneer and subject to the purchaser executing a counterpart containing covenants and provisions corresponding to those contained in the lease or underlease aforesaid
(7) Any statutory covenant to be implied in the conveyance on the part of a vendor shall be so limited as not to affect him with liability for a subsisting breach of any covenant or condition concerning the state or condition of the property, of which state and condition the purchaser is by paragraph (3) of condition 13 deemed to have full notice, and where Land Registration Act 1925, s. 24, applies the purchaser, if required, will join in requesting that an appropriate entry be made in the register.

12 Vendor's duty to produce documents

(1) If an abstracted document refers to any plan material to the description of the property, or to any covenants contained in a document earlier in date than the document with which the title commences, and such plan or earlier document is in the possession or power of the vendor or his trustees or mortgagee, the vendor shall supply a copy thereof with the abstract
(2) If the property is sold subject to restrictive covenants, the deed imposing those covenants or a copy thereof having been made available, the purchaser (whether he has inspected the same or not) shall be deemed to have purchased with full knowledge thereof
(3) The vendor shall not be required to procure the production of any document not in his possession or not in the possession of his mortgagee or trustees, and of which the vendor cannot obtain production, or to trace or state who has the possession of the same.

13 Identity: boundaries: condition of property

(1) The purchaser shall admit the identity of the property with that comprised in the muniments offered by the vendor as the title thereto upon the evidence afforded by the descriptions contained in such muniments, and of a statutory declaration, to be made (if required) at the purchaser's expense, that the property has been enjoyed according to the title for at least twelve years
(2) The vendor shall not be bound to show any title to boundaries, fences, ditches, hedges or walls, or to distinguish parts of the property held under different titles further than he may be able to do from information in his possession
(3) The purchaser shall be deemed to buy with full notice in all respects of the actual state and condition of the property and, save where it is be constructed or converted by the vendor, shall take the property as it is.

14 Property sold subject to easements, etc

Without prejudice to the duty of the vendor to disclose all latent easements and latent liabilities known to the vendor to affect the property, the property is sold subject to any rights of way and water, rights of common, and other rights, easements, quasi-easements, liabilities and public rights affecting the same.

15 Town and Country Planning

(1) In this condition, where the context admits, references to 'authorised use' are references to 'established use', or to use for which permission has been granted under the Planning Acts, or to use for which permission is not required under those Acts, as the case may be
(2) The purchaser shall be entitled to deliver, with his requisitions in respect of the title, requisitions concerning the authorised use of the property for the purposes of the Planning Acts. The vendor in reply shall give all such relevant information as may be in his possession or power
(3) Where the property is in the Special Conditions expressed to be sold on the footing of an authorised use which is specified, then if it appears before actual completion of the purchase that the specified use is not an authorised use of the property for the purposes of the Planning Acts, the purchaser may by notice in writing rescind the contract, and thereupon paragraph (2) of condition 10 shall apply. But, subject to the foregoing provisions of this condition, the purchaser shall be deemed to have accepted that the specified use is an authorised use of the property for the purposes of the Planning Acts
(4) Save as mentioned in the Special Conditions, the property is not to the knowledge of the vendor subject to any charge, notice, order, restriction, agreement or other matter arising under the Planning Acts, but (without prejudice to any right of the purchaser to rescind the contract under paragraph (3) of this condition) the property is sold subject to any such charges, notices, orders, restrictions, agreements and matters affecting the interest sold.
(5) Subject as hereinbefore provided, and without prejudice to the obligations of the vendor to supply information as aforesaid, the purchaser shall be deemed to buy with knowledge in all respects of the authorised use of the property for the purposes of the Planning Acts.

16 Requirements by local authority

(1) If after the date of the contract any requirement in respect of the property be made against the vendor by any local authority, the purchaser shall comply with the same at his own expense, and indemnify the vendor in respect thereof: in so far as the purchaser shall fail to comply with such requirement, the vendor may comply with

the same wholly or in part and any money so expended by the vendor shall be repaid by the purchaser on completion
(2) The vendor shall upon receiving notice of any such requirement forthwith inform the purchaser thereof.

17 Errors, mis-statements or omissions

(1) Without prejudice to any express right of either party, or to any right of the purchaser in reliance on Law of Property Act 1969, s. 24, to rescind the contract before completion and subject to the provisions of paragraph (2) of this condition, no error, mis-statement or omission in any preliminary answer concerning the property, or in the sale plan or the Special Conditions, shall annul the sale, nor (save where the error, mis-statement or omission relates to a matter materially affecting the description or value of the property) shall any damages be payable, or compensation allowed by either party, in respect thereof
(2) Paragraph (1) of this condition shall not apply to any error, mis-statement or, omission which is recklessly or fraudulently made, or to any matter or thing by which the purchaser is prevented from getting substantially what he contracted to buy
(3) In this condition a 'preliminary answer' means and includes any statement made by or on behalf of the vendor to the purchaser or his agents or advisers, whether in answer to formal preliminary enquiries or otherwise, before the purchaser entered into the contract.

18 Leases and tenancies

(1) Abstracts or copies of the leases or agreements (if in writing) under which the tenants hold having been made available, the purchaser (whether he has inspected the same or not) shall be deemed to have notice of and shall take subject to the terms of all the existing tenancies and the rights of the tenants, whether arising during the continuance or after the expiration thereof, and such notice shall not be affected by any partial or incomplete statement in the Special Conditions with reference to the tenancies, and no objection shall be taken on account of there not being an agreement in writing with any tenant
(2) Where a lease or tenancy affects the property sold and other property, the property sold will be conveyed with the benefit of the apportioned rent (if any) mentioned in the Special Conditions or (if not so mentioned) fixed by the auctioneer, and no objection shall be taken on the ground that the consent of the tenant has not been obtained to the apportionment and the purchaser shall not require the rent to be legally apportioned
(3) The purchaser shall keep the vendor indemnified against all claims by the tenant for compensation or otherwise, except in respect of a tenancy which expires or is determined on or before the completion date or in respect of an obligation which ought to have been discharged before the date of the contract
(4) Land in the occupation of the vendor is sold subject to the right (hereby reserved to him) to be paid a fair price for tillages, off-going and other allowances as if he were an outgoing tenant who had entered into occupation of the land after 1st March 1944, and as if the purchaser were the landlord, and in case of dispute such price shall be fixed by the valuation of a valuer, to be nominated in case the parties differ by the President of the Royal Institution of Chartered Surveyors.

19 Preparation of conveyance: priority notices: indemnities

(1) Where the interest sold is leasehold for a term of years to be granted by the vendor, the lease or underlease and counterpart shall be prepared by the vendor's solicitor in accordance (as nearly as the circumstances admit) with a form of draft annexed to the

contract or otherwise sufficiently identified by the signatures of the parties or their solicitors

(2) In any other case the conveyance shall be prepared by the purchaser or his solicitor and the following provisions of this condition shall apply

(3) The draft conveyance shall be delivered at the office of the vendor's solicitor at least 6 working days before the completion date and the engrossment for execution by the vendor and other necessary parties (if any) shall be left at the said office within 3 working days after the draft has been returned to the purchaser approved on behalf of the vendor and other necessary parties (if any)

(4) Where the property is unregistered land not in an area of compulsory registration and the conveyance is to contain restrictive covenants, and the purchaser intends contemporaneously with the conveyance to execute a mortgage or conveyance to a third party, he shall inform the vendor of his intention and, if necessary, allow the vendor to give a priority notice for the registration of the intended covenants at least 15 working days before the contract is completed

(5) Where the property is sold subject to legal incumbrances, the purchaser shall covenant to indemnify the vendor against actions and claims in respect of them: and the purchaser will not make any claim on account of increased expense caused by the concurrence of any legal incumbrancer

(6) Where the property is sold subject to stipulations, or restrictive or other covenants, and breach thereof would expose the vendor to liability, the purchaser shall covenant to observe and perform the same and to indemnify the vendor against actions and claims in respect thereof

(7) Paragraphs (5) and (6) of this condition shall have effect without prejudice to the provisions of Law of Property Act 1925, s. 77, and Land Registration Act 1925, s. 24, where such provisions respectively are applicable, and in respect of matters covered by a covenant implied under either of those sections no express covenant shall be required.

20 Severance of properties formerly in common ownership

Where the property and any adjacent or neighbouring property have hitherto been in common ownership, the purchaser shall not become entitled to any right to light or air over or in respect of any adjacent or neighbouring property which is retained by the vendor and the conveyance shall, if the vendor so requires, reserve to him such easements and rights as would become appurtenant to such last-mentioned property by implication of law, if the vendor had sold it to another purchaser at the same time as he has sold the property to the purchaser.

21 Insurance

(1) With respect to any policy of insurance maintained by the vendor in respect of damage to or destruction of the property, the vendor shall not (save pursuant to an obligation to a third party) be bound to keep such insurance on foot or to give notice to the purchaser of any premium being or becoming due

(2) The purchaser shall be entitled to inspect the policy at any time

(3) The vendor shall, if required, by and at the expense of the purchaser obtain or consent to an endorsement of notice of the purchaser's interest on the policy, and in such case the vendor (keeping the policy on foot) may require the purchaser to pay on completion a proportionate part of the premium from the date of the contract.

22 Special notice to complete

(1) At any time on or after the completion date, either party, being ready and willing to fulfil his own outstanding obligations under the contract, may (without prejudice to any other right or remedy available to him) give to the other party or his solicitor notice in writing requiring completion of the contract in conformity with this condition

(2) Upon service of such notice as aforesaid it shall become and be a term of the contract, in respect of which time shall be the essence thereof, that the party to whom the notice is given shall complete the contract within 16 working days after service of the notice (exclusive of the day of service): but this condition shall operate without prejudice to any right of either party to rescind the contract in the meantime
(3) In case the purchaser refuses or fails to complete in conformity with this condition, then (without prejudice to any other right or remedy available to the vendor) the purchaser's deposit may be forfeited (unless the court otherwise directs) and, if the vendor resells the property within twelve months of the expiration of the said period of 16 working days, he shall be entitled (upon crediting the deposit) to recover from the purchaser hereunder the amount of any loss occasioned to the vendor by expenses of or incidental to such resale, or by diminution in the price.

Index